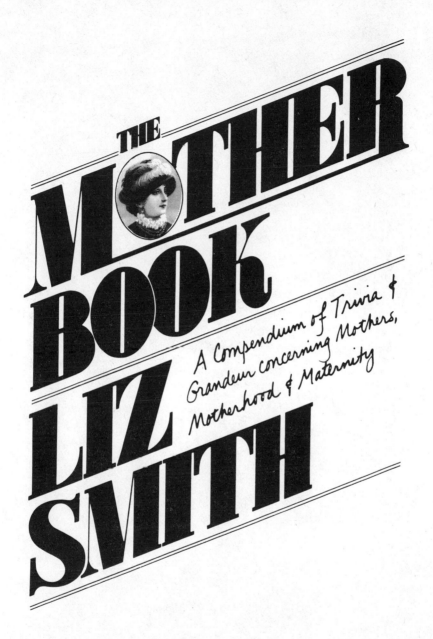

# THE MOTHER BOOK

### LIZ SMITH

*A Compendium of Trivia & Grandeur concerning Mothers, Motherhood & Maternity*

CROWN PUBLISHERS, INC.
*New York*

Copyright © 1984 by Liz Smith

Library of Congress Cataloging in Publication Data

Smith, Liz. The mother book.
Reprint. Originally published: Garden City, N.Y.: Doubleday, 1978.

1. Mothers.  I. Title.

HQ759.S62  1984   306.8'743  83-23950
ISBN: 0-517-55221-3

Designed by Laurence Alexander
10 9 8 7 6 5 4 3 2 1
First Crown Paperback Edition

*For my mother, Sarah Elizabeth, the*
*beautiful McCall girl from Mississippi*
*who married Sloan Smith in Ennis,*
*Texas, in the spring of 1914*

Being a compendium of trivia and grandeur
concerning
MOTHERS . . . MOTHERHOOD . . . MATERNITY
from the sublime to the ridiculous,
past, present and future
including anecdotes about the mothers of
the famous, infamous and unfamous,
as well as obscure facts, fancies,
overblown sentimentalities, sociological speculations,
jokes, japes, jibes, poems, songs,
graffiti, literature,
pieties, profanities and
curiosities about
MOTHER

# Table of Mothers

*Grateful acknowledgment is made to the following for permission to use material owned by them. Every effort has been made to trace the proper copyright holders of the excerpts used herein. If there are any omissions we apologize and will be pleased to make the appropriate acknowledgments in any future printings.*

*American Film,* June 1976, Comment by Antonio Chemasi © *American Film.* January–February 1976, "Movies, Mommies, and the American Dream" by Marjorie Rosen.

Cleveland Amory for excerpts from *The Proper Bostonians* and *The Last Resorts.* Used by permission.

Arbor House Publishing Co., Inc., from *The David Kopay Story* by David Kopay and Perry Deane Young by permission of the publisher, Arbor House Publishing Company, copyright © 1977 by David Kopay and Perry Deane Young.

Ascherberg, Hopwood and Crew, Ltd., London for "And Her Mother Came Too" by Ivor Novello, copyright © 1921 by Ascherberg, Hopwood and Crew, Ltd., London, copyright renewed. Controlled by Chappell & Co., Inc. International. Copyright secured. All rights reserved. Used by permission.

Atheneum Publishers, Inc., from *The Italians* by Luigi Barzini, copyright © 1964 by Luigi Barzini. Reprinted by permission of Atheneum Publishers.

Bantam Books, Inc., from *Toms, Coons, Mulattoes, Mammies and Bucks* copyright © 1973 by Donald Bogle. Published by The Viking Press, Inc., and Bantam Books, Inc.

Basic Books, Inc., from *Children of the Sun:* A Narrative of "Decadence" in England After 1918, by Martin Green, copyright © 1976 by Martin Green, Basic Books, Inc., Publishers, New York.

Basic Books, Inc., from *Letters of Sigmund Freud,* selected and edited by Ernst L. Freud, translated by Tania and James Stern, p. 38, copyright © 1960 by Sigmund Freud Copyrights Ltd., London, Basic Books, Inc., Publishers, New York.

Chappell & Co., Ltd., London, for "Mrs. Worthington" by Noel Coward. Copyright © 1935 by Chappell & Co., Ltd., London. Copyright renewed. Controlled by Chappell & Co., Inc. International. Copyright secured. All rights reserved. Used by permission.

Chappell & Co., Inc., from "That's Entertainment" copyright © 1953 by Chappell & Co., Inc. Used by permission of Howard Dietz.

Edward Colman, executor of the Lord Alfred Douglas literary estate for letter from Lord Alfred Douglas.

Delacorte Press from *My Mother/My Self* by Nancy Friday, copyright © 1977.

The Dial Press from *The Future of Motherhood* by Jessie Bernard copyright © 1974 by Jessie Bernard. Reprinted by permission of The Dial Press.

The Dial Press from *The Unnatural History of the Nanny* by Jonathan Gathorne-Hardy. Copyright © 1972 by Jonathan Gathorne-Hardy and used by permission of the publisher, The Dial Press.

The Dial Press from *Go Tell It on the Mountain* by James Baldwin.

Dodd, Mead & Co., Inc., from *The Women in Their Lives* by Frank Donovan.

From *Diary of a Genius* by Salvador Dali. Copyright © 1964 by Editions de la Table Ronde. English Translation copyright © 1965 by Doubleday & Company, Inc. Reprinted by permission of Georges Borchardt, Inc.

From *Cagney* by James Cagney. Copyright © 1976 by Doubleday & Company, Inc. Reprinted by permission of the publisher.

From *The Movie Stars* by Richard Griffith. Copyright © 1970 by T. G. Scully as Administrator of the Estate of Richard Griffith. Reprinted by permission of Doubleday & Company, Inc.

From *Consenting Adult* by Laura Hobson. Copyright © 1975 by Laura Z. Hobson. Reprinted by permission of Doubleday & Company, Inc.

From *Lena* by Lena Horne. Copyright © 1965 by Lena Horne and Richard Schickel. Reprinted by permission of Doubleday & Company, Inc.

From *Times to Remember* by Rose Kennedy. Copyright © 1974 by The Joseph F. Kennedy, Jr., Foundation. Reprinted by permission of Doubleday & Company, Inc.

"Mehitabel and her Kittens" from *Archy and Mehitabel* by Don Marquis. Copyright 1927 by Doubleday & Company, Inc. Reprinted by permission of the publisher.

# To Begin

Everybody had one with the exception of Adam and Eve. Many of us have them still. We are either blessed or cursed (or a combination of both) and each reader knows into which category his or her perception of or feelings about mother fall.

In a world of shifting constants, the mother idea-ideal, the mother dilemma-delusion remains of great importance, holding within its encompassing maternal femaleness, reflections of the changing times. We have gone from age-old piety ("All that I am or hope to be, I owe to my angel mother."—Lincoln) to present profanity—"you motherfucker" having been shortened simply to "you mother!"

There is Whistler's mother (*An Arrangement in Gray and Black*) and there is the substitute mother, Auntie Mame (a study in marabou and camp). Barring the advent of Aldous Huxley's *Brave New World*, where there will be only test-tube babies and "mother" will be considered a dirty word (the shape of things to come being already here in this instance), the mother bit is a universal experience for animals—a process rendering the female of the species unique, so special that orphans are shaped and traumatized by *missing* Mother.

Whatever one thinks of Mother, whether one loves or hates her, the mothering experience or lack of it, pays off one way or another. I notice that many great poets emerge from motherless child-

1

hoods. They are either early orphans or their mothers are not mentioned at all. It is not so amazing that many of these same artists turned out to be hounded by depression, drugs, and insanity, but did being motherless also drive them to creativity?

*The Mother Book* gives you Mother in what I hope is some fraction of her stunning diversity. As it is sometimes hard to cram Mother into the front seat of the Volkswagen, it is impossible to cram her into the covers of one book. There are miles and miles of books on mothers and motherhood. Just take a look at any shelf 301 in any library using the Dewey Decimal System. Almost every biography and autobiography is a testament to Mother's presence or absence. The literature of Mother abounds.

Within the tiny perimeters of *The Mother Book* is offered only a per cent of Mother in her infinite variety. My selections and reminiscences were strictly arbitrary and personal, subjective and often whimsical. To have tried to be scholarly and comprehensive would have been to tempt madness.

# CAVEAT LECTOR

This book grapples with certain jokes and anecdotes that are distinctly racial, religious, and ethnic. They may appear to be prejudiced. We must face the fact that much in history, legend, myth, and anecdote, as well as in the humor of men and women's lives and times, does concern itself with racial, religious, and ethnic comment.

No offense was intended and repeated stereotypes and putdowns have been included as such. We have tried not to perpetuate too many injustices against any group—mothers included, though they are mainly the ones who take their lumps.

It is my hope that any writer in the popular medium, having struggled for years with the narrow-minded prejudices of magazine and newspaper readers and editors, is to be privileged just once. A strong reason for writing a book is the author's belief that there exists a fair, intelligent readership so that one may insult everybody with good humor and impunity in maturely adult pages.

Now maybe you think I'm not nervous about what my own mother will have to say about all of the sex, profanity, incest, homosexuality, drinking, and insult in this book.

# THE ROSESHIT FACTOR

The division of this book into chapters and the placement of material within certain sections has been highly informal. The very act of *collecting* material often led the same material to its own natural division into a specific category. And, the placement of material has been an ongoing problem, reminding one of the moron who was deemed smart enough to sort potatoes by size. At the end of the first day, this poor soul threw in the towel and said he was quitting. Asked why, he replied: "These decisions are killing me!"

That's how I felt stumbling on the diverse stories in some auto-biographies of the famous. Often a single book would have portions for the grandmother, the ethnic mother, a mother's kitchen, and the mothers and sons or daughters chapters. The reader may well wonder why there are no Puerto Rican or Polish or Latvian or East Indian mothers by chapter? Why not a chapter on Mothers Out of Wedlock Struck by Lightning in the Left Heel? I give up—why not?

But a writer-collector has only one brief life to live. I simply didn't discover enough examples for such chapters to build and sort themselves out. Thus, the diverse tail-ends are in Mother Mix. For instance, I would have enjoyed doing a chapter called Roseshit—this being the name my agent and friend Gloria Safier has given to the unbounded optimism of her mother's outlook. Rose is always there with her fast-growing fertilizer of positive thinking. It never fails to make flowers bloom among the skunk cabbage. If you lost your legs in an accident, Rose would soon remind you of your good fortune in never having to go to the chiropodist again.

She is unflappably an "up." A typical Rose reaction to something negative happened one summer when she was visiting Gloria and friends in Southold, Long Island. The summer house boasted a boat, but Gloria, not being sports-minded, had never been out in it. One day she expressed a desire to "go on the boat." Her housemates looked at her with derision and began to make fun of such sudden aquatic interest. Gloria got exasperated and snapped: "Oh, take the boat and shove it!"

Rose was calmly eating, but put down her fork: "Gloria, you really don't get enough sleep," she said.

But as delightful as Rose is, if I wrote the Roseshit chapter, then I'd have to balance it with one on Mother as Pessimist. Or the

Mother as a Drag. Or Downbeat Mothers. So you see the problem. These are the raveling ends of dealing with the master mother pattern and one doesn't dare start pulling all the threads since they are endlessly interwoven.

## ROSESHIT P.S.

Perhaps I should tell the reader that after compiling this book I am an expert on mothers. However—like those who can, do, and those who can't, teach, I am not, nor have I ever been, a mother. It is now not likely that I shall be one. My own mother considers this a tragedy. But I know I can count on Rose to say: "So? You won't have to be bored to death someday by your kids' problems, since nobody will come to visit you in the Golden Age Rest Home!"

## TABLE OF NON-CONTENTS

Some mother topics you won't find discussed at length in *The Mother Book**

- —The relation between the Great Corn Mother of northern Europe and the Eleusinian Mysteries of the Ancient Greeks
- —Amazon mothers
- —The "nuclear family" as opposed to "the extended family"
- —Breast-feeding
- —How to toilet-train your child
- —Natural childbirth pros and cons
- —Abortion pros and cons
- —Custody rights questions in divorce cases (mother vs. father)

* There are many excellent books covering these subjects but this will not be one of them.

—Precocious sayings of small children to their mothers and grandmothers

—Advice of any sort, except one brief personal aberration on page 38

# Thank You!

*The Mother Book* requires two massive acknowledgments. The inspiration for this work was not my own mother, but the mother of a friend. Though I have never met Betty Shevelove, stories told about this mother by her son, the theatrical director Burt Shevelove, made me begin to collect this material. Burt often tossed off Betty tales at dinner. I knew somehow that they were pearls any swine should at least save. So I did. One day I began to add other mother stories. Eventually there was a file of them crying out to be organized and published, but Mrs. Shevelove was Mother Numero Uno.

One of the best of Burt's mother stories had to do with his moving to live in London. Early on, he placed a transatlantic call to West Orange, New Jersey. Mrs. Shevelove became quite agitated when she heard the overseas operator. She began to stammer. Finally she said, "Is this you—is this you, Burt? Oh my—now, Burt, listen to me—*don't say anything you can write!*" There are other Betty Shevelove stories in these pages. She is also the originator of one type tale, the following, which illustrates a phenomenon of mothering.

During Burt's stay abroad, two of his friends decided to pamper Betty. Nicky and Timmy, as we shall call them, often invited Mrs. Shevelove in to the theater or to their posh town house for dinner. They treated her to all manner of goodies. They fussed over her. One day they asked her to lunch at the Plaza and offered rare theater tickets for a matinee. Betty asked if she might bring her niece Judy. Nicky and Timmy were delighted. They showed off terribly at the Plaza, flashed their cufflinks, and ordered champagne. After lunch, they tucked the "girls" into a limousine and blew good-by kisses. As the limo pulled away from these two elegants on the curb, Betty said thoughtfully:

"Judy, do you think Nicky and Timmy are—fairies?"
Judy answered: "Why, Auntie—of course!"
Mrs. Shevelove blanched: "Oh, my—don't tell Burt!"
(See page 160 for more of the "Don't Tell" Syndrome.)

Burt's mother gave me many laughs. When my friend Jim Elson and I once visited Rome, we went—the Jew and the Southern Baptist—to see Pope Pius XII's daily appearance on his balcony to bless the multitudes. We waited; the crowd clapped and screamed for "Papa." When the Pope appeared, Jimmy and I both gasped. He said, "My God—it's Burt!"

It was true. The Pope bore a distinct resemblance to our friend. We thus brought Burt a souvenir of the robed Pope in a plastic serrated frame. When you moved in the room, the Pope's hand appeared to move also in blessing. Burt loved this and kept it next to his collection of books on demonology. One day his mother was in town. She sat down across from the book shelves and said, "Burt, that's a real good picture of you. But why are you in costume—I thought you had given up acting."

Bless you, Betty Shevelove. If you hadn't been such an inspiration, *The Mother Book* would probably never have been.

The other indispensable person to this proceeding was Elizabeth Pierce who helped me create this book. By rights she is its co-author. Many of the nuggets, much of the organization, probably most of the best writing, are hers. We were engaged together in this labor of love for three years, on and off, and in spite of my erratic work habits, eccentricities, missed deadlines, head colds and whining, Liz Pierce kept on keeping on with me. She didn't nag, she didn't bring chicken soup, she didn't threaten. In no respect was she motherly, except to make me feel *guilty* by the sheer dint of her own work and application. This book could not exist without her own special selective eye and ear, her talent for the off-beat, her appreciative wit and warmth and sense of humor. She is a truly unique, formidable person of superior character and intellect. But what can you expect from one whose own mother, Adela Jacobs Pierce Foulds, sent this travel tip to her daughter prior to their first joint trip to Europe in 1961: "Take as many one-dollar bills as possible. Many times it saves trouble in making change to have a dollar bill. Carry in a case *inside your girdle!*" (Italics mine.)

Unique mothers often produce unique daughters. Adela did.

6

Jointly, Liz Pierce and I want to express our deep appreciation to the New York Public Library, one of the greatest institutions in the world and a reason of its own for living in New York. We owe this Library simply everything.

A special thanks also to my brother Bobby, who provided so much great material. Even the salaciously unprintable was fun. Only Bobby could have gleaned the essence of "his" mother for me, as he did so well, and only he has the total recall which helped me so much in re-creating the past. This elephantine memory has been his pain and his joy all his life. So I feel this book is as much Bobby's as it is mine. I am also grateful to my older brother, James, for not demanding that I suppress publication. He hates to see his name in print. Like my father, James has never understood what I do for a living. He would echo Sloan's long-ago question when I first started writing: "Do you really *know* all of that stuff, or *are you just trying to get rid of it?*"

To every author and publisher who granted permission for use of material, much gratitude.

Finally, I am beholden to Diane Judge and Diane Cleaver, St. Clair Pugh, James Fragale, Larry Alexander, Betty Prashker, and to that glorious ten per center Gloria Safier, for good-natured nagging and unfailing support.

*The Mother Book*? I guess I was "just trying to get rid of it."

# The Language of Mothers

A mother understands what a child does not say.

Jewish proverb

Considering that "Mama" is the first word many of us speak naturally, it's not too surprising that "Mother" has had a tremendous impact on our vocabulary. Nevertheless, it has been astounding to learn the wide variety of "Mother" terms that turn up in the English language. Some of these occur in an affectionate context; some are devastatingly insulting. You know all the obvious examples: *alma mater* . . . mother lode . . . mother tongue . . . mother wit . . . mother-of-pearl . . . mother country (one thinks then of Mother Russia) . . . and so on. One can also get very etymologically complex, pointing out that "mama" and "mammary" come from the same Latin root. (*Mamma* is actually a word for milk gland.) But there are many, many more, as you'll see and be reminded on the pages following.

By way of indicating that "Mother" doesn't always mean what one thinks it does, I'll cite the case of a certain small-town librarian who was more than a little bewildered when a prepubescent Cub Scout came to the check-out desk with a book entitled *What Every Young Mother Should Know*. After looking at him curiously, the librarian asked some questions. It turned out that the lad was looking for a volume to guide him in his hobby of collecting *moths*.

\*

## How to Say "Mother" in 25 Mother Tongues

English—mother
French—mère
German—Mutter
Italian—madre
Spanish—madre
Portuguese—măe
Romanian—mamă
Dutch—moeder
Swedish—moder
Danish—moder
Norwegian—mor
Russian—mat'
Polish—matka

Czech—matka
Serbo-Croatian—majka
Bulgarian—máyka
Hungarian—anya
Finnish—äiti
Estonian—ema
Latvian—mâte
Lithuanian—motina
Greek—mite'ra
Albanian—nâna
Turkish—anne
Arabic—el-oum

\*

". . . All our mothers and grand-mothers used in due course of time to become *with-child*, or, as Shakespeare has it, round-wombed . . . but it is very well known, that no female, above the degree of a chamber-maid or laundress, has been *with-child* these ten years past: every decent married woman now becomes *pregnant;* nor is she ever *brought-to-bed*, or *delivered*, but merely, at the end of nine months, has an *accouchement;* antecedant to which, she always informs her friends that at a certain time she shall be *confined*."

—*The Gentleman's Magazine*,
December 1791

# SOME MORE EUPHEMISMS AND/OR NEOLOGISMS USED FOR THE CONDITION OF IMPENDING MOTHERHOOD*

—*enceinte*

— "to be in an interesting state" (a loan-translation from the Italian)

—expectant

—to be in the pudding club

—bow-windowed

—up the pole

—Irish toothache

—living in seduced circumstances

—infanticipating†

—baby-bound†

—caught with the goods

—belly up

—full of heir

—heir-conditioned

—in the family way

—knocked up

—past her time

—storked†

—wearing the bustle wrong

—awaiting a bundle from heaven

—rehearsing lullabies

—declaring a dividend

—spawning

—a bun in the oven

* According to linguistic scholar Mario Pei, "the *un*euphemistic and thoroughly traditional term . . . is 'with child.'"

† H. L. Mencken in *The American Language* credits all of these to the late New York newspaper columnist Walter Winchell. There are probably more. Along with Louella Parsons and Hedda Hopper, his Hollywood counterparts, Winchell considered it a matter of the gravest importance to be *first* with the news of a forthcoming "blessed event" among the famous. All three gossips viewed it as a tremendous personal affront if not informed early on in a pregnancy.

M is for the million things she gave me
O means only that she's growing old
T is for the tears were shed to save me
H is for her heart of purest gold
E is for her eyes, with love-light shining
R means right, and right she'll always be
Put them all together they spell "Mother,"
A word that means the world to me.

Words by Theodore Morse and
Howard Johnson, 1915

❋

I have come, Sire, to complain of one of your subjects who has
been so audacious as to kick me in the belly.

—Line used by Marie Antoinette to
inform her husband, King Louis XVI
of France, that she was pregnant
with their first child.

❋

Mother is so all-important as a touchstone of verity that oaths
sworn on mother run a close second to oaths sworn on the Bible or
utterances like "As God is my judge."

Tempting eternal damnation by mis-swearing on the deity seems
no less threatening to many than being unfaithful to the sacredness
or ideal represented by Mother. In this increasingly secular age, I
notice that people no longer think they can impress you with their
honesty by saying "I swear to God." When they are really into
being taken seriously, my friends say "I swear on my mother's life."
Or "I swear on my mother's grave" or simply "I swear on my
mother."

Half of this book should convince you that such oaths are sacred and valid. But the other half may make you wonder.

Stutterers in every language have trouble saying the word for "mother."

❊

MOTHER. A World War I Western Front nickname for various big howitzers. A twelve-inch was generally called *grandmother;* a fifteen-inch, a *great-grandmother.*

❊

# WHEN YOU CALL ME THAT, SMILE!

When preceded by the word *mother*, a combination with *fucker* is made that is unique in its ability to incite aggressive anger even among people who have developed an armor of defense against the insults derived from obscenity.* Perhaps mankind's overwhelming fear of incest is challenged when the word *mother-fucker* is heard; or perhaps the image of the mother as pure and inviolate is damaged when the tabooed sounds are spoken. Although an example of a term that is both sexually descriptive and figuratively insulting, *mother-fucker* seems to touch off such a sensitive area, in the speaker and insulter, that it has not passed into the general language of taboos that are violated at the rate of several per minute.

—Edward Sagarin in
*The Anatomy of Dirty Words* †

---

* Demonstrating how emotionally charged this term can be, the psychoanalyst Robert M. Lindner once stated that, while working in prisons, he had "more than once seen a man killed for calling another a 'mother-fucker.'"

† Although Sagarin made his observation in 1962, the term is *still* taboo among people of gentility, even among the mildly profane. But its general "street use" has surely increased.

It seems mandatory here to include the classic black joke about the two mothers meeting. First mother says of second mother's baby: "My, what a good-looking baby. How old?" Second mother: "He's fourteen months." The baby at this point coos and says "Mutha!" First mother: "Do tell—only fourteen months and already he know half a word."

✻

Mama's language has an interesting background. Hebrew was the father's language, since the holy books were in Hebrew, and only Jewish males were taught to read. Yiddish became known as the "mother's tongue," the language of the home.

—Leo Rosten

✻

When First Lady Betty Ford was given a Citizen's Band set, she chose as her code-name for signing on and off, "First Mama."

✻

*Chomo-Lungma*, "God-mother of the Country," or *Chomo-Uri*, "Mother of the Turquoise Peak," is the name of Tibet's—and the world's—highest mountain. Tibetans find it as natural to call the cornerstone of the earth "Mother" as the English to call it by the name of a gentleman, Mount Everest.

—Helen Diner in
*Mothers and Amazons*

✻

## "CAESAREAN SECTION"

Macduff may have been, as Shakespeare put it, "from his mother's womb untimely ripp'd," but Julius Caesar was not, the legend of his so-called "Caesarean birth" notwithstanding. Medical historians now believe that the first instance of a baby taken from a living mother's uterus by surgical means did not occur until around A.D. 1500. Although it was a common practice in early Roman times to

14

remove babies by cutting through the abdominal and uterine walls of *dead* mothers, Caesar's mother, Aurelia, lived on for many years after his birth and so obviously did not undergo such an operation.

The theory is now that the term "Caesarean section" came into being because of an old Roman law making it mandatory for women dying in advanced pregnancy to have their babies removed by surgical means. This *lex Caesarea*, as it was called, gave rise to the custom of referring to all surgically assisted childbirth as being "Caesarean."

✳

## Some Husbands Who Called Their Wives By Maternal Nicknames:

Abraham Lincoln called Mrs. Lincoln "Mother"
Calvin Coolidge called Mrs. Coolidge either "Mammy" or "Mamma"
The Reverend Billy Sunday called Mrs. Sunday "Ma"
Albert Snyder called his wife, Ruth, "Momie"*
Gene Fowler called his wife, "Mother"†
Ronald Reagan calls Nancy "Mommy"
Also: Rousseau called his mistress "Mother"

* This bit of intimate domestic trivia was revealed in the course of one of the most sensational murder trials of the 1920s. In 1927, Snyder was bludgeoned to death with a sashweight by corset salesman Judd Gray, Mrs. Snyder's paramour. Both the lovers were eventually executed in the electric chair for the crime but trial testimony disclosed that Ruth Snyder was the "dominant" member of the passionate partnership. She insisted that her lover, as well as her husband, address her as "Momie" and, after this information became known, Mrs. Snyder received 164 offers of marriage in her jail cell. Shortly before she was strapped to the electric chair she wrote a poem containing these lines:

> You've blackened and besmeared a mother,
> Once a man's plaything—a Toy,
> What have you gained by all you've said,
> And has it brought you Joy?

† Here's the legendary newspaperman Gene Fowler on the two women in his life:
I knew . . . that I loved Dodie [his mother] but I never called her "Mother." I was afraid to, but I wanted to all the time. This is something about myself that I don't understand. Maybe it's the reason I've always called my wife, Agnes, "Mother."

# GRANNY SLANG

The term "granny glasses" is a relatively new addition to our fashion vocabulary, but most of the slang expressions involving grandmother date back a century or more and don't turn up much today. Readers of *Tom Jones,* for instance, are told that "A child may sometimes teach his grandmother to suck eggs." When the novel was published, back in 1749, author Henry Fielding had no doubt that the followers of Tom's adventures would understand that this meant (as Eric Partridge explains in *A Dictionary of Slang and Unconventional English*) "to instruct an expert in his own particular line of business." The seventeenth-century English proverb, "Go teach your grandmother to grope a goose" is a variation.

In Victorian England, downstairs types used the euphemism, "she has her grandmother with her," as a delicate way of saying that a woman was menstruating, whereas "to see one's grandmother" meant "to have a nightmare."

In nineteenth-century New England it was common (albeit a bit vulgar) to speak of "shooting your grandmother," meaning, "to be mistaken or to be disappointed." Sample: "Ah, you've shot your granny this time, for sure!"

Old-time sailors also gave short shrift to grandmother. A "granny's knot," says Eric Partridge, is the nautical term for "a badly-tied knot, apt to jam."

\*

## ACRONYMS

| | |
|---|---|
| mom: | military ordinary mail |
| m-o-m: | middle of month; milk of magnesia; minutes of meeting |
| MOM: | Musée Océánographique Monaco |
| MOMS: | Mothers for Moral Stability |
| MOM/WOW: | Men Our Masters/Women Our Wonders (anti-feminist slogan reading the same upside down) |

## Dirty P.S.

This chapter *could* include a whole colorful subsection devoted solely to "The *Strong* Language of Mothers." Space, alas, does not permit, but here's one example I can't resist.

The first and only time New York writer Frank Gehrecke ever heard his Berlin-born mother use a "dirty word" was during a Christmas holiday he spent with her when she was in her seventies. Mrs. Gehrecke was the proprietor of a greenhouse in Creston, Iowa, and Christmas was one of her busiest seasons. She was especially proud of the poinsettia plants which she supplied every year to the various local churches. It was on the morning the nuns were scheduled to pick up the order for the Catholic church that Mrs. Gehrecke made her once-in-a-lifetime slip into the improper. Frank heard a shriek from inside the greenhouse and rushed to his mother. "Look," said Mother Gehrecke, pointing. "Some bird shit on the sisters' poinsettias!" "Well, Mother," Frank scolded, "that's no reason for you to use that word." "Oh, I know," replied the shattered florist dolefully, "but the white shows up so on the red."

# The Mother as Myth

The hand that rocks the cradle
is the hand that rules the world.

W. R. Wallace, 1865

Here is the chapter everybody seems to fear this entire book might be about. But never fear, the mother as myth, in all her purity and untouchability, her most sacred and saccharine incarnations, is now a no-no. Meaning, nobody wants to hear about it and nobody cares. So I have handled the mythic mother in a fairly cursory manner.

But we must briefly consider the mother deified, illusionary, and mythical, for we cannot understand all the other things that have happened to her through the ages otherwise. Without this little review, we are in no position to evaluate mother's demythicizing, the general disillusion with mother, and/or even mother as reality.

The mother as myth goes all the way back to Eve. Some feminists believe the world was once made up of dominant matriarchies and women only became second-class citizens a little later, as soon as the priests and shamans caught on how to use their mystic powers, and men began to be concerned about female virginity in order to insure that the sons their women produced were their own. When the worship of the phallus replaced worship of the womb, women became "property" and, perhaps to make it up to them, men began to "revere" and "respect" women while oppressing them.

The ripple effect of women's liberation produced shelves of new books and reprints of old ones on the subject of the matriarchal cultures of the past—exploring symbols of the Great Mother, etc. (Boring!) The body of literature on this single subject is truly formidable. So, in this book, we are primarily concerned with the motherhood myth in America: putting mother on a pedestal. Ours is pretty much a nineteenth-century view (with some exceptions). It is chiefly the view of those of us who were born between World Wars I and II.

This chapter could have easily expanded into a book itself. (It often has!) I'm offering the mere tip of the mother-myth iceberg to remind you just a tad of mother's valentine-like, Hallmark greeting card, sweet little old Booth Tarkington era past. Look at what follows as an effort to remind, enlighten and entertain. There is no attempt to exhaust this inexhaustible subject and you will find no somber intellectual dissertations or other manifestations of mother magnified and perfected.

Mythic visions of mother are often cloying, sentimental, overblown, overdone and usually oppressively dull. So no wonder mother was knocked off her pedestal by feminism, the end of Victorianism, the new sexual morality, increased cynicism, pessimism, and realism. She must have been glad to "get down."

✷

Nobody will ever write a book probably about my mother. Well, I guess all of you would say this about your mother. She was a saint.

> —Richard Nixon's tearful farewell
> to cabinet and staff members,
> telecast to the nation, August 9, 1974

✷

It's Mom's Apple Pie.

> —Ronald Reagan—on
> the potency of the Panama Canal
> as a campaign issue

✷

Mama's name was Mary and if your Mother was an old-fashioned Woman and named Mary you don't need to say much for her, everybody knows already.

> —Will Rogers*

✷

Let France have good mothers and she will have good sons.

> —Napoleon

✷

If a woman grows weary and at last dies from childbearing, it matters not. Let her only die from bearing; she is there to do it.

> —Martin Luther

---

* It was also Rogers who observed that, in the U.S.A. of the 1920s, "MOTHER and Baby doing well was our National yell."

In 1920, George Jean Nathan and H. L. Mencken published *The American Credo*, a collection of some of the most popular beliefs held by Americans. Here is one:

"That when a comedian, just before the rise of the curtain, is handed a telegram announcing the death of his mother . . . he goes out on the stage and gives a more comic performance than ever."

Later, Nathan added two others:

"That all poverty-stricken mothers are invariably kind and inspiring to their children, but that all rich mothers leave their young in the care of ignorant servants, and see them only when, in guilty silks and jewels, about to attend the opera or some like orgy of wickedness, they bend for a moment over the cots of the sleeping little ones."

And:

"That if a man loves his mother he will always love his wife."

*

If evolution really works, how come mothers still have only two hands?

—Ed Dussault

*

It may be said that the most important feature in a woman's history is her maternity.

—Mrs. Trollope

*

# Three Mythic Mothers Too Cosmic To Cope With

**DEMETER**

I can't *tell* you how involved this mother gets!

Briefly, the expansive "Mother Earth" of ancient Greek mythology, Demeter was the golden-tressed giver of the fruits and flowers, worshiped as a great benefactress of mankind. The heart of the Demeter legend is the kidnap and rape of her daughter Persephone (Latin form: Proserpina) by Hades (or Pluto) for it symbolizes the death and rebirth of the nourishing produce of the earth.

Demeter was so undone by Persephone's abduction and consumed by sorrow at her loss that she threatened to keep the earth barren until her daughter was restored to her. The gods therefore worked out a compromise that Persephone would spend six months of each year in the dark kingdom of the dead but the rest of the time above ground with her mother. The time Persephone spends with Demeter represents the time of sowing, growing, and harvesting of crops; the period of her absence is the season of the barren fields of winter.

Almost every culture on earth has had a fertility goddess analogous to Demeter, with countless agrarian festivals in her honor. Whatever her name, she represents Mother Nature at her most bountiful and destructive.

## E V E

"The mother of all living," according to Genesis, she was the first female progenitor to get the blame for the woes of her multitudinous offspring. Because of her curiosity and disobedience in wandering from the straight and narrow, God decreed that "In sorrow thou shalt bring forth children" and biblical scholars through the ages have castigated her for bringing sin and death onto man and woman now exiled from Paradise. This aspect of the Semitic creation myth is almost universal; African tribes, North American Indians, Eskimos, Melanesians, and many other farflung peoples all agree that a primordial woman introduced the world to evil.

The Old Testament mentions only three sons of Eve by name, but the Apocrypha says she bore daughters as well, and these presumably were the mothers responsible for all those "begats" that eventually peopled the globe. (The Apocrypha would seem thus to at least relieve Eve from the sin of mother-son incest by providing Cain with sisters for procreation.* But it all depends on whether brother-sister incest seems neater to you than mother-son incest.)

Mother Eve, the mother of us all, is entirely too big a subject for us to tackle.

* For more on this, see page 317 in the chapter *Oedipus and His Brothers*.

23

Paradoxically, little is known about the principal saint, Our Lady, the mother of Jesus Christ, the Virgin Mary. New Testament references to her are sparse and this very lack has contributed to the literally millions of words of apocrypha, discussion, and speculation during the past two thousand years. Arguments as to her exact nature have occupied the minds of the giants of all churches and deal with every aspect—from her reputed "original sinlessness" to whether or not her milk could bring miracles.

The rock-bottom basic importance of this cosmic Mother of Mothers is undeniably her "goodness." In a large mythic scale, she serves as counterpart to the sin-evoking Eve; the Roman Catholics consider her "a second Eve," a co-Redemptress with Jesus Christ. Such veneration helped lead to the Reformation and to Mary's being somewhat discredited among Protestants. Arguments between "Mariology" (the body of teachings about her as the mother of Jesus) and "Mariolatry" (an opprobrious term meaning the worship of her as the Mother of God) have raged ever since. Briefly, this Hebrew "Miriam" was a child of Joachim and Anne, a cousin to Elizabeth, the mother of John the Baptist. Her Jewish family was the House of David, predicted to produce the Messiah. Mary was betrothed to a cousin, a carpenter named Joseph of Nazareth, to be protected by him. The angel Gabriel appeared to her and announced that she would bear the Messiah. The story of the birth of the infant Jesus in a manger in Bethlehem is the staple of the celebration of Christmas. Mary the mother was at the Cross when Christ was crucified and consigned to the care of St. John the Divine. (Jesus: "Mother, behold thy son.")

Put simply, she is the ultimate symbol of purity, divine motherhood, Eve before the fall. Artistic representations of her abound; shrines and cults to her curative powers are all over the world; the "Hail Mary" is a principal prayer of the Catholic Church. In my opinion, one of the most interesting books on the subject is Marina Warner's *Alone of All Her Sex*.

＊

# BUT BITE INTO THIS

The Tooth Mother is the devouring, castrating mother who is always a strong, central—but often hidden or denied—image of woman in a phallic culture. She is *vagina dentata*, the toothed vagina, ready to castrate any male who enters. According to Margaret Mead, the myth of *vagina dentata* is one of the two most widespread in the world. (The other, the flying carpet—sex as joyride? —seems both more sanguine and less dangerous. Perhaps these two myths represent positive and negative views of sex.)

—Signe Hammer in
*The Village Voice*

❋

## THE BEST

Every man is privileged to believe all his life that his own mother is the best and dearest that a child ever had. By some strange racial instinct of taciturnity and repression most of us lack utterance to say our thoughts in this close matter. A man's mother is so tissued and woven into his life and brain that he can no more describe her than describe the air and sunlight that bless his days.

—Christopher Morley in
*Mince Pie*

❋

## *Eight Keepers of the Mythic Flame*

### ANDREW CARNEGIE

Thoughts of "Mother" turned this steely Pittsburgh multimillionaire into molten sentimental molasses. Margaret Hodge Carnegie, he stated, was his "favorite Heroine" and "that power which never failed in any emergency." He vowed never to marry as long as she lived and adhered to this promise to the letter; he did not take a wife until five months after his mother's death when he was fifty-one. Having followed the rags-to-riches Horatio Alger formula in realizing the American Dream, the Scottish-born industrialist, in his autobiography, lighted his personal adulatory flares in honor of *poor* mothers. In Carnegie-endowed libraries across the width and breadth of the land, readers can learn from this volume that "Among the manifold blessings I have to be thankful for is that neither nurse nor governess was my companion in infancy. No wonder the children of the poor are distinguished for the warmest affection and the closest adherence of family ties and are characterized by a filial regard far stronger than that of those who are mistakenly called more fortunate in life. They have passed the impressionable years of childhood and youth in constant loving contact with father and mother . . . no third person coming between. The child . . . whose mother is to him a nurse, seamstress, governess, teacher, companion, heroine, and saint all in one, has a heritage to which the child of wealth remains a stranger."

## EDGAR A. GUEST

Though he was, in the first half of the twentieth century, the most popular and highest-paid verse writer in the world, Guest's poems expressed perfectly the *nineteenth*-century American ideal of Motherhood. His writing schedule of a poem a day (for his syndicated newspaper column and radio broadcasts) left a legacy of some ten thousand poems, a significant proportion of them extolling Mom.

A tiny sample:

> Mothers never change, I guess,
> In their tender thoughtfulness.
> All her gentle long life through
> She is bent on nursing you;
> An' although you may be grown,
> She still claims you for her own,
> An' to her you'll always be
> Just a youngster at her knee.

> (From *Unchangeable Mother*)

## YVETTE GUILBERT

The French *diseuse*, Yvette Guilbert, is most often remembered as a performer of risqué songs in the argot of the Parisian working people, but one of her biggest encore-winners in the Latin Quarter music halls of the 1890s was a tender tribute to mother-love. The words of the song were translated by the French poet Jean Richepin, from a poem written by Jose Echegaray, a Spaniard who won the Nobel prize for literature in 1904. The original source, however, is a Chinese tale dating back thousands of years. There are several English versions of the song, but this is the most striking:

> There was a young man loved a maid
> Who taunted him: "Are you afraid,"
> She asked, "to bring to me today
> Your mother's heart upon a tray?"
>
> He went and slew his mother dead;
> Tore from her breast her heart so red,
> Then towards his lady love he raced
> But tripped and fell in all his haste.
>
> As the heart rolled on the ground
> It gave forth a plaintive sound.
> And it spoke, in accents mild:
> "Did you hurt yourself, my child?"

## WILLIAM RANDOLPH HEARST

Phoebe Hearst gave her son seven and a half million dollars to build up his father's newspaper properties but long before that young Hearst was living proof of the axiom and eternal verity that "a boy's best friend is his mother." He found no one to replace Phoebe until he was forty and idealized her all his life to a degree that most observers considered excessive if not downright "unnatural." This apotheosizing of Motherhood was reflected in the Hearst press to such an extent that the novelist Stephen Crane once observed: "I see no difference between the (New York) *Journal* and Hammerstein's Roof Garden: You get . . . the song about mother's wayward boy in both shows."

## J. EDGAR HOOVER

In the family of the longtime FBI director, his mother, Annie, was, according to biographer Ralph de Toledano, "the dominant—and dominating—influence." Bachelor Hoover lived with Mother in

27

Washington, D.C. until her death at the age of almost eighty.* The determined piety of this martinet mother left Hoover with a strong aversion to mothers who did not share her uncompromising moral standards. Of all the lawbreakers he dealt with during his career, the one who most exacerbated his sense of moral outrage was the notorious "Ma" Barker who masterminded the bank and payroll robberies carried out by her four sons in the 1920s and '30s. "It was at 'Ma' Barker's knee," Hoover once declared, "that her brood became the most vicious and cold-blooded crew of murderers and kidnappers we've known in our time. In the case of the Barker gang, you can say that the major criminal factors were home and mother. She had the most resourceful criminal brain of any man or woman I have observed, and she passed it all on to her sons."

"Ma" Barker was killed in a shoot-out with FBI agents near Lake Weir, Florida, in 1935, her machine gun, still hot, clutched to her breast.

Wrote Hoover after her death: "In her sixty or so years, this woman became a monument to the evils of parental influence."


## HARRY HOUDINI

The life work of escape-artist Harry Houdini was, according to one psychoanalyst, "a manifest symbolization of the birth mechanism" and stemmed from an "overwhelming and almost morbid attachment to his mother." Born Erich Weiss, the fifth son in a Wisconsin rabbi's family, the young man who became Harry Houdini was in his late teens when he promised his dying father always to care for his mother. He kept the promise faithfully. Even after her death at the age of seventy-two, he visited her grave daily and, according to Dr. Louis Bragman, "would lie there face downward and tell her of all his plans, as if she could really hear him." He also tried desperately to communicate with her in séances, and the realization that many of the mediums he consulted used trickery led to his much-publicized campaign exposing such frauds. To the end of his life, Houdini declared that his mother's birthday was "my most holy holiday."

---

* One of Mother Hoover's most treasured gifts from her son was a canary he bought for her from the Birdman of Alcatraz.

# WILLIAM A. ("BILLY") SUNDAY

A popular baseball player in the 1880s, Billy Sunday went out with his teammates one night on a bender, stumbled into a Chicago mission and henceforth turned in his baseball uniform to bat in the league of Jesus Christ. As the most successful evangelist of his era, the many passionate pulpit hours he spent panegyrizing Motherhood had a tremendous influence on the American psyche.

Some Sundayisms:

"I want to tell you women that fooling away your time hugging and kissing a poodle dog, a 'Spitz,' drinking society brandy-mash and a cocktail, and playing cards, is mighty small business compared to molding the life of a child."

"The devil finds no fault with the mother who makes her children play in the street so they won't wear out the carpet."

"If Washington's mother had been like a Happy Hooligan's mother, Washington would have been a Happy Hooligan."

## WOODROW WILSON

A self-proclaimed "mama's boy," the twenty-eighth President of the United States dropped his first name of Thomas to use the maiden name of his "noble, strong and saintly mother" when he started on the trail that eventually led to the White House. Remembering how he "clung to her till I was a great big fellow," Wilson confessed that his "love of the best womanhood came to me and entered my heart through her apron-string." So outspoken was Wilson on his devotion to the former Jessie Woodrow that, in one of Sigmund Freud's more controversial ventures into psychohistory, the Viennese analyst presented her as a veritable Jocasta, from Virginia. No surprise then that in 1914, when Wilson affixed his signature to a resolution setting aside the second Sunday in May to be observed annually as Mother's Day, the proclamation called upon government officials and private citizens alike to display the flag "as a public expression of our love and reverence for the mothers of our country."* It may or may not have been a coincidence that Wilson was also born in Virginia, the commonwealth long known as "the Mother of Presidents."

* Another less celebrated Keeper of the Flame, Representative J. Thomas Heflin of Alabama, asserted on this occasion that "the flag was never used in a more beautiful and sacred cause than when flying above that tender, gentle army, the Mothers of America."

# BUT SERIOUSLY, FOLKS

Mary Anne Ferguson says:

Images of women in literature have always been ambivalent, for every biological role there has been both a negative and a positive view. In the Biblical creation myth, Eve, the mother of us all, is the temptress who brought sin and death into the world. But the Virgin Mary, passively acted upon by the Holy Ghost, pondering in her heart the experience of her Son, is the Queen of Heaven, the Mother of God, and, through Him, of us all. Eve could be tolerated as a necessary evil; Mary was worshiped as a model for all womankind. In Greek mythology, Pandora, sent to earth by the gods to marry and establish the human race, brings with her a magic box or vial; opening it, she releases not only all evil but the greatest gift man can have, hope. Both Eve and Pandora act in defiance of divine law. If they had passively obeyed (experience the world vicariously, as Mary did) man would have been spared the particular kind of life known as human. In both myths, except for the action of a woman, mankind would have been godlike. Because of woman, man is condemned to be mortal; he must die. Yet every human being in his early years sees his mother as the bringer of life, the nurturer, the source of pleasure and comfort. He soon learns that she also takes away pleasure; she says no, and he blames her for denying satisfaction, no matter what her reasons may be. The role of mother is ambiguous. Myths about woman's dual nature are attempts to explain primordial reactions to her double role as the giver of life and death, of pleasure and pain.

*Images of Women in Literature*

※

# THE WISDOM OF SOLOMON

One of the Old Testament's most quoted examples of the unselfish quality of true mother-love is the story of the two harlots who consulted King Solomon in a dispute involving a newborn infant (I Kings 3:16–28). Each had become mothers at the same time, but one's baby had died and now each claimed the living child as her own. Solomon listened to their pleading and when they were finished, called for a sword and ordered, "Divide the living child in two, and give half to the one and half to the other."

One woman assented to the King's plan immediately, stating, "Let it be neither mine or thine." The other woman was aghast at the suggestion for, as the King James version puts it, "her bowels yearned for her son, and she said, 'O my Lord, give her the living child, and in no way slay it.' "

On the basis of this response, Solomon, imbued with "the wisdom of God," decreed that the baby be given to this woman, for, he said, her unselfish answer proved that "she is the mother thereof."

✳

# IT'S ELIZABETH TAYLOR'S FAVORITE NICKNAME

In the figure of Mother Courage, the seventeenth-century canteen woman who follows the armies as they devastate Europe during the Thirty Years' War, [Bertolt] Brecht created a stunning symbol of the human being as victim and survivor.  Pulling  her wagon with her three children, Courage is the "mother torn between battening on disaster and trying—unsuccessfully—to shield her children from the disaster.

> —*Newsweek*, April 7, 1975.
> Review of *Mother Courage
> and Her Children*

✳

# WARTIME CLASSIC

On Thanksgiving Day 1864, a widowed mother dwelling at 15 Dover Street in Boston received a visit from a high army official bearing a holiday dinner, a collection of cash from "the churches and Christian women" of the town, and a letter from the President of the United States. The woman's name was Lydia Parker Bixby. She was the mother of six sons enlisted on the Union side in the War Between the States. Five of them had been reported killed. The letter, reprinted that year in newspapers all over the north, has now become, in the words of Carl Sandburg, "a piece of the American Bible." This was what she read:

Executive Mansion
Washington, November 21, 1864

Mrs. Bixby, Boston, Massachusetts
Dear Madam:

I have been shown in the files of the War Department a statement of the Adjutant-General of Massachusetts that you are the mother of five sons who have died gloriously on the field of battle. I feel how weak and fruitless must be any words of mine which should attempt to beguile you from the grief of a loss so overwhelming. But I cannot refrain from tendering to you the consolation that may be found in the thanks of the Republic they died to save. I pray that our heavenly Father may assuage the anguish of your bereavement, and leave you only the cherished memory of the loved and lost, and the solemn pride that must be yours to have laid so costly a sacrifice upon the altar of freedom.

Yours very sincerely and respectfully,
Abraham Lincoln

Mrs. Lydia Bixby, via this letter, has become a symbol of heroic maternal sacrifice in wartime, and will remain so, even though later research makes the ending of the story happier than it at first seemed. According to Sandburg's classic Lincoln biography, three of Mrs. Bixby's sons were *not* killed after all. Henry Bixby, believed slain at Gettysburg, was taken prisoner, exchanged, and returned to Boston in good health; George Bixby was also taken prisoner and secured his release by enlisting on the Confederate side; the teen-aged Edward Bixby, far from being killed, had deserted the Army and run away to sea.

\*

# BAD BOYS

If I were hanged on the highest hill,
Mother o' mine, O mother o' mine!
I know whose love would follow me still,
Mother o' mine, O mother o' mine.

Rudyard Kipling

For one on the ocean of crime long tossed,
Who loves his mother, is not quite lost.

—Thomas Dunn English

\*

NOTE:  Mothers with problem sons beg intercession from St. Monica, mother of the great church father, St. Augustine who, as a young man, led a dissolute life.

\*

At least one presidential assassin had thoughts of mother in his final hours. The dashingly handsome John Wilkes Booth was the special favorite of all of his mother Mary Ann's nine children and, in turn, Mary Ann said, John was "the fondest of all my boys." Mrs. Booth's son believed that his shooting of Abraham Lincoln in Ford's Theater in Washington, D.C., in 1865 would make him an instant hero. When he was hunted down after the slaying and lay with a bullet in his head, his dying words were, "Tell Mother . . . Tell Mother I died for my country."

\*

# THE WOLF, THE MOTHER, AND THE CHILD

A peasant's house was just outside the village, and the wolf lay in hiding at the door; he had seen all sorts of prey come out—lambs, calves and kids, a flock of turkeys, one good meal after another, so to speak. Yet the thief was beginning to weary of his vigil when he heard a child crying: whereupon the mother petted, punished, threatened him, if he did not stop, to feed him to the wolf. The animal made himself ready, giving thanks to the gods for such a windfall, when the mother, calming her beloved offspring, comforted him thus: "Don't cry—if the wolf comes, we'll kill him." "What's this?" exclaimed the beast, "first fair, then foul—is that a way to treat a beast like me? What kind of fool do they take me for? One day the brat will come into the woods for hickory-nuts . . ." Even as he spoke these words, a watch-dog burst out of the house and caught him by the throat. Pikes and pitchforks soon hemmed him in: "What are you hanging around here for?" and he was foolish

33

enough to explain his reasons. "Mercy!" the mother exclaimed, "you would eat my boy? Do you suppose I brought him into the world to fill the belly of the likes of you?" They killed the poor creature then and there, one villager cut off his head and his right front paw: the master of the village nailed them to his door, and these words were inscribed around the trophies:

> It is a wise wolf that never hears
> A mother scolding her child in tears.

> La Fontaine
> Translated by Richard Howard

*

No bones are ever broken by a mother's beating.

> Russian proverb*

*

# MOTHER E.

Whoever heard of Father Earth?

> —Vance Bourjaily,
> in an article on the "pilgrim mothers"

*

Lucius Junius Brutus, an ancestor of the Brutus who helped assassinate Julius Caesar, is the man who, according to ancient Roman legend, first coined the expression "Mother Earth." During the reign of

* In today's era of the battered child, this truism seems to have bitten the dust.

the tyrant Tarquin around 509 B.C., this early Brutus journeyed with two of the king's sons to the Oracle at Delphi to discover which of the despotic monarch's heirs would succeed to the throne. The Oracle replied: "He who should first kiss his mother." Hearing this, the immediate response of Junius Brutus was to throw himself to the ground with the cry, "I kiss thee, Mother Earth!" Later, after a bloody power struggle, Brutus did indeed become ruler of Rome, as one of the first two Consuls. He is remembered today as "the founder of the Roman Republic."

# Mother Demythicized

The "Mother of the Year" should be a sterilized woman
with two adopted children.

Paul R. Ehrlich
Population expert

There have always been dissenters to the cult of venerating Mother
and there have been iconoclasts dedicated to the tearing down of
her myth. Granted, in the past, they were never in the majority.
Many examples of mother mavericks abound, however, from Nero
to Byron, from George Washington to H. L. Mencken, from Philip
Wylie to Gore Vidal.

Current trends toward legalized abortion, growing acceptance
of birth control, ecological considerations of Zero Population
Growth, youthful revolt and cynicism, the invention of the Pill and
rise of the sexual revolution, the gains of women's liberation, prevalent theories of enlightened self-knowledge and self-interest, and increased consideration of Freudian psychiatric teaching have all
helped to rush the demythicizing of Mother.

This isn't to say that Mother, mothers, and motherhood are no
longer important. If that were true you wouldn't be reading this.
But maybe by simply understanding Mother, mothers, and mother-

hood better, by liberating Mother along with other women, by seeing Mother more realistically and allowing her to be herself, we will no longer expect her to be bounded by unreality. Mother as an ideal is unfair in the same manner as woman as a sex object.

Some people feel so strongly anti-Mother that I encountered occasional objections even to writing this book. Helen Gurley Brown told me: "Liz, it is undoubtedly the worst idea for a book I have ever heard!" Others looked at me with pain in their eyes and asked cautiously if I intended to treat Mother as a sacred cow, go to work for Hallmark, or produce another mound of mother treacle.

A few friends who know I consider myself lucky in the cheerful, independent, and positive mother I have, seemed especially afraid that this might hold true. Perhaps I should explain that since I have now managed, through psychoanalysis, to demythicize my own mother, my relations with her have improved infinitely. I understand her better and can now love her fully and freely at last. (In fact, I highly recommend this course to all who feel their mother is terribly important—negatively or positively—in their lives.)

It is quite clear that many people hate their mothers and even some who do not hate them, hate the *idea* of motherhood. A few stories offered for these pages were too brutal, too unkind, or too unpleasant to be used even in a book that is trying to be adult, evaluative, honest, and to touch all past and present bases.

In a sense, letting Mother down from her pedestal is more what this book is about than anything else. For we are in the middle of a violent re-evaluation of motherhood—historically, sociologically, psychologically, culturally, and physically. The high-water mark of the now not-so-astounding discovery that mother has feet of clay (like everybody else) lies in the fairly recent past. It happened in 1942 with publication of Philip Wylie's scathing essay on "Momism" in his book *Generation of Vipers*.

Wylie's chapter titled "Common Women" put the word "Momism" indelibly into the language. Its publication broke a path through sacred preserves and the author noted that all manner of amateur critics, psychiatrists, and even the U. S. Armed Forces came pouring along after him in agreement.

Wylie was the "motherless" son of a minister who claimed to have gained his insights in the parsonage, observing women in church groups and selling them remnants as a department store clerk. This gadfly said his own mother was "not such a ravening purulence as *they*" (meaning the "moms" he was describing in his essay), so there was nothing personal in his attack. Sexually liberated for his time, Wylie insisted he loved "real" women and "motherhood whenever and wherever it is worthy of respect." In later years he defended himself against the charge that he was a misogynist and said his indictment of "Mom" was meant for only about one American mother in ten. He said he had tried to describe "destroying mothers" and "seductive mothers" who were psychological "types"—not *all* mothers.

Nevertheless, he shot to fame and notoriety on the basis of this one essay and became the object of both veneration and vituperation from those who agreed with his thesis (he said there were an intelligent few thousand of those) and those who detested him for it (he claimed there were millions of these who only thought they knew what he had written).

Wylie insisted he "was speaking of a certain, prevalent subspecies of middle-class American woman" when he stated emphatically "Mom is a jerk!" The notorious essay is today somewhat dated and marred by some of the author's petty personal objections (i.e.—to women in pants) which render it obsolete. In the light of current trends it seems passé, but perhaps it helped prepare the feminist wave, and, if so, one imagines the late author would approve.

Before he died Wylie reconsidered his essay and decided he had been right. "We are deep in the predicted nightmare now and mom sits on its decaying throne—who bore us, who will soon, most likely wrap civilization in mom's final, tender garment: a shroud." He wrote: "I showed her as she is—ridiculous, vain, vicious, a little mad. She is her own fault first of all and she is dangerous. But she is also everybody's fault. When we and our culture and our religions agreed to hold woman the inferior sex, cursed, unclean and sinful—we made her mom. And when we agreed upon the American Ideal Woman, the Dream Girl of National Adolescence, the Queen of Bedpan Week, the Pin-up, the Glamour Puss—we insulted women and disenfranchised millions from love. We thus made mom. The hen-harpy is but the Cinderella chick come home to roost: the taloned, cackling residue of burnt-out puberty in a land that has no use for mature men or women."

So time did not change Wylie's sting from *Generation of Vipers*. No one in this busy world needs to read "Common Women" again, but here are some excerpts from the essay that launched the twentieth century's true demythicizing of mother. They are full of Philip Wylie's florid gift for drama, shock, and hyperbole. Believe me, it was all pretty startling back in 1942 and after it was printed, motherhood was shaken into soul-searching, while "Mom" has never ever been the same popular old girl since.

Highlights (or Lowlights—depending on your point of view) from "Common Women" by Philip Wylie in *Generation of Vipers*:

Mom is the end product of SHE. *She* is Cinderella . . . the shining-haired, the starry-eyed, the ruby-lipped virgo aeternis, of which there is presumably one, and only one, or a one-and-only for each male, whose dream is fixed upon her deflowerment and subsequent perpetual possession. This act is a sacrament in all churches and a civil affair in our society.

I cannot think, offhand, of any civilization except ours in which an entire division of living men has been used, during wartime, or at any time to spell out the word "mom" on a drill field, or to perform any equivalent act.

. . . megaloid momworship has got completely out of hand. Our land, subjectively mapped, would have more silver cords and apron strings crisscrossing it than railroads and telephone wires. Mom is everywhere and everything and damned near everybody, and from her depends all the rest of the U.S. Disguised as good old mom, dear old mom, sweet old mom, your loving mom, and so on, she is the bride at every funeral and the corpse at every wedding. Men live for her and die for her, dote upon her and whisper her name as they pass away, and I believe she has now achieved, in the hierarchy of miscellaneous articles, a spot next to the Bible and the Flag, being reckoned part of both in a way.

. . . mom, the brass-breasted Baal, or mom, the thin and enfeebled martyr whose very urine, nevertheless, will etch glass . . . Mom got herself out of the nursery and the kitchen. She then got out of the house. She did not get out of the church, but, instead, got the stern stuff out of *it*, padded the guild room, and moved in more solidly than ever before . . . she swung the church by the tail as she swung everything else . . . Mom's first gracious presence at the ballot-box was roughly concomitant with the start toward a new all-time low in political scurviness, hoodlumism, gangsterism, labor strife, monopolistic thuggery, moral degeneration, civic corruption, smuggling, bribery, theft, murder, drunkenness, financial depression, chaos and war . . . Her sports are all spectator sports . . . Mom is

40

organization-minded . . . Mom also has patriotism . . . People are feebly aware of this situation and it has been pointed out at one time or another that the phrase "Mother knows best" has practically worn out the staircase to private hell . . . The mealy look of men today is the result of momism and so is the pinched and baffled fury in the eyes of womankind . . . the perfidious materialism of mom . . . Our society is too much an institution built to appease the rapacity of loving mothers . . .

She is a middle-aged puffin with an eye like a hawk that has just seen a rabbit twitch far below. She is about twenty pounds over-weight, with no sprint, but sharp heels and a hard backhand which she does not regard as a foul but a womanly defense. In a thousand of her there is not sex appeal enough to budge a hermit ten paces off a rock ledge. She none the less spends several hundred dollars a year on permanents and transformations, pomades, cleansers, rouges, lipsticks, and the like—and fools nobody except herself. If a man kisses her with any earnestness, it is time for mom to feel for her pocketbook, and this occasionally does happen.

I give you mom. I give you the destroying mother. I give you her justice—from which we have never removed the eye bandage. I give you the angel—and point to the sword in her hand. I give you death—the hundred million deaths that are muttered under Yggdra-sill's ash. I give you Medusa and Stheno and Euryale. I give you the harpies and the witches, and the Fates. I give you the woman in pants, and the new religion: she-popery. I give you Pandora. I give you Proserpine, the Queen of Hell. The five-and-ten-cent-store Lilith, the mother of Cain, the black widow who is poisonous and eats her mate, and I designate at the bottom of your program the grand finale of all the soap operas: the mother of America's Cin-derella.

※

# THE SLIDE

The artistic acceptance of *Whistler's Mother* during the course of its first century in existence is charted by Russell Lynes in his 1955 book, *The Tastemakers.* From the 1870s to 90s (identified as *Arrangement in Gray and Black, No. 1*) it was considered High-brow. From the 1910s to 20s (identified as *Portrait of the Artist's Mother*) it was classified as Middlebrow. By the 1940s to 50s (en-titled, simply, *Whistler's Mother*) it was Lowbrow.

Motherhood is in trouble, and it ought to be. A rude question is long overdue: Who needs it? The answer used to be (1) society and (2) women. But now, with the impending horrors of overpopulation, society desperately doesn't need it. And women don't need it, either. . . .

The notion that the maternal wish and the activity of mothering are instinctive or biologically predestined is baloney. Try asking most sociologists, psychologists, psychoanalysts, biologists—many of whom are mothers—about motherhood being instinctive; it's like asking department-store presidents if their Santa Clauses are real.

—Betty Rollin, quoted in
*The Future of the Family*

Women don't need to be mothers any more than they need spaghetti.

—Dr. Richard Rabkin,
New York psychiatrist

*

# THE FOUNDING FATHERS' MOTHERS

In *The Woman in Their Lives,* a study of "The Distaff Side of the Founding Fathers," author Frank Donovan ponders the views expressed by Franklin, Washington, Adams, Jefferson, Hamilton, and Madison with reference to their female parents. His conclusion? "Surely the women who bore the men who led in establishing the United States must have had something to do with the qualities that made their offspring great. But the offspring and their contemporaries either did not appreciate this influence or did not give it recognition. Despite George Washington's sanctimonious remark on the subject* (which is belied by everything else he ever wrote

---

* "I attribute all of my success in life to the moral, intellectual, and physical education which I received from my mother." For more about the Father of His Country and his mother, see page 69.

about his mother), the Founding Fathers did not credit their mothers as being among the important women in their lives."

✳

# CHILDBIRTH AS AN ACT OF CREATION

MARY ELLMANN:

There are, of course, reasons for women to value pregnancy and childbirth, but they are, I think, slowly persuaded to befuddle the issue (in every sense) with creativity. Women may want to be involved in a particular physiological process for nine months: some enjoy the process itself and most rejoice in its conclusion. But not on the grounds of creativity. The astonishment of childbirth is the unimaginable result of having done no more than indulge the body in a prolonged vagary of its own design. And even this detached impression of *uterine* accomplishment is brief: almost at once, the child appears always to have been a separate and complete being, whose body cannot be seen as the product of cellular multiplication. In this sense, prenatal development is *known* but not believed. A hubris of childbirth is the opposite, a moral conviction beyond natural verification. It marks an extraordinary schism between the self and the body in which the self acquires conscious pride in the unconscious working of the container.

*Thinking About Women*

✳

# MATERNAL INSTINCT?

WARREN FARRELL:

Is there a maternal instinct? In an experiment undertaken by B. Seay, B. K. Alexander, and H. F. Harlow, monkeys were deprived of their mothers immediately after birth so that they had no *environmental* models of motherhood. When they became mothers themselves, they were not able to care for or handle their children. In fact, one monkey "often terminated periods of nursing with violent assaults on her baby. She dragged her infant across the floor, ignoring its screams, and struck it without provocation. On several

43

occasions, this monkey was observed to hang from the ceiling of her cage and beat the infant with her hands." Seay found that *all* of the monkeys without maternal experience were totally inadequate mothers themselves, and none of their babies would have survived without intervention from the laboratory staff. "Two mothers were violent and abusive and the other two were primarily indifferent and withdrawn." Men and women may both have instincts for parenting, but these must be developed through teaching. Our culture teaches women, discourages men, and then claims the instinct for parenting is unique to women.

*The Liberated Man*

\*

# ERIK FOLLOWS PHILIP

By 1950, Philip Wylie's attack on "Mom" had breached all the barricades of sacred reserve, and Mother's blame, Mother's guilt, Mother's role in modern life was up for endless dissection. At this time Erik H. Erikson produced *Childhood and Society* with its now classic, much-quoted-by-feminists passage, "Reflections on the American Identity," as applied to "Mom." Erikson didn't try to restore mother to her mythic pedestal but he did apply psychoanalysis to the field of cultural anthropology to bring a touch of realism into the hue and cry against mother. Briefly, here is an excerpt of Erikson's fair play plea for mothers now thoroughly demythicized and demoralized:

> . . . The psychiatrists tend to blame "Mom." Case history after case history states that the patient had a cold mother, a dominant mother, a rejecting mother—or a hyperpossessive, over-protective one. They imply that the patient, as a baby, was not made to feel at home in this world except under the condition that he behave himself in certain definite ways, which was inconsistent with the timetable of an infant's needs and potentialities, and contradictory in themselves. They imply that the mother dominated the father, and that while the father offered more tenderness and understanding to the children than the mother did, he disappointed his children in the end because of what he "took" from the mother. Gradually what had begun as a spontaneous movement in thousands of clinical files has become a

manifest literary sport in books decrying the mothers of this country as "Moms" and as a "generation of vipers."

Who is this "Mom"? How did she lose her good, her simple name? How could she become an excuse for all that is rotten in the state of the nation and a subject of literary temper tantrums? *Is* Mom really to blame?

In a clinical sense, of course, to blame may mean just to point to what the informer worker sincerely considers the primary cause of the calamity. But there is in much of our psychiatric work an undertone of revengeful triumph, as if a villain had been spotted and cornered. The blame attached to the mothers in this country (namely, that they are frigid sexually, rejective of their children, and unduly dominant in their homes) has in itself a specific moralistic punitiveness. No doubt both patients and psychiatric workers were blamed too much when they were children; now they blame all mothers, because all causality has become linked with blame.

It was, of course, a vindictive injustice to give the name of "Mom" to a certain dangerous type of mother, a type apparently characterized by a number of fatal contradictions in her motherhood . . . "Mom" . . . is a composite image of traits, none of which are present all at once in one single woman. No woman consciously aspires to be such a "Mom," and yet she may find that her experience converges on this Gestalt, as if she were forced to assume a role.

To the clinical worker, "Mom" is something comparable to a classical psychiatric syndrome which you come to use as a yardstick although you have never seen it in pure form. In cartoons she becomes a caricature, immediately convincing to all. Before analyzing "Mom," then, as a historical phenomenon, let us focus on her from the point of view of the pathogenic demands which she makes on her children and by which we recognize her presence in our clinical work:

1. "Mom" is the unquestioned authority in matters of mores and morals in her home, and (through clubs) in the community; yet she permits herself to remain, in her own way, vain in her appearance, egotistical in her demands, and infantile in her emotions.

2. In any situation in which this discrepancy clashes with the respect which she demands from her children, she blames her children; she never blames herself.

3. She thus artficially maintains what Ruth Benedict would call the discontinuity between the child's and the adult's status without endowing this differentiation with the higher meaning emanating from superior examples.

4. She shows a determined hostility to any free expression of the

most naive forms of sensual and sexual pleasure on the part of her children, and she makes it clear enough that the father, when sexually demanding, is a bore. Yet as she grows older she seems unwilling to sacrifice such external signs of sexual competition as too youthful dresses, frills of exhibitionism, and "make-up." In addition, she is avidly addicted to sexual display in books, movies, and gossip.

5. She teaches self-restraint and self-control, but she is unable to restrict her intake of calories in order to remain within the bounds of the dresses she prefers.

6. She expects her children to be hard on themselves, but she is hypochondriacally concerned with her own well-being.

7. She stands for the superior values of tradition, yet she herself does not want to become "old." In fact, she is mortally afraid of that status which in the past was the fruit of a rich life, namely the status of the grandmother.

This will be sufficient to indicate that "Mom" is a woman in whose life cycle remnants of infantility join advanced senility to crowd out the middle range of mature womanhood, which thus becomes self-absorbed and stagnant. In fact, she mistrusts her own feelings as a woman and mother. Even her overconcern does not provide trust, but lasting mistrust. But let it be said that this Mom . . . is not happy; she does not like herself; she is ridden by the anxiety that her life was a waste. She knows that her children do not love her, despite Mother's Day offerings. "Mom" is a victim, not a victor.

Assuming, then, that this is a "type," a composite image of sufficient relevance for the epidemiology of neurotic conflict in this country; to explain it would obviously call for the collaboration of historian, sociologist, and psychologist, and for a new kind of history, a kind which at the moment is admittedly in its impressionistic and sensational stages. "Mom," of course, is only a stereotype caricature of existing contradictions which have emerged from intense, rapid, and as yet unintegrated changes in American history. . . .

In her original attributes . . . the American woman was a fitting and heroic companion to the post-revolutionary man, who was possessed with the idea of freedom from any man's autocracy and haunted by the fear that the nostalgia for some homeland and the surrender to some king could ever make him give in to political slavery. Mother became "Mom" only when Father became "Pop" under the impact of the identical historical discontinuities. For, if you come down to it, Momism is only misplaced paternalism. American mother stepped into the role of the grandfathers as the fathers abdicated their dominant place in the family, in the field of education, and in cultural life. The post-revolutionary descendants of the Founding Fathers forced their women to be mothers *and* fathers, while they continued to cultivate the role of freeborn sons.

# MOTHER UP AGAINST THE WALL

## by Russell Baker

Unpleasant questions are being raised about Mother's Day. Is this day necessary? its critics are asking. Isn't it bad public policy? Isn't it, in fact, dangerous to grant Mother a celebratory day on which she is heaped with all the gratitude flowers and candy can express?

The criticism arises from persons alarmed about world population problems. In their view Mother is the enemy, or at least half the enemy, and unless she is restrained she will bring the world to famine, barbarism, and rampant catastrophe.

The real heroines on this particular barricade are the women who decline motherhood, or so runs the argument, for in their abstention they are helping save the world from the evils being brought on by Mother.

Sound public policy would thus seem to call for abolishing Mother's Day, since it glorifies the authoress of the population miseries, thereby encouraging more motherhood all around.

No politician with half his senses, which a majority of politicians have, is likely to vote for the abolition, however. As a class, mothers are tender and loving, but as a voting bloc they would not hesitate for an instant to pull the seat out from under any Congressman who suggests that Mother is not entitled to a box of chocolates each year in the middle of May.

Congressmen, all of whom have mothers, know how sensitive this class of woman can become when the institution of motherhood is slighted. Congressmen also have an especially soft spot in their hearts for mothers, for they know that mothers are so humane they will forgive their children anything, even the fact that they sometimes become Congressmen.

In short, there is not much hope for abolition. Mother's Day opponents recognize this and concentrate, instead, on other schemes for taking the gloss off motherhood.

One scheme is to flood the greeting-card market with Mother's Day cards intended to make women think twice about the glory of motherhood. "Greetings on Mother's Day," says the message on a typical card for women who are thinking about having their first child. "If your litter be twins, or even a bit littler, you could have a son like Adolf Hitler."

Another aimed at mothers thinking of expanding their families says, "Queen Hecuba of ancient Troy gave birth to fifty baby boys, and would have gone to fifty-one if she'd ever got the laundry done."

The more promising scheme calls for establishing a counter-celebration to Mother's Day. The purpose would be to grant equal veneration to women who do not become mothers. The holiday would be called Unmother's Day.

On Unmother's Day, tribute would be paid to all women who have refrained from contributing to the population problem. In this way, the country would recognize the great contribution these women make in not contributing to the people glut, and they would receive equal glory with mothers.

The difficulty with this proposal lies in finding a suitable way of rewarding them. Unlike mothers, they have no broods to present them with potted plants and gumdrops. Many do not even have husbands.

The question is how they can be given recognition when they don't have anyone to do the recognizing. Well, they can recognize each other, of course, in an exchange of Unmother's Day cards but that is not likely to work very well. It is easy enough for a child to forget Mother's Day even under the social pressure created by the knowledge that Mother may reply with a bout of ostentatious sulking. What comparable pressure is there on an unmother to remember her sister unmother on the big day? None.


The best solution here is for mothers to undertake this duty to their daughters. Here we would have the same pressures acting on Mother to remember her child on Unmother's Day that now compel the child to remember Mother on Mother's Day. She will know all too well that if she slips in her duty, daughter will look at her with a sad unloved expression that says, "You didn't even remember your poor old daughter on Unmother's Day. That's the gratitude I get for not bringing any more people into the world."

A mother with an embittered turn of mind might even find Unmother's Day a good chance to let off some healthy steam, sending a bouquet with a card that says, "Thanks to my daughter on Unmother's Day for not having any more children like her."

Actually, no mother would ever send such a card. And any who did would not be a mother. At least not in America. Ask any Congressman. Ask any mother.

# AN ASTONISHED MELANCHOLY

## by Simone de Beauvoir

The first relations of the mother with her newborn child are variable. Some women suffer from the emptiness they now feel in their bodies: it seems to them that their treasure has been stolen. In her poems Cecile Sauvage expresses this feeling: "I am the hive whence the swarm has departed," and also: "He is born, I have lost my young beloved, now he is born, I am alone."

At the same time, however, there is an amazed curiosity in every young mother. It is strangely miraculous to see and to hold a living being formed within oneself and issued forth from oneself. But just what part has the mother had in the extraordinary event that brings into the world a new existence? She does not know. The newborn would not exist had it not been for her, and yet he leaves her. There is an astonished melancholy in seeing him outside, cut off from her. And almost always disappointment. The woman would like to feel the new being as surely *hers* as is her own hand; but everything he experiences is shut up inside him; he is opaque, impenetrable, apart; she does not even recognize him because she does not know him. She has experienced her pregnancy without him: she has no past in common with this little stranger. She expected that he would be at once familiar, but now, he is a newcomer, and she is surprised at the indifference with which she receives him. In the reveries of her pregnancy he was a mental image with infinite possibilities, and the mother enjoyed her future maternity in thought; now he is a tiny, finite individual, and he is there in reality—dependent, delicate, demanding. Her quite real joy in his finally being there is mingled with regret to find him no more than that.

*—The Second Sex*

\*

To have a child is no more creditable than to have rheumatism —and no more discreditable.

—H. L. Mencken

# DEAR ABBY'S SISTER

In 1976, advice columnist Ann Landers conducted a survey among her readers posing the question: "If you had it all to do over again, would you have children?" The answer was a resounding "No!" According to the columnist's report on the survey in *Good Housekeeping*, 70 per cent of the ten thousand women respondents answered they would not. "The sky fell in," said Landers. "The word came . . . straight from the gut of young parents and old parents, from Anchorage to San Antonio. I heard from Junior Leaguers and welfare mothers. The Boston Brahmins wrote, and so did the hill people of Kentucky." The "no" mail, Landers added, included letters from many mothers and fathers who said that their children had ruined their marriage.

✳

The Great American Mom—a juggernaut whose toll of crippled lives is greater than all our wounded in two world wars.

> —Jacket blurb for 1946 volume *Their Mothers' Sons*, by Dr. Edward A. Streiker, a psychiatric consultant to U.S. armed forces

✳

# FUTURE SHOCK

When Aldous Huxley wrote his novel *Brave New World* in 1932, he was creating social satire. The book became exceptionally popular, not because people believed in its stark vision of the future, but because it was terribly funny.

In the future imagined by Huxley the great god worshiped was Ford . . . people went to the "feelies" as well as the "movies" . . . pills produced happiness and euphoria . . . and babies were produced in bottles, emerging from the Decanting Room to Neo-Pavlovian conditioning by the state. The brave new world would be a benevolent despotism given to increased mechanization and computerism.

No doubt even Huxley did not know how prophetic he was.

Today, America and much of western civilization is strangling in its love of and dependence on the automobile . . . cinema has and does try to give us sensation as well as picture (Sensurround) . . . mood-changing pills and drugs are commonly in use . . . we are increasingly dependent on government paternalism, on mechanization and computerization. And, if you read Alvin Toffler's excerpt from *Future Shock* (below), you will see a truly prophetic writer already worrying about the changes that may occur when science dispenses with Mother and the Decanting Room becomes a fact.

The most unforgettable thing in *Brave New World* is indeed this chilling vision of a society in which human beings are no longer produced by "birth." In the novel, teachers tell their classes the facts of life and the students almost blush knowing that they are skirting the fine line between scientific knowledge and smut when they discuss "being born," "parents," and "viviparous" human beings in the past. The teacher tells his class, "These are unpleasant facts, I know it. But then most historical facts *are* unpleasant."

In *Brave New World*, the greatest obscenity of the English language is the word—*Mother!* Philip Wylie would not write his diatribe against "Mom" for another decade, but the demythicizing of Mother in fiction and in essay was well on its way.

＊

# MOTHER OBSOLETE?

As Alvin Toffler sees it:

. . . advances in science and technology, or in reproductive biology alone, could, within a short time, smash all orthodox ideas about the family and its responsibilities. When babies can be grown in a laboratory jar what happens to the very notion of maternity? And what happens to the self-image of the female in societies which, since the very beginnings of man, have taught her that her primary mission is the propagation of and nurture of the race?

Few social scientists have begun as yet to concern themselves with such questions. One who has is psychiatrist Hyman G. Weitzen, director of Neuropsychiatric Service at Polyclinic Hospital in New York. The cycle of birth, Dr. Weitzen suggests, "fulfills for most women a major creative need . . . Most women are proud of their ability to bear children . . . The special aura that glorifies the pregnant woman has figured largely in the art and literature of both East and West."

What happens to the cult of motherhood, Weitzen asks, if "her offspring might literally not be hers, but that of a genetically 'superior' ovum, implanted in her womb from another woman, or even grown in a Petri dish?"

*—Future Shock*

✳

# ON A SCALE OF 1 TO 10 . . .

How important is motherhood on the scale of human happiness? Not very, according to a nationwide survey taken in 1976 by social scientists at Columbia University. A group of more than 52,000 Americans from the ages of fifteen to ninety-five filled out questionnaires on the subject of happiness, rating its most important ingredients, and parenthood turned out to be much less important to either women or men than health, personal growth, social life, success, and recognition. On the over-all happiness scale, married women rated being a mother way down in tenth position.

✳

Being a housewife and a mother is the biggest job in the world, but if it doesn't interest you, don't do it. It didn't interest me, so I didn't do it. Anyway, I would have made a terrible parent. The first time my child didn't do what I wanted, I'd kill him.

Katharine Hepburn in *People*

✳

Never play cards with a man called Doc. Never eat at a place called Mom's. Never sleep with a woman whose troubles are worse than your own.

—Nelson Algren,
quoting a convict's advice which he now
passes on to young writers

# Mothers and Sons

The god to whom little boys say their prayers has a face very much like their mother's.

Sir James M. Barrie

Mothers and Sons just growed, like Topsy. There was no stopping this chapter; it expanded like an adolescent boy wolfing down milk, eggs, and assorted groceries. The reason possibly is that recorded life stories tend to be predominantly male. Women are now writing more and more about themselves, but they have a long way to go to catch up. You find almost every man who ever sat down to write an autobiography has something to say about his mother. And more biographies have been written about men. There are still fewer female life stories told than male ones. Today more and more contemporary novels are focusing on the mother-daughter relationship, yet even these are not a patch on the great surfeit of mother-son works of fiction, some of them classic.

About all I know of mothers and sons is what I read, for I have never quite figured out exactly what my brothers think or feel about my mother and they are not big on analyzing or discussing their feelings. They seem to offer her all the expected emotions— love, devotion, amusement, tenderness, teasing, protectiveness, and occasional exasperation. The house often rings with their out-of-patience, "Good *night,* Mother!" expression—as if she were the child and they the parent.

Both of my brothers live only seventy miles from my mother and visit frequently. My older brother telephones every single day to be sure she is okay, but this is concern since she got older, not a hang-up on his part. During World War II she was lucky to hear from him once every three months when he would write his unvarying joke, "Dear Mother, You sure are looking good!" and that was about all. Both my brothers spend frequent weekends with my mother. They do her grocery shopping, yard work, and all the things too tough for her to handle since my father died. In this respect, I suppose they are exemplary sons.

My younger brother has become increasingly possessive of her. He frequently refers to her as "*my* mother"—even to me. Now and then she becomes "*your* mother," as in, "your mother thinks it's about time you came to see her." He collects things she says and does and sends them to me. He finds her very funny; her naïveté being one of the joys of his life.

Bobby's favorite story of "his" mother is of the time a Mr. Dwyer roomed with us. In our house no alcohol was served. One day the roomer exuberantly opened the door of his room and, leaning out clad only in his undershorts, asked: "Miz Smith, how'd you like a Tom Collins?" Because mother didn't think she quite approved of Mr. Dwyer, who was, after all, a traveling salesman, and because she knew she didn't approve of his state of undress, she said cautiously: "Well, I don't know, Mr. Dwyer. Is it anything like a Dr. Pepper?" This story is guaranteed to make my brothers roll on the floor, though it has been told hundreds of times and has become a family catch phrase for anything anybody isn't sure about.

I notice James was the only one of us ever to call her "Mama" but he changed to "Mother" somewhere along the line. Maybe it was after she spanked him for the last time and broke the gold hairbrush of her dresser set on his corduroyed behind. She often speaks of this: "I knew I would never spank James again. He was getting too big to spank." But she kept the hairbrush as she has kept a lot of damaged mementos, including the old bird's-eye maple dresser on which "Mary E—" is erratically scratched by a nail file. She says that when she asked, "Mary Elizabeth, why didn't you write your whole name?," I cried and said, "Because it's too long!"

Oops, sorry. You see I just trespassed on Mothers and Sons with something that belongs in either Mothers and Daughters or Mothers and Guilt.

*

## SONNY BOYS

Men are what their mothers made them.

—Ralph Waldo Emerson

My mother was the making of me. She was so true and so sure of me, I felt that I had someone to live for—someone I must not disappoint. The memory of my mother will always be a blessing to me.

—Thomas A. Edison

I am the part of the woman the same as the man,
And I say it is as great to be a woman as to be a man,
And I say there is nothing greater than the mother of a man.

Walt Whitman

It is the general rule, that all superior men inherit the elements of superiority from their mothers.

—Michelet

*

Comparing one man with another,
You'll find this maxim true.
That the man who is good to his mother
Will always be good to you.

Fred Emerson Brooks

# "ADOLF . . . ADOLF HITLER!"

Adolf was a mother's boy, a *Muttersöhnchen*, one of those who are incurably devoted to their mothers and therefore capable of latent and sometimes open hostility to the father. He was perfectly aware of it and seems to have thought it was a natural state of affairs, not to be questioned . . . To the very end of his life, when he was living in a subterranean bunker in the heart of burning Berlin, he kept his mother's photograph with him and found himself continually gazing at it.

—Robert Payne in *The Life and Death of Adolf Hitler*

\*

The older I become, the more I think about my mother.

—Ingmar Bergman

\*

# WHISTLER'S MAMA'S BOY

James Whistler was a strong believer in "art for art's sake," and was dismayed when critics viewed the painting of his mother as a sentimental symbol, a sort of maternal "Mona Lisa." "Art," he wrote, "should be independent of all claptrap—should stand alone, and appeal to the artistic sense of eye or ear without confounding this with emotions entirely foreign to it, as devotion, pity, love, patriotism, and the like . . . Take the picture of my mother, exhibited at the Royal Academy as an *Arrangement in Gray and Black*. Now that is what it is. To me it is interesting as a picture of my mother; but what can or ought the public to care about the identity of the portrait?"

Later, according to his biographer, Roy McMullen, Whistler softened his views a bit in a conversation with a friend. ". . . we were looking at the *Mother*," the friend reported. "I said some string of words about the beauty of the face and figure, and for some moments Jimmy looked and looked, but he said nothing . . .

It was, perhaps, two minutes before he spoke. 'Yes,' very slowly, and very softly—'Yes, one *does* like to make one's mummy just as nice as possible.'"

✳

# THE COMPETITION

Mother is not exactly a new subject. She is everywhere in history, fiction, and biography. There have been some quite comprehensive books on Mother, and one I took pains not to read came out while this work was in progress. Titled *Mothers—100 Mothers of the Famous and Infamous*, it surely deserves mention and recognition, but had I read it, I might have stolen from it. Or I might have been intimidated by it. So I didn't. The fine essayist Harriet Van Horne gave us some of the juice of this work in her column as it related to Mothers and Sons:

> If you doubt that the child shows the man, consider this: eighteen-month-old Cassius Clay (now Muhammad Ali) was being cuddled on Mummy's lap one day when a tiny fist shot straight up and knocked out one of Mummy's teeth.
>
> Pauline Einstein worried that her Albert was subnormal. At the age of nine he still couldn't speak plainly.
>
> Lord Byron's mother had fleshy jowls, a coarse accent, a fishwife temper and a whisky breath. The boy "suffered blows and kisses in quick succession." He grew up in an atmosphere of "reproaches and flying plates." Let nobody wonder henceforth why Byron took up with shrews and treated them shabbily. He was paying back Old Mum.
>
> When Al Capone was found guilty of tax evasion in 1931 his beloved Mama came down to the jail with a hot casserole of spaghetti and cheese. In prison, Capone learned to play the banjo and composed a song entitled "Mother." Mama Capone's best-remembered saying is, "Al is a good boy."
>
> Whistler's mother, Anna, was a North Carolina lady of stern morality. She chose to live on the top floor of her house, explaining that there she was closer to her Maker. She stopped wandering into Jamie's studio when she discovered the parlormaid posing in the

nude. (She was thankful, she said, that the girl was at least standing up.)

Mildred Spock raised her son Benjamin with an iron hand. When he showed her—in fear and trembling—his first book on baby care, she surprised him by saying, "Why, Bennie, I think it's quite sensible."

*

# ERIC

Doris Lund's best-seller about her son's courageous fight for life and eventual death from leukemia tells one way the experience affected the mother-son relationship:

The myth or reality of male power and female weakness dominated our household that summer. Eric had many reasons for identifying with his father. His own recent brush with death, his witnessing of the deaths of so many friends, had left him vulnerable; to compensate he now put on the armor of the cold warrior. Nothing could touch Sidney (his father), therefore nothing could touch Eric. No matter how much I suppressed my concern and tenderness, Eric still suspected me of harboring some. He was not abusive, not overtly cruel, he simply behaved most of the time as if I did not matter and did not really exist. I tried to laugh it off, to see how it was for him. Sometimes it was hard.

"You know," I said one day to a friend who was an analyst, "Eric behaves as if the word 'mother' was a dirty word."

"It is, for him," said my analyst friend calmly. "You are the threat. Men have often seen woman as the death figure."

"But why? We give life."

"Well, that's just it. That *is* why. We all come from the unknown, from darkness, from the mother. And we go back into darkness when we die. Don't you remember how the Egyptians painted a mother-figure inside the sarcophagus?"

No, I didn't remember.

"It's not *your* fault, see?" said my friend, laughing a bit, with his wry, gentle detachment. "Man has always been scared of the dark mysterious womb. So now you get the blame."

"It's not fair, is it?" I said, smiling.

"No, it's not," he agreed. "But maybe it helps if you understand it."

*

## MY SON, THE STAR

Cary Grant's mother died in her native Bristol, England, in 1973 at the age of ninety-five. The romantic film idol, whose hair is now a glittering silver, told a reporter about his last visit with her there. "She looked me over critically and said, 'Archie, you ought to dye your hair.' At the age of ninety-five, mind you, she said, 'It makes you look so *old*.'"

Grant had earlier had a twenty-year rift with his mum, but after it was healed he phoned her every week. In an interview with a London journalist, the four-times-married actor asserted that his mother had taught him more than all the women he had ever known.

"Like what?" the reporter asked eagerly.

Replied Cary: "I can't remember."

*

Sportscaster Howard Cosell published a 390-page autobiography in 1973 in which he did not once mention his mother's name.

*

## Some Presidents and Their Mothers

There was an enormously strong intellectual-emotional bond between Dad and his mother—the sort of bond which, I have discovered from my delvings into presidential lore, has existed between an astonishing number of presidents and their mothers. No less than twenty-one of the thirty-six American presidents to date have been their mothers' first boy and almost every one of them were the favorite sons of strong-minded women.

59

Any boy who spent a lot of time with a mother like Martha Ellen Truman could only emerge from the experience the very opposite of a conventional mama's boy. This is one among many reasons why my father always bridled when a writer or reporter tried to pin this image on him. The rest of the family, knowing Mamma Truman, simply guffawed at the notion."

—Margaret Truman in
*Harry S. Truman*

＊

People have asked me if I ever spanked Jack when he was a boy. I suppose it is part of the mystique surrounding the presidency that anyone who occupies the office is endowed with qualities that are extraordinary and he must have passed through childhood in a glow of virtue. I can state that this was not the case with Jack, nor was it with Bobby or Teddy or any of the others, and whenever they needed it they got a good old-fashioned spanking, which I believe is one of the most effective means of instruction.

—Rose Kennedy in *Times to Remember*

＊

Mrs. Hannah Nixon was proud of her boy Richard for more than his political success. He was also, she told a reporter, "the best potato masher one could wish for." Mrs. Nixon disclosed that when she visited her son and his wife in Washington, or when they visited her, "he will take over the potato mashing. My feeling is that he really enjoys it."

＊

He has been very thoughtful to me. Occasionally he ignores me and I call him down. He says, "Mother, I don't have to prove my love to you. Thank goodness you're the one person I don't have to prove it to." He has always been a polite, kind son, and politeness to me means more than anything. I'm not his life—that's his wife and children—but I'm next to them. He lets me know that."

—Mrs. Lillian Carter discussing
her son Jimmy*

✱

The presidential campaign of 1828, which pitted challenger Andrew Jackson against incumbent John Quincy Adams, was one of the most vicious in U.S. political history. Jackson, who had won the popular vote in a race with Adams in 1824 but lost in the Electoral College, was the object of a cannonade of personal attacks, ranging over his war record, his political past, and even his marriage.

The warrior known as "Old Hickory" took most of the slanders in stride but when he came upon a newspaper story casting aspersions on the honor of his long-deceased widowed mother, he crumpled. "Myself I can defend," he told his wife Rachel. "You, I can defend. But now they have assailed even the memory of my mother." It was the one time in the old soldier's life his wife ever saw him cry.

✱

Although the mothers of five of the first nineteen Presidents were living at the time their sons became U. S. Chief Executive, the first actually to see her son take the oath of office was seventy-nine-year-old Eliza Garfield, mother of James Garfield, sworn in as the twentieth President in 1881. Just four months later, she became the first presidential mother to experience the horror of learning that her son had been struck down by an assassin's bullet.

✱

NOTE FOR FACT-FREAKS: The first five mothers to be alive when their sons became President were: Mary Ball Washington, Susanna

* According to presidential mother-expert Doris Faber, Jimmy Carter was the first President in American history to be born in a hospital—actually a tiny clinic in Plains, Georgia. The mothers of every single one of the previous thirty-seven presidents, from George Washington through Gerald Ford, gave birth to their babies at home.

Boylston Adams, Nelly Conway Madison, Jane Knox Polk, and Hannah Simpson Grant.

*

Nancy Allison McKinley was a devoted, if often stern, Methodist mother who inculcated her nine children with a deep sense of civic responsibility. Yet when her son William progressed from prosperous small-town lawyer to governor of Ohio to twenty-fifth President of the United States, she refused to take any of the credit. "I tried," she told reporters, "to bring up the boy to be a good man, and that is the best a mother can do. The first thing I knew, my son turned around and began to raise *me* to be the mother of a President!" A spry eighty-seven-year-old at the time she watched her boy sworn in as President, Mother McKinley took the cheering crowds and the omnipresent news photographers right in stride but an old dream apparently died hard. On inauguration eve, friends overheard the President's brother Abner comforting her: "But, Mother, this is better than a bishopric!"

*

# UNDER THE SKIN

" 'Dear Mum' or 'In memory of my dear mother' sweeping around a heart, a cross, a tombstone, or merely on a banner lying across a bunch of flowers," writes tattooing historian Hanns Ebensten, "are the inscriptions repeatedly chosen by very young men. Upon asking a much-tattooed man which of his many designs was his first he will nearly always indicate either such a one or a similar picture addressed to either a sister, brother or friend."

George Burchett, who, as "King of Tattooists," practiced his trade in London for many decades, agrees. "Many young men commissioned a small design expressing their 'Love to Mother,'" he writes in his autobiography. "Many young men? There were thousands of them! It was always mother, never father . . . These customers came from every walk of life; some were rough fellows, sailors, or labourers; others were palefaced, bespectacled youths working at an office desk. The week before Mother's Day each year brought a queue of these customers to my waiting room."

"Not infrequently," Burchett says, "I was asked for a memento

62

Popular Tattoo During Spanish-American War

of a dead mother. I tattooed such designs in the form of tomb-
stones or crosses, with a garland of flowers or a small wreath and an
inscription of a simple kind, like 'In Memory of My Dear Mother,'
sometimes with the date of her death. I always felt this work to be a
great responsibility."

*

## BOYS, BOYS, BOYS

My mother had a great deal of trouble with me but I think she
enjoyed it.

—Samuel Clemens

My mother made a brilliant impression upon my childhood life.
She shone for me like the evening star—I loved her dearly, but at a
distance.

—Winston Churchill*

✷

BERNARD:
I grew up to have my father's looks—my father's speech patterns—my father's posture—my father's walk—my father's opinions
and my mother's contempt for my father.

—Protagonist in
Jules Feiffer's play, *Hold Me*

✷

## Some Generals and Their Mothers

The tie between General Douglas MacArthur and his mother was,
he once wrote, "one of the dominant factors of my life." Well-
versed in military ways as an army officer's wife, Mary MacArthur
exerted all the influence she could muster to help her son's career,
including penning a personal letter to General John J. Pershing in
the middle of World War I asking him to promote "my Boy," then
thirty-seven, to the rank of brigadier general. Later, in the 1920s,
she wrote to Pershing again, requesting her son's elevation to major
general. (Whether or not the letters helped is not known, but Mac-
Arthur received both of the promotions.) Mother and son lived together at Fort Myer, Virginia, during the period MacArthur served
in Washington as Army Chief of Staff and he did not marry until
after her death at eighty-three when he was fifty-seven.

✷

In Woodward and Bernstein's *The Final Days*, the authors tell a
story of how General Alexander Haig spoke to his brother Frank
during the dark days of Watergate. They discussed their eighty-
four-year-old mother.

---

* As a schoolboy at Harrow, Churchill often supplemented his allowance by
selling autographs of his mother, Lady Randolph Churchill. In one letter
home, he asked for six.

At this time, Alexander Haig had already enjoyed a distinguished Army career, he was President Nixon's chief of staff, and would go on to be the head of NATO. Frank recalled that their mother had said, "If only Al had had sense enough to go to law school, he might have made something of himself."

Frank, mindful that his brother was then running the United States, asked his mother, "What more could he be?"

Mrs. Haig said, "He could be Senator from Pennsylvania."

＊

As a public man, General George S. Patton, Jr., was thunderously profane, a tough spit-and-polish disciplinarian famous for what his friend and commanding officer Dwight Eisenhower called his "unflagging aggressiveness." He once said of war, "I do like to see arms and legs fly." In private the World War II general who once slapped two enlisted men for breaking down under the strain of battle, could demonstrate unexpected tenderness. In 1931, saddened by the death of a beloved aunt, Patton paid a visit to his old family home in California and placed a letter to his mother in a box of her most treasured trinkets. At the time her only son wrote the letter, Ruth Wilson Patton had herself been dead for three years.

The letter reads:

Darling Mama. Here with your things before me you are very near. I never showed you in life the love I really felt nor my admiration for your courage and sporting acceptance of illness and losses. Children are cruel things. Forgive me. I had always prayed to show my love by doing something famous for you, to justify what you called me when I got back from France. "My hero son." Perhaps I still may but time grows short. I am 46. In a few moments we will bury the ashes of Aunt Nannie. All the three who I loved and who loved me so much are now gone.

But you know that I still love you and in the presence of your soul I feel very new and very young and helpless even as I must have been 46 years ago.

Nothing you ever did to me was anything but loving. I have no other memories of you but love and devotion. It is so sad that we must grow old and separate.

When we meet again I hope you will be lenient for my frailties. In most things I have been worthy.

Perhaps this is foolish but I think you understand.

I loved and love you very much.

Your devoted son G. S. Patton, Jr.

Before the journalist John Reed sailed off for Russia to witness the events that led to his 1919 classic, *Ten Days That Shook the World*, he served as a war correspondent with Pancho Villa's revolutionary forces in Mexico. One of Reed's first south-of-the-border goals was a private interview with the peon insurgent general, Tomas Urbina, who was ensconced in a two-million-acre hacienda which he had recently "liberated" and appropriated as a headquarters. Underlings there told the young journalist that Urbina was "a good man, all heart . . . very brave. The bullets bounce off him like rain from a sombrero." Urbina's doctor, however, put Reed off, explaining that "There has been some little trouble. The general has not been able to walk for two months from rheumatism . . . and sometimes he is in great pain and comforts himself with *aguardiente*. Tonight he tried to shoot his mother. He always tries to shoot his mother . . . because he loves her very much."

. . . my own childhood was unhappy. This was due to a clash of wills between my mother and myself. My early life was a series of fierce battles, from which my mother invariably emerged the victor. If I could not be seen anywhere, she would say—"Go and find out what Bernard is doing and tell him to stop it!" But the constant defeats and the beatings with a cane, and these were frequent, in no way deterred me. . . . I never lied about my misdeeds; I took my punishment. There were obvious faults on both sides. For myself, although I began to know fear early in life, much too early, the net result of the treatment was probably beneficial. If my strong will and indiscipline had gone unchecked, the result might have been even more intolerable than some people have found me. But I have often wondered whether my mother's treatment for me was not a bit too much of a good thing: whether, in fact, it was a good thing at all. I rather doubt it.

> Opening page of *The Memoirs of Field Marshal The Viscount Montgomery of Alamein, K.G.*

✳

Two decades after the end of World War II, a collection of Pentagon files originally marked TOP SECRET were restamped as DECLASSIFIED. Among them was a directive dispatched from the headquarters of the Allied High Command in May 1944, shortly before the D-Day invasion of France. The order, on official yellow message paper, called for sending a Mother's Day greeting to Mrs. Ida Eisenhower in Kansas from her son Dwight, supreme commander of the Allied Forces.

✳

## OTHER SONS

In *Popular Music in America*, Sigmund Spaeth cites this 1910 song hit by Harry Von Tilzer and Will Dillon as "the safest bet today for getting harmony out of any group of voices, male or mixed."

> I want a girl, just like the girl
>     that married dear old Dad.
> She was a pearl and the only girl
>     that Daddy ever had.
> A good old-fashioned girl with heart so true
> One who loves nobody else but you.
> I want a girl, just like the girl
>     that married dear old Dad.

© 1911 Harry Von Tilzer Music Publishing Co. Copyright renewed. Used by permission.

✳

A man who has been the indisputable favorite of his mother keeps for life the feeling of a conqueror, that confidence of success which frequently induces real success.

—Sigmund Freud

✳

## Some Sons Who Feuded With Their Mothers

### NERO

The over-watchful, over-critical eye that Agrippina kept on whatever Nero said or did proved more than he could stand. He first tried to embarrass her by frequent threats to abdicate and go into retirement in Rhodes. Then, having deprived her of all power, and even of her Roman and German bodyguard, he expelled her from his Palace; after which he did everything possible to annoy her, sending people to pester her with law-suits while she stayed in Rome, and when she took refuge on her riverside estate, making them constantly drive or sail past the windows, disturbing her with jeers and cat-calls. In the end her threats and violent behavior terrified him into deciding that she must die. He tried to poison her three times, but she had always taken the antidote in advance; so he rigged up a machine in the ceiling of her bedroom which would dislodge the panels and drop them on her while she slept. However, someone gave the secret away. Then he had a collapsible cabin-boat designed which would either sink or fall in on top of her. Under pretence of a reconciliation, he sent the most friendly note inviting her to celebrate the Feast of Minerva with him at Baiae, and on her arrival made one of his captains stage an accidental collision with the galley in which she had sailed. Then he protracted the feast until a late hour, and when at last she said: "I really must get back to Baiae," offered her his collapsible boat instead of the damaged galley. Nero was in a very happy mood as he led Agrippina down to the quay, and even kissed her breasts before she stepped aboard. He sat up all night, on tenterhooks of anxiety, waiting for news of her death. At dawn Lucius Agermus, her freedman, entered joyfully to report that although the ship had foundered, his mother had swum to safety, and he need have no fears on her account. For want of a better plan, Nero ordered one of his men to drop a dagger surreptitiously beside Agermus, whom he arrested at once on a charge of attempted murder. After this he arranged for Agrippina to be killed, and made it seem as if she had sent Agermus to assassinate him but committed suicide on hearing that the plot had miscarried. Other more gruesome details are supplied by reliable authorities: it appears that Nero rushed off to examine Agrippina's corpse, handling her legs and arms critically and, between drinks, discussing their good and bad points. Though encouraged by the congratulations which poured in from the Army, the Senate and the people, he was never thereafter able to free his conscience from the guilt of this crime. He often admitted that the Furies were pursuing him with whips and burning torches; and set Persian mages at work to conjure up the ghost and make her stop haunting him. During his tour of Greece he came to Athens, where the Eleusinian Mysteries were being held, but dared not participate when a herald ordered all criminals present to withdraw before the ceremonies began.

> From *The Twelve Caesars*
> Gaius Suetonius Tranquillus,
> translated by Robert Graves

*The Bedside Book of Bastards* adds these details:

Once, when asked by an officer to set the password for the day, Nero gave it as *optima mater*—the best of mothers. After several attempts by Nero to have his mother murdered, one of his men hit her over the head with a club and she realized what was about to happen. As a centurion bared his sword, she tore her clothing apart exclaiming, "Smite the womb that bore Nero."

## GEORGE WASHINGTON

Perhaps "feuded" is too strong a term in this case, but what existed between George Washington and his mother, the former Mary Ball,* was a coolth that bordered on the frigid. Douglas Southall Freeman, in his multivolume biographical study of the Father of Our Country, calls his lack of affection for his mother "the strangest mystery of Washington's life." Lonesome George did not, apparently, write his mum a single letter during the entire period of the American Revolution; she sent him neither her blessing nor encouragement when he was chosen as the new nation's first chief executive. Most of their correspondence concerned money—she, beseeching him for more of it; he, complaining about sending it to her. One of his most quoted epistles to her sets forth some of his reasons for not wanting her to move in with him at Mount Vernon. "Nor, indeed," he concluded, "could you be retired in any room in my house; for what with the sitting up of company, the noise and bustle of servants, and many other things, you would not be able to enjoy that calmness and serenity of mind, which in my opinion you ought now to prefer to every other consideration in life."

Tradition nevertheless has it that Mary Washington's dying thoughts were of her famous firstborn son. "I only wish," she whis-

---

* ROOTS FOOTNOTE:  You know how people are always bragging about being related to this or that famous person? Well, I can't resist saying that my wonderful maternal grandma, Sally Ball McCall, was descended from this very lady.

pered, "to hear from him with his own hand that he is well."
She didn't.

## LORD BYRON

As a student at Harrow, the young poet railed endlessly against his mother, "whose *diabolical* disposition," he wrote, "seems to increase with age, and to acquire new force with Time." Later, after an inheritance provided him with one of the most abundant incomes at Cambridge, he gleefully reported: "—I shall be perfectly independent of her, and, as she has long since trampled upon, and harrowed up every affectionate tie, it is my serious determination never again to visit, or be upon any friendly terms with her." (As for Lady Byron, she once hurled a coal scuttle and tongs at her wayward son's head and complained—in terms familiar to many lesser-born moms—"That boy will be the death of me, and drive me mad.")

But when she died, the twenty-three-year-old Byron wept by her coffin sighing, "I had but one friend in the world and she is gone."

## GORE VIDAL

In *Season of Comfort*, an early novel now mostly forgotten, Gore Vidal wrote of a boy's struggle against the domination of his mother. The 1949 book has a climactic scene at the end in which the boy, grown to manhood, tells his beautiful mother he has always hated her.*

Of the real-life Nina Gore Olds, her acerbic son has said little. "She had a gift for not doing the right thing," is what he offered *Time* magazine in 1976. But this was enough to spur Mother Olds to respond in an indignant Letter to the Editor. In it, Nina asserted that her son had never lacked love nor been abandoned by her. She quoted the late writer John LaTouche saying: "I have never seen such a sense of competition as Gore has with you." And, she ended, "I feel so sorry for him, for one day he will have regrets and sorrow."

Some of this maternal outrage was prompted by *Time*'s quotes from Gore's close friend, the late Anaïs Nin, who confided to her

* The title is taken from a quotation by the poet Arthur Rimbaud who, according to the book's protagonist, also hated his mother.

famous *Diary* that Gore "knows the meaning of his mother abandoning him when he was ten to remarry and have other children . . . He had wanted his mother to die."

Mother Nina is the daughter of Oklahoma Senator Thomas P. Gore, a Populist Democrat who was devoted to his intelligent grandson. Nina divorced Gore's glamorous aviator-athlete father in 1935, amid growing tensions, and remarried Hugh D. Auchincloss, later the stepfather of Jackie Kennedy.

Writer Nin thought that Gore's mother had harmed him more deeply than he knew. And Gore did once say of his mother to a reporter, "She was a traumatic experience for anyone who came her way."

Nevertheless, Gore is said to keep a picture of mother Nina in his study at Ravello, Italy.

## HENRY MILLER

The novelist venerated by Lawrence Durrell as the man with whom "American literature today begins and ends" also gave "Mom" short shrift, and the feeling was mutual. Miller's mother was a rigid, puritanical woman who refused to read anything her son ever wrote and who never forgave him for not becoming a tailor like his father. Avoiding both ambivalence and ambiguity, Miller laid it right on the line: "I hated my mother all my life."

※

The son-to-mother communication transmitted over the longest distance was the birthday greeting sent on December 28, 1968, by astronaut James Lovell to his mother. At the time of its transmission, he was 140,000 miles out in space on his way to the moon.

※

My mother's love for me was so great that I have worked hard to justify it.

—Painter Marc Chagall, just before his ninetieth birthday

# LEE'S MOTHER

Mrs. Marguerite Oswald, mother of the (as she insists on expressing it) "alleged assassin" of President John F. Kennedy, has a strong sense of her importance as "a mother in history." In a 1973 interview with W. C. Martin for *Esquire* she explained some of the ramifications of this. "I seldom sign my name to anything," she said. "My signature is worth something. If I am going to sign my name, I am going to get $100 for it to buy some groceries. I also refuse to let anyone record my voice or take my picture without paying.

"Everything in my house, even an ashtray, is a historical item, and it will cost anybody to get one . . . I would also like to sell the headstone from Lee's grave, but I hope it will go to a museum or library. They know they are not going to get it for nothing.

"I know all this sounds bad, but I have no other way to live . . . Is that wrong? I don't think it is. I am doing the best I can for myself and for my son. I think any man in America would be proud to have a mother like me."

❄

# ANOTHER LEE'S MOTHER

QUOTH LIBERACE:

There are so many little things about my Mother that I hold precious. I could probably write a whole book about her. And I feel terrible sometimes that my appreciation and admiration of her as a lovable and very special person have been ridiculed.

I have always felt there was a sort of regal aura around Mother and I found out I wasn't the only one who saw this the evening I was invited to entertain Queen Juliana and Prince Bernhard of the Netherlands at a Command Performance held at the Coconut Grove in Los Angeles. Mother was invited to this affair. And when she and I came down the famous steps at the Coconut Grove everyone in the room was sure it was the Queen herself and gave my Mother a standing ovation. I thought she deserved it and I must say she really looked like a queen that night with her beautiful white hair elegantly coiffed, a white gown, sparkling jewelry and luxurious fur wrap. To this day I have never told her that the standing ovation she received was actually intended for Queen Juliana. Mom thought it was for me. When Queen Juliana really arrived it was almost anticlimactic.

It makes me very happy, and I think it's a lovely compliment to Mother, that she has become so internationally known that no matter where I go the first question I'm asked by famous personages such as the Queen of England and her Mother, the President of the United States, governors and mayors is, "How's your dear Mother?"

✳

# A FEW WORDS ABOUT NINA KACEW (STAGE NAME: Borisovkaia), MOTHER OF ROMAIN GARY

### by Holland Taylor

Alone with her infant son in World War I Russia, stranded by her pale-eyed lover, this actress ended her career, began her picaresque journey to France, and launched into a life of such histrionic extreme and emotional *profondeur* as to leave a Duse gasping. She turned the million-sun candlepower of her love on no one but her boy—condemning him to stumble, after her death, in a world of shadow. Gauloise-puffing, dignified, even when reduced to kenneling dogs, cats, *and* birds in their flat, she was a true child of the nineteenth-century Russian novel, whose romance, passion, and honor she fed to her son along with the daily beefsteak. This latter, her dogged hustling never failed to produce. Gifted with a talent for tenderness, encouragement, and self-sacrifice, she escaped being the quintessential Jewish mother in that she never presented the bill. But her heart could be as hard as it was strong, and at twelve, Romain learned that she expected him to return home from any defense of her honor "on a stretcher, or dead." Not one to keep a boy in short pants, her hopes for him (heroism, literary fame, ambassadorships, English suits—all of which he inexorably achieves) included rendering him *un homme fatal*, but not a cad. ("You may take anything from women, even a Rolls-Royce, if necessary—but never money.") The boy spent his youth feeling he would "die of shallowness, helplessness and love." He spent the ravaging years of

World War II ignorant of his divine mother's last, sublime umbilical subterfuge (she wrote him hundreds of letters as she was dying and had them dispatched by an accomplice so he would not realize she was dead). Because of his mother, Romain Gary lived his manhood "condemned to gaiety and hope"—living up, willy-nilly, to Nina Kacew's balmy and extravagant dreams. He immortalized her in a book *Promise at Dawn*.

❊

## AND A FEW WORDS ABOUT LYDIA BEARDSALL LAWRENCE, MOTHER OF D.H.

Literary critics and Ph.D. candidates have amassed their own Five Foot Shelf of works speculating on the interrelationship between this refined English coal-miner's wife and her writer son's preoccupation with mother-son themes in such novels as *Sons and Lovers* and *Women in Love*. All are in agreement that Lydia Lawrence was a dominant force in both her son's life and works and, as such, made her mark on the psyches of countless impressionable devotees who have striven to pattern their lives on Lawrencian philosophical principles. Lawrence himself never managed to extricate himself from his guilty preoccupation with his mother's life and death. His wife Frieda wrote to him in exasperation: "A sad old woman's misery you have chosen, you poor man, and you cling to it with all your power. I have tried, I have fought, I have nearly killed myself to get you in connection with myself and other people, early I proved to myself that I can love, but never you . . ."

❊

O thou, who used to warm my cold feet in thy hands, O my mother!

—Denis Diderot

# NOEL'S VIOLET

Violet Agnes Veitch married Arthur Sabin Coward in 1890 and they produced Noel Coward. The very first recorded instance of Noel Coward prose was a letter written at age seven to "Darling Mother" and until her death at ninety-one in 1954, Mrs. Coward kept in "Mum's Suitcase" every relevant scrap of information from Noel's birth to early manhood. His friend, secretary, and biographer Cole Lesley writes in *Remembered Laughter* that is was "as though she foresaw he was to become—as Alexander Woollcott later named him—Destiny's Tot."

The Coward family did not get along and Noel claimed not to have cared much for his father or his younger brother, Erick. But he and Mother were close. Here is a note Mrs. Coward made of the days before her son became famous:

"Noel loved to look after me when he was a boy, he was so capable that I depended on him perhaps more than I should, when he was so young. He always knew the right thing to do, his opinion was really law to me, for he was always right. When I was at my wits' end and quite desperate . . . several times for money, he would talk and reassure me, and go off and get money somewhere and bring relief and joy to me. Oh dear those were happy days when the boys were young and I had them all to myself. Fortunately mothers don't realize that those times will come to an end and that when the children grow up they must live their own lives, and the mother who was simply everything to them in their young days must stand aside and try to make another life of her own without them."

In 1921 Noel Coward sailed for New York from England, but he had become aware how fearful his mother always was for his safety. She prayed daily for him and he had learned to tease her about her fears. Here is a letter he sent:

"This is just a short line to reasssure your yearning mother heart. I am well considering I had three operations for appendicitis yesterday—was run over by a bus on Tuesday—smitten down by peritonitis on Sunday and am going into consumption tomorrow. But you mustn't worry because apart from these things I'm *all right.* There are certain to be Icebergs, Hurricanes, Typhoons and Torpedos but Douglas Fairbanks I am sure will save me if you write him a nice letter. By the way there is a dreadfully dangerous lift in this apartment, several people are killed daily just getting in and out—and as the drains are notoriously bad Diphtheria and Typhoid are inevitable! But *Don't Worry*."

❋

Psychologist Bill Bourke of New York and Sagaponack, Long Island, sent this vignette:

1946: I go to graduate school at Tulane in order to get distance from a "posssessive" mother.

I see a lot of a red-haired girl named Maude-Ellen.

My mother asks one day: "Does Maude-Ellen have warts? Every girl I've known named Maude-Ellen has had warts."

Right: Maude-Ellen had warts.

❋

A foolish son is grief to his mother.

Proverbs 10:1

❋

# WHAT'S IN A MOTHER'S NAME?

On August 6, 1945, a B-29 named *Enola Gay* dropped the atomic bomb on Hiroshima, wiping out most of this great Japanese city, killing 80,000 people, injuring 70,000 more. Thus the *Enola Gay* entered history by participating in one of the first steps of the nuclear arms race and became a part of the ongoing controversy as to whether or not President Truman should have decided to drop this bomb on civilians.

The men of the *Enola Gay* were from the 509th Composite Group, led by Colonel Paul Tibbets.

The colonel had named his fateful plane after his mother.

❋

# MAMA'S BOY

The novelist Gustave Flaubert made his home with his mother through most of his adult life. While he was on a trip away from her at the age of twenty-nine, she wrote him a letter inquiring when he intended to get married. This was part of his reply:

"No, no; when I think of your sweet face, so sad, so loving, and of the joy I have in living with you, who are so full of serenity, so full of a serious, grave kind of charm, I know very well that I shall never love another as I do you. You will never have a rival, never fear! The senses or the fancy of a moment will not take the place of that which lies enclosed in triple sanctuary. Some will perhaps mount to the threshold of the temple, but none will enter."

He never changed his mind and remained a bachelor to the end of his days.

✳

# AS MOTHER SAW THEM

I guess *South Pacific* was never going to behave exactly as I wanted it to. Even my mother got into the act. During dinner several nights later, she said, "You know something, Josh, you should write." And when I said, "Mother, I just won the Pulitzer Prize for writing *South Pacific*," she said, "Oh, *that*."

—Josh Logan in *Josh*

✳

James Roosevelt, the eldest son of Mr. and Mrs. FDR, states in his book *My Parents*, that despite Eleanor Roosevelt's busy public life, "she never stopped being a mother." He recalls one night sitting on the dais with her at a formal dinner in her honor. The glowing tributes of the speakers didn't keep Mrs. Roosevelt from noticing that her son wasn't eating much. "Though I was by then in my early fifties," writes James, "Mother leaned over and whispered an order: 'James, eat your peas!' "

✳

# LITTLE BOYS LOST

Sons clinging to mother are nothing new—either in life or literature. Marcel Proust idolized his beautiful and cultured mother who adored and spoiled her worshiping completely dependent child in return. Later, Proust immortalized the Alsatian Jewess in *Swann's*

77

*Way*, the first book of his massive great novel *Remembrance of Things Past*. One of his most famous passages is of the little boy whose mother has forgotten his customary good-night kiss. He lies disconsolately "in the shroud of my nightshirt."

So much did I love that goodnight that I reached the stage of hoping it would come as late as possible, so as to prolong the time of respite during which Mamma would not yet have appeared. Sometimes when, after kissing me, she opened the door to go, I longed to call her back, to say to her "Kiss me just once more." But I knew that then she would look displeased, for the concession which she made to my wretchedness and agitation always annoyed my father, who thought such ceremonies absurd . . . And to see her look displeased destroyed all the sense of tranquility she had brought me a moment before, when she bent her loving face down over my bed, and held it out to me like a Host, for an act of Communion in which my lips might drink deeply the sense of her real presence, and with it the power to sleep.

Proust never recovered from his dependency. He grew up to be an effeminate, sickly neurotic. When his mother died, biographer Charlotte Haldane writes that he became an orphan at age thirty-four and "remained until the end of his days, a little boy lost."

In the words of Dorothy Parker, Tonstant Weader could frow up over any comparison between the sublime *Remembrance of Things Past* and the ridiculous Victorian sickliness of the popular novel *Little Lord Fauntleroy*. Yet we find the same mother-son obsession. Fauntleroy calls his mother "Dearest" and protests to his grandfather that the one thing he wants is his mother.

"But you see her almost every day," the grandfather says. "Is that not enough?" Fauntleroy answers in an absurd mimic of Proust: "I used to see her all the time. She used to kiss me when I went to sleep at night, and in the morning she was always there, and we could tell each other things without waiting." The grandfather then asked, "Do you *never* forget about your mother?" And an about-to-be-super neurotic, Fauntleroy answers: "No, never; and she never forgets about me."

\*

# USELESS BUT DIVINE TRIVIA

The maiden name of the mother of lunar astronaut Buzz Aldrin was Moon.

# MOTHER RUSSIAN

The late Russian novelist Boris Pasternak told reporter Jhan Robbins his theory about the impossibility of studying effectively when one is too comfortable, a concept he learned from his mother. When he was a young schoolboy, Pasternak said, his mother would open the windows wide on very cold days to keep him less comfortable. Once she put him in a room that had just been painted; its smell gave just the right degree of discomfort. Sometimes, the novelist recalled, she would even set him to work in poor light so that he would concentrate harder.

*

Much has been written about the sadness of the long "exile" of the late Duke of Windsor from his native England after he abdicated the throne as Edward VIII. Yet it has recently been revealed that in private conversation, the man who was the much beloved Prince of Wales and Britain's most popular momentary monarch, said that he missed neither England nor friends: "My mother was the only person I missed."

*

Charles Wadsworth of the Orlando, Florida, *Sentinel* discovered a local automobile salesman with a surefire sales pitch for uncertain female car buyers. "This car," he says in a confidential whisper, "is the same make and model as the one Ralph Nader's mother drives."

*

# JOE WILLIE'S ROSE

Joe Willie Namath frequently pays tribute to his mother, who was a maid in Patterson Heights, a fancy section of Beaver Falls, when he was growing up. At night she stayed up late cutting down Joe's brother's old baseball and football uniforms to fit her younger son. Joe notes with some pride that today his mother herself lives in Patterson Heights, Pa.

In his autobiography with Dick Schaap, *I Can't Wait Until To-morrow . . . 'Cause I Get Better Looking Every Day*, Joe says: "My mother—her name is Rose Szolnoki now—raised me, and she had her hands full. I think she did a helluva job. She taught me to be polite and to respect my elders. She's a great lady, and she loves to talk. She talks very slowly and very properly. We have a running gag among my friends that whenever my mother calls on the phone she uses up the first three minutes just to say hello. And she does some of the funniest things in the world. When she watches the Jets play on television, she prays to two saints, one when we've got the ball and one when the other team's got the ball. She's the only person I know who has an offensive saint and a defensive saint."

✳

# GBS ON MOM

Her almost complete neglect of me had the advantage that I could idolize her to the utmost pitch of my imagination and had no sordid or disillusioning contacts with her. It was a privilege to be taken for a walk or a visit with her, or on an excursion . . . Though I was not ill-treated—my parents being quite incapable of any sort of inhumanity—the fact that nobody cared for me particularly gave me a frightful self-sufficiency, or rather a power of starving on imaginary feasts, that may have delayed my development a good deal, and leaves me to this hour a treacherous brute in matters of pure affection.

—George Bernard Shaw

# Mothers and Daughters

What the daughter does, the mother did.

Jewish proverb

The writer Barbara Grizzuti Harrison says that when she looks at photographs of her mother as a beautiful young bride, she sees a stranger in the picture—fragile, shy, with a look of dewy vulnerability. Barbara says the woman in the picture bears "no resemblance to the self-contained, armored, aloof woman I call mother now."

Well, there are mothers and daughters and mothers and daughters. My experience is the opposite. When I look at the recent small-town-newspaper picture of my eighty-four-year-old mother accepting an award for having raised the most library money in her town and then look back at the sepia-tinted photographs of her at sixteen in a Mississippi State College gym costume, or on her wedding day in 1914, or even as a plump, bosomy young mother a few years later, *I see exactly the same woman.*

Anne Sexton writes, "A woman *is* her mother. That's the main thing." And it is true, for when I look at my mother's pictures, young or old, I see something of myself in all the stages of her face, just as I see her fleetingly sometimes when passing a mirror. But I only see the similarity physically.

My mother has always been painfully consistent in her character and personality. I have been zigging and zagging all over the place and have had about a thousand total changes, of persona, character body counts, and switching philosophies. I admire my mother's serenity and her deep convictions, but her certainties are not for me.

Mothers and daughters who are able to be honest about themselves and their "situation" will admit that however much they may love and be devoted, a high pain quotient is exchanged. I feel this isn't *generally* true of mothers and sons, but I think it must almost *always* be true of mothers and daughters. (All of you exceptions are happily excused from the room.) Mothers and daughters are not only natural allies; they are natural enemies. They are at odds for the attentions of the men in their families—fathers, husbands, sons, brothers—just as women are often at odds for the attentions of men anywhere. Families are basic training ground for the combat of later life.

Mothers are often jealous of daughters and daughter is, of course, at least subconsciously jealous of mother's hold over father. My mother was never jealous or envious of me but caused me a great deal of pain because the standards she lived by were so idealistic and moral, so valiant and vigilant, that I simply could never live up to them. And I caused my mother a lot of pain because I was nobody's idea of a darling daughter. I was rebellious and offbeat.

This book is full of all kinds of mothers to all kinds of daughters. But I can only speak directly of the one mother I have known best and been something of a failed daughter to—my own. The word has fallen into disrepute now—nevertheless, "lady" is the word inextricably bound up with the word "mother" in *this* daughter's mind. The issue of being a lady and behaving in a ladylike manner was occasionally appealing, more often distressing, when I was growing up. My more pressing desires were always to emulate my energetic and dynamic father as well as my two normally rowdy brothers. So I grew up with a lot of ambivalence about behavior. All my life I have "misbehaved," then pulled back, set up standards and knocked them down, tried and failed, castigated myself and then my mother alternatively.

I would like to beg indulgence in a book on mothers, and in an introduction to a chapter on mothers and daughters, in order to say a few words about my father, for he created much of this daughter's conflict with her mother. His old-fashioned attitudes supplied the reinforcement my mother required for her views on ladylike behavior, civilized demeanor, manners, and mores, while at the same time his own iconoclastic rebellion and kinetic energy were things he encouraged his children to emulate.

He was always giving us a crash course in life survival. "If anyone tries to mess with you, don't let me catch you fighting them fair. Pick up a wrench or a rock and knock their brains out!" My mother would protest, cry and tell us later to turn the other cheek. It was bewildering to say the least.

My father believed there were only two kinds of women—ladies, and the other kind. One of the reasons he married my mother, of course, was because he was a poor, uneducated boy from the hardscrabble West Texas plains and she was a soft-spoken, magnolia-voiced lady whose family abounded with doctors, whose mother had been a teacher, and whose gentility appealed to his rougher background. My parents were, in fact, classic lovers—an incredible case of opposites attracting. He was short, she was stately; he was ugly, she was beautiful; she never lost her temper, he never kept his; she was naïve, he was street-smart.

When a tall, gorgeous southern belle with full bosom and bright blue eyes marries a short, strung-out, runty-looking little live-wire who in his wedding pictures resembles a kind of cute orangutan dressed for an outing, one may well wonder why. "I was in love with him," she says simply. I always considered their mating crazy, thinking that the electricity between Elizabeth McCall and Sloan Smith in the fevered years of the First World War had brought about only the desired effect of me and my brothers.

My mother remembers that my father was "fun" and "different" from the other nice boys her doctor brothers were introducing her to in Ennis, Texas. They had imported her fresh from college to keep house for them. As next-door neighbors, Sloan and Elizabeth began to date. My feisty, hot-tempered father weighed only a hundred pounds and could not pass the U. S. Army physical. My mother was glad of that, for she had fallen in love with this courtly little roughneck. They married. He went on buying cotton, which was his trade, and spent almost fifty years trying to change my mother into an energetic, impulsive, live-for-the-moment Texan. She remained stubbornly the lovely thing he had most prized her for—a lady, slow, gentle, cultured, and worried about conforming and what the neighbors would say.

They almost never agreed on anything. She was so glad to be out of "the country" she refused even to go on a picnic. My father loved the outdoors, animals, and nature. My mother wanted a home with music, books, several bathrooms, and annuities tucked away for college educations. My father bought polo ponies, brought home hitchhikers, loaned all his money, filled the house with wild-life picked up on the road, didn't believe in insurance, and gambled.

My father was so sharp and fast that I recall as a child cringing night after night as he beat my mother in whatever game they were playing—dominoes, gin, checkers, canasta. I used to cross my fingers and pray, "This time, let her win." I mistakenly felt sorry for her and hadn't a clue that she had no more desire to win than to wear pants.

When my father died, I was long grown up and had spent a deluded lifetime of seeing my parents as inextricably unsuited, unhappy even. I had listened to their very real differences (she wanted him to go to church; he wanted to sleep on Sunday mornings), I had observed her carefully saving and scrimping so he could give everything away in some misbegotten burst of generosity. There were often hot words, pouts, and tears in our house.

But the one thing on which my father and mother *did* agree was that I should grow up to be a *lady*. In fact, the path to adulthood in my house was marked by admonitions of behavior. A lady didn't smoke in the street. A lady didn't allow herself to get sunburned. A lady didn't sit with her legs apart, nor notice the vulgarity when her brothers snickered and called it "taking your picture." A lady didn't swear, of course, nor did she drink anything stronger than an occasional glass of wine. A lady didn't interrupt.

It drove me berserk.

Now that the word *lady* is gone with the wind, however, I find myself appreciating and cherishing it. This explains a lot about me, my rebellions, my failures, and possibly some of my successes.

The best definition of a lady is one related by a southern aristocrat named Mrs. Fort Elmo Land. Cleveland Amory says she recalls the attributes of a lady as handed down by her own mother. They involved four S's: simplicity, sympathy, sincerity, and serenity. This describes my mother exactly, both as mother and lady.

(Like principles of operative Christianity which may work

even for agnostics, atheists, and secular thinkers, Mrs. Land's mother was definitely onto something good, in my opinion.)

When my father died at seventy-four, I went home for his funeral with all my prejudices about my parents intact. Except for their curious agreement about daughters being ladylike, I still felt that they had been drastically mismatched. I did not even consider their marriage a success.

But in the days following his funeral, I saw that theirs had been a real romance, a love match of such overwhelming satisfaction to both of them that it had never mattered that their children were too ignorant to see it. The staggering reality of my mother's loss, her love, her grief, and her satisfaction at having loved the same man for almost fifty years was overwhelming.

I had never really appreciated my mother until then. I had always definitely been Daddy's girl. In the time I spent at home after my father's death I received a kind of great awakening and a gift— the full realization of my mother's worth, her wonder, her splendor. My father had gone on wherever he had to go, but he had left behind his love for my mother and to my great happiness I was able to make it my own. I have had the most incredibly fulfilling relationship with my mother since then. I would wish every daughter such a happy experience.

✳

## DO WE HAVE A CHOICE?

Mothers of daughters are daughters of mothers and have remained so, in circles joined to circles, since time began. They are bound together by a shared destiny. Daughters have been expected simply to assume the identity of their mothers, "naturally" growing up to become wives and mothers in their "own right." The sense of biological inevitability underlying this expectation has been taken for granted by both sexes until quite recently; in fact, the generation of daughters now growing up may be the first one in history to feel that motherhood can be one choice among many that a woman can make.

—Signe Hammer in
*Mothers and Daughters*

As is the mother, so is the daughter.

Ezekiel XVI:44

⁂

# NANCY'S MOTHER AND HERSELF

Nancy Friday won critical acclaim in 1977 with her personal evaluation of the mother-daughter relationship in her book *My Mother/ Myself*. Here are brief excerpts:

I have heard daughters say that they do not love their mothers. I have *never* heard a mother say she does not love her daughter. Psychoanalysts have told me that a woman patient would rather consider herself "crazy" than admit that she simply does not like her daughter. She can be honest about anything else, but the myth that mothers always love their children is so controlling that even the daughter who can admit disliking her mother, when her own time comes, will deny all but positive emotions toward her children.

⁂

### The Adversary

A mother's hardest to forgive
Life is the fruit she longs to hand you,
Ripe on a plate. And while you live,
Relentlessly she understands you.

Phyllis McGinley
*Times Three*

⁂

. . . the truth is that when one woman gives birth to another, to someone who is like her, they are linked together for life in a very special way. Mother is the prime love object, the first attachment for both male and female infants. But it is their sex, their sameness that distinguishes what a mother has with her daughter. No two people have such an opportunity for support and identification, and yet no human relationship is so mutually limiting. If a mother suggests to her daughter that motherhood was not the glorious culmination she had been promised, that life had not opened out

86

for her but been somehow diminished instead, this is saying to the girl: I should not have had you.

✳

## MOTHERS OF DAUGHTERS WHO WRITE, SURVIVE

In her autobiographical book, *Flying,* the feminist writer Kate Millett told of a visit she had with author Doris Lessing:

I am dulled by her kindness and the strawberries. Slender maternal figure before me in her chair as I sit on the floor. Primed with my greatest confusion. Mother. "You see, if I write this book my mother's going to die. She has already given me notice." Lessing laughs. "Mothers do not die as easily as they claim. My own announced her intentions with every book I wrote. And I went on hoping eventually I might manage to please her, that I could finally make her proud of me. Only to produce another funeral. Women who write books have a particular obstacle in their mothers. I suppose it is universal." "There's Colette and Sidonie." "Ah, but they never quite convinced me. In any case, I did not have their luck. My mother finally did die, for reasons of her own. But I find she never quite went away."

✳

I still feel with my mother like I'm an oyster. One gulp—and I'm gone!

—Judy Feiffer,
book editor of her seventy-three-
year-old violin-prodigy mother,
Claire Scheftel Kroyt

✳

## MTM'S MOM

Mary Tyler Moore recalls as a teen-ager being a bit jealous of her mother's youthful beauty, not to mention her mother's popularity with her boy friends. "They always became smitten with Mom,"

Mary told readers of the *Ladies' Home Journal,* "and wanted to hang around the house instead of taking me out. I would tell myself, 'That's all right. One of these days she is going to be old and fat and unattractive.' But it never happened. Mom still has a better figure than I do."

Mary always identified more with her quiet father than her mother and it wasn't until some time after she had stopped working on *The Mary Tyler Moore Show* that she came to realize that her vivacious, outgoing mother was the model she had been unconsciously using for her character of Mary Richards, as well as for the character she had played years earlier on *The Dick Van Dyke Show.* "Maybe," Mary says, "Mom is my alter ego and the woman I am able to be when I'm working."

＊

There are many things I will never forgive my mother for, but heading the list is the fact that she did the Double-Crostic in ink.

—Nora Ephron in *Esquire*

＊

# A FRANK ANNE

While living in The Secret Annexe upper floors of the Amsterdam building where her family hid for two years from the Nazis, thirteen-year-old Anne Frank found time not only to celebrate the secret sweetness of her beginning menstrual periods, but to see her much jeopardized future as one of infinite possibility. She rejected the "cramped and narrow" life of her mother as a role model while at the same time chiding herself for writing about "Mummy" in such a "hot-headed way" in her diary.

Mummy Frank came in for lots of evaluation. Anne wrote: "I've grumbled a lot about Mummy, yet still tried to be nice to her again. Now it is suddenly clear to me what she lacks. Mummy herself has told us that she looked upon us more as her friends than her daughters. Now that is all very fine, but still, a friend can't take a mother's place. I need my mother as an example which I can follow. I want to be able to respect her . . . I imagine a mother as a woman who, in the first place, shows great tact, especially towards her children when they reach our age, and who does not laugh at me if I cry about something—not pain, but other things—like 'Mums' does. . . ."

*

## JO'S MARMEE ABBA

A fictional portrait of the artist's mother that *was* "kindly done" is a key component in what is still, more than a century after its publication, the most popular girls' book ever written in America. Novelist Louisa May Alcott based her 1868 best-seller *Little Women* on her own growing-up years in Concord, Massachusetts, and the characters Meg, Jo, Beth, and Amy March were close approximations of Alcott sisters Anna, Lizzie, May and the author herself.

But the beloved persona of sweet-tempered, adoring "Marmee" bore little resemblance to the real-life mother of the girls. As Catharine Moore points out in her study of *Victorian Wives*, "Abba Alcott was restless, hot-tempered, possessive, disliking home duties and often neglectful of them, unsatisfied and critical of her husband." The truth was, says Moore, Abba was "not maternal by nature and when the children were tiny their father attended to them more tenderly and carefully than their mother."

So kindly was the portrait of Abba Alcott touched up for *Little Women* that she is absolved of all responsibility for one of the family's saddest losses—the death of the third daughter, Lizzie, immortalized as the book's beloved Beth. In the fictionalized version of the Alcott sisters' life, the scarlet fever which took Beth away was contracted when "Marmee" was away from home. In actual fact, it was Abba who carried the scarlet fever into the house. Abba Alcott never forgave herself for this tragedy; daughter Louisa obviously did forgive her.

*

## MOTHERLESS CHILD

In his 1942 book *The Lonely Ones*, artist William Steig introduced the world to a group of individuals who, in the words of Wolcott Gibbs, "have been set off from the rest of the world by certain private obsessions." Steig presented these people, said Gibbs, in the "queer, distorted, but absolutely faithful definition of a character available to most of us only in alcohol or a dream." The illustration below is one of the book's classics.

MOTHER LOVED ME BUT SHE DIED

*

# ALMOST A SONNET

Mother, do you know, almost all people love their mothers, but I have never met anybody in my life, I think, who loved his mother as much as I love you. I don't believe there ever was anybody who did, quite so much, and quite in so many wonderful ways. I was telling somebody yesterday that the reason I am a poet is entirely because you wanted me to be and intended I should be, even from the very first. You brought me up in the tradition of poetry, and everything I did you encouraged. I cannot remember once in my life when you were not interested in what I was working on, or even suggested that I should put it aside for something else. Some parents of children that are "different" have so much to reproach themselves with. But not you, Great Spirit . . .

If I didn't keep calling you mother, anybody reading this would think I was writing to my sweetheart. And he would be quite right.

—Edna St. Vincent Millay,
letter, June 15, 1921

＊

# ADVERSARY RELATIONSHIP

Reading the lethal caricature of herself in her daughter Sylvia Plath's autobiographical novel, *The Bell Jar,* was so painful to Mrs. Aurelia Schober Plath that the Massachusetts widow tried to stop its publication, calling it "the basest ingratitude." "Sylvia wrote *The Bell Jar* to get it out of her," she told Gail Jennes of *People.* "Also, she needed the money and thought it would sell. There's no more salable conflict than that between parent and child. I'd given her that instruction myself."

Later, obviously believing that a more lighthearted mother-daughter relationship might also be salable, Mother Plath waded through "boxes and boxes" of her daughter's papers and came forth with 391 of some 700 letters which Sylvia wrote to her mother before her death reflecting the loving side of their relationship. The letters were published in a volume entitled *Letters Home.* Sylvia, says her mother, "was an artist first. All experiences were filed away in her memory to undergo a sea change. Sometimes it was not kindly done."

＊

# COLETTE AND SIDO

### *by Holland Taylor*

It is impossible to divine what in the mid-nineteenth-century provincial French background of Adèle-Eugénie-Sidonie Landoy Colette, other than a few adolescent years in a Belgian artists' colony, can have created a mother so gifted as to produce, nurture, inspire, and then *remain* the love-object, muse, and endlessly fascinating mystery for a daughter of such majestic talent as La Grande Colette. Surely this *éminence grise*, celebrated for her descriptive powers—in nature's affairs and matters of love—acquired her finesse through a lifetime of regarding, remembering and reveling in her infinitely subtle and various mother.

Sido was independent emotionally and intellectually, tucking her paperback Corneille into a leatherbound book stamped with a gold cross at mass. She was a great naturalist, blithely lost in admiration as the crow's claw skillfully pitted her precious cherry crop; fey and spirited, writing a letter to her daughter by the light of a burning barn, capable of "that divine cruelty which was innocent of wrath."

Perhaps Sido's most beguiling aspect was not some predictable and sentimental affectionate quality, but something more discreet, a cooler separateness that drew her lovers (children and husband) to her, instead of enclosing and imposing on them.

She spent the last two thirds of her life raising four children ("the savages"), tending innumerable plants and animals, and trying to go about her business despite the distracting unending glow of admiration from her retired Zouave army husband, whose concern was ever the fear that she might "leave" before him. This lifelong ardor for the plain woman with the "radiant garden-face and anxious indoor-face" left him little impetus for his own literary and scientific talents, and drew from Sido, ever distressed by love's lavish waste, cries of disdain and outrage: "What frivolity! Love is not a sentiment worthy of respect!"

Seventy-six when she died, Sido looked in those years no farther than the four corners of her Saint Sauveur-en-Puisaye garden to find the rewards of life and secrets of the universe. Oblivious to the delirious excitement brought on by a freak July snowstorm, she would be found examining a handful of icy crystals through the big brass-rimmed magnifying glass, her characteristic curiosity scarcely bettering the child's keen eye for detail—the child who would remember a lifetime later, that the snow on the still sun-hot red carnations melted first. Sido's curiosity was as innate as a true scientist's fascination, yet she was equally susceptible to beauty, to the point where a ravishing child left her as "disturbed" as a great lover. Her capacities for passion and truth-cold realism trembled in the balance which was her genius; for she knew that one "possesses by abstaining, and only through abstaining." "Regarde! Regarde!" she would cry to her Minet-Chéri, in their garden, their "earthly paradise"—her nose covered in yellow pollen, "her face innocent of powder and her neck moist"—Look, look! was her injunction and her bequest. Look at it *all*, but don't touch. "Don't touch the butterfly's wing!" she catechized her daughter, like most children a natural assassin. Sido had a way of lifting roses "by the chin, to look them full in the face." Gazing thus at her cunning young savage, she would ask, "Do you think you are getting a little less untruthful as you grow older?" This adored child was to become Colette, whose "wings," dazzlingly iridescent, were never damaged by a mother with a talent for respect.

＊

# HIGH ANXIETY

The wearing of glasses on the job has been a subject of long-standing debate between CBS newscaster Lesley Stahl and her mother. This disagreement hit a new peak on the night in 1972 when Lesley made her very first appearance on the full CBS network. Mrs. Stahl called up her daughter after the broadcast and said: "Forty-nine million Americans saw you on television tonight. One of them is the father of my future grandchild, but he's never going to call you for a date because you wore your glasses!"

＊

Mother, may I go out to swim?
Yes, my darling daughter,
Hang your clothes on a hickory limb
And don't go near the water.

Nursery rhyme

＊

Thou art thy mother's glass, and she in thee
Calls back the lovely April of her prime . . .

William Shakespeare, Sonnet III

# SMALLTALK

Tracy Ellis, age four: "Mommy, I want you to be with me always!"

Diana Ross, mother of Tracy: "I'll be with you always; and even when you don't want me to be."

※

# MOTHER MUSIC

Ivor Novello's 1925 saga of mother and daughter was revived by Bobby Short for his "historic soul-touching" Town Hall concert with Mabel Mercer in 1968. The sophisticates who flock to Bobby's pounding piano and urbane delivery never tire of requesting this song:

## And Her Mother Came Too

I seem to be the victim of a cruel jest
It all concerns the person that I love the best
She's just the dearest thing that I have ever known
Somehow we never get a chance to be alone.

My car will meet her, and her mother comes too.
It's a two-seater; still her mother comes too.
And when they're visiting me, we finish afternoon tea
She likes to sit on my knee—and her mother does, too.

We buy her trousseau and her mother comes too.
Asked not to do so, still her mother comes too.
She simply can't take a snub; I go and sulk at the club,
There have a bath and a rub—and her *brother* comes too.

We lunch at Maxim's, and her mother comes too.
How long a snack seems, when her mother comes too.
At Ciro's when I am free, we'll often go for a spree
She likes to shimmy with me—and her mother does too.

To golf, we started, and her mother came too.
Three bags I carted, when her mother came too
She fainted off the first tee, my baby whispered to me,
"Thank God, at last we are free!" . . . then . . .
(Want to sing it in unison?)
Her mother came to.

# NORMAL

In Neil Simon's *California Suite*, a divorced couple are quarreling over their seventeen-year-old daughter, Jenny. The screenwriter husband, Billy, asks the bright and successful *Newsweek* editor, his ex-wife, if she'd like to know what Jenny has to say about her.

HANNAH: "She's told me. She thinks I'm a son-of-a-bitch. She also thinks I'm a *funny* son-of-a-bitch. She loves me but she doesn't like me. She's afraid of me. She's intimidated by me. She respects me but wouldn't want to become like me. We have a normal mother and daughter relationship."

＊

# TO MOTHER

Novelist Edna Ferber, who adored her mother, dedicated one of her books:

> To my mother
> who thinks it doesn't
> interrupt if she whispers.

＊

Thank you mother—for whatever you did.

> —Carol Channing's
> speech on receiving a Tony
> award for *Hello, Dolly* in 1964

＊

The dedication to Mae West's somewhat ribald autobiography, *Goodness Had Nothing to Do With It*, is:

> In loving memory of my
> MOTHER
> without whom I might have been
> somebody else.

In the book, Mae reveals her devotion to the Bavarian-born Mrs.

Matilda Doelger West. "She tried in every way to understand me," writes Mae, "and she succeeded. It was this deep, loving understanding as long as she lived that more than anything else helped and sustained me on my way to success."

❋

## SHE ME I SHE

My love for her and my hate for her are so bafflingly intertwined that I can hardly *see* her. I never know who is who. She is me and I am she and we're all together. The umbilical cord which connects us has never been cut, so it has sickened and rotted and turned black. The very intensity of our need has made us denounce each other. We want to eat each other up. We want to strangle each other with love. We want to run screaming from each other in panic before either of these things can happen.

From the novel
*Fear of Flying,*
by Erica Jong

❋

An indulgent mother makes a sluttish daughter.

Dutch proverb

❋

Why should it be necessary for a mother to be there like a grindstone at the heart of everything?

—Doris Lessing, *The Summer Before the Dark*

❋

## PROTECTIVE CUSTODY

Sixteen-year-old Cheryl Crane suffered and endured for some time while Johnny Stompanato, the lover of her mother, Lana Turner, threatened and bullied the actress.

One fateful Easter in 1958, Stompanato ranted to Lana that he would destroy her famous face. But the words that *finally* sent Cheryl to the kitchen for the butcher knife with which she returned and stabbed Stompanato to death, were these cruel ones addressed to Lana: "I'll get you where it hurts—your daughter and your mother."

*

# ONE OF MILDRED'S BEST FRIENDS

Carmel Berman Reingold writes:

Mildred Newman and Bernard Berkowitz, co-authors of *How to Be Your Own Best Friend* and *How to Take Charge of Your Life*, are husband and wife as well as psychologists. Both had been divorced when they married each other and both had children from their first unions. "When we decided to get married," says Mildred Newman, "my daughter wouldn't come to the wedding . . . She started to cry, and she cried for seven days and seven nights. Everyone said, 'What are you going to do about this?' And I said, 'She has to cry and I have to get married.' I truly felt that way. It took six months for her to change her attitude. I did not want to give her the responsibility of deciding whether or not I should marry." According to Dr. Berkowitz, accepting a child's dictation "is the equivalent of robbing a child of a parent, by putting this responsibility on a child's shoulders. It's your life, and your decision, and in time Mildred's daughter became one of my best friends."

*Remarriage*

*

It is hard indeed to be separated from one's own mother when one has only just learnt *what* one owes her.

—Comment of the eldest daughter
of Queen Victoria after the birth
of her first son, the future
Kaiser Wilhelm II

# WRAPPED IN THE FLAG

The most renowned mother-and-daughter artifact at the Smithsonian Institution in Washington, D.C., is the flag delivered to Fort McHenry in Maryland on August 19, 1813, by Mrs. Mary Young Pickersgill of Baltimore. Assisted by her mother, Mrs. Roberta Young, and her daughter Caroline, Mrs. Pickersgill spent six weeks spinning and stitching 440 yards of bunting into the mammoth "Star-Spangled Banner" which, during the War of 1812, inspired Francis Scott Key to write the words to what would become the U.S. national anthem. For creating this stunning thirty-six-by-forty-two-foot ensign of fifteen stripes and fifteen stars, Mrs. P. and her helpers were paid $405.90.

※

# OVERKILL

"If too much love felt by a mother towards a daughter be a fault, then Madame de Sévigné was one of the most offending souls that ever lived." So the 1911 Encyclopaedia Britannica tells us. Here are two examples of Madame de Sévigné's letter-writing to her daughter:

"Love me always and forever; my existence depends on it, my soul yearns for it; as I told you the other day you are all my joy and all my sorrow. What remains of my life is overshadowed by grief when I consider how much of it will be spent far from you." (1671)

"Farewell, dearest and best. Words fail me adequately to express the strength of my passion for you; they are, I find, wholly inadequate." (1688)

Yet had it not been for what she once described as a "love for her daughter [that] passes the love of mothers," the widow of Henri, the Marquis de Sévigné, would probably not be remembered more than three hundred years after her birth in France in 1626. As things turned out, this bubbly matron with the "extravagant maternal partiality" has become one of the best-known figures in European literature. When her only daughter, Françoise, became the bride of a provincial nobleman and moved to the country, Madame de Sévigné fought her loneliness by launching a torrent of letters to her which flowed on, unstemmed, for a quarter of a century. Collected and published by a granddaughter after her death, these lively, gossipy accounts of the seventeenth-century French *haut monde*—a total of almost seventeen hundred of them—have now attained the status of classics in the field of epistolary reportage.

And what was daughter Françoise's reaction to such maternal effusions as: "Do you wonder if I cannot refrain from kissing your lovely face and bosom?" We don't know. Her side of the correspondence has not been preserved. We do know, however, that whenever mother and daughter actually spent time together, sometimes for visits lasting many months, they engaged in a good bit of bickering. As Somerset Maugham once observed: "It was only when they were separated that they did not get on one another's nerves." We also know that when, on a visit to her daughter's home in Provence, the seventy-year-old Madame de Sévigné contracted a fever that claimed her life, Françoise was not at mother's bedside.

❋

## MAKING MOM LAUGH

Emily Post, before she became famous as an arbiter of etiquette, tried her hand at many other kinds of writing. One of the periodicals to which she submitted material was the original *Life*, a humor magazine. Since she was a neophyte at joke writing, Mrs. Post worked out a system. Before sending a new joke to the editors, she would read it aloud to her mother. If the older woman laughed, Mrs. Post threw out the joke. If her mother looked blank—or, better still, disapproving—Mrs. Post slipped it into an envelope and mailed it. Through the years, this system proved infallible.

❋

## NEEDING

A rare mother-and-daughter relationship is discussed peripherally but importantly in the Betty Rollin book, *First, You Cry*. The writer's insights say a lot about the special nature of daughters and mothers, their flowerings, wiltings, resentment, joy, to and fro:

My mother is a big feeler, but she has never been much of a

crier. Not in front of me, at least. The only time I can remember her crying was when Arthur and I were living together in my walk-up apartment on 49th Street. It was before we were married, and my mother came up to visit. She was fine until she started to leave, and then, at the doorway, having listened to Arthur make his points about *feeling* married to me even though he wasn't she stood under the ratty brass fixture we had thought would look so great when we bought it in Tangiers, turned the doorknob, and burst into tears. "If you were a mother," she sobbed, "you would understand!" Exit.

Although tears were rare while I was growing up, lines like that were not, and naturally they drove a wedge between my mother and me. For the longest time, we didn't talk to each other about anything important, because she would wind up saying one of those lines, I would overreact to both the style and content of the line, she would react to my overreaction, and everybody would wind up with a headache or a stomachache or both. Part of the problem was that in my mother's ferocious striving to give me "everything," she had never considered that giving me "everything" would make me (1) different (from her), and (2) guilty (about what I got). Different and Guilty are not the stuff on which comradeship is built.

Then things got better between us. Getting older helped. Analysis helped. Getting married helped. And now, in a way that I could not have predicted, this crisis* helped. Arthur had been right. I needed my mother now and she knew it and I knew it. And my mother is very, very good at being needed.

In the hospital she did exactly what I needed her to do. It wasn't only that she was loving and helpful. Of course she'd be loving and helpful. What impressed me—what dazzled and moved me—was how spirited, how bright-eyed and positive and cheerful she was. Not phony cheerful, either . . .

One late afternoon when I was coming off Demerol I looked at my mother, rearranging the flowers for the fourth time that day. She was humming. Hey, Mother, I thought, I love you. Then I decided to say it. "Hey, Mother, I love you and I'm glad you're here and I think you're being terrific."

"Don't be silly," she said briskly, as she clipped off some leaves with a pair of shears she had brought from home. "What are mothers for?"

* A mastectomy

# OVERWHELMING

Katharine Graham, often called the most powerful woman in America, is known as the dynamic newspaper publisher who rescued the Washington *Post* from oblivion after her husband committed suicide. Her courage in backing the journalists exposing Watergate is legendary. Yet this incredible woman grew up in the Shadow of an overwhelming mother who was brilliant, energetic, and intimidating. (Among other pursuits, she translated Thomas Mann and was an expert on Chinese art.) Mrs. Graham told reporter Diane Shah:

"I came from this incredibly high-powered family. My mother was sort of a Viking. Very bright, and utterly contemptuous of everyone else. When I told her I had read *The Three Musketeers*, she said, 'Undoubtedly a waste of time, my dear, unless you read it in the original French."

✳

As it turns out, Mrs. Graham is a mother, too. She insists that her own newspaper's executive editor, Ben Bradlee, ignores her suggestions of "Let's cover this or that" if the news event involves one of her friends. Mrs. Graham's daughter Lally Waymouth compiled a book about Thomas Jefferson that came out at the same time as five others. Two were reviewed in the *Post*, but there was nothing about Lally's book. Mrs. Graham bit her tongue as long as she could, but maternal instinct finally prevailed. She marched into Bradlee's office and declared, "Goddam it, Ben, you've mentioned the two other books. What about. . . ."

Kandy Stroud reported in *W* that "Bradlee stonewalled her, and she knew he wasn't going to do anything. But she felt she had fulfilled her obligation as a mother."

✳

# MOTHER AND DR. FREUD

Mildred Newman, who has been a kind of high-powered mother to the adult me and has changed my life infinitely for the better, tells of the first day she was ever to treat a patient in private psychiatric practice. She was nervous and excited, but the last thing her mother said as she went to the appointment was, "Now don't you go getting those poor girls to hate their mothers!"

*

# *Joke*

Nellie Ann, raised in the tradition of high-minded Southern womanhood, found herself in a state of perpetual shock when exposed to the new liberality of language exhibited by her girl friends. "I keep trying to get over it," she told one of them, "but I'm just too inhibited. I say d-a-m-n and then I think, 'Oh, what would my dear mother say if she heard me?' and I'm *miserable*."

Said the friend, "You should go to a psychiatrist. It's nice to be ladylike, but you carry it too far."

The two girls did not meet again for some time and when they did, the friend asked Nellie Ann if she had taken her advice.

"Yes, I did," Nellie Ann told her. "I've been going to a psychiatrist three times a week for six months."

"And did it help?"

"It certainly did. Only the other morning when I was provoked, I just came right out and screamed 'Bullshit!' at my m-o-t-h-e-r."

# Mothers of Multiples

I always say, "You show me a woman with fifteen children, and I'll show you an overbearing woman."

Phyllis Diller

It couldn't happen today, when the public's idols seem to be those flashing overnight overexposed TV names who burn themselves out in a season or a moment. In my childhood, idols were longer-lived in the public's adoration. They were also disgustingly wholesome. Our parents had thrived on the heroic purity of Charles Lindbergh; they raised us on the determined, rise-above-it character of Helen Keller, and everybody admired Will Rogers right up to and past the day when a newspaper "extra" announced that he and Wiley Post had died in an Alaskan plane crash.

But the most astounding newspaper-magazine-newsreel personalities of the thirties were the Dionne Quintuplets. Why does that seem faintly funny now? Listen, they were *important!* With the advent of the Pill and the development of fertility drugs (science at cross-purposes?)—although the birth rate has fallen—multiple births at one confinement are no longer so terribly rare as they were back in the days when the phenomenon represented not only a miracle of biology but of nurturing. Tiny babies born in fours and five seldom survived.

True, a mother of our time can still make the AP or UPI wire by producing quads, but she'd probably have to bust the sextuplet limit for her brood to get much sustained attention. So, most probably there will never be another multiple-birth event to match the popularity of the Dionnes. For years, they were as famous as FDR and Eleanor and Fala. We even knew all their first names and how each little girl differed in personality from her sisters.

The Dionne Quints arrived on a primitive Canadian farm, delivered by an astonished general practitioner who became as well-known as his charges. (When the quints were finally starred in a feature movie, which we all rushed to see in the same way we crammed in to the theaters for Shirley Temple, Dr. Dafoe was played onscreen by Jean Hersholt.) The Dionnes had drama. They had been thrillingly unexpected, unpredicted, and their survival had cliffhanger qualities of rotogravure excitement. Nobody knew what to do with them until the government took over. Their father was a wispy little Caspar Milquetoast; their mother a robust, strapping woman twice his size. The Catholic Dionnes became the staple of many cartoons and jokes. Much of the WASP middle class looked down on large families and considered multiple births "vulgar." (Some of it still does.) But the little girls up in Ontario were irresistible.

We read everything about the Dionne Quints, put up pictures of them, wrote them, and sent gifts. As I type this, I am looking at a Karo Syrup advertisement from 1937, showing them as "The World's Darlings" with their brown eyes shining under glamorous, Maybellined, drawn-in eyelashes. I recall that everybody worried endlessly about Marie, who was the smallest and the "runt" of the litter. We loved the Dionne Quints until they reached the awkward age and began to grow into puberty. Then we forgot about them.

So, the following chapter is one of my favorites. It includes not only examples of multiple births at a single accouchement, but stories of fruitful mothers who multiplied on many diverse occasions—a practice that has fallen into disrepute with the practitioners of Zero Population Growth. A joke of my childhood concerned the beleaguered mother of many "stairstep children" born in rapid succession. Asked if she shouldn't practice birth control, the wiped-out woman, nursing one, with others hanging on her apron, said, "What? And give up my only annual rest in the hospital?"

A bull's-eye story in this section is the illuminating follow-up speculating on the meaning of the nursery rhyme about the Old Woman Who Lived in a Shoe. (See page 109.) For some reason, this nonsensical bit of trivia just knocks me out.

# WOW!

Of children in all she bore twenty-four
Thank the Lord there will be no more.

> Epitaph in a churchyard near
> Canterbury, England

\*

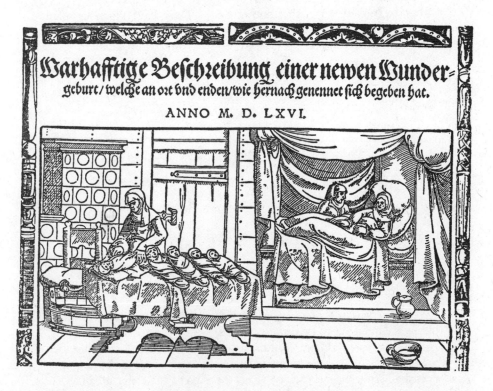

Earliest pictorial record of the birth of quintuplets. Woodcut: Bavaria, 1565.

# THE MOST CHILDREN

The greatest number of children produced by a mother in an independently attested case is 69 by the first wife of Fyodor Vassilet (1816–72) a peasant of the Moscow Jurisdiction, Russia, who in twenty-seven confinements, gave birth to sixteen pairs of twins, seven sets of triplets and four sets of quadruplets. Most of the children attained their majority. Mme. Vassilet became so renowned that she was presented at the court of Czar Alexander II.

Currently the highest reliably reported figure is a thirty-eighth child born to Raimundo Carnauba, fifty-eight, and Josimar Carnauba, fifty-four, of Belem, Brazil. She was married at fifteen and so far has had fourteen sons and twenty-four daughters at yearly intervals. In May 1972, the mother said, "They have given us a lot of work and worry but they are worth it," and the father: "I don't know why people make such a fuss."

The Guinness Book of World Records

\*

A woman with a few children allus has an alibi.

—Kin Hubbard

\*

# NEGATIVE VIEW

To many primitive peoples, ignorant of biological facts, multiple births are believed to be due to infidelity on the part of the mother. According to folklorist Claudia de Lys, in places where this idea prevails, the life of the twins is spared, but the mother is not only punished severely, but driven from the village for a period of isolation and not allowed to speak to anyone, except from a distance. In some parts of Africa, where dual births are still frowned on, the worst insult to a woman is to hold up two fingers as a reminder of the fact that she once brought twins into the world.

# POSITIVE VIEW

An important facet of Adolf Hitler's grandiose dream of peopling the Third Reich with a "Master Race" was his institution in 1938 of the *Mutterkreuz*, a special German Mother's Cross honoring the nation's most fertile females. A military-style amalgam of the Nazi party badge, Pour le Mérite, and Iron Cross, and bearing the inscription "The child ennobles the mother," its purpose was to endow prolific begetters with as much national prestige as soldiers who performed well on the battlefield. The *Mutterkreuz* had several classes: bronze for four or five children; silver for six or seven; gold for eight or more. The emblems were bestowed every year on August 12, the birthday of Hitler's own mother.

*

Italian law permits expectant mothers sentenced to prison to stay free until they have delivered their babies and in the film comedy, *Yesterday, Today and Tomorrow*, Sophia Loren portrayed a Neapolitan slum wife who used this loophole when arrested for selling contraband cigarettes. The story was loosely based on the career of a Naples resident, Concetta Mussbardo, better known by the nickname, "Black Market Connie." Sentenced to seventy days for cigarette peddling, Connie managed to stay out of jail by having a baby —her fourth. While enjoying this prenatal reprieve, she continued her black-market dealing and received more sentences. But each time the police came to take her off to jail, she was pregnant.

When *Yesterday, Today and Tomorrow* proved to be a big commercial success, Connie came storming to producer Carlo Ponti with a request for suitable compensation. She eventually settled for about four thousand dollars but has in recent years been considerably outclassed. Another Italian woman using the same dodge has given birth to eleven children—all while under sentence for arrest, an all-time record.

*

# FIRST WITH THE MOST

The American First Lady with the most children was Anna Symmes Harrison, wife of President William Henry Harrison. The

Harrisons had six sons and four daughters, but neither Mrs. Harrison nor the children ever lived in the White House. She was sixty-five when her husband was sworn in as the ninth U. S. President and was unable to accompany him to his inauguration because of poor health. Preparing to join him in Washington a month later, she received word of his death.

Mrs. Harrison produced more grandchildren (48) and great-grandchildren (106) than any other President's wife. One of her grandchildren, Benjamin Harrison, became the twenty-third President of the U.S.

\*

## More First Multiple Mothers

LUCY HAYES (Mrs. Rutherford B.)—seven sons, one daughter
LUCRETIA GARFIELD (Mrs. James)—five sons, two daughters
ELEANOR ROOSEVELT (Mrs. Franklin D.)—five sons, one daughter
LETITIA TYLER (Mrs. John)—three sons, five daughters
JULIA TYLER (second wife)—five sons, two daughters

\*

## ROYAL FLUSH

Marie Leszczynska, consort of King Louis XV of France, married the king when she was twenty-two and within the next dozen years had born him ten children, of whom six daughters and a son reached maturity. After her tenth accouchement, complaining that she was forever "in bed, or pregnant, or brought to bed," Marie began to look for excuses to keep her royal husband out of her chamber. Writes Nancy Mitford about the queen in her biography of Madame de Pompadour: "As she was extremely pious, he had never been allowed there on the days of the major saints. By degree the saints for whom he was excluded became more numerous and less important; finally, he was kept out by one so utterly unknown that he flew into a temper." Thereafter, Louis contented himself primarily with mistresses, including, eventually, Pompadour and DuBarry, and Queen Marie had her bedroom to herself.

The reign of England's Queen Anne, whom crusty old Jonathan Swift memorialized as "the real nursing-mother of her kingdom," was one of the most brilliant in British history but, though she was pregnant fifteen times, the matronly monarch left not a single heir. Wed to Prince George of Denmark, Anne suffered through a total of ten miscarriages, lost four babies in infancy and one son at the age of eleven.

*

# NUMBERS GAME

The seventh child has been regarded traditionally with some peoples as the most favored by nature. Benjamin Franklin was the fifteenth child, John Wesley the eighteenth, Ignatius Loyola was the eighth, Catherine of Siena, one of the greatest intellectual women who ever lived, was the twenty-fourth. It has been suggested that one of the reasons for the lack of genius in our day is that we are not getting the ends of the families.

—Archbishop Patrick J. Hayes,
defending his efforts to prohibit
a birth control lecture by
Margaret Sanger, scheduled for
New York's Town Hall in 1921.

*

Desire not a multitude of unprofitable children.

Ecclesiasticus 16:1
in the Apocrypha

*

# MOTHER DISGUISED

There was an old woman who lived in a shoe
She had so many children she didn't know what to do.
She gave them some broth without any bread;
She whipped them all soundly and put them to bed.

Mother Goose

It's the theory of some scholars that the "old woman" in the rhyme was actually Parliament; the "shoe" was the British Isles, and the "many children" were the empire's multiple farflung colonies. According to William S. and Ceil Baring-Gould in their *Annotated Mother Goose,* the "bitter cup of broth" was the much-disliked person of James I of Scotland as King.

\*

## NAMES AND NUMBERS

Mrs. Ann Lear, the mother of nonsense-writer Edward Lear, gave birth to twenty-one children in twenty-four years. Thirteen of them died. Because the Lears persisted in using a name until one of the youngsters survived, there were three Sarahs, three Henrys, two Catherines, plus an Ann, Mary, Eleanor, Jane, Olivier, Harriett, Cordelia, Frederick, Florence, Charles, and Edward. Two others, a boy and a girl died unnamed. It may or may not be relevant that, when Mrs. Lear finally passed to the great beyond, the cause of her death was listed as "general decay."

I've had eleven children, all unwanted.

> Remark attributed to Mrs. Chiswell
> Dabney Langhorne, mother of the
> famous "Langhorne Sisters of Virginia,"
> Nancy, Lady Astor, and
> Mrs. Charles Dana Gibson.

\*

## EPITAPH

The grave of the mother of John Marshall, Chief Justice of the Supreme Court, 1801–35, bears this marking:

> Mary Randolph Keith Marshall
> wife of Thomas Marshall, by whom she had
> Fifteen Children,
> was born in 1737 and died in 1807,
> She was good but not brilliant
> Useful but not great.

> Charles Wallis in *American Epitaphs*

# MOTHER OF DOUGHBOYS

The great Wagnerian opera and concert singer Ernestine Schumann-Heink was called World War I's "Mother of the Doughboys," despite the fact that she had sons not only in the AEF but in the German Army and on a U-boat. Born near Prague in what was then part of Austria, the singer felt strongly that her first loyalty should be to her adopted country, the United States, and she sang tirelessly at camp concerts for American soldiers throughout the war. (Appropriately, Brahms's "Lullaby" was one of the favorites of her repertoire.)

By Armistice Day 1918, two of Mme. Schumann-Heink's sons had been killed—one fighting for the Allies, the other for Germany.

The star claimed that, after each of her eight confinements, she added an additional note to her singing range.

*

# A UNIQUE AMERICAN BINARY SYSTEM

Two North Carolina sisters named Adelaide and Sarah Yates Bunker mothered, between them, during the years 1843 and 1874, twenty-two children, and are presently survived by well over a thousand living grandchildren, great-grandchildren and great-great-grandchildren. This, in itself, is not so unusual in a nation where large families were once the norm. What makes these two "Mothers of Multiples" unique in U.S. history is that these many offspring resulted from their union with the two most closely knit brothers ever to debark on American shores. They were Chang and Eng, the original "Siamese Twins," exhibited extensively in the early nineteenth century by showman P. T. Barnum.

The twins, joined across the chest by a thick band of flesh containing a common navel, liked the country so much they decided to settle here after retiring from show business in 1840 with a nest egg of sixty thousand dollars and the adopted surname of Bunker. Exposed to the charms of North Carolina on one of their tours, Chang proposed to farmer's daughter Adelaide Yates; Eng, to her sister Sarah. The brothers were accepted. After the double wedding in 1843, the couples settled down on two neat farms near White

Plains, N.C., about a mile apart. For the next thirty-one years the inseparable brothers followed a routine of spending three days and nights in one house with one wife followed by three days and nights in the second house with the other, a regimen which led, eventually, to the birth of seven boys and five girls to Eng and Sarah, and seven boys and three girls to Chang and Adelaide. Though the twins, themselves, sometimes quarreled and went for days without speaking to one another, their marriages were remarkably successful and their conjugal schedule continued without interruption until the death of the brothers (on the same day) in 1874. The two widows continued to live in North Carolina and many of their multitude of descendants still live there today.

*

# MOTHER MUM

What, in the eyes of many, is the world's most beautiful building was erected to honor the memory of a mother of fourteen children. She was Mumtaz Mahal, favorite wife of the seventeenth-century Mogul emperor Shah Jahan. Her monument was the magnificent Taj Mahal in Agra, India. An estimated twenty thousand laborers quarried the materials to create this "dream in marble" built by a grieving husband.

The romance memorialized by the Taj Mahal began as a classic case of love at first sight. The Shah, as a sixteen-year-old prince, spied his fifteen-year-old beloved at a bazaar. He maneuvered her family into an engagement the very next day but, following local custom, did not marry her until he was twenty-one. During the five years waiting time the husband and wife-to-be did not see each other once, but after the marriage ceremony on March 27, 1612, they were seldom apart. In the nineteen years of their idyllic marriage, Mumtaz Mahal—"The Chosen One of the Palace"—gave birth to fourteen of the Shah's children, seven of whom survived. When she herself died, as a result of complications following the fourteenth confinement, it was recalled that an omen had warned her of her fate: attendants reported Mumtaz Mahal had heard the baby crying in her womb.

*"Occupation?"*
*"Woman."*

Drawing by Chon Day; © 1940, 1968 The New Yorker Magazine, Inc.

## Twenty-five Noteworthy Mothers of Multiples

**MOTHER:** Alexandra, wife of Czar Nicholas II
**NUMBER OF CHILDREN:** Five
**WHAT'S SO SPECIAL:** The empress of Russia caused a scandal by her relationship with the Siberian mystic Rasputin, whom she hoped would heal her hemophiliac son. She was probably executed with

her family at Ekterinburg by the Bolsheviks in 1918; legends persist that at least one daughter, Anastasia, escaped the massacre.

MOTHER: Lydia Bixby
NUMBER OF CHILDREN: Six
WHAT'S SO SPECIAL: After five of her sons were reported slain during the Civil War, she became a symbol of heroic maternal sacrifice in wartime.* Lincoln's letter to her is one of the most-quoted documents in American history.

MOTHER: Aloise Steiner Buckley
NUMBER OF CHILDREN: Ten
WHAT'S SO SPECIAL: Called by the New York *Times*, "a kind of matriarch of conservatism in the country," she numbers among her eight surviving children former New York Senator James and columnist William Buckley. "There is not a liberal in my family," she says. "There'd better not be! The rest of them would jump on him."

MOTHER: Queen Charlotte, consort to King George III
NUMBER OF CHILDREN: Fifteen
WHAT'S SO SPECIAL: Called by Lord Chesterfield, "a good woman, a good wife, a tender mother, and an unmeddling Queen," her brood included two future kings, George IV and William IV.

MOTHER: Adeline Younger Dalton
NUMBER OF CHILDREN: Fifteen
WHAT'S SO SPECIAL: While eleven of her offspring led blameless lives, four of her sons grew up to become the infamous Dalton Brothers, known throughout the Midwest in the post-Civil War years for their daring bank and train robberies.† She contributed a good deal toward the state of Missouri's earning its unfortunate nickname, "The Mother of Bandits."

MOTHER: Lavinia Stockwell Day
NUMBER OF CHILDREN: Four
WHAT'S SO SPECIAL: Her sparkly and wise relationship with her four carrot-topped boys, not to mention their irascible sire, was the

* For more about Mrs. Bixby, see page 31.

† Outlaw "Butch" Cassidy, a contemporary of the Daltons, also came from a large family. *His* mother had *ten* children.

Bey diesem sagt man den Kindern vor: Dieses Kindlein hat nichts gelernet, darum wird es geschlagen, und schreyet Weh: hier muß man gleich auf das W. deuten, und dem und sagen: hier sihe, diß heisset W.

Nach diesem wann das Kind den Buchstaber wol betrachtet, frage man nochmal: wo ist ein W. Wann es darauf deutet, soll man nochmal fragen: Wie derselbe Buchstabe heiße.

A page from the spelling book of King Frederick the Great of Prussia
—even then spanking was mother's helper in producing guilt.

"What about us working mothers?"

Mary Harvey and her stillborn child, 1785. Gravestone rubbing by Ann Parker and Avon Neal from a slate slab burial marker in a cemetery in Old Deerfield, Massachusetts.

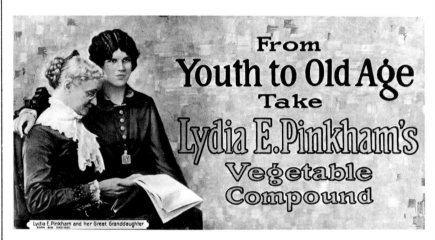

Lydia Pinkham advertisement from 1930, showing the famous working mother with a great-granddaughter she actually never lived to see.

The fashionable mamma in the late eighteenth century always did her breast feeding in style. Her free-flowing classical "new look" of 1793 was associated with an offhand approach to "beau monde" motherhood.

"Oh, and speaking of Mother, just send her the bills. She takes care of all those things."

"Founding Fathers! How come no Founding Mothers?"

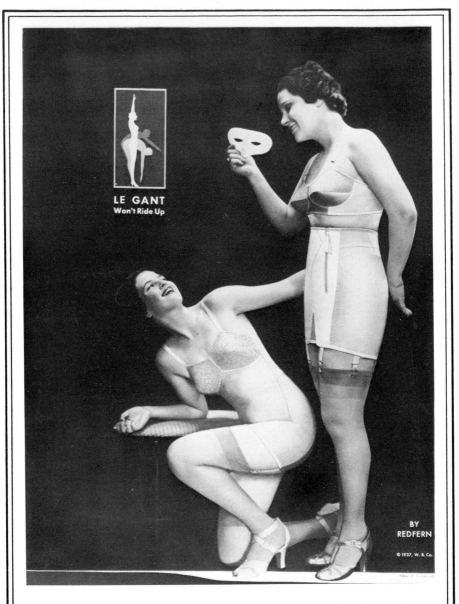

This 1937 Vogue underwear ad pictured mother and daughter with a caption that had the younger saying, "Why, Mother! You slim young thing! I thought you were one of the girls!" Mother's response: "Indeed, miss! And since when has LeGant been restricted to your generation?" Did mothers and daughters ever talk like this?

inspiration in part for *Life With Father*, one of the great family comedies of the American theater. Dorothy Stickney was the original "Vinnie," in the play crafted by Howard Lindsay and Russel Crouse from Clarence Day, Jr.'s memoir of American family life in the eighteen-seventies and eighties.

MOTHER:  Olivia Dionne
NUMBER OF CHILDREN:  Nine
WHAT'S SO SPECIAL:  This Ontario farmer's wife made international headlines on May 28, 1934, when she gave birth to five identical baby girls, later named Émilie, Marie, Yvonne, Cécile, and Annette. As infants, these famed Dionne Quintuplets* were separated from her to be raised by the family physician, Dr. Allan Dafoe, in conjunction with a troop of nurses and nuns subsidized by the Canadian government.

MOTHER:  Madeline Morando Foy
NUMBER OF CHILDREN:  Seven
WHAT'S SO SPECIAL:  She gave up her career as a ballet dancer to wed vaudevillian Eddie Foy; produced the "Seven Little Foys" who, starting in 1913, began to troupe with Eddie in theaters all over America. The Foy story was a 1955 film vehicle for Bob Hope.

MOTHER:  Lady Antonia Fraser
NUMBER OF CHILDREN:  Six
WHAT'S SO SPECIAL:  Provided with what she called "the admirable example" of a mother (The Countess of Longford) who managed to raise a family of eight while writing best-selling historical biographies of Queen Victoria and the Duke of Wellington, Lady Antonia stepped down from the London Beautiful People merry-go-round and proceeded along the same path. Now herself a mother of six, she entered the best-seller circle first with her biography of Mary, Queen of Scots; went on to Oliver Cromwell and James I.

MOTHER:  Lillian Gilbreth
NUMBER OF CHILDREN:  Twelve
WHAT'S SO SPECIAL:  The foremost American woman industrial engineer of her time, she applied her time-and-motion technique on family as well as factories; was maternal heroine of her son and daughter's book (later a movie) *Cheaper by the Dozen*. In the film, she was portrayed by Hollywood's "perfect wife," Myrna Loy.

*For more on the five, see introduction to this chapter.

115

MOTHER: Mrs. Elizabeth Goose
NUMBER OF CHILDREN: Ten stepchildren; six of her own
WHAT'S SO SPECIAL: Presumed by some to be the original "Mother Goose."*

MOTHER: Katherine Jackson
NUMBER OF CHILDREN: Nine
WHAT'S SO SPECIAL: The matriarch of this tightly knit black family went from report-card checking to *Billboard* chart-watching in 1969 when her youngsters became Motown hit-makers as The Jackson Five. Now most of the family is in the act.

MOTHER: Ethel Kennedy
NUMBER OF CHILDREN: Eleven
WHAT'S SO SPECIAL: Daughter-in-law of Rose Kennedy and widow of her son Robert, former U. S. Attorney-General, Ethel is the mother of Kathleen, Joseph, Robert, Jr., David, Mary Courtney, Michael, Mary K., Christopher, Matthew, Douglas and Rory Elizabeth, born six months after her father's death in 1968. The mistress of Hickory Hill in suburban McLean, Virginia, has also focused her maternal attention on an assortment of livestock which has included horses, ponies, a donkey, dogs, kittens, ducks, chickens, roosters, geese, rabbits, pigeons, sparrows, turtles, goldfish, tadpoles, and "two snakes Mom doesn't know about." Her favorite nickname for herself is "Old Moms."

MOTHER: Rose Fitzgerald Kennedy
NUMBER OF CHILDREN: Nine
WHAT'S SO SPECIAL: "She was the glue" her late son, President John F. Kennedy once said, "that held us together." Said the mother of Joseph, Jr., John, Rosemary, Kathleen, Eunice, Patricia, Robert, Jean, and Edward about herself: "I would much rather be known as the mother of a great son or a great daughter than the author of a great book or the painter of a great masterpiece."†

MOTHER: Jean Kerr
NUMBER OF CHILDREN: Six
WHAT'S SO SPECIAL: Wife of drama critic Walter Kerr, she was inspired by her five boys to write (among many other things) *Please*

* For more on her, see page 438.
† For more, see page 133.

116

*Don't Eat the Daisies*, first a best-selling book, then a film (starring Doris Day) and later a popular TV series. She is now also the mother of a daughter. When her children were younger, Mrs. Kerr was known occasionally to lock herself and her writing materials inside the family car to get away from them.

MOTHER: Leah
NUMBER OF CHILDREN: Seven
WHAT'S SO SPECIAL: The "beautiful and well-favored" Rachel gave the Old Testament patriarch Jacob his two most beloved sons, Joseph and Benjamin, but her older sister Leah was the more prolific of Jacob's two wives. As the begetter of Reuben, Simeon, Levi, Judah, Issachar, and Zebulun, Leah was responsible for launching six of the twelve tribes of Israel. She also had a daughter, Dinah.

MOTHER: Anne Morrow Lindbergh
NUMBER OF CHILDREN: Six
WHAT'S SO SPECIAL: This gentle, sensitive poet had to endure one of the most publicized "heavy and brown" (her words) family tragedies of the century in the 1932 kidnapping death of her first-born son Charles, Jr. But she also has flown to great adventure, romance (as wife of the "Lone Eagle," Charles Lindbergh), and literary success (as author of such best-sellers as *Listen! the Wind* and *Gift from the Sea*). "I believe," once observed the mother of Jon, Land, Anne, Scott, and Reeve, "that what woman resents is not so much giving herself in pieces as giving herself purposelessly."

MOTHER: Loretta Lynn
NUMBER OF CHILDREN: Six (including one set of twins)
WHAT'S SO SPECIAL: Married at thirteen and a mother the following year, by the time she was twenty-nine she was both a grandmother and one of the nation's top country music recording stars. Fittingly, two of her biggest hits have motherhood as a theme. The first was "One's On the Way"; the other, "The Pill." After her twins were born, Loretta's husband Doolittle (as she put it in her autobiography *Coal Miner's Daughter*) "got himself clipped." How come? "When they start coming in pairs," she says, "it's time to quit."

MOTHER: Anna Murray McDonnell
NUMBER OF CHILDREN: Fourteen
WHAT'S SO SPECIAL: Matriarch of one of America's F.I.F. (First

Irish Families), she raised her brood in the nineteen-twenties and thirties in what was then the largest single apartment in New York City—twenty-nine rooms, with a separate kitchen for the children. She used her fifty-room Long Island mansion as a base for transforming the sleepy village of Southampton into a superfashionable summer resort.

MOTHER: Empress Maria Theresa
NUMBER OF CHILDREN: Sixteen
WHAT'S SO SPECIAL: For forty dedicated years she was, as she once described herself, "the general and chief mother" of the Habsburg empire and one of the central figures in the wars and politics of eighteenth-century Europe. In her private life she taught her children to follow her example as a servant of the state. One of those who learned the lesson the hard way was her daughter Marie Antoinette, guillotined during the French Revolution.

MOTHER: Nefretete (Nefertiti)
NUMBER OF CHILDREN: Six
WHAT'S SO SPECIAL: The stunning queen of Egypt's King Akhnaten in the fourteenth century B.C. bore the Pharaoh six daughters. The beautiful painted limestone bust of her, discovered in ancient ruins near the Nile and now in a West Berlin museum, has become one of the world's most reproduced works of art and established her as a symbol of imperishable beauty. Thanks to a royal marriage of her daughter Ankhesenpaaton, Queen Nefretete also deserves a niche in maternal history as the mother-in-law of King Tutankhamen.

MOTHER: Abby Aldrich Rockefeller
NUMBER OF CHILDREN: Six
WHAT'S SO SPECIAL: The gracious lady whom husband John D. Rockefeller, Jr., loved for her "unexpectedness" mothered the five famous Rockefeller brothers, John III, Laurance, Winthrop, David, and Nelson, and a daughter Abby. Late in life, she said of them: "John and I have gotten to a point where we feel that perhaps the children have brought *us* up."

MOTHER: Harriet Beecher Stowe
NUMBER OF CHILDREN: Seven (including one set of twins)
WHAT'S SO SPECIAL: The unprecedented popularity of her anti-slavery novel, *Uncle Tom's Cabin*, written between baby-tending chores, made it one of the "moving causes" of the Civil War. Busy

throughout her life with writing and mothering, she once observed: "My children I would not change for all the leisure and pleasure that I could have without them."

MOTHER: Maria Augusta Trapp
NUMBER OF CHILDREN: Ten (including seven stepchildren)
WHAT'S SO SPECIAL: Mother of the singing group once rated as "the most heavily booked single attraction in the entire concert history of the U.S." Julie Andrews played her in *The Sound of Music*, the Broadway musical of her story, later also one of Hollywood's biggest money-making films.

MOTHER: Queen Victoria of England
NUMBER OF CHILDREN: Nine
WHAT'S SO SPECIAL: In the first quarter of the twentieth century, her progeny occupied the thrones of half the countries of Europe. Although the Queen was genuinely fond of her four sons and five daughters once they were grown, she took a dim view of young babies at what she called the "frog stage." And she *hated* being pregnant. When her oldest daughter, the Princess Royal, wrote to her expressing delight at the prospect of giving birth, she replied: "What you say of the pride of giving life to an immortal soul is very fine, dear, but I own I cannot enter into that; I think much more of our being like a cow or a dog at such moments; when our poor nature becomes so very animal and unecstatic."*

---

* For Victoria as Grandmother, see pages 401–2.

# In-laws or Out-laws

Of all men, Adam was the happiest; he had no mother-in-law.

> François Parfaict,
> French historian, 1698–1753

Talk about love and hate! Mothers-in-law have always generated these obverse emotions, and this chapter is both sublime and ridiculous.

I have had my own personal mother-in-law experience; it was a pleasant one—right up until the divorce. And my general philosophy about in-laws has always been that it is better to make a rapprochement with them than to live in a state of siege. In other words, why not *try* to love them and get along with them since you are stuck with them. This pragmatic rationale for a quid pro quo, or a "you stay off of mine and I'll stay off of yours" tradeoff, doesn't always work.

I watched my parents grapple with the mother-in-law problem at close range. (You can read all about the women they were grappling with in the introduction titled "To Grandma's.") My father was always a bit awed by his mother-in-law because she was such a gentle soul, one of those "too good to be true" people. He felt she encouraged my mother to be "babyish" and this annoyed him, but

121

he respected and loved her in spite of the minor problem. When she died he commented that she was "one of the finest ladies I've ever known."

On the other hand, my mother was often steamrolled in the classic manner by her terrible-tempered mother-in-law, who lived *with* us more years than without us. After aeons of in-house sniping, back-biting, snide behavior, and scratchy irritations, they developed a grudging respect for each other. This woman, my paternal grandmother, died among her own daughters, begging to be taken "home to Elizabeth, who is so good to me." So we had a late-blooming Ruth and Naomi situation in reverse, a tribute to my mother as a daughter-in-law.

The varieties of feelings, philosophies, jokes, experiences, and characters making up this chapter are wildly different, but none are indifferent. It is difficult to be indifferent to a mother-in-law or even to the idea of one.

✳

# *These Are Only a Few of the Jokes!*

"You don't look so good, old man. What's wrong?"
"I got domestic trouble."
"But Harry, you always said your wife was a pearl."
"Yeah, she is. It's the mother-of-pearl that's the problem."

✳

"Do you know that your dog bit my mother-in-law yesterday?"
"No, I didn't. Now I suppose you want to sue me for damages."
"Not at all. What will you take for the dog?"

✳

"My husband got angry last night and told me to go to the devil."
"What are you going to do about it?"
"I'm going straight home to mother."

WIFE on her deathbed to her husband: Would you grant me one final wish?

HUSBAND: Anything, darling.

DYING WIFE: Promise me you'll ride with mother at my funeral.

HUSBAND: Well, okay, but it'll ruin my entire day.

✻

# BUT SERIOUSLY, FOLKS . . .

The American humorist George Ade contended that there were only three basic jokes. "But," he said, "since the mother-in-law joke is not a joke but a very serious question, there are actually only two."

✻

The awe and dread with which the untutored savage contemplates his mother-in-law are amongst the most familiar facts of anthropology.

—Sir James Frazer

✻

# IT'S TABOO

Or, so writes Claudia de Lys:

Among the taboos with which primitive man surrounds marriage, none is stranger than the mother-in-law taboo. It varies with different peoples, as do the penalties for breaking it—but in general, the mother-in-law is scrupulously shunned.

The Navajo and Apache Indians, for instance, never looked directly at their mothers-in-law for fear of becoming blind. Other American Indians adopted a quaint method of avoiding the mother-in-law taboo: the groom went through the marriage ceremony with the bride's mother prior to marrying the real bride.

Nearly all of the primitive Australians, Melanesians, Polynesians, as well as Negro races of Africa, have created rules for the subjugation of the mother-in-law. For example, the Zulu-Kaffirs require a man wishing to address his mother-in-law to stand at a dis-

123

tance. He may not address her by name, for such familiarity might imply she still has authority over her daughter. Often he prefers to communicate with her by means of a third person. Furthermore, he is not allowed to look at her, for he must conform with the Zulu proverb that "man should not look upon the breast that has nursed his wife." If, by chance, they meet, they pretend not to know one another.

In the region of the Nile, a Negro of the Basogas tribe will converse with his mother-in-law only when a wall separates them, or through a third person.

Other tribes forbid any intercourse between husband and mother-in-law whatever. When a man of the Celebes Islands meets his wife's mother, by chance, he expectorates in order to rid himself of the evil influence which may result from seeing her.

*A Treasury of American Superstitions*

*

# M-I-L BITS

Behind every successful man stands a surprised mother-in-law.

> —Hubert Humphrey in a speech during the 1964 presidential campaign.

*

When you bury a rich mother-in-law you can afford to spend a few extra *groschen*.

> —Sholom Aleichem, *Eternal Life*

*

A mother-in-law is like the dry rot; far easier to get into a house than to get it out again.

> —*Punch*

Distrust all mothers-in-law. They are simply unscrupulous in what they say in court. The wife's mother is always more prejudiced against the husband than even the most ill-treated wife. If I had my way, I am afraid I would abolish mothers-in-law entirely.

> —Sir Geoffrey Wrangham, British
> High Court Justice and specialist
> in divorce cases, 1960

\*

Sigmund Freud discusses his future mother-in-law in a letter:

I do not think I am being unfair to her; I see her as a person of great mental and moral power standing in our midst, capable of high accomplishments, without a trace of the absurd weaknesses of old women, but there is no denying that she is taking a line against us all, like an old man. Because her charm and vitality have lasted so long, she still demands in return her full share of life—not the share of old age—and expects to be the center, the ruler, an end in herself. Every *man* who has grown old honorably wants the same, only in a woman one is not used to it. As a mother she ought to be content to know that her three children are fairly happy, and she ought to sacrifice her wishes to their needs.

\*

# MORE M-I-L BITS

I know a mother-in-law who sleeps with her glasses on, the better to see her son-in-law suffer in her dreams.

> —Ernest Coquelin

\*

If a daughter-in-law is ugly, she can't conceal the fact from her mother-in-law.

> Chinese proverb

\*

A daughter-in-law can no more live under the same roof with her mother-in-law than a goat can live in the same barn with a tiger.

> Jewish proverb

# SUBSTITUTE MAMA

Edgar Allan Poe was one writer who did not harbor anti-mother-in-law sentiments. His own mother died when he was only two years old but, as an adult, he found another in the form of his father's sister, Mrs. Marie Poe Clemm, who was also the mother of his wife, Virginia. This tribute to his beloved "Muddie" has been called, "the best tribute to a mother-in-law ever written."

## TO MY MOTHER

Because I feel that, in the Heavens above,
    The angels, whispering to one another,
Can find, among their burning terms of love,
    None so devotional as that of "Mother,"
Therefore by that dear name I long have called you—
    You who are more than mother unto me.
And fill my heart of hearts, where Death installed you
    In setting my Virginia's spirit free.
My mother—my own mother, who died early,
    Was but the mother of myself; but you
Are mother to the one I loved so dearly,
    And thus are dearer than the mother I knew
By that infinity with which my wife
    Was dearer to my soul than its soul-life.

*

# CHAPTER 1, VERSES 16 AND 17

In view of the widespread "battle ax" mother-in-law stereotype, it's ironic that probably the most famous mother-in-law in recorded history is Naomi, whose relationship with Ruth, the wife of her dead son, provides one of the Old Testament's greatest stories of constancy and devotion. Through the years, Ruth's plea to Naomi has become such a classic in the literature of loving declarations that it often turns up in marriage ceremonies.

And Ruth said, Intreat me not to leave thee, or to return from following after thee: for whither thou goest, I will go; and where thou lodgest, I will lodge; thy people shall be my people, and thy God, my God. Where thou diest, will I die, and there will I be buried: the Lord do so to me, and more also, if ought but death part thee and me."

Ruth 1:16,17

✻

My wife is the kind of girl who'll not go anywhere without her mother, and her mother will go anywhere.

—John Barrymore

✻

A mother-in-law and a daughter-in-law in one house are like two cats in a bag.

Yiddish proverb

✻

Mother-in-law, daughter-in-law—storm and hail.

Italian proverb

✻

The best mother-in-law is she on whom your geese feed (i.e. on the grass that grows over her grave).

Spanish proverb

✻

# MAMMY, HOW I LOVE YA!

Mary Martin credits her mother-in-law, whom she called "Mammy," with helping to save her marriage to Richard Halliday, the Paramount script editor who later took over her career. The marriage was foundering because the young actress knew nothing about homemaking, while Halliday had been formally reared. So Mary telegraphed her mother-in-law: "Mammy, if you love your son you must help me. I love him with all my heart, but I don't

127

know how to run this house, make his home. I love him, but believe me if you don't fly out here, right this minute, it will be over in a week." Halliday's mother flew to Los Angeles, made an excuse to her son why she was there and began to teach Mary how to organize and be a homemaker. Miss Martin says: "Bless Mammy, she did it . . . But most important of all, we became the closest of friends for the rest of her life."

✳

Every cloud has a silver lining; when you get a divorce, you also get rid of your mother-in-law.

—Evan Esar

✳

## LARRY'S MA-IN-LAW

Painter Larry Rivers is possibly the only artist in modern history to select as his favorite nude model his former mother-in-law. After his divorce from his first wife, Augusta Berger, Rivers maintained a warm, affectionate relationship with her mother and, before the older woman died, in 1957, executed a number of nude paintings of her, the most famous of which is *Double Portrait of Berdie*, in the collection of New York City's Whitney Museum. (You can see it in the picture section.)

✳

## AS DOROTHY PARKER
## ONCE SAID . . .

Dorothy Parker used to do wicked imitations of her husband Alan Campbell's mother's southern accent. Dotty's favorite was a conversation she overheard her mother-in-law having with a telephone operator in which the senior Mrs. Campbell said: "I'll have you remember, young lady, that *I* am a mother!"

The rapier-tongued Miss Parker lodged many complaints against the elder Mrs. Campbell, chief being that her mama-in-law thought she was the only mother who ever lived! Dotty told her good friend, the writer Wyatt Cooper, how much she abhorred "the way she gushed over me when we got married, calling me 'my little daughter' (I wasn't her little daughter; I wasn't her little anything) while she went around telling everybody I had 'snatched that boy out of the cradle' just because I happened to be a year and a half older than Alan."

When Alan died, his mother insisted on having the funeral in Richmond, Virginia, where he had come from and where Mrs. C. lived. Said Dotty snidely: "Alan's funeral was to be her coming out party, I believe." She also railed: "After all those years of going to the Episcopal Church, she buried Alan in the Hebrew Cemetery." (Wyatt was so astounded by this that he looked into it and discovered that Mrs. Campbell the elder had never attended the Episcopal Church or in any way denied that she was Jewish.)

Dotty ranted for years that she had received a huge bill for Alan's funeral. But she got lots of mileage—Parker style—out of not having attended, under doctor's orders, and then asking, "What did they have—fireworks?"

When a person becomes as well-known as Dorothy Parker, so many anecdotes collect around the name that it is hard to distinguish the apocryphal from the true. However, thanks to Wyatt Cooper, who was one of Miss Parker's first and most accurate biographers, some of these tales have never been printed before. But I would be derelict not to retell the best-known Parker anti-mother-in-law mordancy.

Lillian Hellman noted in her book *An Unfinished Woman,* that the following has been attributed variously to Mischa Elman and to Jascha Heifetz, but she insists it was Dorothy Parker who said it:

Lillian and Dorothy were conversing before the fireplace downstairs in the country house Dotty shared with Alan Campbell. Alan was upstairs having a row with his visiting mother. As the day progressed, it began to snow lightly and Dorothy threw a few more logs on the fire. Finally, the angry melee upstairs subsided and Alan appeared in the living room, saw the blazing grate, and snapped: "It's hot as hell in here."

Replied Dorothy Parker: "Not for orphans."

# JULES' VIEW

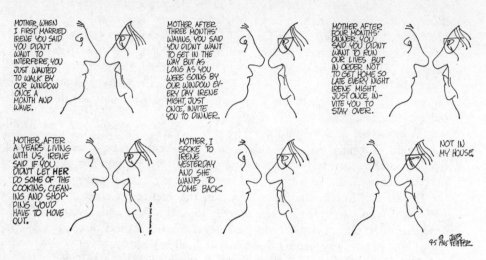

---

*

## DAN'S VIEW

No one could improve on Dan Greenburg's vision of the Jewish mother and the potential or actual daughter-in-law.

> To permit a completely objective evaluation, never speak to the young lady directly, but use your son as an intermediary:
> "Does she like mashed potatoes?" This form of address is known as The Third Person Invisible. Should your son ever decide to marry the girl, this device adapts very nicely to Basic Daughter-in-Law technique, otherwise known as The I-Forget-Her-Name Gambit:
> "Is what's-her-name—is your wife coming over also?"

*　　　　　　•

The port city of Norfolk, Virginia, has been called The Mother-in-Law of the Navy.

# HELLO, DOLLEY!

For twenty-eight years, after her husband's death, Nelly Madison, the mother of the fourth President of the United States, made her home at Montpelier, her son's Virginia mansion, in a special apartment in the "old wing." During much of this time, James and Dolley Madison were in Washington, but during the last decade of the old woman's life, they were all under one roof. The senior Mrs. Madison took her meals by herself and seldom joined the family circle, but was visited daily by her son and daughter-in-law at her two o'clock "audience hour." A visitor who once sat in on one of these gatherings asked the old woman how she passed her time. "I am never at a loss," she replied. "This and these," she said, touching her knitting and her books, "keep me always busy; look at my fingers and you will perceive I have not been idle." Her eyes, she reported, had not yet failed her, "but in other respects I am feeble and helpless and owe everything to *her*"—pointing to Dolley Madison seated nearby. "She is *my* mother *now*, and tenderly cares for all my wants."

✳

# MORE M-I-L'S

Never rely on the glory of the morning or the smile of your mother-in-law.

Japanese proverb

✳

The mother-in-law does not remember she was once a daughter-in-law.

Spanish and Portuguese proverb

✳

Peter remained on friendly terms with Christ notwithstanding Christ's having healed his mother-in-law.

—Samuel Butler

The incident Butler refers to took place shortly after Peter, then known as Simon, relinquished his life as a fisherman to become a disciple. Here is the account, according to St. Mark:

. . . Simon's wife's mother lay sick of a fever, and anon they tell him of her. And he came and took her by the hand, and lifted her up; and immediately the fever left her . . .

# MÈRE-IN-LAW RAMPANT

Could a mother's mind be at rest, knowing her daughter to be under the same roof?

—Lady de Montreuil, mother-in-law of the Marquis de Sade.

The French aristocrat whose name has become a symbol for delectation in cruelty was imprisoned in the Bastille for his perverted sexual excesses, in a large part through the influence of his righteously indignant mother-in-law. Though the connoisseur of pain often railed against this "foul termagant" from his rat-infested prison cell, he demonstrated remarkable gallantry toward her when the chips were down. Released from jail after the French Revolution and placed in a position of influence, he unexpectedly found himself called upon to decide whether she should be sent to the guillotine on political grounds. The Marquis de Sade decided against it.

❊

# DIVORCE ITALIAN STYLE

Lady Mary Wortley Montagu, in 1751, writes to her daughter, the Countess of Bute:

. . . they have long been in fashion in Genoa; several of the finest and greatest ladies there having two husbands alive. The constant pretext is impotency, to which the man often pleads guilty, and though he marries again, and has children by another wife, the plea remains good by saying he was so in regard to his first; and when I told them that in England a complaint of that kind was esteemed so impudent no reasonable woman would submit to make it, I was answered we lived without religion, and that their consciences obliged them rather to strain a point of modesty than live in a state of damnation. However, as this method is not without inconveniences (it being impractical when there is (*sic*) children), they have taken another here: the husband deposes upon oath that he has had a commerce with his mother-in-law, on which the marriage is declared incestuous and nullified, though the children remain legitimate. You will think this hard on the old lady, who is scandalized; but it is no scandal at all, nobody supposing it to be true . . .

The husband's mother is the wife's devil.

German proverb

\*

# Four Formidable Mothers-in-law

## ROSE FITZGERALD KENNEDY

The mother of the thirty-fifth President of the United States is also the mother of two dead war heroes (JFK and Joe, Jr.) and produced, along with her total of nine children, three U.S. senators. With her acute sense of duty, her deeply held religious convictions, her incredible knack for keeping up with her bewildering array of children and grandchildren, Rose has been definitely a formidable mother-in-law to Joan, Ethel, and Jacqueline. In fact, when anyone compliments Senator Edward Kennedy's wife after she speaks in public or plays at a recital, Joan invariably answers: "Oh, thank you —I wish you'd write and tell my mother-in-law that!"

Rose Kennedy has always preferred not to be called "Mother" by the spouses of her children, but requests to be addressed instead as "Grandma." (The exception is Jackie, as you'll see.) Once, fresh from the beauty parlor and wearing a new Paris gown, Rose made an entrance at a party in high good humor because her maid had just said, "Madam, you don't look a day over fifty."

Son-in-law Sargent Shriver, himself silver-maned and in his fifties, greeted her with a rousing, "Hello, Grandma!" at which point, says Rose, "I was immediately deglamorized and very conscious of my eighty years."

One of the most charming tributes written to a mother-in-law is included in Rose Kennedy's book *Times to Remember* and comes from her famous daughter-in-law Jacqueline, who has always preferred to call Rose "Belle Mère," the French term for mother-in-law:

". . . I think it's so sick when you hear those mother-in-law jokes on the radio or any of the media. They used to make me sad even before I had a mother-in-law. They really used to make me almost angry when I heard them; because I'd think, are people really like that? And then this woman, my mother-in-law, she just bent

133

over backwards *not* to interfere. If she gave a suggestion, it was in the sweetest way. She sort of set you—set Jack and me—up as an entity.

"I think it's doubly extraordinary coming from that strong family where all the ties were so centripetal.

"And so: everything. I loved her very much. And I do now. She was just the most extraordinary mother-in-law, Belle Mère."


## QUEEN MARIE OF ROMANIA

The English-born wife of King Ferdinand I of Romania was, to both Europeans and Americans of the 1920s, the epitome of queenly glamour, but in her own eyes she was first and foremost "a passionate mother." And mother-in-law. With daughter Lisabetta married to King George of Greece and daughter Mignon to King Alexander of Yugoslavia, Marie was called "the mother-in-law of the Balkans" and was viewed for a time as one of the most powerful women in Europe, the possible precursor of a vast Balkan empire. Like many a less blue-blooded mom, however, Queen Marie had to suffer through the "she's-not-good-enough-for-you" syndrome with regard to the beloved of her eldest son, Prince Carol. Magda Lupescu, wrote Marie, was a creature "who is as low-born as she is ambitious, a woman who is disastrous to the man who sacrifices honor, honesty, loyalty, duty to feed her ever-growing greed." Marie's experience with Carol made it possible for her to offer solace to another queenly mother whose royal son also persisted in a liaison with a commoner. "My thoughts were with you in intense sympathy," she wrote in 1937 to Queen Mary of England, mother of the abdicating Edward VIII, "and with an understanding only possible to one who has been hit in the same way."


## FANNY, DUCHESS OF MARLBOROUGH

"At the rustle of her silk dress, the household trembled," reported Jenny Jerome Churchill about her aristocratic mother-in-law, Fanny, the Duchess of Marlborough. The mistress of Blenheim Castle had her hands full, checking out prospective sons-in-law for her six daughters, but she still found time to oversee the lifestyle of her famous daughter-in-law, the Brooklyn-born wife of her favorite son, Randolph. In 1873, when, after a fevered three-day courtship, Randolph proposed to the daughter of a businessman from the States, most highborn English viewed an American woman (in Jenny's words) "as a strange and abnormal creature with habits and manners something between a Red Indian and a Gaiety Girl." The Duchess of Marlborough was no exception. Her dismay at Randolph's "American alliance" never completely dissolved even when Jenny presented her with a cherubic Churchill grandson named Winston. A letter Jenny wrote to her own mother during a stay under her mother-in-law's roof in the 1880s expresses emotions familiar to the possessors of formidable mothers-in-law the world over:

"The fact is, I *loathe* living here. It's not on account of its dullness, *that* I don't mind, but it is gall and wormwood to me to accept anything or to be living on anyone I hate. It is no use disguising it, the Duchess hates me simply for what I am—perhaps a little prettier and more attractive than her daughters. Everything I do or say or wear is found fault with. We are always studiously polite to each other, but it is rather like a volcano, ready to burst out at any moment. . . ."

## SARA DELANO ROOSEVELT

When Franklin Delano Roosevelt first ventured to Washington, D.C., in 1913 as Assistant Secretary of the Navy, he and the family moved into a house on N Street selected by his mother. Stated Sara Delano Roosevelt in her journal shortly thereafter: "Moved chairs and tables and began to feel at home." Wrote Franklin's wife Eleanor in *her* diary: "My mother-in-law, as usual, helped us to get settled." This was a pattern that repeated itself with little variation from the moment Sara reluctantly accepted Eleanor as a daughter-in-law in 1905 until the older woman's death in September 1941, four months before the beginning of her son's agonizing period as the leader of America during World War II.

Sara Roosevelt supervised her beloved only son's married life with the same smothering attention she had demonstrated in bringing him up. The first home of newlyweds Franklin and Eleanor was a townhouse on Manhattan's Thirty-sixth Street, which Sara found, furnished, and paid for. It was located only three blocks from her own residence. Later, Sara put up a new, bigger house for the couple—and built herself an identical dwelling next door, joined on the lower and upper floors. Sara instructed her insecure daughter-in-law in the proper operation of a household, hired and fired the English nannies of Eleanor's children, spoiled the youngsters shamelessly, and, according to grandson James, once told them: "Your mother only bore you. I am more your mother than your mother is." When Eleanor bristled at Sara's flagrant overriding of parental discipline, Franklin usually watched amused from the sidelines and it was only Eleanor's increasing involvement in FDR's rising political career that gave Sara's daughter-in-law the leverage to cope with the commanding matriarchal overseer of the family estate at Hyde Park.

In time, Franklin's wife and mother eased into a relationship of comparative harmony, but it had its limits. "It is dreadful," observed Eleanor at the time of her mother-in-law's death, "to have lived so close to someone for thirty-six years and feel no deep affection or sense of loss."

✳

Robert E. Lee writes about his mother-in-law, Mary Custis:

She was to me all that a mother could be, and I yield to none in admiration for her character, love of her virtues, and veneration for her memory.

✳

# FOUR AND A HALF

Though her influence as a mother-in-law has not been quite as pervasive as the aforementioned Formidables, Jolie Gabor, mother of the famous Hungarian sisters of that name, deserves at least a footnote in this category by virtue of the *quantity* of her in-law relationships, if nothing else. Because of the proclivity of Zsa Zsa, Eva, and Magda toward multiple marriages, Jolie's three daughters have given their ebullient mother a total of sixteen different sons-in-law. Actually, the sisters have had, between them, a total of *seventeen* husbands but because he followed up his marriage to Zsa Zsa with an elopement with Magda, the late George Sanders was Jolie's son-in-law twice. States Jolie about this turn of events in her autobiography: "I was ecstatic. I always think it's nice when you get a son-in-law back."*

* If you want a treat, read this funny book, *Jolie Gabor*, as told to Cindy Adams.

# *Joke*

This is to me the epitome of a *new* mother-in-law joke:

Two mothers fell into each other's arms at their twenty-fifth high school reunion. Talk quickly moved to the children. Said Mrs. Doe to Mrs. Roe, "I know your eldest daughter is married now. Is it a good match?"

Mrs. Roe was rapturous. "Marvelous," she replied. "No girl ever had such a wonderful husband. He treats her like a princess. She stays in bed until eleven and then the maid brings her breakfast on a tray. In the afternoon, she goes shopping on Fifth Avenue—and her wardrobe is right out of *Vogue!* And in the evening, she meets her husband for cocktails at the Plaza. It's really a marriage made in heaven!"

"And how," asked Mrs. Doe next, "is your son Richard? I hear he's recently married too."

At this question, Mrs. Roe's face fell. "Don't even *ask* about him!" she told her old friend. "He married one of those girls who thinks money grows on trees. She won't lift a finger around the house. She lolls around in bed until eleven, waiting for the maid to bring her breakfast. Then, off she goes to Saks and Bonwit's and Bergdorf's buying more clothes for a closet that's already bulging with them. And then, in the evening, does she go home for a quiet dinner with Richard? No, she drags him off to the Palm Court for cocktails. Really! I don't know what I've done to be punished with such a daughter-in-law!"

y

# Beautiful Black Mothers

Oh, take me to my kind old mudder
Dere let me live and die.

Stephen Foster,
*Old Folks at Home*

I was one of the luckiest white children ever born on the face of this earth, because for all of the important moments of my early babyhood, childhood, and prepuberty, I had two wonderful mothers—my own, and a woman named Dott Burns.

Dott was black, but hardly anybody's idea of the traditional "mammy" type. Nevertheless, she was definitely my mammy; there are no two ways about it. Because she was so young when she came to work for us, I always called her Dott and she was *my person*, the other mother I had until I was almost thirteen years old.

Dott Burns was also beautiful, physically beautiful, back in a time of accepted segregation and racism, before black people called themselves black, when they felt lucky to be called "Negro" instead of something worse, and usually settled—down South—for gentility's tacky terms "colored" or "nigra." Actually, Dott wasn't black at all—more *café au lait*. Years later when I met Lena Horne, I

139

loved her instantly, not for her glamour, her blazing talent, or her sultry looks and funny nonsensical charm, but because I felt instantly happy in her presence. She reminded me physically of Dott Burns, my number two mother.

I have no idea how the Sloan Smith family managed to get its hands on Dott Burns and keep her through so many years when my brothers, James and Bobby, and I were growing up at 1919 Hemphill Street in Fort Worth, Texas. It was indeed a miracle of luck for us, though I have often wondered how Dott viewed it. She may not have thought much about it. My father's gentlemanly bigotry was "normal" for the times, and my mother was kind and sweet. Both my parents were too steeped in southern Christian ideals ever to mistreat a servant. So Dott may have considered herself lucky even, but the fact is, she was simply a young black woman caught in the socioeconomic facts of Texas life. There was no escape route for her from playing nursemaid to white middle-class children, as well as chief cook and bottlewasher to their demanding parents. And she didn't seek one. It staggers the mind to realize what an important key role she played in our lives, and yet my mother can't even recall how she came to hire Dott. "Oh," she said recently when I asked for Dott's history, "she just came to us. I don't remember how. But I couldn't have done without her."

So the historyless Dott lived with her husband, Raford, in a little shack out in the back yard behind our fine, green, asbestos-shingled, three-bedroom cottage with its flawless lawn and apricot and magnolia trees and hedges and flower beds about which my father was a fanatic. When we wanted to play in the back, we took over Dott's porch and nailed things onto her railings and banged pots and pans and marched in and out of her house like little lords and masters. I can't believe she never scolded us or told us to get lost or to shut up. She cooked and cleaned and babysat and said "Yes, ma'am" and "No, sir" and was always spotless and shining and *there* for us.

Dott traveled to the Rio Grande Valley with us every summer when my father went down to buy cotton, but she would never go across the border to Mexico because the border patrol had told my father that she would have trouble getting back into the United States. Her light color might be mistaken for "Mexican," they said, speaking about her as if she couldn't hear. So she would go back to the tourist court or hotel and wait for us and my mother would

140

have to manage with all the whining and screaming for a while. My father was an intelligent man, but nothing was ever said about getting Dott papers or a passport or something to prove she was a bonafide U.S. citizen. It wasn't done. "Colored" folks just didn't *have* papers and credentials.

Dott was a worry in only one way to my parents. My father did not approve of Dott's husband, Raford. This did not mitigate my interest in the strapping six-footer who took me down to the corner each night to "stomp bugs" under the street light. He had been an object of total fascination to my brothers and me from the moment we observed him singlehandedly lifting Dott's little Model A Ford with the yellow wire wheels off the ground to change a tire without a jack.

My father was sure Raford would come to no good end and couldn't imagine why a nice woman like Dott wanted to be married to such a "sorry rascal." After Raford was stabbed in a bar brawl, he won the nickname "Icepick Red" and was on his way to living up to all my father's predictions. "Now you see," my father would say, "why I won't let him work for me."

Eventually, Raford *was* killed in another knife fight. I have no memory of Dott's pain or any active concern on our part for her feelings. But I do remember Daddy taking us down to the Negro funeral parlor to look at Raford lying in all his rugged mahogany majesty on a plain metal table with a white sheet draped up over his naked body to his chest. We stood mesmerized. My father said *this* would teach us a lesson. I never knew what lesson it taught except that Raford was as mysterious, wonderful, and glamorous in death as he had been in life. If I know my tactless father, what he probably said to Dott was something helpful like, "Good riddance" or "you're better off without him."

Raford had been the racy part of Dott's life. Otherwise she was just the quiet, refined, sensible, and totally dependable servant who "looked after the Smith children." She seemed to have few desires outside the periphery of our lives. (Her purchase of the Model A car was her one act of individualism.) When we'd been infants Dott had insisted on rocking me and later Bobby out in the front porch swing no matter how cold the day. Mother would tell her not to go out. "Oh no, I dress up warm and I snuggle up the baby warm and I swing her in the treetops and she'll go right to sleep." ("In the treetops" was her name for "Rockabye, Baby.")

In her starched white uniform, Dott was acceptable to pass through Fort Worth's racist front doors while delivering her little charges to parties, or to sit at the table with us to feed us, but *not* to eat with us. When she took us to the Tivoli Theater, it was understood that she could sit wherever she liked. "Maids with white children may sit downstairs" read a management sign. But Bobby and I always wanted to sit upstairs in the "colored" balcony. "Are you sure?" Dott would frown. "Your mother wouldn't like it." We would yell, "Mother won't know!" and burst up the stairs where—without Dott—we were not allowed to go. It was in this balcony that I became initiated into a few of the mysteries of what the great white jazzman Mezz Mezzrow was to call so feelingly "The Race."

It was an initiation into what became an abiding fascination with blacks—their pain, their sorrow, their music, their laughter, their philosophy. It must have cost Dott plenty to put up with us and all our careless curiosity and our rotten little white kid jokes. We drank from the "colored" water fountains to show off our rebellion, knowing no one would arrest us for doing what was forbidden to blacks as a vice versa. Dott disapproved of such flouting of the rules. She cautioned us but never punished us. We were her charges, but she was our possession. It was a cost never to be paid back to her or made up to her. There is no way to erase the fact that she was a servant of our whims, a slave to white middle-class thoughtlessness.

Years later, after protesting, badgering, striking, marching, and working to see the first black student admitted to the University of Texas, I recall thinking I had struck a small blow for Dott but it was a mighty puny one in retrospect. No doubt she would have equated it with the drinking-fountain rebellion.

Through all the time Dott was a part of our lives it occurs to me she had no resources telling her she would "overcome." She just wanted to get by. Yet I never saw her exhibit anger, resentment, impatience, or weariness. At the most she displayed worry over our rambunctious ways. She was, in retrospect, the dream mother my own mother didn't always have the time to be and the memory of being rocked in Dott's arms on the porch is still vivid. Bobby recalls that for years she made him white icing birthday cakes decorated with red-hot candies spelling his name. James remembers that when she no longer worked for us, Dott came and spent weeks nursing my mother when she was ill. She refused a salary.

I am happy to say that Dott eventually escaped from our thoughtless bondage. She married a good-looking farmer who was well-to-do and well educated. He was as handsome and elegant as Raford had been randy and rugged. It somewhat scandalized my father who said over and over, "Why, he is whiter than Dott!" Dott and her husband prospered in nearby Roanoke, Texas. They frequently brought us fine hams and sausage for which they refused payment. This remarkable woman still works part-time at the popular Austin Patio Dude Ranch in Grapevine, Texas, where the owners say they could not manage without her.

I can understand this feeling. One of the saddest days of my life was the day she left our employ. Dott Burns never had any children—except for James, Bobby, and Mary Elizabeth Smith.

I hope we have been some credit to her.

*

# THE GOSPEL ACCORDING TO FLO

"We were poor, but we refused to be pitiful, and although we were Black, we felt precious." That's how the black feminist activist Florynce Kennedy sums up her childhood as one of five sisters growing up in Kansas City during the Depression. The feeling of being "precious" (which gave her, among other things, the courage to become one of the first black women ever to graduate from Columbia Law School) came, she says, in a large part from her mother, Zella. Joy and Faye Kennedy, both published authors and the other two thirds of the trio dubbed "the Black Brontës," agree with Flo in this evaluation.

"We never felt like losers," Florynce Kennedy writes in her autobiography, *Color Me Flo*. "We were the exact opposite of the Marilyn Monroe syndrome, the beautiful golden goddess who because of her bad childhood and sense of worthlessness was never able to feel like a goddess. We were little black pickaninnies, but because of the way we were treated by our family, we felt very favored. I remember how at Christmastime Zella would call all the creditors and tell them she wouldn't be able to pay them because she had to buy something for her kids. She always made it clear to

143

us and to everybody else that we were something special and to be indulged. Some families have the wherewithal, but they act as if it were some kind of betrayal of parental responsibilities to indulge their kids. Her feeling was, 'I want these children to know we care about them, that we give them the best we have. . . .'"

*

# DICK'S MOMMA

DICK GREGORY:

. . . I wonder about my Momma sometimes, and all the other Negro mothers who got up at 6 A.M. to go to the white man's house with sacks over their shoes because it was so wet and cold. I wonder how they made it. They worked very hard for the man, they made his breakfast and they scrubbed his floors and they dispersed his babies. They didn't have too much time for us.

I wonder about my Momma, who walked out of a white woman's clean house at midnight and came back to her own where the lights had been out for three months, and the pipes were frozen and the wind came in through the cracks. She'd have to make deals with the rats; leave some food out for them so they wouldn't gnaw on the doors or bite the babies. The roaches, they were just like part of the family.

From *nigger, an autobiography,*
with Robert Lipsyte

*

# TONY WINNER'S MA

Virginia Capers, winner of an Antoinette Perry Award for the best performance by an actress in the Broadway musical, *Raisin,* gives her mother much of the credit for her success. She explained why to reporter Judith Cummings:

"When I was small and she would take me out for a walk where the curtains were clean and things were nice and pretty, she used to tell me that hope lived in those windows. Her teaching me that hope comes from within, that it's something that grows inside you, was one of the main reasons that I hung on for twenty-three years until this moment."

❋

## JIMMY BALDWIN WRITES

"You getting to be," she said, putting her hand beneath his chin and holding his face away from her, "a right big boy. You going to be a mighty fine man, you know that? Your mamma's counting on you." And he knew again that she was not saying everything she meant; in a kind of secret language she was telling him something that he must remember and understand tomorrow. He watched her face, his heart swollen with love for her and with an anguish, not yet his own, that he did not understand and that frightened him. "Yes, Ma," he said, hoping that she would realize, despite his stammering tongue, the depth of his passion to please her.

*Go Tell It on the Mountain*

❋

### *MY MAMMY*

Mammy, Mammy,
The sun shines East, the sun shines West
But I've just learned where the sun shines best,
Mammy, Mammy,
My heart strings are tangled around Alabammy
I'se a'comin', sorry I made you wait;
I'se a'comin', hope and pray I'm not too late.
Mammy, Mammy,
I'd walk a million miles for one of your smiles
My Mammy.

By Sam Lewis, Joe Young,
and Walter Donaldson

# JOLSON'S MAMMY

Songs about "Mammy" were a Tin Pan Alley staple starting in the 1890s* and, like the popular vaudeville phenomenon of the "Mammy Singer," originated far from the plantations of the South. The first and greatest of the Mammy specialists was Al Jolson, born in Russia and raised on New York City's Lower East Side. The song, "My Mammy," which, according to music historian Sigmund Spaeth, "gave the generic name of 'Mammy Singer' to all those who bent the knee and spread the arms in the familiar Jolson style," has a special niche not only in vaudeville but in movie history for it was included in *The Jazz Singer*, which revolutionized the movie industry by introducing sound in 1927. Most of the picture's sound track was music but, significantly, there was a bit of dialogue too, between the Jolson character and his mother. (See photo section.)

Jolson's real mother died when he was ten. "My Mammy" did *not* initiate his blackface act. He started in blackface back in 1903 and was not seen on stage without it for the next 25 years. The mannerism of getting down on one knee was, according to Maurice Zolotow, prompted by a prosaic accident. One night an ingrown toenail hurt unbearably, so Al knelt to get the pressure off his toe. The trick was so effective that he adopted it permanently.

᪉

# HOW I LOVE YA'
# HOW I LOVE YA'

Following is an extract from a charming consideration of the Mammy by a talented black writer who prefers to remain unidentified:

> I saw *Gone With the Wind* last week for the fourth time which means that I like the film very much . . . But I don't like this film

* Most were on the order of the Harry Von Tilzer 1899 favorite, "Mammy's Kinky-Headed Coon," but there were some satiric versions, too. Eddie Cantor once co-authored a number entitled, "My Yiddisha Mammy."

because of Scarlett . . . or Rhett . . . or Melanie . . . or Ashley. What I really like about this film is Hattie McDaniel, the Mammy.

A Mammy, I think, is different from your mother because while your mother is expected to love you, Mammies love you for no reason at all. A Mammy is fair, loving, loyal, nurturing, supportive, protective, generous, and devoted. Ideally, she is a big black woman, who wears big, full skirts that are good for burying your face in. Aunt Jemima was one of the best Mammies and even if she was not really responsible for giving us the pancake, the credit does not look very good on anyone else.

A Mammy is the sort of person who will pretend to be listening to you as you jabber about all the insane things happening in your life, but what she's really doing is just looking at you and thinking, isn't she wonderful, isn't she great? . . .

Black people do not like the image of a Mammy anymore, but they haven't liked anything wonderful about themselves in a long time. At least not publicly. They don't seem to like acknowledging . . . that no one else has quite mastered the beauty of rolling the eyes, hands on the hips, shaking the head from side to side, and muttering *hmmm, hmmmm,* all in one stroke . . .

(For more on the mammy, as personified by Hattie McDaniel, see "Mom and Hollywood.")

✳

# MAYA ANGELOU WRITES OF GRANDMA

People spoke of Momma as a good-looking woman and some, who remembered her youth, said she used to be right pretty. I saw only her power and strength. She was taller than any woman in my personal world, and her hands were so large they could span my head from ear to ear. Her voice was soft only because she chose to keep it so. In church, when she was called upon to sing, she seemed to pull out plugs from behind her jaws and the huge, almost rough sound would pour over the listeners and throb in the air.

Each Sunday, after she had taken her seat, the minister would announce, "We will now be led in a hymn by Sister Henderson." And each Sunday she looked up with amazement at the preacher and asked silently, "Me?" After a second of assuring herself that she indeed was being called upon, she laid down her handbag and slowly folded her handkerchief. This was placed neatly on top of the purse, then she leaned on the bench in front and pushed herself to a standing position, and then she opened her mouth and the song jumped out as if it had only been waiting for the right time to make an appearance. Week after week and year after year the performance never changed, yet I don't remember anyone's ever remarking on her sincerity or readiness to sing.

Momma intended to teach Bailey and me to use the paths in life that she and her generation and all the Negroes gone before had found, and found to be safe ones. She didn't cotton to the idea that whitefolks could be talked to at all without risking one's life. And certainly they couldn't be spoken to insolently. In fact, even in their absence they could not be spoken of too harshly unless we used the sobriquet "They." If she had been asked and had chosen to answer the question of whether she was cowardly or not, she would have said that she was a realist. Didn't she stand up to "them" year after year? Wasn't she the only Negro woman in Stamps referred to once as Mrs.?

That incident became one of Stamps' little legends. Some years before Bailey and I arrived in town, a man was hunted down for assaulting white womanhood. In trying to escape he ran to the Store. Momma and Uncle Willie hid him behind the chifforobe until night, gave him supplies for an overland journey and sent him on his way. He was, however, apprehended, and in court when he was questioned as to his movements on the day of the crime, he replied that after he heard that he was being sought he took refuge in Mrs. Henderson's store.

The judge asked that Mrs. Henderson be subpoenaed, and when Momma arrived and said she was Mrs. Henderson, the judge, the bailiff and other whites in the audience laughed. The judge had really made a gaffe calling a Negro woman Mrs., but then he was from Pine Bluff and couldn't have been expected to know that a woman who owned a store in that village would also turn out to be colored. The whites tickled their funny bones with the incident for a long time, and the Negroes thought it proved the worth and majesty of my grandmother.

*I Know Why*
*The Caged Bird Sings*

# ORPHAN'S LAMENT

Sometimes I feel like a motherless child,
Sometimes I feel like a motherless child,
Sometimes I feel like a motherless child,
A long ways from home. . . .

This traditional Negro spiritual is a specialty in the concert reper-
tories of both Harry Belafonte and Leontyne Price and was also a
performing favorite of the late Mahalia Jackson. John Lovell, Jr., in
his scholarly study, *Black Song: The Forge and the Flame,* calls it
"the most famous 'blue' spiritual of them all." Its author is unknown.

*

## MOTHER TO SON

Well, son, I'll tell you;
Life for me ain't been no crystal stair.
It's had tacks in it,
And splinters,
And boards torn up,
And places with no carpet on the floor—
Bare.
But all the time
I'se been a-climbin' on,
And reachin' landin's,
And turnin' corners,
And sometimes goin' in the dark
Where there ain't been no light.
So boy, don't you turn back.
Don't you set down on the steps
'Cause you finds it's kinder hard.
Don't you fall now—
For I'se still goin', honey,
I'se still climbin',
And life for me ain't been no crystal stair.

Langston Hughes

# DON'T WALLOW!

Maxims imparted to the Reverend Jesse Jackson, as a boy, by his maternal grandmother, Matilda ("Aunt Tibby") Burns of Greenville, North Carolina:

"If you fall, boy, you don't have to wallow. Ain't nobody going to think you somebody unless you think so yourself. Don't listen to their talk, boy, they don't have a pot to pee in or a window to throw it out. For God's sake, Jesse, promise me you'll be somebody. Ain't no such word as *cain't, cain't* got drowned in a soda bottle. Don't let the Joneses get you down. Nothing is impossible for those who love the Lord. Come hell or high water, if you got the guts, boy, ain't nothing or nobody can turn you around."

Barbara Reynolds in *Jesse Jackson*

\*

# "MOMS"

This section on Black mothers needs at least a brief mention of the late Jackie "Moms" Mabley, hardy perennial of Harlem's Apollo Theater in its golden days and originator of a rambunctious genre of black rhyming slang that found its way into many jazz-song titles. A mother for the first time at age sixteen, she raised a total of three children, but to several generations of Harlemites she was "Moms" by acclamation. Her comedy persona had little to do with motherhood per se although she did have one hilariously raunchy routine posing the question, "At what age do you 'hip' a child?" meaning, when do you tell your youngsters the facts of life.

"Moms" Mabley was a symbol of one important aspect of black motherhood in the first half of the twentieth century: the irreverent spunkiness which helped many blacks to endure and prevail against tremendous odds.

# Jewish Mothers

God could not be everywhere, so he created mothers.

Jewish proverb

I would be derelict in my duty trying to introduce this "very lovely" chapter if I did not tell you of its forerunner, a humorous classic by Dan Greenburg called *How To Be a Jewish Mother (A Very Lovely Training Manual)*. On the back of Dan's book jacket are pictures of Mama Greenburg in 1938 feeding little Dan from a spoon and also of Mama Greenburg in 1964 feeding big Dan from a spoon. (Possibly the same spoon!) The jacket copy notes that "though twenty-eight years of age, he (Dan) is still unmarried and does not know how to stand up straight or eat properly."

By rights, the whole of Dan's landmark book should be reproduced here. *How To Be a Jewish Mother* has stood the test of time better than Dan himself. He is no longer twenty-eight, has been married and divorced (*Oy vey!*), and somehow, in spite of his lovely Jewish mother, has spent recent years chasing fires, writing about sex experiments, and dabbling in the occult. He still can't stand up straight and doesn't know how to eat properly. What's worse—he is jaded.

But *mox nix*. As Dan wrote in his lovely little book back in 1964:

151

There is more to being a Jewish mother than being Jewish and a mother. (On the other hand, you don't have to be either Jewish or a mother to be a Jewish mother. An Irish waitress or an Italian barber could also be a Jewish mother.) Properly practiced, Jewish motherhood is an art—a complex network of subtle and highly sophisticated techniques.

Master these techniques and you will be an unqualified success —the envy of your friends and the backbone of your family.

Fail to master these techniques and you hasten the black day you discover your children can get along without you.*

The Jewish mother, from Mrs. Noah to Gertrude Berg, from Mrs. Portnoy to Barbra Streisand, has had more jokes written about her, more fun poked at her, more stereotypes created around her, than just about any of our other categories. She is the lightning rod of mothers, the symbol of motherhood as high tragedy or high camp. In matters of sheer survival, as Irving Howe tells us in his poignant and magnificent work *World of Our Fathers*, she represents motherhood magnified—angel's wings, warts, and all.

Though I am the most obvious of WASPS and hardly ever saw or knew a Jewish mother until I grew up and left Texas, I have had the privilege since 1949 of knowing many Jewish mothers. Most of them were characteristically nifty and even the ones I didn't care for were nifty characters. Lest we forget, it was a Jewish mother (of course) whose story started this book in the first place, so this chapter has special significance.

I have known prototypical Jewish mothers who wear aprons, call you "Dolly" and actually say, "Eat, eat a little." And I have known some mighty elegant classy gorgeous steppers such as the handsome and intellectual Ruth Elson of Tulsa or the remarkable Rose Shumofsky of "Roseshit" philosophy fame or the attractive dowager Ruby Schinazi of the Hotel Pierre in New York and the dedicated community-conscious former Los Angeles social worker Lillian Newcomb, whose daughter Patricia is a friend of mine. I have warmed my heart at the table of my Jewish "sister" Shirley Herz's mother, Sybil, and my sense of humor at that of Betty Lee Hunt's mother, the fractious May Perlman. These mothers, uncommonly unalike, seem to share at least a twinkle in common.

It must be kind of fun to be a Jewish mother and know you are

* The Gotham Book Mart, 41 W. 47, NYC could order this Price/Stern/Sloan collector's item for you.

having such an incredible impact on your children. The WASP mother is apt to feel quite ineffectual in comparison. Though times are changing and there are no simple truths any more, I can still say that *I* have never yet known a Jewish mother who was ignored by her children. (A few are hated, but not ignored.)

And finally, of course, the Jewish mother is most of the mothers I meet, including my own, who invariably wants me to eat a piece of fruit ("It's good for you and makes your eyelashes curly") or wrap up a piece of cake to take home, who makes chicken soup when someone is sick and desperately wanted her sons to grow up to be doctors and dentists, and prayed that I would marry a "professional" man—or anybody "respectable who will take care of you."

\*

# THE DEFINITIVE IRVING HOWE

Learning to relish the privileges of suffering, the Jewish mother could become absurdly, outrageously protective. From that condition, especially if linked, as it well might be, with contempt for her husband, she could decline into a brassy courage, with her grating bark or soul-destroying whine, silver-blue hair, and unfocused aggression. Nor was it unusual for her to employ ingenuity in order to keep her brood in a state of prolonged dependence, as she grew expert at groaning, cajoling, intimidating. Daughters paled, sons fled.

Yet even behind the most insufferable ways of the Jewish mother there was almost always a hard-earned perception of reality. Did she overfeed? Her mind was haunted by memories of a hungry childhood. Did she fuss about health? Infant mortality had been a plague in the old country and the horror of diphtheria overwhelming in this country. Did she dominate everyone within reach? A disarranged family structure endowed her with powers she had never known before, and burdens too; it was to be expected that she would abuse the powers and find advantage in the burdens. The weight of centuries bore down. In her bones, the Jewish mother knew that she and hers, simply by being Jewish, had always to live with a sense of precariousness. When she worried about her little boy going down to play, it was not merely the dangers of Rivington or Cherry Street that she saw—though there *were* dangers on such streets; it was the streets of Kishinev and Bialystok and other towns in which the blood of Jewish children had been spilled. Later, such memories would fade among those she had meant to shield and it would become customary to regard her as a grotesque figure of excess.

Venerated to absurdity, assaulted with a venom that testifies obliquely to her continuing moral and emotional power, the immigrant mother cut her path through the perils and entanglements of American life. Everyone spoke about her, against her, to her, but she herself has left no word to posterity, certainly none in her own voice, perhaps because all the talk about her "role" seemed to her finally trivial, the indulgence of those who had escaped life's primal tasks. Talk was a luxury that her labor would enable her sons to taste.

*World of Our Fathers*

✳

A mother is not a dust rag.

—Sholom Aleichem
in *Modern Children*

✳

# A MOTHER'S CURSES

Performer David Steinberg says a mother's curse in a Jewish home is nothing like one in a gentile home. A Jewish mother would say: "May you inherit a huge estate and own that huge estate and have on it a hundred mansions and a hundred beds in every one and may you flip from bed to bed with malarial fever."

✳

# MEL ON MOM

Mel Brooks, talking about his mother on *The David Susskind Show*, said he never saw her furniture. "It was always covered to keep the dust off. Also, I never drank out of a glass until I was thirty-four. We only had jelly jars." Mel said his mother now lives in Miami, and he asked her if she was frightened to move there. She told him: "I come from Russia. *That* was a move. New York to Florida? That's nothing!" The comic-writer-director says that when he introduced his mother to his present wife, Anne Bancroft, a Catholic, his mother said pleasantly: "Sit down and take a piece of fruit. I'll be out in the kitchen—and my head will be in the oven."

❄

## SAMMY'S MAMMY

My mother was the Jewish Lourdes. People always came to her with their problems.

—Songwriter Sammy Cahn

❄

## LENNY'S FAY

The screen and playwright Leonard Gershe, who wrote about overprotective mother love for a blind son in *Butterflies Are Free*, offers this story:

My mother was the only truly innocent person I have met in my life. She was good and thought everyone else was that way, too. Once when I was visiting New York from California, she insisted on buying me a sweater at Bloomingdale's and she wrote out a check. They then asked for identification and she presented the clerk with a postcard she'd just received from Miami that morning. The clerk said, "But this isn't identification." Mother said, "Yes, it is . . . look, it's from my best friend Lilly Silber and it's made out to me. How could I possibly have that postcard if I weren't Fay Gershe?" Seeing the logic of this, the clerk let it go and accepted her check!

155

# MOTHER OF THE TIMES

One of the most elegant and effective of our mothers in this chapter is Mrs. Arthur H. Sulzberger, who is the largest single stockholder in The New York *Times* corporation, a millionaire more than a hundred times over. Born Iphigene Ochs, she was the daughter of Adolph S. Ochs, who founded the nation's most prestigious newspaper in 1896. The *Times* has been run since then by her husband, her son-in-law Orvil E. Dryfoos and her son Arthur Ochs Sulzberger, but some believe that the octogenarian Mrs. Sulzberger is still involved behind the scenes.

For many years she was on the board of the NYT and attended all meetings, offering a strong voice in decisions affecting the famous paper. In her book *Doers and Dowagers*, Felicia Warburg Roosevelt noted of Mrs. Sulzberger: "She has written letters to the Editor on a variety of subjects, from decrying the unnecessary killing of rabbits to stating her liberal Democratic views. Many times she uses deceased relatives' names, unknown to the public but self-evident to the editorial staff."


Iphigene, who created a humorous family crest stating NOTHING IS IMPOSSIBLE, is also outspoken on the subject of motherhood. "Sons," she says, "either have an Oedipus complex about their mothers or hate the ole gal for giving them too much chicken soup. But then I believe in telling my children what I think."


*

# MAMA MAILER

Norman Mailer once singled out the one aspect of his personality he "found insupportable—the nice Jewish boy from Brooklyn . . . a man early accustomed to mother-love." In all his prolific literary output, Mailer has written scarcely anything about the woman who produced him. This poem, from the collection *Deaths for the Ladies* (*and other Disasters*) is one of his rare "mother writings."

the worst to be said
about mothers
is that they
are prone
to give
kisses
of con-
grat-
u-
lation
which make you feel
like a battleship
on which someone
is breaking
a bottle

\*

# NEW YORK MAGAZINE CONTEST
# HONORABLE MENTION

The Jewish Mother doll: wind it up and it orders slipcovers.

—Larry Laiken, Bayside, New York

\*

Inside every Jewish father is a Jewish mother.\*

—Josh Greenfeld, telling
the story of his afflicted
child in *Be Not Afraid*

\* Mr. Greenfeld must surely be right. The other day I received a ton of fruit sent up from Florida by the generous Irving Mansfield, husband of the late Jacqueline Susann. In it was a card: "Dear Liz Who sez a girl from Texas can't have a dirty old man for a Jewish mother? Love, Irving."

# ANOTHER MOTHER MARY

Her book *Nobody Calls at This Hour Just to Say Hello*, is Irene Kampen's tribute to her mother, Mary Trepel. In this version the Jewish mother is a worrier, a charmer, an overstater of fact, a rescuer of chipmunks, cats, and children, a woman with good reasons for everything she says and does. She is a Cassandra at predicting and expecting the worst, while saying reassuringly to her family, "Everything will be all right." Author Kampen says it was always impossible to convince her mother that she had telephoned just to say hello.

MOTHER: Irene? What's wrong?
DAUGHTER: Nothing is wrong, Mother. I felt like saying hello to you.
MOTHER: Something has happened out there in Cleveland. Tell me what it is.
DAUGHTER: Everything is fine. Nothing has happened.
MOTHER: I can tell by the sound of your voice that something is wrong.
Etc., etc., etc.
MOTHER (*subsiding*): Well, you sound to me as though you're coming down with a cold.

Irene relates the following as typical of her mother:
"Never mind," Mother tells me. "Tomorrow is Columbus Day. Christopher Columbus was Jewish." Mother specializes in who famous is Jewish.
"Christopher Columbus?" I say. "Oh, Mother!"
"Never mind," Mother says . . . "I'll tell you who else is Jewish. Richard Burton, that's who."
"Oh, Mother!" I say.
"Never mind," Mother says. "Mark my words."
"Richard Burton is not Jewish," I tell her patiently. "Richard Burton is Welsh. He was born in Wales of Welsh parents. He grew up in Wales. He went to school in Wales. His father was a Welsh coal miner."
"Never mind," Mother says again. "I happen to know."*

*Mother was right. Richard Burton is Jewish. Part Jewish, anyway, Jewish grandmother.

I say later to my sister, Joyce, "Guess who's Jewish now? Christopher Columbus and Richard Burton!"

We both have a good laugh over this, but the next day Joyce tells me she looked Christopher Columbus up in the Encyclopaedia Britannica, just for her own amusement. "He was Jewish," Joyce says.

There is a silence. What can we say? "At least," I tell Joyce, "give me an at least."

Joyce thinks about it for a moment. "At least Mother isn't going around claiming that the Queen of England is Jewish," she says.

I repeat Joyce's remark to Mother. Mother says, "Never mind, with that nose of hers it wouldn't surprise me at all."

*

# EXTREMES?

JANE LAZARRE:

What was locked in that extremity of expression that I so loved as a child? When the grownups became annoyed with our childish fights and shrieks and sent us out of the house yelling, "Go play in traffic!" Why did I feel deeply secure, certain of their undying love? Was it that by their yelling, their faces puffing red, their fingers pointing dramatically toward the door, their hateful words screaming out at the tops of their lungs, that I knew how much they loved us? Yes, it was that. But it was more. I sensed, I now know, that they, by their own expression, acknowledged the devil in us all, established their toleration for the reality of our humanness. "You are my hell on earth, my endless burden!" the mother shrieks at the child she patently adores. And the child, if not the neighbors, hears the silent addition: "my reason for staying alive."

*The Mother Knot*

*

# THAT WOMAN!

The mother of New York theatrical attorney L. Arnold Weissberger read an interview with Maria Callas's mother in which she complained about what a monster her daughter was and how badly Callas had treated her. A week later, Weissberger told his mother he had priceless tickets to the Met for them to hear Callas in *Lucia*. Anna Weissberger protested, citing Callas as a horror she would not want to see. Arnold was exasperated. "These tickets are the hottest of the year and you're going." Mrs. Weissberger finally gave in. At the end of the first big aria, the audience rose, applauding and cheering madly, but Mrs. Weissberger sat in silence. When Arnold sat down after the applause subsided, Anna turned to her son and whispered: "It's quite obvious that nobody in this audience but me cares how that woman treats her mother!"

✳

## "DON'T TELL" AGAIN

A successful unmarried career woman I know had a married sister named Joan, who was a typical housewife whose life centered around her husband and kids.

The mother of these two unalike females was talking to the unmarried one. "I worry about you. I do. You're not married. You don't have a man to take care of you. What's going to become of us?"

The single woman snapped, "Mother, for heaven's sake, I'm living exactly as I like. I do as I please. I make plenty of money and I can spend it on myself. I don't have to worry about what some man wants. I go to Europe twice a year. I entertain. I have all the friends I want. I'm not tied down to housework or kids. My life is glamorous and wonderful."

There was a pause and then the Mother said, "I know. Don't tell Joan."

NOTE: The above anecdote has become known as the "Don't Tell Joan" syndrome of motherhood. This same story with variation appears elsewhere in this book. It is also known as the "Don't Tell Burt" syndrome and sometimes as the "Don't Tell Your Father" syndrome.

To me its implication is clear and important. A mother may

protest, a mother may try to change things, a mother may deplore, but when the chips are down, *a mother can take it,* while she isn't so sure that anybody else can.

*

# MEIN SIGI

Ernest Jones writes in *The Life and Work of Sigmund Freud:*

Amalie Freud was nineteen when she married, bore her first son, Sigmund, when she was twenty-one and subsequently became the mother of two other sons and five daughters. According to Freud's friend and biographer Ernest Jones, she maintained a close relationship with her eldest son throughout her long life and even in the presence of the Master's young disciples, referred to the Father of Psychoanalysis as "mein goldener Sigi." Says Jones: "When young she was slender and pretty and she retained to the last her gaiety, alertness and sharp-witted intelligence." She held onto her vanity, too. "When she was ninety," Jones writes, "she declined the gift of a beautiful shawl, saying it would 'make her look too old.' When she was ninety-five, six weeks before she died, her photograph appeared in the newspaper, her comment was: 'A bad reproduction; it makes me look a hundred.'"

*

# AGE CANNOT WITHER

The mother of Broadway director Burt Shevelove went to the doctor for a minor ailment. The doctor asked her age and she told him sixty-eight. "But why did you do that, Mother," asked Burt. "Why lie to the doctor?" Mrs. Shevelove shrugged. "Why did I do it? I figured if I told him I was eighty-seven he might have said—'Enough already!'"

*

Mrs. Jacob Adler of the famous Yiddish theater family decided to return to acting after a long interval. A reporter interviewing her asked, "By the way, Mrs. Adler, how old are you?"

"I am sixty-one," she said.

"How odd," said the reporter. "I interviewed your son Jack last week, and he told me *he* was fifty."

Mrs. Adler shrugged: "Oh well, he lives his life and I live mine."

✻

# A GREAT JEWISH STAGE MOTHER

Here is one of the all-time fantastic mother stories about Sarah Adler—the erudite and brilliant wife of the Yiddish theater idol Jacob Adler. She was the mother of a theater dynasty that produced Luther, Stella, Frances, Jack, and Julia Adler. Sylvia Sidney, once her daughter-in-law, describes her as "one of the greatest women I ever knew; a truly extraordinary talent and teacher. Even in her maturity when she entered a room, every man there wanted to sit at her feet."

After years as his leading lady, Sarah found her famous husband had decided he needed younger partners onstage. He replaced her as his leading lady with their volatile daughter Frances. This caused a coldness between Sarah, the mother, and the daughter whom the family had nicknamed "Nunya."

After years of estrangement, Sarah Adler lay dying. Suddenly the long absent "Nunya" arrived at the hospital. The door of the room didn't just open; it flew open dramatically. Nunya sobbed aloud and rushed to Sarah's side. She knelt sobbing grasping her mother's hands. Sarah looked resigned. Finally she weakly signaled to the nurse with a free hand. The nurse came to the bedside while "Nunya" continued to wail on her knees.

The great Sarah whispered: "Nurse—nurse—did you ever see a play called *Medea?*"

The nurse nodded.

Sarah Adler shrugged in her bed. She said: "One day in the life of 'Nunya'!"

# Four Favorite "Jewish Mothers" of Modern Fiction

MOTHER: Bessie (Mrs. Les) Glass
IMMORTALIZER: J. D. Salinger (in *Franny and Zooey*)
CHARACTERISTICS: The "svelte twilight soubrette" who is the mother of Seymour, Buddy, BooBoo, Walt, Waker, Zooey, and Franny Glass came to motherhood from a career as a vaudeville hoofer. Though Irish by descent and Jewish only by marriage, she closely resembles the stereotypical "Jewish mother," urging her youngest son to get married and seeking to nourish her youngest daughter through an emotional crisis with "a nice cup of chicken broth." Her customary at-home garb is an ancient midnight-blue Japanese kimono with two enormous pockets—"the repository for the paraphernalia of a very heavy cigarette smoker and an amateur handyman." In addition to several packs of cigarettes and matches, the pockets usually contain "a screwdriver, a claw-and-hammer, a Boy Scout knife that had once belonged to one of her sons, and an enamel faucet handle or two, plus an assortment of screws, nails, hinges, and ball-bearing casters"—all of which tend to make her "chink faintly" as she progresses through her *kibbutz*-like domain. Family members also recognize a "particular facial expression that her eldest daughter, BooBoo, had once described as meaning one of two things: that she had just talked with one of her sons on the telephone or that she had just had a report, on the best authority, that the bowels of every single human being in the world were scheduled to move with perfect hygienic regularity for a period of one full week." Though her son Zooey often views her as "an impenetrable mass of prejudices, clichés and bromides," he also recognizes within her the source of an occasional skyrocketing truth. Her chicken broth, he tells his sister, is "consecrated."

MOTHER: Sophie (Mrs. Jack) Portnoy
IMMORTALIZER: Philip Roth (in *Portnoy's Complaint*)
CHARACTERISTICS: Coping with the manifold crises of domestic life in northern New Jersey in the 1930s, this hyper-energetic "Jewish mother" often seems, to her son Alexander, "some doomed dazzling combination of Marie Curie, Anna Karenina, and Amelia Earhart." Though daughter Hannah ranks first chronologically, Alexander is

her true favorite—the child of choice in everything from helping her to set up the mah-jong tiles on Tuesday nights to bringing honor to the family as "Albert Einstein the Second." She still fondly refers to him as her "lover" when he is well into his thirties. Intensely concerned with his physical as well as his intellectual development, she examines the "poopie" he deposits in the toilet bowl with the same eagerness she applies to the grades on his report card and her watch-its and be-carefuls regarding food are extensive. ("Not everybody is careful the way your mother is about spoilage.") All these "*meshuggeneh* rules and regulations," coupled with her attempts to be (in Alexander's words) "the patron saint of self-sacrifice," have managed, through the years, to render guilt from her son "like fat from a chicken." They are significant contributing factors in the etiology of what psychoanalyst O. Spielvogel terms "Portnoy's Complaint"—a disorder in which "acts of exhibitionism, voyeurism, fetishism, auto-eroticism and oral coitus are plentiful; as a consequence of the patient's 'morality', however, neither fantasy nor act issues in genuine sexual gratification, but rather in overriding feelings of shame and the dream of retribution, particularly in the form of castration."

MOTHER: Judith Steloff White
IMMORTALIZER: Erica Jong (in *Fear of Flying*)
CHARACTERISTICS: "I would have been a famous artist if it hadn't been for you kids," declares the tall, red-headed mother of the four poetically named daughters, Gundra Miranda, Isadora Zelda, Lelah Justine and Chlore Camille. Isadora agrees, saying, "Thirty-five years of buying and spending and raising kids and screaming . . . and what did my mother have to show for it? Her sable, her mink, and her resentment." (The sable and the mink smell of Joy and Diorissimo, nevertheless.) Wed to a former Catskills comic currently in the *tsatska* (little items?) business, her artistic impulses are directed toward redecorating her sprawling fourteen-room duplex on Central Park West, alternately screaming at and loving her children in the "good mother–bad mother" tradition and assembling startling costumes for herself. Isadora sees her style as a "Charles Adamsy look" and is mortified when mother turns up on Parents Day in tapestried toreador pants, a Pucci pink silk sweater, and Mexican serape. Unlike the prototypical Jewish Mother, Judith White is seldom in the kitchen. As a child, Isadora longs for her to be more conventional—"a bleached-blond, mink-coated Mama who

played bridge." When Isadora attempts to distill the basics taught to her by Judith she is left with only: (1) Above all, never be *ordinary*. (To Judith this was the greatest sin and insult.) (2) The world is a predatory place. Eat faster! So Judith takes it in stride when one daughter marries an Arab, another a Negro, a third, an Oriental. She tells her children that the Christmas tree commemorates not the birth of Christ, but "the Winter Solstice." When the girls play with Easter eggs, they're not celebrating the resurrection but "the Vernal Equinox." Concludes Isadora: "Listening to my mother, you would have thought we were Druids."

MOTHER: Meg (no last name given)
IMMORTALIZER: Bruce Jay Friedman (in *A Mother's Kisses*)
CHARACTERISTICS: Like Sophie Portnoy (whom she preceded into print by more than half a decade), this Bensonhurst matriarch has a daughter as well as a son, but it is her boy, Joseph, who is the focal point of 99.44 per cent of her *kvetching* maternal attention. Whether it's at the summer camp where Joseph waits tables or on the post-World War II campus of the college where he spends his freshman year, henna-haired Mother Meg, with her ample bosom exuding clouds of perfume, is the omnipotent, omnipresent, good-natured meddler in all his affairs. "He'll kill me for this," she shrugs on a typical incursion. "But what can I do? I'm one of those crazy mothers." Volatile, extravagant, flamboyant, and sexy, she embarrasses Joseph. The kisses of the book title are "wide and gurgling" and as he receives each one, Joseph feels "as though a large, freshly exposed open-meloned internal organ (has) washed against his face." Coos larger-than-life, really "stacked" Mother Meg, with each affectionate pinch, "Ooooooh, that child. I could die. My life." If and when Joseph ever protests against the marsupial ministrations designed to keep him in the pouch, Meg reports that he is merely "going through a stage." Most of her dialogue is offered in the form of questions. "Oh I don't know what's on your mind, do I? I haven't been your mother for seventeen years for nothing" . . . "Is *that* a person? Is that an angel?" . . . "Did your mother ever let you down?" . . . "Sometimes he wishes he had another kind of mother, a gray-haired little old one, don't you, darling?" When not talking about her son, Meg's conversation as likely as not turns to girdle and underwear protocol. Because of this, Joseph considers "all female garments that weren't hers as ill-fitting, ridiculous and somehow a little bit shabby and unclean."

# And One Radio-TV Favorite

MOTHER: Molly Goldberg

IMMORTALIZER: Gertrude Berg

HISTORICAL HIGHLIGHTS: The cry, "Yoo-hoo, Mrs. Bloom!" ringing out from the window of a make-believe apartment in the Bronx was, for more than twenty years, the signal for, first radio, and later TV audiences all across the country to plunge into the richly comic family life of the most famous Jewish Mother in the U.S.A. Introduced on NBC radio in 1929, Molly Goldberg and her clan went on to glory in early television, a 1948 Broadway play (*Molly and Me*) and a 1951 movie (*Molly*). Gertrude Berg created, wrote, and starred in her saga of *The Goldbergs* and brooded over the casting and production details of the series with the same mama-hen dedication exhibited by the fictional Molly with regard to her tailor-husband Jake, live-in Uncle David, and the children, Sammy and Rosalie. Berg became so closely identified with her creation that fans forgot her real name and even the stagehands called her "Molly." Mrs. Goldberg delivered her maternal nuggets ("Better a crust of bread and enjoy it than a cake that gives you indigestion") in the cadence of the Bronx neighbors from Gertrude Berg's childhood but judging from Molly's enduring national popularity, the truths she uttered were universal.

*

# MAMA NIEMAN-MARCUS

Stanley Marcus, chairman and chief executive officer of the world-famous Dallas department store, Nieman-Marcus, tells in his autobiography, *Minding the Store*, about some of his mother's activities after she became a widow. "She had a green thumb," he writes, "and it was her interest in plants that encouraged my father to bring exotic tropical specimens into the store for their decorative contributions. . . . Upon my father's death, mother was elected to the Board of Directors, and was named vice-president in charge of horticulture. . . . At that time there were 1,800 plants in 60 different locations in the two existing stores. She supervised the activities of the gardeners, calling their attention to the plants which needed to be cut back, fertilized, and watered. She was always on the lookout for exciting new specimens which would enhance the store's display . . .

"Once she was observed pulling dead leaves off an *Aurelia elegantisima* by a customer who wrote, 'There's a very nice-looking woman whom I frequently see in your store picking dead leaves from your plants. Surely you can find a better position for a person of such obvious quality.' We thanked her, explaining that the only higher rank she could have would be my job."

❋

Every Jewish girl is born with two in help—her mother and her father.

—Lyn Tornabene in
*How to Be a Jewish Princess*

❋

## NEGATIVE IONS

The songwriter Sam Coslow ("Cocktails for Two") and his singer wife, Frances, decided to get out of show business once he had launched a successful Wall Street financial letter. By this time they had a precious six-year-old daughter, so they went house-hunting and bought a beauty in Englewood, New Jersey.

Sam then called his eighty-eight-year-old mother to tell her the good news. "Fantastic ranch-style house, swimming pool, wood-burning fireplaces, perfect school nearby in the most wonderful of suburbs."

Sam's mother listened, then scraped the bottom of the barrel for a negative: "New *Jersey*?!!! Oh, my God, isn't that where the Lindbergh baby was kidnaped???!!!"

❋

## GOLDA'S MAMA

Golda Meir spent most of her adolescent years in Milwaukee and in 1917, at her parents' home there, became the bride of Morris

Meyerson. In her 1976 autobiography, *My Life*, the former Prime Minister of Israel writes of the tumultuous relationship with her mother regarding this nuptial day:

"Our marriage was preceded by a long and emotional argument with my mother. Morris and I wanted a civil ceremony, no guests and no fuss. We were socialists, tolerant of tradition, but in no way bound by ritual. We neither wanted nor needed a religious ceremony. But my mother informed me in no uncertain terms that a civil marriage would ruin her, that she would have to leave Milwaukee at once, that I would be shaming the entire family—to say nothing of the Jewish people—if I didn't have a traditional wedding. Besides, would it harm us? So, Morris and I gave in; indeed, what damage could fifteen minutes under the *chuppah*, the bridal canopy, do to us?

"We invited a few people, my mother prepared refreshments and Rabbi Schonfeld, one of the true Jewish scholars of Milwaukee, officiated. To her dying day, my mother talked with pride about the fact that Rabbi Schonfeld had come to our house for my wedding, had made a short speech wishing us well and, though he was known for his strictness in religious matters and as a rule refused to drink—let alone eat—anything outside his own home, he had *tasted* a piece of her cake. I have often thought about how much that day meant to her and how I nearly ruined it for her by being married at City Hall."

✳

# MA!

As Ida Morgenstern of the TV series *Rhoda*, Nancy Walker portrayed a meddlesome, nosy Jewish mother whose prime project for years was getting her daughter ceremoniously married. Not so, Nancy, the real-life mother, wife of director David Craig. Vivian Cadden of *McCall's* reports that when, after five years of living with a young man, daughter Miranda Craig announced to her mother that they were about to be married and wanted a real "wedding-wedding," Nancy replied, "Oh, how nice. But why don't you just elope and I'll give you the money?" After it became clear that the young people were set on the sort of ceremony they wanted, the California-based Nancy said to Miranda, "Your father and I really want to come to New York for your wedding, my darling, and to see *A Chorus Line*—you know, the new Broadway hit show—but not necessarily in that order."

Nancy sums up her relationship with Miranda observing, "My daughter owes me nothing. I had such a good time conceiving her. I sent for her—she didn't send for me."

＊

On TV, Nancy demonstrated the Jewish mother's art of *kvetching* to perfection, but her fiction didn't outdo the facts. Once, during a *Rhoda* rehearsal, Valerie Harper topped a Walker bit with this example of her own: "I swear this is true. After Winston Churchill died at the age of ninety-two with all those wars and world crises behind him, what did Avery Schreiber's mother say? She said that Churchill's *children* killed him from aggravation, that's what Avery Schreiber's mother said."

＊

## THE IMMACULATE CONCEPTION

W. H. AUDEN:
Behind this ingenious doctrine lies, I cannot help suspecting, a not very savory wish to make the Mother of God an Honorary Gentile. As if we didn't all know perfectly well that the Holy Ghost and Our Lady both speak British English, He with an Oxford, She with a Yiddish, accent.

*A Certain World*

＊

## TWO VERSIONS OF MAMA

The attitudes of Alexander Portnoy and his ilk make us forget, sometimes, that the "Jewish Mother" has also been a subject of unabashedly sentimental veneration and devotion. The 1925 song "My Yiddishe Momme" says it all. But lyricist Jack Yellen had an eye for the big and brassy as well as for "that dear little lady so old and gray." In 1928, he wrote "I'm the Last of the Red Hot Mamas," which became the belting trademark of the late Sophie Tucker. It's an interesting paradox that Sophie, who sang "My Yiddishe Momme" at the Palace the year it was written and kept it in her repertoire for over forty years, was the epitome of the rhinestone-and-glitter Miami Beach "Jewish Mother" stereotype. But even in a gaudy nightclub setting she could, with her tribute to the old-fashioned Yiddishe Momme, stir the customers to fountains of tears.

※

## WALTER'S WILD JEWISH ROSE

"The truth is," says actor Walter Matthau, "that in middle age, I'm turning into a Jewish Mother. I'm a very good Jewish Mother. Only make that 'Methodist' so it will read more American."

The actor's mother was a seamstress named Rose who married an emigré from Kiev, Russia, named Mike Matuschanskayask. Rose liked to describe son Walter as "the Ukrainian Cary Grant." After seeing him in *Candy*, the first of the soft-core porn films, she said to him: "What's *that? That's* how you make a living?"

Walter told me he calls Rose at least once every two days and says she still yells at him as if he were twelve years old. "I guess you could say we have a sadomasochistic relationship without the sex."

※

## DOUBLE ENTRY

I am hard pressed to know where to put the following and you'll see my point, so I'm including it in two places. This is the first place:

Joan Rivers says: "The only difference between a Jewish mother and an Italian mother is black stockings!"

170

## MOM'S M.A.D.

How many miles away should you allow your child to move? To compute the Maximum Allowable Distance, or M.A.D., multiply the speed in miles per hour of existing transportation to the new location by the amount of time in hours it takes for a frozen lambchop to defrost in your purse; or:

DISTANCE equals M.P.H. times Lambchop Defrosting Time.

—*How to Be a Jewish Mother*
by Dan Greenburg

✳

# HOW DO YOU GET TO
# CARNEGIE HALL?

It is not always possible to predict the response of a doting Jewish mother. Witness the occasion on which the late piano virtuoso Oscar Levant telephoned his mother with some important news. He had proposed to his beloved and been accepted. Replied Mother Levant: "Good, Oscar, I'm happy to hear it. But did you practice today?"

✳

## PROUD FLESH

Neil Simon's mother, now living in California, actually is said to have introduced her other comedy-writing child, Danny Simon, to a friend like this: "Meet my son—the brother!"

This reminds me that Barbra Streisand's mother is also the mother of a lesser known singer, Rosalind Kind. This Jewish mother has been quoted as saying: "But I am *Barbra's* mother first!"

# A CLASSIC

When the son leaves home to start his freshman year at college, his doting mother gives him two cashmere sweaters as going-away presents. Wanting to show his appreciation, the boy comes home for Thanksgiving, wearing one of the sweaters.

The mother greets him at the door. She takes a long, anxious look and says: "What's the matter? The other sweater you didn't like?"

&#42;

And then there's the mother who, after dragging her small son into Macy's with her on a Saturday, admonishes him: "Now I'm warning you, Seymour, hold tight to my hand! If you get lost don't come crying to me!"

&#42;

A more recent story that surely *will* become a classic concerns three Jewish mothers engaged in that exquisitely pleasurable occupation of boasting about their sons' affection for them.

Mrs. Schwartz begins. "Have I got a good son! The minute the first snow falls, he's phoning the airport it should send me for two weeks to Florida. He's putting me up in the best hotel in Miami. And not a penny it's costing me. That's my son!"

Mrs. Weiss picks up the theme. "You should pardon me for saying it, but my son, he's even *more* considerate. The minute the first snow falls, he's not just *phoning* the airport. He's coming to my apartment in a limousine and *driving* me to the plane to Miami. And he's not just putting me up in a hotel, he's getting me a private house on the beach. What a son!"

Now it's Mrs. Gelber's turn. "No question, it's two lovely boys you got, but *my* son, well, this is what *my* son does. Every week he's going to a man and he's paying the man fifty dollars. For what? Just so he can lay down on a couch and talk. And what is my son talking about at such fancy prices? *Me!*"

# Mothers Machree

A man loves his sweetheart the most, his wife the best, but his mother the longest.

Irish proverb

It doesn't do to generalize about the Irish because they are one of the true mysteries of the human race. Who else could have given us leprechauns and Irish whiskey and their own special brand of Roman Catholicism as well as militant Protestantism, managed to keep themselves separate from the interests of Western Europe, survived famine, forced migration, and religious war in the twentieth century, while maintaining a dynamic ethnic apartness?

These are a people whose fiercely surviving mothers helped write their nation's history in blood; a people whose mothers produced not only the hod-carriers and laborers of a young America but also some great Irish geniuses intoxicated by literature, drama, and poetry. I am thinking of George Bernard Shaw, James Joyce, Sean O'Casey, Oscar Wilde, William Butler Yeats, Brendan Behan, John Millington Synge, Lady Augusta Gregory, and so many others. And let us not forget Ireland's gift to the American theater, Eugene O'Neill.

Some years back when the Irishman Samuel Beckett's *Waiting for Godot* was produced on Broadway, it was fashionable to try to fathom the meaning of this allegorical play. Many said it was metaphysical, about man's search for God; others said it was in the style of Voltaire, about man's inhumanity, etc. But I will never forget Bert Lahr, who acted in the original. He once said to me somberly, as we sat in a TV rehearsal, that he thought the play was so mysterious because "it is really about the Irish rebellion." I thought *that* was as good an insight as any into the Irish mystique. It was even possibly true.

So the women who produced the men of the Emerald Isle and transfused a great portion of their national sinews and heart to this continent, bolstering up our immigrant strain during the potato famine, are mysteries in themselves. They are often incredible beauties, apt to be transformed overnight by hard work, poverty, climate, and too many children into Mothers Machree. (As you trill this song, imitating a million Irish tenors, it might interest you to know that "machree" comes from two old Irish words meaning "my heart.")

Irish writers have given us mothers distinctly various. Take Molly Bloom, whose only child dies in infancy. For James Joyce, she became the symbol of the loose, lewd woman. Take Sean O'Casey's Juno, the mother in his drama of Dublin slum life, *Juno and the Paycock*. She is one of the noble characters of the modern stage. (O'Casey was the last of thirteen children, eight of whom died in infancy.) Then Eugene O'Neill offered up the torments of his own mother's drug-ridden life in *Long Day's Journey into Night*. The essence of his drama is wrung from the stuff of his real life as a boy who yearned desperately for his mother's love and could not overcome the feeling that she had failed him. Mother Mary Tyrone wanders through the night carrying a long-forgotten wedding dress (token of her innocence) asking, "What is it I'm looking for? I know it's something I lost."

The mother surely is the omnipresent heart of much Irish culture, whether she looks like Maureen O'Hara in *The Quiet Man* or like Anne Revere in *Young Cassidy*. Portraying playwright Sean O'Casey's mother, Revere was toil-worn, caring, sympathetic, proud of her son, ambitious for him, and dying of poverty, overwork, and illness in a literal garret. She was unforgettable. Likewise, Barry Fitzgerald won his Oscar as the Irish priest in *Going My Way* and the high point of the film is when Bing Crosby imports Barry's ninety-year-old mother from Ireland for one last wavering look at her "boy."

So, as you see, many of my perceptions of Irish mothers were shaped by the movies. I myself have an Irish face, inherited, I expect, from my grandmother Martha Tipton. This sturdy woman is my connecting link to the Irish mother. There is much more about Martha in the introduction on grandmothers, but this is my pet story about her and maybe it qualifies as just Irish enough to be included *here* instead of *there*. As a narrow-minded Southern Baptist who disapproved of almost everything, she naturally worried about her children. (Actually, she may have constituted more of a danger to them than anything they encountered on the Texas plains, for she could slap fire out of a person with a little finger or fell a wayward child with a well-aimed biscuit.)

Only one of Martha Tipton Smith's children ever learned to swim because, as she once put it, succinctly: "Of course any child of mine could have gone swimming but I always told them they could go only if they knew how to swim first."

If that's not mother-logic, what is?

✳

## MOTHER MACHREE

"I kiss the dear fingers, so toil-worn for me . . .
God bless you and keep you, Mother Machree."

Since its original publication in 1910, this song has launched a veritable Niagara of tears in theaters and concert halls all over the world. The words were written by Rida Johnson Young to music by the Irish tenor Chauncey Olcott in collaboration with Ernest Ball. When Olcott first introduced the song in a theater in St. Paul, Minnesota, it was reported that "every eye in the audience was glistening with tears," and the great Erin-born tenor John McCormack managed to open up similar floodgates from the moment he added it to his concert repertoire in 1913. One of McCormack's most memorable performances of "Mother Machree" was on a trip back home to the Emerald Isle. "There wasn't a dry eye in the house," his wife wrote later of his appearance in a Dublin concert hall. "Everyone knew he was singing it to his own mother." All was harmonious until the family gathered afterward for a party at home and the tenor's father remarked, somewhat testily, "John, have you no songs at all about a poor father?" The singer said nothing, but at his next concert, sang "A Father's Early Love" as an encore, "to the delight of his father, mother and the whole audience."

175

"Here's to the salmon. She lays two million eggs and nobody ever calls her Mother."

—Toast by a character in 1938 movie, *Spawn of the North*

In this film, starring George Raft and Dorothy Lamour, we are shown a group of Alaskan fishermen at play, making glaciers shudder and fall with the sound of their voices. The song they invariably sing to bring the ice crashing is "Mother Machree."

❋

He is bare of news who speaks ill of his mother.

Irish proverb

❋

# TWO IRISH PLAYWRIGHTS ON MOTHERHOOD

I myself was never on bad terms with my mother: we lived together until I was forty-two years old, absolutely without the smallest friction of any kind: yet when her death set me thinking curiously about our relations, I realized that I knew very little about her. . . . But a mother is like a broomstick or like the sun in the heavens, it does not matter which as far as one's knowledge of her is concerned: the broomstick is there and the sun is there; and whether the child is beaten by it or warmed and enlightened by it, it accepts it as a fact in nature, and does not conceive it as having had youth, passions, and weaknesses, or as still growing, yearning, suffering, and learning.

—George Bernard Shaw, preface to *Misalliance*

❋

What a rest to speak of bicycles and horns. Unfortunately it is not of them I have to speak, but of her who brought me into the world, through the hole in her arse if my memory is correct. First taste of shit.

—Samuel Beckett in *Molloy*

176

# BUT SERIOUSLY SERIOUSLY . . .

There was a process at work in Irish-American families in the nineteenth century that, as William Shannon puts it in *The American Irish*, "tightened family bonds and departed from the normal American patterns of family life." Because most Irish immigrant fathers were engaged in hard, and often dangerous, manual labor, they often died young, victims of industrial accidents or, more often from such diseases of overwork and exhaustion as tuberculosis and pneumonia. Thus came into being that singular breed of American mother, the Irish widow. Shannon sums her up in these words:

> The mother, as the children's only link to the happier days of the past and symbol of the family's will to survive, occupied the central role. Her sufferings and sacrifices were crucial in keeping the home together in the critical years after the father's death. Those sacrifices earned from her children obedience and respect for her opinions on every important subject. The "widow woman" thereby became a classic figure in the Irish community. The Irish widow exercised an emotional hegemony rarely equaled in other American families. *Few novels on the American Irish have been written that do not include a widow as one of the major characters.**

✳

# AL'S CAT

Catherine Mulvehill Smith, the mother of former New York Governor Al Smith, fits perfectly into the pattern just described.† Although she herself was a native New Yorker who raised her children almost literally "under the Brooklyn Bridge," her parents emigrated to America from Ireland's County Westmeath by clipper ship. Widowed when Al was just thirteen, she left home only a few

---

* Italics mine. L.S.

† Another famous Irish politician raised by a widowed mother was FDR's gregarious Postmaster General, James Aloysius Farley. Mother Farley brought up her brood of five boys after her husband was killed by a horse when young Jim was nine.

hours after her husband's funeral to ask for her old job back at an umbrella factory; later she supported her brood by opening a small candy and grocery store. Although, like so many Irish mothers, Catherine Mulvehill longed for her son to become a priest, she was completely supportive of his political ambitions. Remembering the mother-son relationship as it existed late into Al Smith's life, family friends noted "the speed and ardor with which he sought her out when he entered the house, the way he knelt to receive her blessing, the pride with which he saw that she was in the best seat at functions marking his success in life . . ."

Mother Smith lived to see her son move into the Governor's Mansion in Albany, but died before his unsuccessful try for the presidency in 1928. The experience of her death, said the man known as "The Happy Warrior," then fifty-one, was the "first real sorrow I ever suffered."

✳

# JIMMY'S MOM

James Cagney's mother was born on New York's Lower East Side, but she was as typically a daughter of Erin as if, like her own mother, she'd begun life in the green heart of County Leitrim. She had beautiful red hair, was a good Catholic and was fiercely protective of her brood of four sons and a daughter. In his autobiography, entitled simply *Cagney*, the actor tells this story of one of his mother's last meetings with them:

The greatest piece of pantomime I have ever seen in my life was not performed on any stage or in any film. It was done by my mother on her deathbed. Because the strokes had deprived her of speech, she had only her eyes and one fully functioning hand to use. The four boys were in the room when Jeannie arrived. She came in and embraced Mom. Then we all got around and hugged Mom warmly, and she made a vocal sound that was unintelligible but spoke volumes of love for us.

It happened that two brothers were on each side of Jeannie. Mom then raised her functioning arm, the right. She indicated Harry with the index finger of her useless hand, she indicated me with her second finger, she indicated Eddie with her third finger, and with her fourth finger indicated Bill. Then she took the thumb, moved it to the middle of her palm, and clasped the thumb tightly under the other four fingers. Then she patted this fist with her good hand and made a single wordless sound. We understood at once that Jeannie was the thumb and we four boys were to take care of our girl. It was a movement totally simple, totally eloquent, totally beautiful.

Mom died about two months later. She was sixty-seven—and there was hardly a day of those years that had not been spent in giving.

*

## ED'S MUTH

As a child, Ed McMahon recalls he liked going home with boys from the large Japanese colony in Bayonne, New Jersey. Big Ed says, "I know why I used to like to go home with them after school. There would always be cookies and milk waiting, and there was always some for me. But what I liked more than the waiting snacks was the waiting mother. There was seldom anyone waiting at my house."

Ed's mother, Eleanor, was a somewhat peripatetic if affectionate Irish beauty whom he called "Muth." He says she always got what she wanted when she turned her eyes on a person. The TV personality recalls dropping by his mother's card parties as a kid and being offered a sip of whiskey, "so he won't crave it later."

He says when he told this story to Johnny Carson, the comic said quietly, "She should see you now."

*

## JEAN'S KITTY

Born Kitty O'Neill in Kinsdale, Ireland, the mother of humorist Jean Kerr has, says her daughter, "a way of cutting things down to size." The example of this quality Mrs. Kerr gives in her book *The Snake Has All the Lines* involves the time, a few years back, when she had a collection of short pieces brought out in book form. The author's mother was sent one of the first copies and responded with bubbly delight: "Darling," she wrote, "isn't it marvelous the way those old pieces of yours finally came to the surface like a dead body."

✻

## CHARLES' LOUISE

In *The Sting, Dog Day Afternoon* and countless TV dramas, actor Charles Durning has been cast as the quintessential Irish cop. And, as he describes her, his maternal parent, Mrs. Louise Leonard Durning, is the quintessential Irish mother. "She's something, boy," he says. "Had ten children, lost five—three in two weeks. Scarlet fever and flu." When Durning's father died, Mrs. Durning went to work in the cadet laundry at West Point, insisting that the children remain in school, and when young Charles grew up to pursue an acting career she was profoundly skeptical. She had a great fear of anyone having their photograph taken, believing, like the aborigines and bushmen, that "you lose your soul because it goes into the picture." When Charles told her of his acting aspirations, she told him, "Well, just don't go into the movies." On each of his birthdays, Mrs. Durning would send him a card with a dollar bill taped inside. After many years of this he told her he was doing okay and she shouldn't bother any more. Said Mrs. Durning: "You never know when you'll need it."

✻

## VIV'S MUM

Elaine Dundy reviewed Anne Edwards' biography of the actress Vivien Leigh, saying that Miss Edwards did not include enough on Vivien's mother, Gertrude. Here is Dundy:

> But Gertrude! We need much more of the French-Irish mother (more lace-curtain Irish than French, one suspects) who abandoned her six-year-old Vivien to a convent and remained forever after at her side, always ready with a reprimand. Gertrude was a great dis-

180

approver: of Vivien's early marriage, of her engagement ring, of her attitude toward the church, her liaison with (Laurence) Olivier, her choice of roles.

I have actually listened to Gertrude expound: "There's nothing the matter with Vivien. She doesn't need all those psychiatrists. Why, as a little child at the convent the nuns told me she loved me so much she used to cover up my photograph with her blankets at night so my picture wouldn't get cold." Vivien, too, abandoned her young child to a convent in Canada during the war. And guess who delivered her.

Dundy notes that in spite of the facts of Gertrude's heartlessness (she did not see her tiny child for eighteen months after first putting her into the convent) and her continuing disapproval, Vivien did not, in turn, abandon her mother. "But Vivien had her final revenge on the Catholic Gertrude. In her will she specified that she be cremated."

✳

# MARY'S NORA

Mary Higgins Clark, whose first suspense novel, *Where Are the Children?* became a best-seller, started her career writing romantic magazine fiction. When, as a young New Jersey housewife with five children, she made her first big sale, it was a cause of great celebration. The magazine was the *Saturday Evening Post;* the fee, fifteen hundred dollars. Mary's mother, Nora Higgins, rejoiced at the good news, but her Irish practicality responded, too. "Be sure to put the money in the bank, dear," she told her daughter.

"The bank?" the neophyte writer protested. "Not a prayer. We're going to get new slipcovers, and get away for a few days, and we all need clothes and . . . and anyhow, this is just the beginning. This is my *first* big sale, not my last."

There was a moment of total silence before Nora Higgins replied in a puzzled tone. "But, Mary, *you've used your idea!*"

✳

# JOHN'S DOROTHY

West Coast writer John Gregory Dunne is eloquent on the subject

181

of his Irish mother, Dorothy Burns Dunne:

"My mother . . . was in many ways the quintessential *Mary Tyler Moore* viewer, a strong, tough, funny woman with an eminently rational view of the human condition. In 1972, she changed her mind in the polling booth and voted for George McGovern, whom she detested, because she did not think anyone deserved to get beaten as badly as he was going to be, especially by Richard Nixon. Even in the intimidating presence of death, she never lost her sense of humor. 'One good thing you can say about dying,' she told me shortly before she did in 1974. 'I won't have to read about Patty Hearst anymore.' "

Dunne recalls watching *The Mary Tyler Moore Show* wherein Mary implied she was taking the Pill. "My mother, a devout Catholic, asked me if she had heard correctly?

"I nodded.

" 'Then it must be all right,' my mother said."

✳

# IRISH STATUS

The young New York writer Shaun Considine is a wonderful advertisement for the Irish mother's proudest production. Here's Shaun:

To most Irish mothers, the ideal job for their offspring is in the service of God. To have a daughter a nun or a son who is a priest is top points in community status. And of course after death "the pull" helps their bid for eternal life.

When Mrs. MacMahon died, her two daughters (nuns), three sons (priests), and a brother (a bishop), officiated at her services. After the high mass a neighbor whispered to my mother, "With her connections, there's no doubt she went straight to heaven when she died." "With her connections," my mother whispered back, "I'm surprised she wasn't lifted upstairs while she was still breathing."

✳

# THE CHAMPS' CHAMPION

After Jack Dempsey won the world heavyweight championship

from Jess Willard in 1919 he found himself extremely unpopular because sportswriter Grantland Rice accused him of having been a World War I slacker. (Dempsey was eventually vindicated in a jury trial but at the time the accusation was made, it hurt him and took the edge off his ring victory.)

Once Rice's story broke, thousands of telegrams poured into Dempsey's training camp. The only one he answered came from his religious Scotch-Irish mother who wired:

MY DEAR BOY MOTHER IS PROUD OF YOU
AND WISHES YOU PLENTY OF LUCK.
KEEP YOURSELF CLEAN PHYSICALLY BOY.
BE A PROPER CHAMPION. MOTHER.

✳

# CLEARING MRS. O'LEARY

Connoisseurs of TV's old movies know that the great Chicago fire of 1871 was a direct result of the motherly distress of Alice Brady, when she was distracted from her milking chores by concern over two feuding sons, Don Ameche and Tyrone Power. The Brady portrayal of Katie O'Leary in the 1937 film, *In Old Chicago*, was so effective that it won for her an Academy Award as Best Actress in a Supporting Role. But the Hollywood Katie and the one who dwelt on Chicago's DeKoven Street had little in common beyond their nationality.

The real Mrs. Patrick O'Leary was a "tall, stout Irish woman" in her mid-thirties and the mother of five children, one a babe in arms. Historians now believe she had nothing personally to do with the starting of the Windy City conflagration, although it *was* her cow who kicked over a lantern to get things going. When she testified at a hearing two weeks after the fire, she presented an appealing picture of maternal solicitude—the infant in her lap, reported one local paper, "kicked its bare legs around and drew nourishment from mammoth reservoirs"—and when she stated that she was fast asleep when the fire began, the judges apparently believed her. In their official report, no blame was fixed. But newspaper readers were too fascinated by the legend of Mrs. O'Leary and her cow to give it up. The Chicago *Evening Journal* summed it up this way: "Even if it were an absurd rumor, forty miles wide of the truth, it would be useless to attempt to alter 'the verdict of history.' Mrs. Leary (*sic*) has made a sworn statement in refutation of the charge, and it is backed by other affidavits; but to little purpose. She is in for it and no mistake. Fame has seized her and appropriated her, name, barn, cows and all. She has won, in spite of herself, what the Ephesian youth panted for."

In the movie version of her story, one of Katie O'Leary's sons grows up to be mayor of Chicago and the other is a professional gambler. At least that latter part was based on fact. One son did indeed become a gambling baron, with a fief of some six hundred betting parlors on Chicago's South Side. He died a millionaire in 1926.

What was mother O'Leary's personal view of the burning of Chicago? Asked by a reporter if the conflagration was rough on her, she sputtered out this reply: "Rough! Why, my God, man, it was a terror to the world!"

❋

## ENDING ON A GRACE NOTE

Betty Williams, an Irish Catholic mother of two, became co-founder of the peace movement in ravaged Northern Ireland in August 1976, after watching in horror as an IRA getaway car—its driver shot dead by a British soldier—jumped a curb in West Belfast and crushed to death three children. Teaming up with Mairead Corrigan, an aunt of the dead children, she managed within two weeks to encourage some thirty thousand Protestant and Catholic women out on the streets to demand an end to violence and the beginning of peace. After years of attrition, it was the first hopeful sign in the hateful Irish conflict and in 1977, these two courageous women were awarded the 1976 Nobel Peace Prize.

# Mamma Mia!

No mother is so wicked but she desires to have good children.

Italian proverb

The stock popular stereotype of the Italian mother, a favorite of the producers of TV commercials for spaghetti sauce, always picture Mama as a short, stout, aproned matron in her kitchen. She may strike her forehead with her open palm, ward off the evil eye from her children, heap pasta on plates, or pray to the Virgin. I have even known a few Italian mothers in this exact mold. For instance, the mother of my friend, the publicist Maria Pucci, keeps two kitchens —one upstairs that looks good for company and one downstairs where she actually cooks. I love it!

When I worked and traveled as a publicist-manager for Kaye Ballard, she used to entertain me with wonderful impressions of Italian mothers in her Cleveland neighborhood and how they acted when one of their children was lost. As soon as the child was found, the mother invariably bopped it with relief. "It was worth your life," says Kaye, "to be lost—but almost worse to be found. If ever you escaped from any danger, the danger then became your mother."

But like all mothers, the Italian mother comes in many shapes, sizes, and social varieties. There is the elegant Suni Agnelli of the Fiat family, herself an Italian mother who gives us a picture of her own aristocratic mother in the autobiography *We Always Wore Sailor Suits*. There is the lush Neapolitan maternity of Sophia Loren and her mother. There are the blonde, liberated Milanese mothers of northern Italy. And there are the oppressed women of Italy's lower boot who only find any measure of "success" or authority by becoming mothers. There are the fashionable women of the black and white nobility in Rome who dance all night at the chicly popular nightclub Jackie O. and later go home to their children who are being watched over by surrogate Italian mothers or grandmothers. There are the whores who are mothers plying their trade on the Via Veneto. There are the Mother Superiors of the Church praying always to a madonna who is especially identified with that Church. There are the leaders of Venetian high society such as the international hostess Countess Annamarie Cicogna, who works to save Venice from sinking into the sea. There is the Italian mother as we have seen her through the eyes of De Sica, Rossellini, Visconti, Pasolini, and Wertmuller—on film.

To lapse into French, the Italian mother is *formidable!* Earthy or elegant, she is almost never timid. In some ways she typifies the Earth Mother; she is legend made manifest.

✻

# THE ETERNAL MAMMA

The fact that woman is the predominant character of Italian life, even if not the most conspicuous, can be read in many small signs. Almost as many popular songs are dedicated every year to *La Mamma* as to voluptuous hussies or romantic beauties. "*Mamma Mia*"*!* is the most common exclamation. What other people call for their mother in time of stress and danger? Do the Germans say "*Mutter*", the French "*Maman*", the English "*Mother of mine*", when faced by a disappointment or an emergency? Wounded Italian soldiers in front-line dressing stations moan "*Mamma, mamma, mamma*", almost inaudibly, like hurt children. "*Mamma*," say men condemned to death as they wait for the firing squad to fire. . . .

Luigi Barzini in
*The Italians*

# BAMBINO WORSHIP

The rich relationship between Italian mother and son is so omnipresent that there is even a term in the language for the mentality of the pampered child. Pronounced with a shade of contempt, it is *mammismo*.

Erazim Kohak wrote of it in *Harper's Magazine:* "The Italian male . . . is adored and pampered from birth. Since bearing a manchild is woman's great claim to recognition, most Italian mothers and wives prop up their males, encouraging them to be beautiful, precocious, vain, irresponsible, and existentially incompetent. In so doing, the Italian woman makes herself indispensable—and dominant. The male may be the master, but he needs his mother, or so the theory goes."

\*

# MOTHER OF *THE GODFATHER*'S FATHER

"I had every desire to go wrong, but I never had a chance. The Italian family structure was too formidable. I never came home to an empty house. There was always the smell of supper cooking, and my mother was there to greet me. Sometimes she had a policeman's club in her hand (nobody ever knew how she acquired it), but she or her authorized deputy, my older sister, was there . . .

"When I came to write my autobiographical novel (*The Fortunate Pilgrim*), the book every writer does about himself, I planned to make myself the sensitive, misunderstood hero, much put upon by his mother and family. To my astonishment, my mother took over the book. But it is, I think, my best work."

Mario Puzo in *McCall's*

\*

# AN ITALIAN MOTHER'S KITCHEN

At one time there was a chance that restaurateur Joe Allen's right-hand man, Richard Polo, would have to go to Paris to help open a new Allen's cafe. It seemed so definite that Polo told his parents.

Then he discovered he wasn't going after all and went home for Sunday dinner. He announced the change in plans.

"Oh," said Mrs. Polo, "I'm so happy. I got so nervous when you told me you were going to Paris to live, I cooked for three days."

\*

# A GEM

The Italian mother most celebrated in art and literature was Cornelia, who resided in Rome in the second century A.D. On the death of her husband, refusing numerous offers of marriage, she devoted herself to the education of her twelve children, two of whom were the tribunes Tiberius and Caius Gracchus. The story is told of her answering the boasts of another Roman matron about her jewels with the simple reply, "These are my jewels"—pointing to her children. This much-quoted remark has guaranteed "The Mother of the Gracchi" a place in any Mothers Hall of Fame.

\*

# FRANK'S DOLLY

Item reprinted in its entirety from Winston Daniel's column in *The National Star*, September 21, 1976:

Frank Sinatra is rarely called anything to his face except "sir." But not last week in New Jersey where a little lady turned on him and blitzed him almost through a wall with the words: "You slob."

Feisty Frank paled and dutifully looked for a hole in the ground to jump in. The lady, of course, was none other than Frank's diminutive little mother, Dolly Sinatra. It appeared Frank trudged into her kitchen, opened up the refrigerator door, pulled a carton of milk to his lips and started drinking it straight from the container.

"Nobody drinks milk like that. Can't you get yourself a glass . . . you slob?" she told him. You see, under that bestial breast of cranky Frankie, beats the heart of a terrified son.

NOTE: A few days after Mrs. Sinatra's death in a plane crash in 1977, a memorial service was held for her at St. Malachy's, the actors' church in the heart of New York's theatrical district. Those who attended heard her eulogized by Rev. Robert Perella as "a great lady and a staunch friend . . . blessed with a vibrancy and a zest for life."

"She lived and died for her son," Father Perella said. "Every breath she ever breathed, every effort she ever made, every prayer she ever prayed was for her son . . . The greatest break that Francis Albert Sinatra ever enjoyed in his entire life, in his entire career, was to have Dolly as a mother."

✳

The real Duce was my mother.

> —Edda Mussolini Ciano,
> writing in her autobiography
> after thirty years of silence.

✳

# ITALIANS ALL

When stripper Ann Corio, often billed as "the girl with the Epic Epidermis," began her career, her Italian mother from Hartford was a total innocent about the world of burlesque. After seeing Ann in action, however, she was emphatically approving. "They look," she told friends proudly, "but they no touch."

✳

Kaye Ballard was always so entranced by her Italian grandmother that she incorporated "Nana" into her night-club act and did impressions of her going to the opera, an instance where "Nana" insisted on explaining the plot aloud to Kaye. "Aïda no lika the queen. The queen, she no lika Aïda." Kaye frequently sang a heartrending Italian ballad dedicated to her grandmother. When Kaye was doing the Jimmy Durante TV show, she sang the song and at the end of it said, "Ciao, Nana," something she'd never done before. The show, taped six weeks in advance, played on the day of her ninety-four-year-old grandmother's funeral in Cleveland.

❋

She was my only refuge from my troubles, and my relief in many labors.

Comment of Lorenzo de' Medici
about his mother on the day
of her death, 1482

❋

As noted in a previous chapter, I couldn't decide where to put the observation below, so it is in two places. This is the second:

Joan Rivers says: "The only difference between a Jewish mother and an Italian mother is black stockings."

❋

The Italian comic with the improbable name Pat Cooper spends a great part of his act extolling the virtues of *his* mother in particular and motherhood in general. He says, "At forty-seven, I am still a baby to my mama. When I go to her house I've got to jump in her lap."

Cooper keeps his audience rolling with his reminiscences of his Italian mother rubbing wine over his gums when he was teething or what it was like to live in a house with forty-five religious statues. "How would you like ninety eyes staring at you all the time?"

He says one day he went home and his mother wanted him to take off his pants so she could mend them. "I said, 'Mama, I don't feel good taking my clothes off.' Mama said, 'What happen? You grew something else since I last saw you?!'"

❋

# THE BELOVED JOHN

Because of the high rate of infant mortality in nineteenth-century Italy, the Church stressed the urgency of baptizing babies as soon as possible. So it was that only a few hours after the birth of her fourth child and first son on November 25, 1881, Signora Maria Anna Mazzola Roncalli of the village of Sotto il Monte pulled herself out of bed, dressed in her best clothes, picked up her baby and, since men never carried babies, personally transported the newborn to the local church to be baptized. This was the beginning of a long

190

association with the Church that was to culminate, in 1958, with Angelo Giuseppe Roncalli's assuming the position of supreme head of the Roman Catholic Church as Pope John XXIII.

The pope-to-be was a Vatican representative in Turkey in 1939 when he learned of the death of his mother back home in Italy. Unable to leave his post to attend the funeral, he closed himself in his study and composed this memorial tribute to her:

> Dear and respected by all,
> Dearer to her children
> Who grew numerous and strong
> In the fear of God and the love of men.
> And to the sons of her sons
> Whom she saw multiplied in joy
> In her home
> Even to the third and fourth generations,
> Blessing her memory.

✻

# ANN CORNELISEN'S MOTHERS

The following has been included in Italian mothers, but the material presents an unusual dilemma, for it belongs also in considerations of working mothers . . . liberated mothers . . . mothers and sex . . . mothers and guilt . . . mothers and sons . . . as well as in any social consideration of the matriarchal societies which still make up so many countries of the world.

In her critically acclaimed book *Women of the Shadows*, Vassar-educated Ann Cornelisen writes of her experiences in Southern Italy setting up Save the Children Fund nurseries, but mostly she writes of ultimate failure in a searing manner that won her recognition as a social critic.

The book describes the grinding poverty, the stifling mores and manners, the isolation, insulation, ignorance, the fear and the failure of both the Church and the Italian political system to offer the people of the South any hope. The author shows us the fresh-faced girls who rush through adolescence to become mothers, struggling through a series of pregnancies, which leave them burnt-out grandmothers at forty. In no other book of our time has the anatomy-is-destiny dictum seemed so oppressively true. One can only gasp with relief at not having been born a Southern Italian woman trapped in local socioeconomics.

This is not to say that the women of this book are not gutsy and admirable. They are incredible! The men are crushed, broken, licked by the system before they start. The women are hideously oppressed, and motherhood is the only possible way to even minimal power. Here is Ann Cornelisen:

> The women earn the most dependable supply of cash. They help with all the crops, raise as many small animals as they can find space and feed for and then market them with acumen. Somehow they are the ones who understand the intricacies of local bureaucracy and politics, so they sense who can be tricked, forced or cajoled into granting a subsidy, a house, a sack of flour. They teach their children, and it is often the soundest teaching they will receive, right from wrong, the "proper" ways of the community and the few skills they possess. Ultimately they decide on the size of their daughters' dowries and then collect the linens piece by piece, for they are the ones who actually control the purse and decide what purchases shall be made each week in the market. Most important of all, these women create security for their children which no spanking or screaming rage will ever undermine. Each has nursed her child, fondled him, rocked him to sleep and cared for him when he was sick until he knows his mother loves him, not in exchange for good behavior or a chore done, but simply because she loves him. He is hers. She is to her children, as the Madonna is to the believing Catholic of her society, all-forgiving, all protecting. This is the aim of most mothers, but they seldom carry the weight of total responsibility. The comparison could be carried still further, though it is hard to know whether the practices of the Catholic Church in Southern Italy are the result of a domestic evolution of theology or simply versatile adaptation to the mores of the parish. The Marian cult exists and has become the core of local belief. The apparitions of the Virgin Mary escape any attempt to catalogue them, much less verify them, but that makes no more difference than the rosy stupidity of the modern plaster statues. Mary, the Earth-Mother figure, can be loved, trusted and prayed to, while God and His son, Jesus, remain cold symbols. The Holy Ghost, so elusive anyway, is quite literally the white plaster bird that hovers uncertainly over all altars. Men find it hard to be humble before other men, even harder to lose face, so praying to a woman for her intercession is less abrasive to the ego. Women can identify immediately with the all-

suffering Mother and perhaps take consolation in her importance to all men. . . .

The women, as they grow older and their children marry, struggle less. They know they will be taken care of. In many ways theirs have been and continue to be surrogate lives. They have snatched power without appearing to and reap happiness from the uncritical devotion of their children, most especially their sons . . .

There are no large decisions to be made by the man and day-to-day existence is left to the women, who unconsciously take over all the practical aspects of life. There are no others. Once a woman has power, however slight her influence appears to be outside the family, she consolidates it into a hold over her sons stronger than that famous boast of the Jesuits. Only death will loosen it, but already her daughter-in-law has learned the art of day-by-day living and day-by-day power and has tied her sons to her as firmly as though they were still swaddled. She has also slowly replaced her husband's mother, and he, accustomed as he is to the strength of women, does not notice it . . .

I was present when a woman, a widow I know extremely well, answered an interviewer with all solemnity: "No I would never do anything my mother did not approve of."

*

Another point Ann Cornelisen makes in her magnificent book is that there has always been a nice bit of medical snobbery in the assumption that peasant women feel less pain and suffer less in childbirth than "other" women. She says this is because we do not understand the peasant woman's strict code of behavior, the shame she feels she will bring on herself if she flails about in pain. "To her the shame is a brand as conspicuous, as permanent as a strawberry birthmark, or a scarlet letter."

She quotes one Southern Italian woman:

Nothing's private in a one-room house. . . . I had nine children in that room, back there, and I suppose I'll die there the same way—with all the men in the family sitting around the fire muttering, "Why doesn't she hurry up about it." When my time came and the pains started, I'd send my husband to call my mother. . . . I'd hear the shuffling in the room and know the men were arriving one by one. My father, my brothers, my husband's brothers, they all sat there by the fire and drank wine and waited.

If you make a sound, if a pain catches you by surprise, or the baby won't come out and you can't stand it and you moan, you've disgraced yourself. You keep a towel shoved in your mouth, and everytime it hurts so bad, you bite down on it and pray to God no noise comes out. . . . I suppose I'll die the same way. The men used to say, "She's a brave one, she is." But I'll never forget the pain. I remember all nine times, just how they felt—and every one is different, I can tell you—and you just lay there and bite the towel and never let out a sound. Not once. So many times it was all for nothing too. Six of mine died. I could have wailed then—that's all right—but there are some hurts that stay inside. Every time one of my babies was about to be born I'd think to myself, you're going to die! This time, you're going to die! Then it'd come out. Somehow—I don't know how to explain it—but somehow it was like I had been born again. Maybe that's what gives a woman strength when she finds out she's pregnant. At least some part of her will go on. I tried to think of that when I wanted to scream. Nothing's private here, not birth, not death, not anything. No matter what anyone says though, you never get used to it.

＊

# THE MAESTRO'S MAMMA

The mother of the late conductor Arturo Toscanini (born in 1867) fits perfectly into the mold of poor-but-proud Italian mothers. The tailor shop maintained by the maestro's father, Claudio, in the family's narrow pink stucco house in Parma was financially a touch-and-go proposition and many days and nights Paola Toscanini's brood went hungry. In all his childhood, the musician could not remember once seeing meat on the table.

Howard Taubman, in his biography of Toscanini, gives a wrenching example of the lengths Paola could go in hiding from neighbors and relatives the depths of the family's poverty. Little Arturo, garbed in a pressed albeit threadbare suit, was instructed before any of his visits to family members in other parts of town never to say he had not eaten. Once, when he was six, he was invited to sit down to a meal at the home of an aunt and declined, as his mother had instructed him. The aunt, however, suspecting the truth, kept on insisting and finally the little boy gave in and filled himself from the platter of hot sausages steaming on the table. When he returned home, his mother asked him if he had eaten at his aunt's and Arturo admitted that he had. Without further comment, Paola whipped her son within an inch of his life.

Writes Taubman about Mother Toscanini: "She did what she had to do for her children, but apparently she had no time to spare for the normal, little tendernesses and affections. The maestro, years later, remarked that he could scarcely remember being kissed by his mother."

*

# ORIANA FALLACI ON HERS

She has been a special relationship. I hate the word "love." There is no nuance in English. I was the oldest. I was a good, a very good child, but I was expecting her to serve me somehow, even mentally, which is what oppression of women in the family is about. I knew how intelligent she was, how much she could have given if she had been a free woman, if she had not been enslaved by the family. Her dream was to become an astronomer. She knew everything about Leonardo da Vinci. So that's why I am here now, trying to pay back all she has given. We are four sisters. The youngest is fourteen. It is still too soon to judge her. But we three old ones are all, from your point of view, successful journalists. We are her revenge. All of us.

From an interview with the
international journalist in <i>W</i>

*

# MOTHERING FIRST

Although the majority of filmgoers may think of Sophia Loren first and foremost as a sexually alluring enchantress, she herself claims that "the role of mother has always been my favorite both on and off the screen." The on-screen maternal Sophia was seen most memorably in *Two Women*, for which the actress won an Academy Award in 1961. A glimpse of the *off*-screen mother is given by Donald Zec in his biography, *Sophia:*

"Once," he writes, "during some major crisis involving a mere couple of million dollars or so, producers, lawyers and others converged upon the villa for urgent discussions with her. They were told to wait. It was a long wait. As they sat frowning at their watches, around the enormous Roman pool, they naturally assumed the 'queen' was engaged in even more vital business.

"She was. She stood some distance away, outside a fumed-oak toilet, involved in an intimate dialogue with Cipi, her son.

" 'Cipi, darling, it's Mamma.'

" 'Yes, Mamma?'

" 'Have you done good business?'

" 'Si, Mamma, very good."

" 'Bravo, Cipi. Ciao.'

" 'Ciao.'

"She then strolled into the conference, smiling broadly at the agitated moguls. 'Okay, gentlemen,' she said, 'shall we start?' "

*

# SO WONDERFULLY ITALIAN

Historically speaking, of course, the Virgin Mary must be classified as a "Jewish mother," but this evocation of her seems so quintessentially Italian in spirit that it is included here:

Mary has wept! Mary has wept! . . . Weeping is fecund. There has never been a sterile tear. As the rain that falls from on high irrigates the countryside and prepares it to receive, in all fertility, the crops and seed and fruit that will in time come to ripeness, so it happens in the realm of the spirit. A woman who weeps always becomes, in the very act, a mother. And if Mary weeps beside the Cross of Jesus—I can tell you that her weeping was fertile and made her a mother.

—Monsignor Salvatore Giardina,
of Syracuse, Sicily, after a mass-produced
plaster of Paris plaque of the Virgin Mary
on the bedroom wall of a local worker wept,
in 1953, for four consecutive days

# *The* WASP *Nest*

Who ran to help me when I fell,
And would some pretty story tell,
Or kiss the place to make it well?
My Mother

Ann Taylor, 1804

Every time I have tried to begin the introduction to the WASP mother, I've found my mind wandering in the direction of the Jewish mother. After trying to figure out such circumflexions, I decided that the reason is simple. As I wrote in the introduction to the Jewish mothers chapter, I see the Jewish mother in most mothers, including my very own white Anglo-Saxon Protestant mama. Like any good Jewish mother, my dear WASP mother also shares the common mother mania—fear that an accident of some sort will reveal one of us, or worse still—herself, with torn underwear, a pin in a slip strap, panties that have lost their elastic.

When my parents were in a car wreck which broke my mother's neck, I rushed to the hospital where she was in traction. The sight of her suffering was unbearable, but I went to the bed and, leaning over her, whispered, "Well, how was your underwear?" She searched my face, puzzled, then started laughing. "Oh, honey," she said, "I had on my new Christmas things. It was all right." Happily, she recovered to go on worrying about the state of everyone's underwear.

My father had an unfortunate penchant for gambling. This almost drove my mother crazy since she thought it was sinful, immoral, and wasteful. It flew in the face of all her beliefs, conventions and common sense. One day I found her with the mail in her hand, crying. I asked what was the matter. "Oh," she said, "I just can't bear the thought of *The Daily Racing Form* and *The Baptist Standard* coming in the same mailbox."

✼

My mother has several expressions I'm rather fond of. I've no idea where she got them but they go about as far as she ever would in expressing WASP exasperation, mild profanity being out of the question for her.

    1. "You don't pay me any more mind than if I was a *goat* barking!"

    2. "You have about as much business with that (or doing that) as a monkey with a football!"

✼

The wonderful woman who married my father has now become a fan of the soap opera *As the World Turns*. She is disgusted with herself for watching it and refuses to even look at any other soaps for fear of getting hooked. While she takes time out each day for "my program," as she calls it, she clearly resents her addiction. Here are some running comments when the soap is playing: "Well, that sappy girl is so silly, I don't know why he doesn't slap her winding . . . Come on, now get on with it . . . I've got rat-killing to do . . . You know, sometimes I think they just run this old show to get all those commercials on the air."

✼

One of the joys of growing up with a devoted WASP mother still alive is the fun of leaving home. Then one can "get letters", as they say. Believe it or not, here is an actual excerpt from one of those weekly reports from Gonzales, Texas (pop. 5,000), where my mother once lived happily with her widowed sister:
    "Darling baby,
    I have just finished watching Lawrence Welk on television while playing a game of Canasta with Helen.
    Went to Sunday School and Church yesterday. It was on the Crucifixion—so sad!"

It doesn't matter that I am far past the age of consent. My mother's salutations are a cornucopia of affectionate nonsense. They begin, as often as not, "My baby pie" or "Baby dumpling" or "Dearest little Lillibet." One of my favorite sentences is the closing to a letter chronicling the local state of health and giving the week's menus:

"Darling angel. I'm sorry this letter is all about food and illness. Tacky!"

*

As she has grown older and more set in her ways, my mother finds her all too frequently visiting children's and grandchildren's careless approach to chores exasperating. A typical remark goes like this: "Now, I don't want you to take this garbage out like you've been shot out of a cannon; I just want you to do it pretty quick!"

*

And, finally, my mother recently went to my younger brother, puzzled. She said, "Bobby, I hate to sound ignorant but what does WASP mean when they say it about people?"

He patiently explained. She looked thoughtful. "Oh, so, if anybody asks me, I'll just tell them that I *am* one, right?"

*

Right!

*

# PREMIER WASPS

The first WASP mother in America was the ill-fated Ellinor or Elenor Dare, who gave birth to her daughter Virginia in 1587 in what has since become known as "the lost colony" on Roanoke Island off the coast of Virginia. The ill-prepared residents of this ragtag settlement disappeared without a trace.

Another early WASP mom whose descendants still people the land was Mrs. Susannah White, a passenger on the *Mayflower*. Her baby son was born when that historic carrier was still bobbing at anchor in the waters of Cape Cod, a month and a day before the first Pilgrim climbed ashore at Plymouth Rock. After Susannah's husband died during that first hard New England winter, she mar-

199

ried another *Mayflower* passenger who had lost his wife, thereby becoming the first bride of the Plymouth Colony as well as the first mother. Her son Peregrine, in the eyes of his contemporaries, led a somewhat "extravagant" youth, but he was "much reformed in his later years, and died hopefully."

✳

# SNOBBISM

The WASP mother ranges, of course, from Low Redneck to High Episcopal, just as Italian mothers go from titled white Roman to black-shawled Sicilian.

In discussing the use of the phrase "well-connected" in his massive work *Who Killed Society?*, Cleveland Amory presents one of the ultimate mother stories, citing the late Rebecca Shippen of Baltimore. Born a Nicholson and descended from the Lloyds of Wye House, Mrs. Shippen was asked by a friend if it had ever occurred to her that if Our Lord had visited Baltimore she would never have met Him—since his father was, after all, merely a carpenter. "But my dear," replied Mrs. Shippen, "you forget. On His Mother's side, He was well-connected!"

And then there was the southern matron, returning from her first trip to Europe, who was quizzed by a widely traveled, more sophisticated friend who asked her how she liked Paris. "Oh, it was all right, I guess," was the reply. "And the marvelous Louvre Museum," her friend continued, "didn't you adore that?" "Well, we have the Metropolitan in New York and the National Gallery in Washington," answered the southern lady. Undaunted, the friend kept on. "But what did you think of the world-famous painting of 'Whistler's Mother'?" "Oh, it was all right," said the returnee. "But you know, she was only a McNeill from North Carolina."

✳

# UP AGAINST THE WALL,
# REDNECK MOTHER

He's born in Oklahoma and his wife's name is Betty Lou Thelma Liz,
He ain't responsible for what he's doin' 'cause his mother

made him what he is.
And it's up against the wall, Redneck Mother,
Mother who raised a son so well,
He's 34 and drinkin' in a honky-tonk,
Just kickin' hippies' ass and raisin' hell.
He shore does like to drink that Falstaff Beer and chase it
    down with that Wild Turkey likker
He drives a 57 G.M.C. pickup truck with a gunrack and a
    "Goat ropers need love" bumper sticker.

    M – is for the mud flaps she got him for his pickup truck
    O – is for the oil he puts on his hair
    T – is for Thunderbird
    H – is for Haggard
    E – is for eggs
And R – is for Redneck

And it's up against the wall, Redneck Mother,
Mother who raised her son so well,
He's 34 and drinkin' in a honky-tonk,
Just kickin' hippies' ass and raisin' hell.

Country and western hit by
Ray Wylie Hubbard

✻

# HOW TO RAISE A PRIG

My mother was a woman who used to say, in a studiously quiet voice, "I pride myself on my reserve." . . . My mother wanted everybody to think that our household was one of unimpeachable dignity, where all human passion was completely under control . . . My mother cooked and scrubbed and varnished floors and washed and ironed and sewed, like the other women in the neighborhood. But in her mind she was a "perfect lady" and an aristocrat. That was why she never raised her voice, never cried and never showed emotion. In her lexicon the sin against the Holy Ghost was to do anything that made you conspicuous. People did not talk about role-playing in those days, but never was a role played to the hilt like my mother's secret role as the Lady Prioress of Lincoln Park.

Margaret Halsey in
*No Laughing Matter, The*
*Autobiography of a WASP*

# THE NON SEQUITURS

The following does not apply *only* to WASP mothers, but as both examples come from same, let's tuck it in here. A common "mother" thing seems to be the writing of letters with startling information that rises from nowhere and sinks never to rise again.

My column associate and friend St. Clair Pugh treasures his mother's letters. She once wrote him from Smithfield, North Carolina, that a cousin had been "bitten by a poisoned fly." All of St. Clair's attempts to follow up on the cousin's condition came to naught. Neither could Saint later discover from his mother any explanation of what "a poisoned fly" might be, nor did she even recollect writing him about such an event. It has driven him crazy for years.

The late writer Wyatt Cooper told of the time he lived in Italy with no access to family news other than his mother's letters from Mississippi. In one of them, she included this: "The man your Uncle Howard shot didn't die." Wyatt could not get a satisfactory explanation until he ceased to be an expatriate. He said: "I felt Mother liked to deal with various family calamities, such as unwanted pregnancies, by tossing them into a letter in connection with something else. In this way, she got the message across without having to discuss the problem itself."

✻

# THE REFORMATION

That astute observer Harriet Van Horne has noted: "Martin Luther was severely beaten by his mother. It is easy-Freud to view his denigration of the Holy Mother as an expression of hatred for his own parent, but there it is."

Deductive reasoning leads one to the inescapable conclusion, therefore, that Luther's mother caused the Reformation and helped create that fixture of our time, the WASP mother.

✻

# MAIN LINE MATER

The actress Anne Francine comes from a fine Philadelphia family.

Her mother went to see her perform in Cordelia Biddle Robertson's play *My Philadelphia Father*, which concerns itself with intermarriage between the Duke and Biddle families. Afterward, Mrs. Francine, who resembled a ship's figurehead, swept backstage. She came into Anne's dressing room and inquired rather petulantly: "But, Anne, why is it you're playing a Duke, when it's the Biddles we know!"

＊

# KING'S STING

Florence King is such a specialist on the humor to be found in the South and among WASPs that her two books to date are titled *Southern Ladies & Gentlemen* and *Oh, WASP, Where Is Thy Sting?*

From the latter came her absolutely last word sum-up of "The WASP Mother," subtitled, when it appeared in *Playgirl*, like this: "She lies, she drinks, she cusses like a mule skinner; but she knows where her children are at 10 p.m."

Florence has kindly given permission to reprint the highlights:

> The ethnic mother has had it in the media. We have heard everything about the long-suffering Jewish mother, the long-suffering Irish mother, and the long-suffering Latin mother. It is now time to examine the non-suffering WASP mother.
>
> According to the observations of Philip Roth's Portnoy on his sole trip west of the Hudson, the WASP mother is a pleasant woman whose relationship with her child begins and ends with an absent-minded "Good morning, dear." This is often true, but it only scratches the surface. There *must* be more to the WASP mother than that. After all, Winston Churchill had one, and so did Lizzie Borden.
>
> There are actually two basic versions of the archetypal WASP mother. The first is the New England suburbanite.
>
> She has what she believes is a plain, no-nonsense traditional Anglo-Saxon name like Sarah, Rebecca or Hannah. She also has a perpetual suntan because she will ski, golf, and play tennis until she drops—except she never does. . . .
>
> She never gains weight; at fifty she can easily pass for thirty-five. She controls her figure by sheer will power, one of her outstanding gifts . . . But she never gets drunk because, as she puts it, she "sweats it off."

The Southern version of the archetypal WASP mother can be one of two types. One is the aging belle who makes a career out of having the change of life. She can orchestrate a menopause to such a pitch that it would make *The Trojan Women* sound like *Little Women*. Referred to constantly as "a raving beauty in her day," now she is simply raving. Her sturdier sister is the terrifying "foxhunt matron" of Virginia who spends a lifetime yelling, "Where're the dogs?" . . .

To outsiders, the most striking thing about the WASP family is the lack of closeness. The self-absorbed WASP mother may often say "dear" or "darling" to her children, but usually such endearments pop out when she has something else on her mind and isn't thinking straight. Moments of true sentiment are rare; yet it's quite common for her to address her offspring as "droopy drawers," "stinkweed," or "snotnose" in the most affectionate tones. This clashes with the stereotype of WASP elegance for which our mothers are unjustly famed. Though she is extremely fussy about outward appearances and the patina of good manners, it is only for show. A muleskinner cusser, she is entirely capable of going from Anglo to Saxon in a trice. . . .

She enjoys her children most when they hit eighteen and take "c/o American Express" as their permanent abode. It is said that when the Jewish child expresses a desire to bop off to Europe and find himself, his mother will have an attack, a migraine, and a long talk with that lovely man at the Pinkerton Agency. The WASP mother will have a surprise party to give Johnny the Eurailpass that she has bought him. . . .

Another hang-up of the WASP mother is her conviction that males *must* enjoy regular stag festivities away from women. Our WASP-ische Mama panics if the males in her life aren't bonding enough. Somewhere, somehow, she has acquired the astounding theory that her own company is too "softening," so she encourages her son to go out with the boys. She thinks that men should play together, sing together, fight together. Even childhood sadistic rites don't shake her up, so long as they are the boys-and-boys together variety. If her son is being beaten up by a gang of schoolmates who throw his books, and then him, into a gravel pit, she will not interfere and go to his rescue. It's *good* for him to get beaten to a pulp; the other boys will respect him afterwards . . .

The worst sin in WASPland is invasion of privacy. When *Marjorie Morningstar* came out in 1956, everyone in our all-WASP sorority read it. We identified with Marjorie because she was universal; what we couldn't fathom was her mother. Mrs. Morgenstern read her daughter's mail. Whenever one of our blonde Peggys or Nancys looked up from the book with a shocked "Imagine!" we knew she had come to the part about the letter.

Even more incredible was another of Mrs. Morgenstern's characteristics: she was constantly giving advice. Never once in the entire six hundred pages did she utter any of those maternal exit lines we had all grown up hearing:

"It's none of my business."
"It's your life, you have to live it."
"You don't have to explain, I trust you."
"I know you'll do the right thing."
"I refuse to interfere."
"It's not my place to sit in judgment."
"You're free to choose your own friends."
"I don't care what you major in."
"Why tell me?"
"I'm sure he's a nice boy if his father is a Sears executive. Sears stands behind everything."

There *is* one occasion, however, when our WASP-ische Mama will give advice. If a WASP wants to kill her mother, the best way to do it is to get married too soon. Announcing an early engagement will turn her into a keening matriarch in no time. Her chants include:

"You're only young once."
"You have your whole life in front of you."
"Sleep with him first, then see how you feel."

Marriage before twenty-five is, as she puts it, "the pits." She herself was "almost thirty" when she married—"almost thirty" being the official WASP marrying age in her mind, if not exactly in fact. If she married younger, she will rewrite history until she has herself convinced that she nearly died on the vine.

The WASP mother's aloofness is often engaging.

Her detached attitude is a plus when her children are ill or have accidents. She maintains a Battle of Britain calm that enables her to do what is necessary. However, let something happen to the dog and she panics. "Oh, my God! Muffin's nose is hot! Call the vet, quick! Somebody call the vet!"

❋

# NONPAREIL

Here is Cleveland Amory on the most formidable WASPs of the Eastern Seaboard:

To Proper Bostonians the frozen formality of their First Family femininity is as accepted a part of the city's social picture as the fact that there is a right and a wrong side to Commonwealth Avenue. . . . There are many variations on this female manners-formality theme, but one story, authenticated by the senior partner of one of Boston's better-bred law firms, runs as follows:

A young lawyer in the firm, a man from the West who had settled in Boston, was invited to play bridge one winter night some years ago in Brookline. Finding the street on which his hostess lived blocked with snow, he left his car and made his way toward her house on foot. Almost there, he was attracted by the barking of a dog to a snowbank in which he found to his amazement the shivering form of a little girl. The young man picked up the child and rushed to his hostess' door. There the child was recognized as a member of a First Family who lived close by. With his hostess to aid him he took the little girl to her own home and there put her in the charge of a servant who hastened to summon a doctor. Apparently the child had wandered outdoors unnoticed. But the man had arrived in the nick of time; the girl was numb with cold.

The next day the mother of the child came to call on the man's hostess and thanked her for her part in the rescue. "I wish I could thank that young man, too," she added, "but then I've never met him. Would you mind conveying my gratitude to him?" This was done of course, but to this day . . . the young man from the West has not received so much as a personal phone call from the lady whose daughter's life he may well have saved.

※

# Three Funny WASP Mothers with "K" in Their Names

EDITH BUNKER
MA KETTLE
MAMMY YOKUM

# Three Serious WASP Mothers
## with "K" in Their Names

**PEARL BUCK**

Raised in China, this daughter of Presbyterian missionaries began putting her oriental background into novels after discovering that one of her two daughters was retarded and would need extra financial support. Later, the writer and her second husband adopted nine more children, including some of mixed races, and many of the funds from her enormous literary success found their way into an adoption agency called Welcome House, which she founded for children of American GIs and Asian mothers. In *The Good Earth*, the 1931 Pulitzer Prize-winning novel which later helped earn the author the Nobel Prize for Literature, Mrs. Buck created one of the most famous fictional mothers of the 1930s—the Chinese peasant's wife who worked with her husband in the fields until the very day of the birth of her first child and was back at work the following day. When the refined European actress Luise Rainer played this Chinese mother on film, Viennese accent and all, she was awarded an Oscar.

**MARY BAKER EDDY**

This founding mother of the Christian Science religion believed in a "Father-Mother God" and her First Church of Christ, Scientist, chartered in Boston in 1879, is known the world over as the Mother Church. A mother herself of one son, Mrs. Eddy asserted that "A mother is the strongest educator either for or against crime."

**"MA" PERKINS**

Durable maternal heroine of one of radio's longest-running soap operas.

# "K" P.S.

A WASP mother with a "K" in her name who has been viewed both seriously *and* humorously through the years is Mrs. Ada Jukes, female head of "a strictly American family" of the Finger Lakes region in upper New York State. In 1874, amazed to discover that a disproportionately large number of convicted criminals in an upstate jail bore the same name, sociologist Richard Dugdale made a genealogical study of the prisoners' families going back more than five generations trying to determine if such traits as criminality, "harlotry," and pauperism were inherited characteristics. So many of the convicted felons traced their ancestry to Ada Jukes (a fictional name), she became famous in sociological circles as "the mother of criminals." (Among the crimes committed by her descendants were assault and battery, murder, robbery, rape, and forgery, not to mention cruelty to animals. Many of her female descendants were prostitutes.) Few contemporary sociologists now hold much truck with Dugdale's findings, but the name "Jukes" has become firmly entrenched in the language as a term for any ill-bred, no-account American family. Mrs. Martin Kallikak of New Jersey, whose descendants were the subject of a related study, made her mark in a similar fashion.

*

# WASPS ACROSS THE SEA

One of England's great eccentrics writes about her mother in *Taken Care Of—The Autobiography of Edith Sitwell:*

> I do not wish to be cruel about a poor dead woman. I have forgiven the unhappiness long ago, and now write of it only because otherwise, after my death, much in me will be misunderstood. I now feel only pity for my mother, a poor young creature, married against her will into a kind of slave-bondage to an equally unfortunate and pitiable young man. Neither seems to have had the slightest knowledge of "the facts of life." My mother ran away a few days after the marriage and returned to her parents. But my grandmother sent her back. Changeling that I am, I was born nine months after that slavery began. No wonder that my mother hated me throughout my childhood and youth, though she became touchingly reconciled to me after disaster befell her—reconciled after a year in which

she tried the worst kind of bullying, taking the form, mainly, of making the most horrible accusations against my moral character.

Then, suddenly, she forgave me for my existence. One night after this . . . she called to me:

"Edith, have you ever been happy?"

"Yes, mother," I answered. "Haven't you?"

"Never *bird*-happy," she replied. "Still, I have three very nice children." Then, sighing, she went to sleep again.

In spite of her rages (the result of half-forgotten miseries, of disappointments), there were moments, just before the ambush into which she fell materialised, when she softened towards me—such moments as those when she planned the suppers for the Hospital Ball at Scarborough: "Of course, darling we *must have* quails!" Or when, with a far-away idealistic look in her eyes, she would say, "Of course, what I would *really* like would be to get your father put in a lunatic asylum."

✻

# UNIVERSAL

When Liberace met England's Queen Mother for the first time in London in 1972, she, like many another celebrity he meets, asked him about his mother. He explained that she had just celebrated her eightieth birthday and the trip to England had seemed too much for her. "But," he added, "she sends her love to you. She loves everybody who is nice to me."

Replied that Royal WASP, the Queen Mother: "That's the way all us Mothers are."

✻

# THE END

I knew this neighborhood was ruined when they gave us all house numbers!

—Cleveland Amory's mother

# The Mother as Auntie Mame or The Exotics

A mad place, truly!—with a monkey in my bathroom, a llama on the lawn, and our corridors shrill with the curses of our parrot (learned from a diplomat). In the stables when my children wished to play at being grownups they could find there midget horses and the coach, brightly painted, that had once belonged to General Tom Thumb.

> Evalyn Walsh McLean, owner of
> the Hope Diamond, about her
> Washington home, "Friendship."

In her eighties, my mother is still a beautiful woman. But with her soft southern voice and gentle manner, she does sometimes come across as something sent from Central Casting. When she last visited New York, the social butterfly writer Philip van Rensselaer took us to lunch. I thought we were a little tame for him but he seemed enchanted. When lunch ended, Philip took me aside and congratulated me. "You are so lucky, Liz—imagine—you have a *real* mother—not one of those Auntie Mames like everybody else has these days!"

211

In spite of this, I *have* known one mother-as-Auntie-Mame quite well and she was actually called "Mother" in my circle of friends, at her own request. Francis Carpenter (the society columns always note that she spells it with an "i") had two children of her own, a son and a daughter, but as these grown offspring did not live near, she adopted my entire summer group and behaved toward us in a most frivolously unmaternal and beguiling manner as if she had invented the book written by Patrick Dennis.

Actually, Francis was only about fifteen years older than the oldest of us and her sexy glamour made her more than a match for anyone younger. But she said, "You shall call me 'Mother' for you are all my darling children." It was reassuring to have such an exotic extra "mother" and no one questioned being adopted into the charmed circle. In fact, there was busy jealous rivalry to keep new "siblings" at bay. Outsiders were never allowed to call her "Mother." "That," she would say with a tilt of her gorgeous Kay Kendall nose, "is for family."

Francis Carpenter is a rich and beautiful life-lover, one of the refreshing breezes that occasionally manages to blow through the stultified lives of the rich to help kill Society. When I met her, she was something of a displaced person, having just been divorced after twenty years of marriage into the conservative duPont clan of Wilmington. For an interim, Francis made her home in a lovely Mansard-roofed "cottage" near the ocean in Bridgehampton, Long Island. There surrounded by Pekingese dogs, a sculptured flower garden, expensive espalier trees, shining cars, an entire top floor converted into a closet, and a shell-shaped swimming pool, she contemplated what to do with the rest of her life, as well as "tonight."

Mrs. Carpenter had already lived several different lives and was legendary when we were invited to think of her as "Mother." She was (is) breathtakingly attractive, smartly turned out, full of *joie de vivre* and Positive Thinking, endlessly funny, malapropic, and fascinating. Her lifestyle was then and is still a mélange of *trompe l'oeil* and David Barrett decoration, high fashion and high-kicking foolishness. In her youth, she had shocked the staid duPonts almost out of their chemical compositions by "living it up," asking for madder music and more wine, keeping a pet ocelet on her estate, and being spoiled by her sportsman husband William K. (Bill) Carpenter, who always referred to his wife as "The Black Banana" in deference to a soigné Norman Norell wardrobe.

It is a tribute to the charm and staying power of Francis that in spite of the lifted eyebrows of Wilmington, after the divorce, she and Bill remained good friends. Likewise, his mother, *the* Mrs. Carpenter, whose brothers were the founders of the duPont dynasty, cherished "Franny." And the moment Francis had a grandchild, she insisted it, too, must call her "Franny." (It was rather funny watching a baby clutched to "Mother's" marvelous maribou-negligéed bosom while some young man in attendance poured the champagne and listened to Francis insisting that she was "just plain Grandma.")

In the time I knew her well, "Mother" once took a cruise to the Orient with a new Young Lover. She and the Y.L. were to be the only paying passengers aboard a freighter leaving New York and going East via the Canal. Mrs. Carpenter's minions arrived at the port with cases of bubbly and booze, exotic canned goods, long-playing records. She and the Y.L. disappeared into their cabin and were said not to have emerged until the boat got to Hawaii. The frustrated captain of the vessel was later reported a suicide.

Eventually, there was a quarrel causing the Y.L. to drive his Mercedes (a gift from Francis) across her newly sodded twelve-thousand-dollar lawn, leaving two vicious ruts. "Mother," who never employed profanity, ordered Y.L. off the premises in the middle of a startled lawn party, warning, "If you don't get out of here, I shall kick your ass up through your shoulder blades." Y.L stormed into the car and blasted off, leaving two more ruts. "Mother" sighed and turned back to her guests: "And to think, I took *that* around the world!"

The first time I ever saw Francis was at a party given in the St. Regis Hotel by the agent Gus Schirmer, Jr. Resplendent, ladylike, and refined in black and diamonds, she eventually left with a tall, slender stranger who had taken her fancy. As she passed through the door, she dropped all her jewelry into the hand of her host, saying, "Keep these for me, darling. 'Mother' doesn't know where she is going tonight or even with whom."

On one occasion, "Mother" presented us with a new friend for the summer—an ex-athlete gone to seed. She would often intone as she gazed at this diamond-in-the-rough across a crowded cocktail hour, "Isn't it too too divine?" We would murmur appreciatively, surprised that the ex-athlete was not exactly her youthful type. The happy couple went off to Hollywood for Francis to visit with her old friend Gayelord Hauser, whereupon, one day Francis happened to put on her eyeglasses to read a telephone number and got a good look at her paramour. At least, this was the explanation given for why the ex-athlete suddenly turned up somewhat glumly back in the East, fresh off the champagne circuit and a Greyhound bus.

My favorite memory is of Francis when she was thinking of selling her Long Island house (to the dismay of sybarites and free-loaders in the area) and moving to Nantucket. Like many rich people, she was always beset with "servant" and "money" problems. So, complaining of being pressed for cash, she said she might sell the Rolls. I suggested she sell instead the two Purdy elephant guns I knew were stashed in the attic—relics of the days when she and Bill went on safari and at night she bathed in a canvas tub and then put on all her emeralds for dinner in the Serengeti.

Francis was shocked: "Sell my guns??!!"

I pointed out, "Well, 'Mother,' you are not likely to need them again in Long Island or Nantucket."

"But," she gasped, "I could never do that. They were tailor-made for me!"

Wherever they are clanking glasses today and talking fun and nonsense, "Mother" Carpenter, I salute you. You left a lot of orphans with maribou poisoning in Long Island when you moved your frivolous operation elsewhere. And I'll bet you still have your handmade guns, tailored for your own reach, in case an elephant ever wanders onto the lawn in Nantucket.

✳

## "MOTHER" MAME

Life is a banquet and most poor sons-of-bitches are *starving* to death.

—Auntie Mame

If the record didn't show that writer Patrick Dennis based his free-spirited "Auntie Mame" character on his own aunt Marion Tanner, one could easily suspect he had been inspired by a real-life "Mame" of Society's Golden Age. In the days when the girl who was up to the minute had an hourglass figure, the wife of financier Stuyvesant Fish—born Mary Ann Anthon—made her nickname of "Mame" a synonym for wit and high jinks in the social set. This adult *enfant terrible*, more than any other hostess of her time, was responsible for bursting the protective bubble around that exclusive entity known as "the Four Hundred."

The major battlefields for Mame Fish's campaign against social stodginess were her Venetian palazzo on upper Madison Avenue and her handsome colonial "cottage" (it had two ballrooms) in fashionable Newport. Recoiling from the effort of remembering all her blueblooded guests' names, Mame addressed everyone indiscriminately as "sweet pea," or "lamb," or "pet." Bored by the long-drawn-out multicourse dinner parties of her period, she customarily served her guests in fifty minutes flat, her record being an eight-course extravaganza in a half hour. She defied tradition further by serving champagne instead of wine, from the oysters on. "You have to liven these people up," she explained. "Wine just makes them sleepy."

As Cleveland Amory points out in *The Last Resorts*, Mame Fish was also the first hostess of the front rank to include in her invitations all kinds of celebrities, from European royalty to John L. Sullivan to the chorus of Broadway's *Merry Widow* and even to an occasional tapdancer from Harlem. At one party, the guest of honor was a monkey, complete in white tie and tails. On another ballroom occasion, a troupe of circus performers did their stuff while a baby elephant circulated among the guests passing peanuts.

Innovative as she was as a hostess, however, Mrs. Fish, as a mother, was strictly Old Guard. Her eldest son, Stuyvesant Fish, Jr., recalled a life of "children seen and not heard." He and his siblings never saw their mother at breakfast, which she invariably ate in bed. They *were*, however, permitted a ritual audience to say "Good morning." At tea, occasionally, the children were exhibited to the guests; after supper, if they behaved themselves, they were allowed to watch their dynamic mother dress for the party she was going to that evening. If the party was at home, the youngsters were permitted to peek through the banisters and watch the guests arrive. Sometimes, they could even stay up long enough to raid the dinner table of the banquet's remains. But did the children ever really *mingle* with their elders? "Only," Mrs. Fish's son told Cleveland Amory, "at the beach."

Mrs. Fish's children-should-be-seen-and-not-heard philosophy extended itself also to babies as a subject of conversation. No ladies' luncheon topic bored Mame more. Typical was her response to a luncheon companion's query regarding a large and expanding family in Mame's Newport neighborhood. "Have you seen Mrs. So-and-so's last baby?" the friend inquired. "Pet," replied Mame, with a pained look, "I don't expect to live that long."

※

Don't let's go to the dogs to-night,
For mother will be there.

Sir Alan Patrick Herbert

※

# DINA'S MOTHER

Dina Merrill, the talented and beautiful actress, is the child of financier E. F. Hutton and the late Marjorie Merriweather Post, a famous society beauty whose own grandfather, C. W. Post, had founded a food fortune.

Dina says a romantic interlude in her childhood occurred at about age eight, when she and her parents were sailing around the Galapagos Islands on a square-rigger. "My mother decided she wanted a stuffed flamingo, so my father got his gun and shot her one. It was in the days before conservation had the meaning it has now. I remember there was a doctor on board ship and he was sitting there ineptly attempting to skin the bird.

"Finally, Mother said, 'Oh, for God's sake, give it to me,' and she took up the knife and began doing a really expert job of skinning the flamingo. I was astonished and said, 'But, Mother, how do you know what you're doing? How did you learn to do that?'

"She snorted, 'Bear-hunting, with your grandfather!'"

※

On another occasion, Dina remembers a trip on the square-rigger when her glamorous and statuesque mother was invited to come ashore in Scandinavia for dinner with friends who were entertaining King Gustav of Sweden. "Mother loved to get all dressed up in her tiara and evening dress. So this night she was done to the nines to see the King, but there was a terrible storm and she had to go ashore in a dinghy. Taking a sou'wester and oilskin leggings from the crew, and tucking her long dress underneath, off she went in the rain and wind. The boat made shore, Mother climbed out, headed for the seashore house, and knocked. She couldn't take off her outer clothes because it was still storming. Then the door opened and it was the King himself. He took one look at her and started to laugh and they fell into each other's arms, hysterical. It was one of Mother's greatest entrances."

✳

## NOT RHODA MORGENSTERN'S MA

Lady Rhoda Birley was an intellectual who married at nineteen the English portrait painter Sir Oswald Birley. She produced some stunning progeny—a son, Mark, who owns London's Club Annabel; a famous fashion designer daughter, Maxime de la Falaise, and two lovely grandchildren, Loulou and Alexis de la Falaise. Of her, exotic daughter Maxime says: "My mother had a wonderful solution for teen-age children at parties. I would wear the dress she had chosen until she said good night to me, and then I would go upstairs, change my clothes, and for the rest of the night she wouldn't officially recognize me." Lady Birley was always a great one for mixing her guests as well as putting children and adults together. She was as apt to invite the butcher as a member of the Royal Family. She once declared: "Everybody should be on the same level of good manners and affection and understanding. High society is for people who are not professionals." Of motherhood, she commented: "I am always happy to hear what my children and grandchildren are doing, but I don't interfere with their lives. *Mothers are a great bore*, don't you think?"

✳

## MOTHER MIMI

When Mary Martin married Richard Halliday in California at twenty-five, she already had an eight-year-old son, Larry Hagman, by a previous teen-age marriage. After the wedding in Las Vegas Mary came home to see Larry and tell him. "It had been too late to wake him the night before, when we drove away.

". . . Larry was sitting in the bathtub, scrubbing up for bed. I walked in and said, 'Luke, I just got married.' Luke was my pet name for him; he called me 'Mimi.'

" 'Which one, Mimi?' he asked. 'The one with the zebras?'

" 'No,' I said, 'I married Richard Halliday.'

"Larry just said, 'Oh?'

"In retrospect, this dialogue seems very cryptic. But my son and I were more like brother and sister, or perhaps very close friends who sometimes got to play together. We didn't have mother-son discussions."

From *My Heart Belongs*

*

# ANOTHER MOTHER MARY

Michael Chase, who toils in the vineyards of public television and is wed to the writer and wit Chris Chase, finds writing women with lots of talent and a giddy approach to life appealing. His mother, Mary Chase, who won the Pulitzer Prize for her play about a rabbit, *Harvey*, has provided her son with endless excitement and amusement. He recalls that upon her success as a playwright she bought herself a new mink coat and decided to embark on a trip around the world. At that point, she sat down and wrote Michael:

"Remember when you were a little boy and you cried because you couldn't have some toy and I told you we were saving all our money for you when you were older. Well, dear, I was lying."

Two other letters from Mary Chase to Michael are true pearls: "Dearest Michael—When you were only a little boy you would often come screaming out of your room at night crying, 'There's an owl in my room.' And we would lead you back into the room and slap you and say, 'There is no owl in this room,' and then kick you and put you back to bed. Often you would sob for hours and your father would say, 'I'd sure like to put an owl in that kid's room for him.' Well, to make a long story short, we finally found an owl—after all these years—walking through a store and so we've sent him to you, so now you *will* have an owl in your room! Isn't that nice? Merry Christmas and love from Mother."

And this one, in a more touching vein:

"Michael Dearest—I hope this valentine gets to you on your birthday even though it will say what I've said to you so many times

before and yet becomes increasingly true. You were not so handsome when I first saw you—forty-two years ago, on the 21st of
January—as you are today. But you had something and it took
hold of me and held me and has never let me go. I could sell that
line for a lyric, but I give it to you freely—Happy birthday. Love
always, Mother.

P.S. And in case you're asking, where's the gift? Let me remind
you, kind hearts are more than coronets."

*

# STORK CLUB MAMA

That charming man-about-New York Billy Livingston, who was a
fixture of Cafe Society back in the Brenda Frazier days, also served
a stint as a marine on Guadalcanal during World War II. One day,
in the long-delayed mail from the States, a sweating and bored Billy,
now light-years from the Stork Club, received a birthday gift from
Abercrombie & Fitch. The package contained a mysterious object
resembling a leather doughnut. In answer to a tedious V-mail exchange in which Billy queried his mother, "What is it?" he received the information that the incredible Ninie had thoughtfully
sent him a special "Fox Hole Headrest" which was very big at
Abercrombie's that season.

Ninie also informed Billy that she was terribly busy knitting
with a charity society group called "Remember, Purl Harder!"

Mrs. Livingston, as she was called for a time, was a true belle, a
fixture of Charleston society, adorning the resorts of the rich and
famous for years. In the process, she acquired five different husbands.

When Ninie was married for the last time, in Maryland, the
ceremony was performed by a female judge who happened to be a
spinster. Afterward, Ninie burst into tears to the consternation of
her new husband who was surprised to find his bride so sentimental.
"No, it's not that," sobbed Ninie, "I just feel so sorry for the
judge. You and I have had eight marriages between us and she
hasn't had any!"

For some years Ninie had only one grandson and whenever she
wrote the father and mother, she always added thoughtfully: "And
give my love to little what's-his-name."

# MADDER MARRIAGE MUSIC

Letter excerpt from my friend Thomas Wm. Bianchi of Columbia
Pictures about his six-times-married mother:

My mother's fourth marriage lasted but seven weeks after it
began in one of those neon wedding chapels in Las Vegas. In an attempt to found her fifth marriage on more solid ground, she
reverted to her penchant for traditional church weddings. My assigned task was to deliver my grandmother down the aisle to the
seat of the mother-of-the-bride. When we reached our pew, I asked
my grandmother, who was then seventy-eight, whether it had ever
occurred to her that at her age she would again be playing this role.
"Occurred to me?" she snapped. "Sweetheart, I am saving this dress.
I'm sure we'll be back doing this again next year."

When I called my grandmother recently to determine whether
she had worn that dress again at the sixth wedding two years later,
she advised me that she had. She said, however, "But, Tom, if you
let them print that, I will have to get another dress for the next
wedding. Surely, now someone will notice how worn that dress is."

My mother herself has a sense of humor about her many trips
down the aisle. Several weeks after her fifth divorce she announced
that her sixth wedding was imminent. In response to this news, I
asked if she did not think it was appropriate to wait awhile—at least
until "the body was cold." Her reply: "That was the problem. That
body has been cold since the night after the honeymoon!"

# A Mother's Kitchen

The best fork is mother's hand.

Jewish proverb.

All her life my own mother detested cooking but loved housekeeping. It was her cross to bear that instead of the cleaning and organization she loved, she usually had a hungry household of visiting relatives, live-in in-laws, aging parents, children, and a long marriage to a quirky husband who frequently sat down impatiently at the table a full hour before the meal was to be served. Likewise, my father never went to bed without innocently asking my mother to fix him a snack. He invariably prefaced this with his favorite verse:

> To bed, to bed, said Sleepyhead
> Wait a while, said Slow
> Put on the pot, said Greedygut,
> We'll have a bite before we go.

At times in the forty-seven years she heard this rhyme, it drove my mother quite crazy. Sometimes she simply refused, but usually she gave in. And she became a good cook in spite of herself.

As she grew older, her approach to cuisine became haphazard. However, her candy-making remains near perfect and no Christmas complete without her fluffy white divinity and creamy chocolate fudge. Not long ago, however, this doughty eighty-four-year-old made a batch of fudge with lemon extract because she had run out of vanilla. "Oh, I didn't think you children would notice the difference," she said when everyone remarked on the peculiarity of the fudge.

Though I love to eat at home, my mother's menu planning would try the soul of a nutritionist. To wit:

## GUARANTEED TO MAKE YOU BLOW UP LIKE A JAPA-NESE WRESTLER—
## ELIZABETH McCALL SMITH'S ALL STARCH AND FAT 5,000-CALORIE DINNER

Spaghetti Red—spaghetti with canned tomatoes, onions and ground meat

Hotwater cornbread—cornmeal formed into cakes with boiling water, fried in bacon fat

Leftover creamed corn (only enough for two people)

Creamed gravy

Lima beans in scalded milk and butter (this is my mother's idea of a "green" vegetable)

Chicken fried steak, fried chicken, fried pork chops, or ham

Escalloped potatoes

Side order of enchiladas

"Salad" of avocado and mayonnaise

Three kinds of pie

✳

Anyone who did not experience the great Depression of the 1930s probably can't imagine what it was like in those days when derelicts, drifters, and just plain people out of work would come to the back door asking for odd jobs and hand-outs. My mother never turned anyone away without a meal of some sort and my brother recalls that she once saw a man walking through the alley. She called and said, "Bobby, ask that man if he needs a meal. And even if he doesn't; his paper sack looks so soggy. Take him this clean sack so he can carry off whatever he's got properly."

# YES, VIRGINIA, THERE WAS A REAL MOTHER HUBBARD

Old Mother Hubbard went to the cupboard
To get her poor dog a bone.
When she got there the cupboard was bare
And so the poor dog had none.

Mother Goose rhyme

Tradition has it that, midway through the reign of King George III, she served as a housekeeper in the Devonshire home of a Member of Parliament with the provocative name of John Pollexfen Bastard. The poem commemorating her (which extends to a full thirteen verses) was, most scholars believe, composed by a whimsical house guest named Sarah Catherine Martin, the onetime beloved of one of King George's sons, the future William IV. Ms. Martin missed out on being a Queen, but her doggy 1804 doggerel has unquestionably made Mother Hubbard's the most famous kitchen cupboard in Western literature.

\*

# FIRST YOU FRY AN ONION

"The kitchen," writes Irving Howe in *World of Our Fathers*, "was the one place where immigrants might recall to themselves that they were not mere creatures of toil and circumstances, but also human beings defined by their sociability. The kitchen testified to the utterly plebeian character of immigrant Jewish life; the kitchen was warm, close, and bound all to the matrix of the family; sometimes of course it could also be maddeningly noisy and crowded—'my own private Coney Island,' Zero Mostel has remembered. . . ."

Howe continues: "It was from her place in the kitchen that the Jewish housewife became the looming figure who would inspire, haunt, and devastate generations of sons. She realized intuitively that insofar as the outer world tyrannized and wore down her men, reducing them to postures of docility, she alone could create an oasis of order. It was she who would cling to received values and resist the pressures of dispersion; she who would sustain the morale of all around her, mediating quarrels, soothing hurts, drawing a circle of safety in which her children could breathe, and sometimes, as time went on, crushing her loved ones under the weight of her affection. The successful entry of the immigrant Jews into the American business world would require a reassertion of the 'male principle,' a regathering of authority and aggression—at least outside the home. But in the early days of a family's life in America, it was often the mother who held things together and coped best with the strange new world."

\*

## "THE JEWISH MOTHER'S GUIDE TO FOOD DISTRIBUTION"

Dan Greenburg says: "Just as Mother Nature abhors a vacuum, the Jewish Mother abhors an empty mouth." He continues:

*Bread with Everything*
Never forget the importance of bread in the diet. Urge that it be eaten with all foods, even snacks:
"Irving, wait. Take a little bread with that."
"Bread? With strawberry ice cream?"
"Just a little piece. To help wash it down."

*How to Administer the Third Helping*
"You are too full to eat any more?"
"Yes, yes, yes."
"All right. This I can understand . . . So I'll wrap it up in wax paper and you'll take it for later."

*Watch Between-Meal Treats*
Between meals, follow guests about the house with trays of fruit, nuts, candies, cookies, cakes, and sour pickles. Eating should never be restricted to the dining table. . . .

*How to Accept a Compliment*
Never accept a compliment:
"Irving, tell me how is the chopped liver?"
"Mmmm! Sylvia, it's delicious!"
"I don't know. First the chicken livers that the butcher gave me were dry. Then the timer on the oven didn't work. Then at the last minute I ran out of onions. Tell me how could it be good?"

*Definitions*
    *for later*   To be eaten within the next two weeks.
    *poison*   What a Jewish Mother is not trying to feed you.
    *nourishing*   Fattening.
    *scarecrow*   Anybody who weighs less than 250 lbs.
    *shameful waste*   Throwing out a teabag after using it only once.
    *sliver*   Any portion of food smaller than a breadbox.
    *wash down*   To keep it company in your stomach.

                                        —*How to Be a Jewish Mother*

*

# *Miz Smart's Salad, Bunky, Louisiana**

(*This is a typical Southern idea of what a "salad" should be*)
            One iceberg lettuce leaf
            Ring of canned pineapple
            Half a banana (erect)
            Half maraschino cherry on top
            Grated cheddar cheese
            Mayonnaise spill-over

*

# BE CAREFUL, BE CAREFUL

Comedian Milton Berle's autobiography reveals some examples of
the way his mother, the illustrious Sandra, made her mark on his
eating habits:

When I was six or seven, I went to the grocery store one day
with my mother. I pointed to a pile of long green things. "What are
those, Mama?"

"Don't eat them, they're no good for you."

I figured she was right; she was my mother. So I never eat cu-

* From the collection of Wydell Martin.

225

cumbers. Maybe they just didn't sit well with her.

Radishes are another thing. "You can eat radishes, but always put butter on them." Why? I don't know. Maybe it helps digest them better. And maybe not, but to this day, I put butter on radishes.

And I won't drink from somebody else's glass, and I won't touch ice water, or anything with ice in it . . . All from Mama.

❋

She riseth also while it is yet night, and giveth meat to her household . . . her candle goeth not out by night . . . She openeth her mouth with wisdom; and in her tongue is the law of kindness . . . She looketh well to the ways of her household, and eateth not the bread of idleness . . . Her children arise up, and call her blessed . . .

Proverbs

❋

When my mother had to get dinner for eight she'd just make enough for sixteen and only serve half.

—Gracie Allen

❋

You can't chop your mama up in Massachusetts
Not even if you're tired of her cuisine.
No, you can't chop your mama up in Massachusetts
You know it's almost sure to cause a scene.

Michael Brown's
"Lizzie Borden,"
*New Faces of 1952*

❋

# LIBERACE'S FAVORITE

A few years back, Liberace published a cookbook. "I wanted," he said, "to call it *Mother, I'd Rather Do It Myself!* But the publishers decided *Liberace Cooks* was more to the point."

226

The pianist admits to deep, sentimental feelings about his mother's kitchens—plural. "Sometimes people wonder," he says in his autobiography, "why my home, any one of them, has two kitchens. It's because I think I should have it as nice, now that I can afford it, as I had it when we would hardly afford anything." Liberace explains that when he was a youngster growing up in Milwaukee, his mother always had two kitchens in the house. "One," he says, "we used when we had company and one just for the family." (LIZ'S NOTE: Just like the Pucci's in the intro to Italian Mothers!)

*

## Some Moms Not Famous For Their Apple Pie

*Harry Truman's mother Martha.* In her younger days, according to granddaughter Margaret, she was the overseer of a kitchen that fed as many as twenty field hands, but the actual cooking was done by paid help. Says Margaret: "Mamma Truman hated to cook, and only made one dish that was praiseworthy—fried chicken."

*The mother of playwright Preston Jones.* The creator of the much-heralded *A Texas Trilogy* reports that his Lone Star mom "was the world's worst cook. What is more, she hated cooking with a passion. When the TV dinner first came out, she considered it the greatest boon to mankind of all time—so did the rest of the family."

*Ernest Hemingway's mother.* In her memoir, *At the Hemingways: A Family Portrait,* the novelist's older sister, Marcelline, discloses that Mother Hemingway was a mature woman before she made her debut as a baker. The big breakthrough came with an English teacake, the recipe for which Grace Hall Hemingway discovered in a cookbook of her own mother dating back to the 1880s. A neighbor helped work out the correct proportions. "Seldom," writes Marcelline Hemingway, "have I seen such joy on anyone's face as on Mother's when she baked her first highly successful English teacakes all by herself in the kitchen at Windemere. Ernest and I were in high school by the time this cooking debut of Mother's took place; Sunny and Ursula were of grammar school age, and Baby Carol was in her high chair. Daddy had just come in from fishing and rushed to wash his hands at the pump as Mother, flushed and excited, finished buttering the hot raisin-filled teacakes and sliced wedge-shaped pieces for each of us to taste.

" 'Delicious! Gracie, delicious!' Daddy gave his verdict with his mouth full. 'You got any more in the kitchen? Where have you been hiding this talent all these years?'

" 'It *is* good, isn't it?' said Mother modestly. We all joined in extravagant praise. But the teacake was worthy of every adjective. From then on Mother served *her* teacake for every social occasion. She even looked up people she hadn't seen for years and invited them for tea. Later she proudly presented her recipe to the 1921 edition of the Oak Park Third Congregational Church Cook Book, and to this day, though she never baked but one other thing . . . people still remember her as a 'wonderful cook' and mention that delicious teacake.

"Once I suggested that she learn to make a layer cake, a baking powder recipe.

" 'No, dear,' said Mother. 'I proved I could cook with my teacake, and I'm not going to take a chance of spoiling my reputation by trying anything else.' And with few exceptions, she stuck to her word."

❋

"There is no such thing as bad food," Mama used to say. "There are only spoiled-rotten children."

—Sam Levenson

❋

# A DOG'S LIFE

It's been said that a Hungarian cook's best friend is paprika and biographer Lester David's mother is proof of the pudding. Says Lester: "We had a Boston terrier named Colonel who, of course, ate what the family ate. Once I came home from school and found my mother bending over Colonel's dish. She had just scrambled some eggs for his midday meal and was sprinkling paprika over them for him. When she saw my look of amazement, she said, 'Well, whoever heard of eating eggs without paprika?' "

✳

## BUTTERING UP

I hated the servants and liked my mother because, on the one or two rare and delightful occasions when she buttered my bread for me, she buttered it thickly instead of merely wiping a knife on it.

—George Bernard Shaw

✳

## ON THE LEVEL

The renowned Boston Cooking School director, Fannie Farmer, was a lifelong spinster, but, because of her efforts to bring order to the chaos of nineteenth-century cooking directions, historians of American cuisine call her "The Mother of Level Measurements."

✳

## *Lena Horne's Apprenticeship in Haute Cuisine*

**LENA HORNE:**
. . . one of my vivid memories of Florida is buying crayfish, bought from some guy who had a roadside stand, or who peddled it from door to door, then eating it after the herbs, garlic, onions, and maybe a little shrimp were added. It was, therefore, natural for me to welcome bouillabaisse years later in Villefranche like an old friend. Similarly, as a child in the South, guavas off the trees, all pale pink and green, sapodillas, mangoes, figs (purple and green), prepared me for the fabulous fruit that Italy offered. And chitlins—I

229

always adored them—put in a pot with all the right things and cooked all day, making the house funky, prepared me for calamare in San Francisco and squid in Italy and snails everywhere. In my mind, at least, the only thing you can compare those things to is chitlins.

Negro dishes are directly comparable to the famous delicacies of Europe. Rabbit, fricasseed, for instance, was standard Sunday fare at my Uncle Frank's home in Fort Valley and it did not taste appreciably different at Lapin Agile where I had it in Paris. By the same token, grits tastes to me almost exactly like farina in Rio or polenta in Italy, and a great French cassoulet calls to mind the taste of turkey neckbones and fatback and dumplings all cooked together, in Macon, Georgia.

It sometimes amuses and amazes me that poverty is a better preparation for *haute cuisine* than is a good, solid, middle-class upbringing.

✳

Lena's grandmother Cora Calhoun Horne was a formidable, no-nonsense woman. "She had a Spartan appetite. . . . But she did have a taste for classic Southern cooking. She thought—and I agree —that the gods had a great deal to do with the creation of okra, the divine food. She liked it fresh cooked, not too soft, served in a bowl with butter, salt and pepper on top. She also liked clabber (which is something like yogurt), custard lightly sugared, oysters and clams. Kale and mustard if someone else would wash and cook the greens."

*Lena*

✳

L.S. NOTE: The custom of "sugaring" things is southern and midwestern. My mother often puts sugar on rice or clabber. My grandmother McCall liked sugar on sliced tomatoes. And as children, one of our favorite treats was sliced bread, buttered and sugared, or toasted. Liz Pierce says she learned to eat spinach because her mother put sugar on it.

# MOTHER IS EVERYWHERE

Calling the white ghostly substance in the bottom of a vinegar jug "the mother" is an etymological mistake. It all began when some long-ago dictionary maker mixed up *moeder*, the Dutch word for "mother" with *modder*, the Dutch word for "mud."

*Larousse Gastronomique* points out that vinegar is the result of acetic fermentation of wine. This fermentation is caused by a fungus known as *mycoderma aceti*, which, when added to wine, is apparent in the form of a thick, gelatinlike skin that occurs on the surface of the wine in a crock, cask, or whatever. In French, this is known as *mère de vinaigre* and in English, mother of vinegar. The growth of the fungus and transformation of wine into vinegar is best at 59 to 86 degrees F. The mother, incidentally, can be divided and discarded or transferred to another batch of wine as it expands, otherwise it will fill the cask or crock.*

*

# MOTHER BLATTY AND FDR

William Peter Blatty followed up his fictional megaseller, *The Exorcist*, with a factual book about his immigrant Armenian mother. She was, he wrote, a "destitute, suffering, loving, illiterate, defiant" lion of a mother who raised her five children in a Manhattan tenement partly by peddling her own homemade jelly in the streets. Blatty recalls one day in 1939 when President Franklin Roosevelt came to the neighborhood to officiate at the opening of the Queens Midtown Tunnel:

"On the day of the ceremony, my mother and I were standing at the outer circumference of a cordon of spectators. Mama's left hand held a brown paper shopping bag. I ignored it; the bag was her custom. All eyes at the time were on FDR as he reached from his car with a gold-plated scissors and neatly snipped the broad silken multicolored ribbon that dropped from side to side across the entrance to the tunnel like an unconvinced rainbow. Then, before

---

* Craig Claiborne of The New York *Times* notes that vinegar complete with mother may be ordered from the Franjoh Cellars, Box 7462, Stockton, Ca. 95207 or from Bloomingdale's, NYC 10022.

anyone knew what was happening, my mother was grimly advancing on the President.

"Suddenly, flashbulbs began to explode. FDR dropped the gold-plated scissors in horror, and a covey of startled and uncertain Secret Service men reached for revolvers and surrounded the car.

"Too late. My mother had gotten to the President.

" 'I wanna shake your hand,' she told him warningly in a voice of quiet command; then reached out and took his hand in a grip which had the power of her mesmerizing presence, imbued with an illusion of crunching strength. FDR started numbly . . . When my mother leaned over and reached in the shopping bag, several Secret Service men leaped from their socks . . . but they barely got a glove or a thought on my mother before she had withdrawn from the bag a rather large, sticky jar filled with a murky and rust-colored substance. She handed it over to the dumbfounded President.

" 'Homemade quince jelly,' she grunted. Then she added, 'For when you have company.' "

*

# HEALTH FOOD

In her superb memoir *First, You Cry*, Betty Rollin describes the charmed life she led up until the time she underwent a mastectomy. She says: "It was not only my identity as a journalist that made me feel immune to disaster. There was also the fact of my past perfect health and, therefore, my identity as a perfectly, immutably healthy person.":

> I was always superbly healthy. My mother, true to the stereotype of Jewish mothers, used to make me eat. But, unlike the stereotype, she shoveled sirloin and wheat germ into the mouth of her baby girl, not matzoh brei or fatty chicken soup. When it came to food, Mother's rabbi was Carlton Fredericks, her guru Adelle Davis. My mother's kitchen never housed a potato chip or a slice of white bread. Once in a while, I had a hot dog at another child's birthday party. Usually, guilt would make me confess the transgression. "You ate that junk?" my mother would say. Then she would shake her head as if I were reporting a pregnancy, wondering where she went wrong.

232

One rebels against such a mother. I rebelled against mine. I smoked cigarettes and I had affairs with Christians. But I never ate a Baby Ruth or drank a Coca-Cola.

It must have worked. Both sides of the family were physical wrecks. But we Rollins—my father was subject to the same regimen—were beacons of good health. My mother took pride in my father's and my fitness the way other mothers took pride in their family's talent or good looks. And she loved to tell about what a mess my father was when he ate *his* mother's cooking. "She was a wonderful woman," my mother would say of my Russian grandmother. "But the way she cooked, it's a wonder she didn't kill her children."

❋

# TAKE ONE NUDE CHICKEN

In his little book *Making Chicken Soup*, now something of a collector's item, photographer Les Krims pictures all the ingredients for making chicken soup including a Jewish mother posing half nude behind the kitchen counter. This is the photographer's mother to whom the book is dedicated and whose letter at the close reads:

May 5, 1970

Dear Leslie:

I was making chicken soup today, and making it reminded me that last time I saw you, you didn't look so hot. If your wife would learn to make chicken soup like mine, things would be different.

Do you remember the first time I fed you chicken soup! You were just a year old. I couldn't get myself to give you the prepared kind, so I cooked some fresh. I carefully skimmed all the fat off, broke a piece of Zweiback into it, and fed you the cooked soup a little at a time. You loved it! Chicken soup is one of the healthiest foods you can eat.

I know you're a famous photographer now and you go to all kinds of interesting places, see interesting things and eat fancy food, but remember, you'll never be too famous to eat chicken soup.

Love,
"Mom"

One of the highlights of the first season of Norman Lear's satiric TV soap opera *Mary Hartman, Mary Hartman* was the drowning of the basketball coach of Mary's home-town high school in a bowl of her chicken soup. Because of the circumstances of this demise, Mary, the mother of one, insisted that the funeral services be held in her kitchen.

✳

## AND JUST A FEW WORDS ABOUT MOTHERS AND DRINK

Mrs. Rutherford B. Hayes, wife of the nineteenth President and mother of his eight children, was an ardent supporter of the goals of the Women's Christian Temperance Union. Her prohibition of wines and liquors in the White House earned her the nickname of "Lemonade Lucy." "I have young sons who have never tasted liquor," she once said. "They shall not receive from my hand, or with the sanction that its use in the family would give, the first taste of what might prove their ruin. What I wish for my own sons I must do for the sons of other mothers."

✳

When England's King and Queen paid a 1939 state visit to the United States, their schedule included an overnight stay at the Hyde Park family home of President Franklin Roosevelt. The royal couple was expected late in the afternoon, so Roosevelt ordered a tray of cocktails brought to the library where he, his wife Eleanor and his mother were assembled to wait. Mother Roosevelt was greatly disapproving of this, pointing out that the King and Queen would surely prefer tea at this hour. In her book, *This I Remember*, Mrs. FDR reports that her husband, "who could be as obstinate as his mother," left the cocktail tray exactly where it was. As last the King and Queen arrived. When George VI approached FDR, the President nodded toward the drink tray and said, "My mother does not approve of cocktails and thinks you should have a cup of tea." Replied the King: "Neither does my mother," and took a cocktail.

234

If this story is true, it ruins the great apochryphal one of Mae West being offered sherry by the aforesaid queen, Mary, the Queen Mother. Mae reportedly said, in her highly-imitatable manner: "I don't drink, Your Majesty, and as a matter of fact, I'm *surprised* that you do . . ."

❋

Writer Marya Mannes, in her memoir *Out of My Time*, tells of the effect Prohibition had on the cultured, intellectual household of her musician father, David, and her mother, Clara, sister of the conductor Walter Damrosch:

"The common humanity in the face of Prohibition," she writes, "made lawbreakers of us all." Her favorite instance of this was the sight of her parents making gin in the bathroom and the sound of her mother "calling Professor Robert W. Wood, our long-time physicist friend, in Baltimore, and asking 'Robert—just what proportion of juniper do you use in yours?'"

❋

The mother of President Franklin Pierce was an alcoholic, and his own struggles with John Barleycorn were made more difficult by the fears that he had inherited his mother's problem.

❋

But total abstinence on the part of a mother doesn't always mean salvation. The daughter of crusader Carry Nation, the scourge of the saloonkeepers, wound up in an insane asylum—an alcoholic.

❋

A saloonkeeper and a good mother don't pull on the same rope.

—Billy Sunday

❋

My brothers, James and Bobby, like to recall the end of World War II, when almost everybody was still celebrating the victory for days on end. Home safe after years in the Air Force and the Merchant Marine, neither of the Smith boys was an exception, but they claim to remember Mother on the telephone to one of her friends, saying: "Well, I'm sure Bobby and James don't drink because they are both so thirsty every morning."*

❋

Bobby has unfortunately never forgotten anything about his childhood. One of his most vivid memories is that Mother kept him quiet during church services by giving him one or two . . . never three . . . always two, soda crackers she kept in her purse. "They tasted of face powder," he says, and in a burst of understanding self-enlightenment, "I guess that's why vodka tastes so good *now!*"

* Sorority housemothers have been known to say exactly the same thing.

# Mothers and Sex

I can't even tolerate seeing two birds mating without
wanting to separate them.

> Much-quoted remark of Nancy,
> Lady Astor, mother of six

It will establish me and my mother in time no doubt if I simply say
in preface to this chapter that my mother disapproves of "The
New Morality" and once told me after I had gone to work as a
movie reviewer for *Cosmopolitan:* "I think S-E-X is the ugliest word
in the English language."

If I am not mistaken, this was the only time I ever heard her
even come close to uttering the word. She believes me when I tell
her that Helen Gurley Brown is a perfectly nice person, but takes
pains to tear the covers off *Cosmo* when the magazine arrives in the
mail. "I have impressionable grandchildren," she says. "They do not
need to see these terrible pictures of girls showing their—breasts."

I remember being surprised she had used such a precise word
instead of the more genteel "bosom." Mother referred to anatomy
gingerly—"private parts" was one of her old standbys. She once
shocked us by telling of a male relative who had "three testicles"
which sent my brothers into hysterics and made me feel it was all
more than I needed to know. I recall one night when a faintly fa-

237

mous name came up and Mother said she had known this person in her youth. "He was no gentleman," she said firmly. Pursuit of the matter revealed that he was a cad who got "aroused" while dancing with her. Unforgivable!

Still, she has a sense of humor. For years when doing the wash, she always referred to my brothers' athletic supporters as "wampum belts." Lately I detect a resigned acceptance of the modern realities in my mother's more sophisticated approach to the things she reads, or sees and hears on television. She has been swept into the sexual revolution against her will and possibly as a natural result of being forced for years to cope with the sexual precocities of her three children. When a relative and his ex-wife came to visit her recently and shared a single bedroom, she simply shrugged and indicated that although she had prepared two rooms, "It's none of my business where they sleep." I congratulated her on this as eminently sensible.

"Nevertheless," she said. "I don't think it's exactly right." I pointed out that perhaps they were still "'married in the sight of God," knowing this would appeal to her religious nature. "Maybe so, honey," she said, "I hope so."

To my mother, sex was and is something sacred—an event that should occur only within the boundaries of the tenets of matrimony and not to be taken lightly. She was not, however, like the Victorian woman who endured her wedding night by gritting her teeth and "thinking of England." Though my parents were extremely private about their intimacies, we children were always aware that they were bound together by something mysterious, compelling, and strong. My father once said, "After I married your mother, I never looked at another woman!" And again, when I asked how long he had been married, he laughed: "All my life—why, I don't *remember* when I wasn't married to your mother."

Mother liked to tell of her courtship by the energetic and wiry cotton buyer who took a room in the house next door when she was living with one of her doctor brothers in a little town near Dallas. And how this young man peeked through his window shade at her playing croquet on the lawn. As children, we were tremendously involved in the romantic episodes that led her to drop all her handsome, tall, rich prospects for the little man with the great personality who was a wonderful ballroom dancer. We followed their tender story through his efforts to enlist in World War I and her relief that he was turned down for not weighing enough and through the sagas of the arrivals of their four babies and the tragic loss of their first infant son and on and on. She would entertain us over and over with true details. But Mother's stories always stopped at the bedroom door. That was strictly between Elizabeth, Sloan, and God.

I am afraid I have never since quite properly been able to make all the realistic distinctions between sex and romance. This is good or bad depending on how one looks at it. But in any case, my mother deserves the credit or the blame. And she says she is willing to take it, because like most mothers, she did the very best she knew how and always only tried to do what she thought was right.

*

# CATHERINE WAS GREAT!

Though Catherine the Great of Russia was renowned throughout Europe as a sexual libertine and bestowed her imperial favors on at least twenty-one lovers—the last when she was aged sixty-seven—she grew up in the utmost innocence. Her strict German mother kept her so insulated from the facts of life that at the age of sixteen, only a few months before her marriage to a Russian grand duke, Catherine still was not sure what the anatomical difference was between a man and a woman. The empress reports in her memoirs that her teen-aged ladies-in-waiting, despite their proximity to one of the most licentious courts of the period, shared her ignorance, and at night before going to sleep the girls would giggle for hours, pondering this mystery. Finally, the intrepid Catherine resolved to ask her mother for the facts so they could all know. But no revelations were forthcoming. When the future empress approached her mother, the older woman refused to answer her questions and, instead, chided her severely for such unladylike curiosity.

*

# MIZ LIL

At a press conference during the Democratic Convention in New York City in July 1976, Jimmy Carter's mother Lillian told reporters about her own mother. "My mother was old-fashioned," she said. "Do you know, until I was twenty-one, I never got in a car with a boy by myself? I had a chaperone." There was a short pause, brightened by a grin. "I learned everything I know from a chaperone!"

# TANGLED WEB

Lady Melbourne, mother of the Prime Minister who initiated Queen Victoria into the duties of sovereignship, was a favorite subject of London gossips through most of her adult life. Married at seventeen, the former Elizabeth Milbanke involved herself thereafter in such a complicated web of extramarital love relationships that wags referred to her six children as "Miscellany" because of their uncertain paternity. Her fourth son was believed to be the result of a brief romantic liaison with the Prince of Wales, later King George IV. The Prime Minister himself, her second son, was rumored to be the son of the wealthy patron of the arts, Lord Egremont. As an elderly man, the adviser to Queen Victoria was once observed staring intently at a portrait of his illustrious mother. "A remarkable woman," he mused aloud. "A devoted mother, an excellent wife, but not chaste, not chaste."

\*

# SEX EDUCATION

One of the funniest female writers alive is Florence King whose dissertation on the WASP Mother appears elsewhere in this book. Florence must come by her sense of humor as a matter of heredity, even if her mother's own humor is largely unconscious.

In the matter of oral sex, Florence reports: "Naturally, she never called it by name or said what it was—she merely told me, 'If a man ever asks you to do something funny to him, I want you to give me your word of honor that you'll run screaming into the night.' Then, in one of her finest non-sequiturs, she added, 'That's why the French can't win a war without our help. They're always doing something funny to each other.'"

\*

# AT ARM'S LENGTH

As a young boy, the feisty British sexual libertarian and philosopher

Bertrand Russell was enormously fond of his paternal grandmother, the wife of Lord John Russell, English Prime Minister from 1846 to 1852. By the time he reached his teens, however, Lady Russell's Puritan morality began to seem to him to be "excessive." Here's how he sums up her views on sex in his autobiography:

"Marriage," she felt, "was a puzzling institution. It was clearly the duty of husbands and wives to love one another, but it was a duty they ought not to perform too easily, for if sex attraction drew them together there must be something not quite nice about them. Not, of course, that she would have phrased the matter in these terms. What she would have said, and in fact did say, was: 'You know, I never think that the affection of husbands and wives is quite such a good thing as the affection of parents for their children, because there is sometimes something a little selfish about it.'

"That," says Bertrand Russell, "was as near as her thoughts could come to such a topic as sex."

*

# DAN AGAIN

It's funny, my own mother doesn't *look* Jewish, but here she is turning up again in Dan Greenburg's book *How to Be a Jewish Mother:*

There are only two things a Jewish Mother
needs to know about sex and marriage:

(1) Who is having sex?
(2) Why aren't they married?

*

# CARING

Barbara Walters, interviewing Lillian Hellman on the television program *Not for Women Only,* asked the playwright if she thought that her thirty-year live-in relationship with novelist Dashiell Hammett shocked people while it was going on? Ms. Hellman said she didn't think anybody was really shocked, but admitted she had been "rather careful" in the early days with regard to her parents, at least to the extent of maintaining a separate address. Interviewer Walters was surprised at this answer, recalling that the Hellman-Hammett liaison took place during an era when people still "cared" about such things. Walters added: "My mother still cares." There was a momentary break in the conversation. Then, said Lillian Hellman: "Everybody's mother still cares."

*

## Victorian Porn

A young woman got married at Chester
Her mother she kissed and she blessed her.
  Says she, "You're in luck,
  He's a stunning good f—,
For I've had him myself down in Leicester."

> Nursery Rhyme printed in
> *The Pearl, A Journal of Facetiae
> and Voluptuous Reading,* 1879.

*

I'm basically an old-fashioned woman. I am. I think for a school to introduce contraceptives is . . . well, the pendulum has just swung too far. The business of trying anything once! In my day, that meant jumping out of a cherry tree.

> —Mrs. Alice Bahman,
> mother of Jonathan Winters

*

## SWEET!

Neil Simon's successful play and film *Barefoot in the Park* presents a scene between the honeymooning, just happily married daughter

242

"What's the celebration about, M's Milligan?"
"Sure, me boy's comin home today. He was sentenced to ten years in the penitentiary, but he got three years off for good conduct."
"Ah! I wish *I* had a son like that!"

Boardman Robinson illustration
of Irish Mothers in Masses, 1915

"We can't ask him to take it down if it's his mother."

Drawing by New Hilton in *Collier's*, 1941.

Painter Larry Rivers is possibly the only artist in history to select as his favorite nude model his former mother-in-law. Here she is in *Double Portrait of Berdie.* (Collection of Whitney Museum of American Art, New York)

Baby-delivering storks as pictured in a nineteenth-century magazine illustration. Storks themselves are very good mothers and thus appropriately titled in the "animal queendom." (See chapter so titled.)

The wolf who suckled Romulus, the founder of Rome, and his twin, Remus, was not only an animal mother but an "other" mother par excellence.

Bronze sculpture in the Museo Nuovo, Palazza dei Conservatori, Rome.

Al Jolson and his film mother in *The Jazz Singer* (1927). When movies first talked mom was there wearing her Hollywood goody two-shoes.

Sylvia Sydney and Joanne Woodward played mother and daughter in *Summer Wishes, Winter Dreams* (1973), a more up-to-date and realistic vision of one of life's most intense relationships.

Barbara Stanwyck and Anne Shirley in *Stella Dallas* (1937). The suffering "bad" mother has been a staple of Mom and movies. Hollywood's mothers have paid and paid.

and her widowed mother. The daughter, played onstage by Liz Ashley and in the movie by Jane Fonda, lectures the mother, played in both places by Mildred Natwick, about the facts of life:

CORIE: Do you know what I think you *really* need?

MOTHER: Yes, and I don't want to hear it. (*She gets up and moves away.*)

CORIE: (*Goes to her*) Because you're afraid to hear the truth.

MOTHER: It's not the truth I'm afraid to hear. It's the *word* you're going to use.

CORIE: You're darn right I'm going to use that word . . . It's love!

MOTHER: Oh . . . thank you.

CORIE: A week ago I didn't know what it meant. And then I checked into the Plaza Hotel. For six wonderful days . . . And do you know what happened to me there?

MOTHER: I promised myself I wouldn't ask.

CORIE: I found *love* . . . spiritual, emotional, and physical love. And I don't think anyone on earth should be without it.

MOTHER: I'm not. I have you.

CORIE: I don't mean *that* kind of love. I'm talking about late at night in . . .

MOTHER: (*Quickly*) I *know* what you're talking about.

CORIE: Don't you even want to discuss it?

MOTHER: Not with *you* in the room.

✳

# HARD TO PLEASE

What did Ernest Hemingway's mother think of Lady Brett, the loose-living heroine of his novel *The Sun Also Rises?* Not much, according to the author's older sister. In her book *At the Hemingways: A Family Portrait*, Marcelline Hemingway discloses that her mother refused to finish reading the book, declaring that she couldn't "make head nor tail over such crazy people." It was a mystery to Mrs. Grace Hall Hemingway why her son wanted to write about "such vulgar people and such messy subjects." Sister Marcelline did her best to explain the high value Brother Ernest placed on "realism and truthfulness" in his writing, but Mother Hemingway wasn't impressed. "I can't stand filth," she retorted, and that was the end of it.

❋

## EASY TO PLEASE

In 1976, *Esquire* conducted a survey among the publishers of nine of the nation's leading "skin" magazines to learn how their mothers felt about their labors in the milieu of nude centerfolds and other explicit pictorial erotica. The reported responses ranged from "mildly receptive" to "happy" to "thrilled," this latter reaction coming from the mother of Al Goldstein of *Screw* who, he said, wants to *be* a centerfold. Only one of the publishers stated that he had a mother who was vigorously opposed to his work. Said Peter Wolf of *Cheri:* "She knows what I do and doesn't like it. She wishes I'd write *Love Story*."

❋

## *Joke of the 1960s*

Q: What do you call a girl who will not take the Pill?
A: Mother.

❋

## GRAFFITI

Any lady who believes her mother about clap, etc. from the toilet seats should not be in bars.

Ladies Room wall in
Greenwich Village

# MAD MOTHER OF TWO

You have put me in here a cub, but I will come out roaring like a lion, and I will make all hell howl.

—Carry Moore Nation,
reacting to her first jail term
in 1900

The hatchet-toting crusader against Demon Rum took almost as much umbrage to any public display of the unclad female form. One of her earliest forays as a saloon-smasher—the one that first sent her to jail—was in the barroom of the Carey Hotel in Wichita. The aspect of this establishment that incited her wrath as much or more than the bottles of booze was an oil painting behind the bar of a voluptuous nude called *Cleopatra at the Bath.* Aghast at this display of the Nile temptress in the altogether, replete with pubic hair, Carry reacted with what some witnesses heard as a "screek," and others a "shrill, thin 'Yawk!'" "Disgraceful," she shouted to the young man polishing glasses behind the bar. "You're insulting your mother by having her form stripped naked and hung up in a place where it is not even decent for a woman to be when she has her clothes on!" The next day she came back and decimated the place.

\*

# PLAYING DOCTOR

My mother's morality was ten times as heavy a threat as is desirable. There's no need of making a person impotent until the age of twenty.

—Dr. Benjamin Spock
in *The First Time* by Karl
and Anne Taylor Fleming

# FRANKLY . . .

"The President," stated White House press secretary Ron Nessen, "has long ceased to be perturbed or surprised by his wife's remarks." Not so, indignant church officials and outraged mothers who in August of 1975 were more than a little perturbed by First Lady Betty Ford's remarks on the subject of sex, in and out of marriage. In an interview with Morley Safer on CBS-TV's *60 Minutes*, the mother of Gerald Ford's four children allowed as how premarital sex might just lower the divorce rate and said she "wouldn't be surprised" if her daughter Susan, eighteen, decided to have an affair.* The stately New York *Times* headlined the news:

### BETTY FORD WOULD ACCEPT
### "AN AFFAIR" BY DAUGHTER

and volcanic controversy erupted across the width and breadth of the land. White House mail, both pro and con, arrived in tidal wave proportions. Observed the President eleven days later: "When I first heard it, I thought I'd lost ten million votes. When I read it in the paper the next morning, I raised it to twenty million."

In the meantime, modern Mother Ford kept on her frank and forthright path. "They've asked me everything but how often I sleep with my husband," she told Myra MacPherson. "And if they'd asked me that, I would have told them, 'as often as possible.'"

\*

# IMPROPER VICTORIANS

In *The Unnatural History of the Nanny*, Jonathan Gathorne-Hardy passes on a revealing glimpse he was given by his grandmother of the boudoir life of *her* mother, wife of the Earl of Glasgow. A naval captain in the late eighteen-sixties and seventies, the Earl was often away from home. Frequently, Gathorne-Hardy was

---

* Quoth another prominent mother Mrs. Walter Cronkite, on the occasion of her son's twentieth birthday. "I've never told any of my children to get married. I've always encouraged them to live with the person first."

told, "his disappearances seemed to coincide with visits from a young man, a cousin of theirs aged about eighteen. One morning when she was seven she went in to her mother. She found her completely naked (the mother must then have been about thirty) sitting on the knee of their cousin who was also naked. Her mother turned round and they all stared at each other. 'Go away, Dorothy,' her mother said, 'I'm busy.' "

Obviously, Lady Glasgow was considerably more liberated than most of her Victorian contemporaries. Gathorne-Hardy also recalls his grandmother, who was married in 1899, describing to him how on her wedding day her mother drew her aside with this bit of advice. "There's just one thing I must tell you, Dorothy. Remember, whatever Gathorne does to you is *right*."

# Mothers and Gaiety

GRAFFITI:

My mother made me a homosexual!

If I get her the wool,
will she make me one, too?

An increasingly urban society with relaxed attitudes about sexual behavior has produced this facetiously named chapter. Ten years ago, it would probably not have appeared in print. Yet most of the material to follow concerning homosexuals and their mothers, or homosexuality and motherhood, is not the result of Gay Liberation or the emergence of homosexuals into the open—just the opposite.

What follows represents the homosexual's acute area of emotional response to a situation often fraught with fear, guilt, repression, and/or deeply urgent feelings. After all, the homosexual's first brush with the pejorative or surprising aspect of his or her condition occurs in relation to Mother, and few children can be indifferent to the reaction of their mothers to the central fact of their adolescent (or mature) sexuality. In fact, homosexuals have generally *over*-reacted to Mother, as every psychiatrist knows.

A bit of Mothers and Gaiety is serious, reflecting the very real dilemma of mothers of homosexuals and of homosexuals trying to love, honor, and respect (if not obey) their mothers. But most of Mothers and Gaiety came into being because social oppression and moral disapproval and government regulation and religious strictures *always* create a body of response, often defiant; frequently humorous. Just as Black humor is and was often based on self-depreca-

249

tion, irony, satire and the intimate or elitist feelings generated by being an "outside" minority marching to its different drum, so a great body of gay humor, anecdote, and apocryphal myth has sprung up.

Gay people almost invariably deal with society by first dealing with their mothers—so the stories literally pour out of them. Hurt, guilt, fear, feelings of inferiority, and sometimes triumphs of love and understanding are strong motivations for an entire body of folk tale only beginning now to be revealed, years after the supposed death of Victorianism.

This chapter makes me sad. It makes me happy. It represents perfectly the collision of past and future and bewilderment of the human condition facing us so drastically in the complicated present.

*

# MOTHER-LOVE IS BLIND

A friend who chooses to remain anonymous had a mother who had known for some time that he was gay but had never truly come to terms with it. One day, when she came to visit him, they had the following exchange:

MOTHER: You look particularly well today. Has something especially good happened?
SON: Perhaps it's because I'm in love.
MOTHER: How wonderful. Who is she?
SON: His name is David.
MOTHER: Oh, what does she do?
SON: He works for Eastern Air Lines.
MOTHER: Is she a stewardess?
SON: No, a pilot.

*

# MERLE'S MOTHER

The author Merle Miller made a spectacular debut out of the closet into openly avowed homosexuality back in 1971 when his mother in

Marshalltown, Iowa, was eighty-four years old. Miller had told his mother he was gay before writing about it in the New York *Times Magazine*. "When I told her, she said, 'I suspected something was wrong when I came to see you in Brewster, New York, and you were with that fellow.'"

When Merle warned his mother that he would be on Dick Cavett's TV show discussing his situation, Mrs. Miller gasped, "Oh, Merle, not that!"

The writer said, "But, Mother, I'm only going to tell the truth. You always said I should tell the truth."

Mrs. Miller sniffed. "I don't like that kind of truth." She then proceeded to refuse his phone calls and had him disinherited. But finally motherhood won out and a year later his telephone rang.

"Is my son there?" asked Mrs. Miller.

"*I'm* here, if that's what you mean," said Merle.

"That's what I mean," said the older and wiser Mrs. Miller, who asked him to come home for Christmas. "But what will the neighbors say?" asked Merle.

Mrs. Miller shot back with comic timing, "We've already discussed that and we don't think you will do 'anything' while you are here."

Merle expresses tremendous sympathy and understanding concerning the position into which his "truth" put his mother. "I could not deprecate her," he says. "It was a difficult thing for her—especially given her age and background. I think she has handled it pretty well. Of course, she still disapproves and whenever she telephones me long distance, her first words to me are, 'Merle—are you alone?' Because, of course, that's what she really wants."

✳

## OH, NEVER MIND

Actor Leonard Frye elected to play an outrageously campy, blatantly "minty" homosexual in the controversial play *Boys in the Band*. His parents attended the opening and Leonard was a little worried about their reaction. They came backstage after and talked around the play, discussing the dressing room, etc. Finally, Leonard said, "Well, Mother, did you like the play? Did you understand it?"

His mother waved her hand. "Well, I don't know. I don't even understand the Vietnam War!"

# ENOUGH IS ENOUGH

The story goes that Truman Capote was once living briefly with his mother and receiving phone calls from friends. Some of these were males who spoke in deep voices but left messages that "Miss So-and-So" had called.

One day Mrs. Capote took a call when Truman was out. "Tell him Miss Bankhead called," said Tallulah. Mrs. Capote lost her temper, "I want you boys to stop that. I've had quite enough. If you can't use your right names, don't leave them at all!"

\*

# HISTORICAL IMPERATIVE

Martin Green's book *Children of the Sun* was subtitled, "A Narrative of 'Decadence' in England after 1918." It borrowed its title from the philosophy of Johann Jakob Bachofen, and Green meant it to refer to the *Sonnenkinder*, the brilliant, influential generation of young men who, in the aftermath of World War I, refused to become husbands, fathers, and heads of households. They cultivated alternative styles of youthful manhood, such as that of the dandy, the rogue, and the naïf. (Not always homosexual, the *Sonnenkinder* were nevertheless influenced by the aestheticism around them and many of the *Sonnenkinder were* homosexuals.)

Involved in this assessment are such talents as Evelyn Waugh, Harold Acton, Cecil Beaton, Christopher Isherwood, Graham Greene, Oliver Messel, Brian Howard, Peter Quennell, Alan Pryce-Jones, Randolph Churchill, Guy Burgess, Kim Philby, the Sitwells, Nancy Mitford, Nancy Cunard, Cyril Connolly, Donald MacLean, W. H. Auden, and many more. Not all were alike—some were dazzling public figures such as the Prince of Wales and Lawrence of Arabia—but Green sees them influenced by the cult of the *Sonnenkind*.

The *Sonnenkinder* revolted against their fathers. While some mothers were powerful influences on their sons, Green calls it "an influence too close, too insidious, to be objectified, depicted and repudiated, like that of the fathers. Their mothers were figures of affection and reassurance to nearly all of these people; however they may have undermined their children's confidence in their bolder gestures, they offered no significant challenge or inspiration. Beside the fathers, they counted for nothing. This is striking when one looks back to the then so-recent work of D. H. Lawrence, E. M. Forster, and Thomas Hardy in which the figure of the mother, or of woman, and of the earth, nature and life itself identified with woman, is so overwhelmingly important. That erotic movement, which had seemed in the years just before the war about to release the English imagination from its enchainment to the world of men, to redeem it from its slavish slothfulness, was completely defeated . . . it was the fathers who counted—as enemies. The world of men was undermined not only in the persons of the fathers (and families), but also in the schools (and other institutions)."

Green's fascinating book goes on to say that the *Sonnenkind* (not always homosexual, but influenced by homosexuality and aestheticism) "despite his brave show of independence, defiance, and brilliant innovation, really holds his power always by grace of the mother behind him, and that certainly seems to have been true of our two principal figures (the poets Harold Acton and Brian Howard) . . ."

*

# MORALS

Here's one from an anonymous donor in his own words:

During the furtive fifties, I was at a university in the Texas Bible Belt and was involved in a witch-hunt, the prey being homosexuals. Anyone connected with the Fine Arts Department was suspect.

Having the academic McCarthy finger pointed at me was not easy to take and I turned to my mother and stepfather who lived in a nearby city.

I called home and said I needed them, but was reluctant to say why on the phone. They quickly drove to see me and I explained privately to my stepfather what was going on at the campus. He went with me to the dean and said that most young men had some homosexual experience along the way and that my academic record seemed to be in excellent shape and if the school proceeded to harass his son, he would get a lawyer and call the local papers. The dean assured him I would in no way be bothered again.

Later, when my stepfather told my mother about the source of the trouble, her response was: "Thank God! I thought he had stolen something."

✳

# DAVID AND HIS MOTHER

As executive director of the Fortune Society, a helping organization for ex-convicts, New Yorker David Rothenberg devotes a good bit of his time advising former prison inmates to be open and honest about their time spent behind bars. In 1974, at the age of forty, David came to the realization that he himself was being less than forthright about a hidden aspect of his own life: his homosexuality. Before entering into a public discussion on this subject with a panel of gays on *The David Susskind Show* on TV, David wrote a private letter to his mother in Florida. Here is part of it:

> For the first time in my life, I am beginning to get a sense of contentment and of self-acceptance. This is important in *our* relationship, son to mother, mother to son. I have held back with you, filled my being with moody silences that I now realize were underlined with fears of rejection. It is my deep hope that as I have learned to accept myself, it will fill in some of the blank spaces of our friendship and love.
>
> This is all by way of saying to you that I have, at last, accepted a truth about myself—and in so doing, it makes my life bearable. An enormous weight has been lifted. It is that I am, and always have been, homosexual.
>
> Growing up in New Jersey—unknowing and affected by small-town mores, I felt cursed . . . Now I have learned that I am a total human being with much to be proud of, much which I can offer, and my personal sexual orientation is a problem only if I permit it to be and if I am obsessed with the rejection of an unknowing outside world. . . .
>
> I have talked with parents of other gay people about talking or sharing this fact with you. They have urged me to do so. I do so, in hope that you will accept me as I have accepted myself—and, in turn, am a happier person. Parents, I have heard, often lament, "Where have I failed?", but since my life has been filled with pur-

pose and meaning *your* question should be, rather, "How have I contributed to this success?" . . .

This letter is written to you with an enormity that I hope you can understand, with tears running down my face because at last I am asking you, whom I love with every ounce of breath, to accept me as I am, not in pretense.

I am your son, with a growing sense of freedom, who loves you.

David Rothenberg says his mother's response was a loving and caring letter in which she stated that "she cried when she read the letter, because of all the years that I felt I could not share with her. I went down and spent some days with her—and it was the first time in thirty years that we were able to have a totally honest conversation."

※

# QUESTIONS

People telling these stories generally preferred not to identify their mothers for fear of humiliating them. But there is one about a mother talking to her sister, discussing two local gay boys who ran an antique shop. In spite of changing times, the mother said, "But Louise, what is it they do?"

Her sister replied, "I think it's something oral."

The mother: "Well—whatever could they possibly say to each other??!!"

※

# THE UNUSUAL HARRY
# STACK SULLIVAN

Harry Stack Sullivan, who died in 1949, has been called "the most original influential Americanborn psychiatrist . . . the foremost developer of what is known as the interpersonal approach to psychiatry." His influence is so pervasive (but unrecognized) that Leston Havens of the Harvard Medical School has said that Sullivan "almost secretly" dominates American psychiatry.

Yet Sullivan was a homosexual, who grew up on an upstate New York farm. The predominant figure in his childhood was his mother. In his biography, *Harry Stack Sullivan, The Man and His Work*, A. H. Chapman says of Harry's mother: "She was a continually complaining, semi-invalid, and Sullivan bore the major brunt of her laments and unhappiness. She much resented the fact that in Ireland her family, the Stacks, had produced mainly educators, physicians, lawyers, priests and other professional and middle-class people, but had sunk in social, educational, and economic status upon immigration to America. Moreover, she felt that her social state had been further lowered, or at least had been made irreparable, by the failures of her husband, who never rose above the level of a factory worker and a poor farmer. Throughout his childhood she unloaded on her son her helpless anger, her tales of her family's former prominence, and impractical dreams of a better future. Sullivan many years later stated bitterly that he had escaped the problems of being an only child because his mother never took the trouble to notice the characteristics of her son, but used him as a coatrack on which to hang 'an elaborate pattern of illusions.'"

*

# GAY MOMS

Jarred by an observation made at a gay community meeting in New York City in 1976 that "if they were really lesbians they wouldn't be mothers," a group of lesbian feminist mothers decided to launch their own activist organization. Comprised of gay mothers and their children, lesbians who want to be parents, and gay women working in the child care and teaching fields, they call themselves, "Dykes and Tykes."

*

# A STRUGGLE

Laura Z. Hobson's novel *Consenting Adult* opens with a letter from a teen-aged boy telling his mother that he is a homosexual. The rest of the book concerns the mother's struggle to come to terms with this revelation, in particular with her own agonizing self-accusations. Here is Ms. Hobson's rendering of a train of thought familiar to many mothers of gays:

> No matter how often she was given a reprieve by something she read, it never remained in force for long. The next expert she came upon would rescind the reprieve and doom her once again . . . Now there was a rapid proliferation of new articles and books on homosexuality, and each time she came across another rejection of mother-fixation as too simplistic, she would again feel that blessed exoneration, a gift, a benison.
>
> But never did this freedom from blame become a fixed star in her emotional cosmos. On dark nights that star would no longer be in the heavens to guide her. If she asked herself why it should matter so much, this exoneration, she would think, I do not know why it matters so much but it matters. I could not bear it if it was I who did this to him. And then she would grow ashamed that she should be so avid to establish her own "innocence."
>
> She felt the slow rise of shame now and thought, It's nobody's guilt, it's nobody's innocence, it happened, it is life.

✳

# A MOTHER STEPS OVER THE LINE

Mothers of gays often dwell just as timorously in the shadows as their sons and daughters. An articulate exception is Mrs. Betty Fairchild of Denver who has progressed from dismayed shock to warm acceptance of her son's homosexuality. Perhaps the nation's most visible mother of a gay, Mrs. Fairchild makes countless appearances on radio and TV on behalf of the nationwide "Parents of Gays" organization and has written a widely circulated booklet for the mothers and fathers of homosexuals. Says Mrs. Fairchild: "One of the things we work toward in our groups is that [homosexuality] really doesn't matter. The past is past. It's much more effective not to ask, 'Why did this happen?' but to ask, 'What can I do now to help him or her?'—to devote energy to the present. Once people believe that homosexuality is a variation on human sexuality, it loses its negative connotation."

# CALL OF THE WILDE

Lord Alfred Douglas, whose relationship with Oscar Wilde precipitated the trial which ultimately sent the playwright to prison, has often been pictured as vain, shallow, and selfish. Yet even in the Victorian era of repression in which Wilde and Douglas lived, "Bosie," as Douglas was called, wrote a generous and fervid defense of homophile friendship to his mother, the Marchioness of Queensberry, after she begged him to break the Wilde relationship off. This is a part of the letter he wrote to her from Egypt in 1893 explaining why he would not and could not do what she asked:

"If I looked upon you as an ordinary mother or an ordinary woman, I should do what sons generally do when they disagree with their mothers on a vital point, shrug my shoulders, drop the subject and say to myself, 'what can one expect, they are all the same, unreasoning, illogical, it is no use talking.' It is just because I do not think this about you, and because I know you to be different from ordinary women and vastly superior to them . . . that I write and reopen a subject on which perhaps you think everything has been said that can be said. And in doing this I have two objects in view, and I cannot say which is the most important, one is to defend my friend and to try and get you to treat him and think of him with ordinary fair play and common justice, the second is to try and remove you from a position which is unworthy of you. . . .

"Now in the first place you said to me the other night . . . that even I had never tried to make you think that Oscar Wilde was a *good* man. In answer to that I say 'have I ever tried to make you think that any of my friends were good, have I not all my life been consistent in my desire to protest against the dividing of people into good and bad?' Oscar Wilde says in his preface to Dorian Gray 'There is no such thing as a moral or immoral book, a book is well written or badly written, that is all.' Now transpose that principle a little and it is equally true of men, and it is my way of looking at men. 'There is no such thing as a moral or immoral man, a man is well written or badly written, that is all.' . . .

"Here I should like by the way to point out to you a curious thing. It was not you that taught me to see that a good man can be splendid, it was not the pastors and masters of my youth, it was not Francis with his dissertations on Sociology, no it was simply Oscar Wilde who taught it to me and no one else. And again who was it who taught me to believe if not absolutely in a God and the Christian religion, at least in the possibility of them, who taught me that it was ignorant and vulgar to scoff at mysteries which one did not understand, who animated for me the dry bones of the ugly dull religion I was brought up in, the religion which I had by the time I was eighteen flung aside with contempt and derision? Not you, and the good people who surrounded me, not even the good Ottley at Oxford for whom I had such a strong admiration, no, again simply Oscar Wilde. This is the man who according to you has ruined my soul. Why, I tell you I don't believe I had a soul before I met him. He has taught me everything that I know that is worth knowing, he has taught me to judge of things by their essential points, to know what is fine from what is low and vulgar, it is owing to him that I am able to admire Newman on the one hand, Milton on the other. The high priest of mystery and the propagandist of low church puritanism. These are the big things, now look at the smaller points. Why have I given up gambling and betting and going to race-meetings? Simply because Oscar Wilde told me that it was unworthy of me, that it was too ordinary, too silly. What have you got to accuse him of? You know perfectly well that he did not *teach* me to be extravagant.

"Then to return to the subject of the goodness, on which you lay so much stress. When you wrote that letter to Fleming in which the unfortunate expression occurred that Oscar Wilde saw, I remember being both astonished, upset and very angry . . . I remember I sat down and wrote you an awful letter, full of bitter words, a letter that must have pained you very much. I refused to show it to Oscar Wilde, for a long time, but finally he got it, read it and tore it up at once, he begged me not to write at all. I remember what he said exactly it was this 'After all Bosie nobody has a right to be unkind to his mother'. . . .

"And now let me ask you, what you propose to give me in exchange for this man, where am I to go for my quickening? Who is going to 'feed my soul with honey of sweet bitter thought'? Who is going to make me happy when I am sad depressed and ill at ease? Who is going to transport me out of the tedious world into a fairyland of fancy, conceit, paradox and beauty by the power of a golden speech? (A thing that you have never heard, for want of sympathy in a listener completely mars his conversation). What do you propose to give me instead? That is what I ask. I am spoilt for society. I am a bohemian by nature, and must remain one. Why can't you leave us alone, why can't you help me to do what I must do? Be nice to my friend, be just and kind. Your present attitude towards him is so banal, illogical, so shallow. Do try and look at the thing from another point of view. Remember for instance, that Oscar Wilde's mother exists as well as mine, that she loves her son just as you do yours, and that perhaps she has something to say on the subject which might put the thing in a different light. Believe me there is nothing so ludicrous, touching as it might be, as the one sided point of view of a mother, its always *her* son who is being led astray, other people are all brutes and blackguards. There is one more thing that I must say something about, that is that you cannot do anything against the power of my affection for Oscar Wilde and of his for me. I am passionately fond of him, and he of me. . . . There is nothing I would not do for him, and if he dies before I do I shall not care to live any longer. The thought of such a thing makes everything black before my eyes. Surely there is nothing but what is fine and beautiful in such a love as that of two people for one another, the love of the disciple and the philosopher. I think when Oscar's life comes to be written, as the life of a man of genius and a man who has stamped his age, it will be remembered and written about as one of the most beautiful things in the world, as beautiful as the love of Shakespeare and the unknown Mr. W. H. or that of Plato and Socrates, and far more beautiful than the love of Alcibiades for Socrates . . .

"I cannot say any more now, so goodby. Please try and like my friend who is so dear to me.

> With heaps of love
> Ever your very loving son
> Bosie"

✳

# INCREDULOUS

Some years ago, when a revealing film biography of Oscar Wilde played in New York, writer Frank Gehrecke occupied a seat behind two white-haired, motherly types. The ladies watched the dramatization of Wilde's love affair with young Lord Alfred Douglas without a whisper, but when they walked up the aisle after the movie, one of them did have a comment to make. "I heard," she confided to her friend, "there's a man like that living right here in New York City."

This incredulity on the part of mothers emerges as a recurring theme. The story surfaces in various forms, some no doubt apocryphal. After emerging from the closet, Merle Miller received a deluge of mail from secret homosexuals who wanted to tell him of their feelings, experiences, and aspirations. One boy wrote to say he had taken his mother to see the movie *The Boys in the Band* hoping she would "get the message" about his life.

He asked his mother afterward how she liked the film. "Well," said the mother, "I thought it was wonderful. I know there are people like that. I think there must be about fifty of them in Chicago, Los Angeles, and New York."

✳

These days, mothers are getting smarter. A mother I know recently saw a well-known actor on TV, one with a reputation as a closet gay. The mother said knowingly to her grown children: "That one—he's one of those, you know, a homosexualist."

The children were shocked and a little embarrassed. "How do you know that, Mother?"

Mother sniffed. "I just know. But we must be tolerant. You know they can't help it, those homosexualists. It's something in their throats."

✳

# PAINFULLY OUT OF THE CLOSET

Dave Kopay, ten-year veteran running back for the San Francisco Forty-Niners, Detroit Lions, Washington Redskins, New Orleans Saints and Green Bay Packers shocked the sports world in December 1975, when he became the first professional athlete to reveal his homosexuality. In a subsequent autobiography, he revealed some of the torments involved in that decision, including the following scene with his mother and father:

"You keep asking me why I'm going to an analyst. Well, I've been very depressed, and I've told you that. I'm trying to figure out why I'm so depressed and so fearful of everything. Look," I finally said, "I'm a homosexual."

My mother sat there, stunned. "David, you are not a homosexual." I said, "Mother. I know I am." Dad seemed very calm about it . . . "Well," he said, "there's nothing I can do about it now."

Mother then became hysterical. She yelled at me, "Why do you feel this way? Why are you saying this? Are you blaming this on me?" I said, "I'm not blaming anybody, Mother. It's a fact." She asked if Mary Ann Riley knew. I said she did. She asked if my other friends knew. I said they did.

"Look," I said, crying myself by then, "sometimes there are no explanations." Mother was screaming, "You're not, you're not . . . David, when did this happen? . . . . when you went away to school?" I told her I had been a homosexual for a long time, that homosexuality wasn't uncommon among professional ball players. She asked about Ted Robinson. I told her he and I had slept together. "I hope he burns in hell," she said. I told her that was a horrible thing to say. "He made you a homosexual." "No, he definitely did not make me a homosexual."

"I created you and I can destroy you," she said, and then I grabbed her and we just held each other for a long time, with her sobbing, "No, no, no . . ." As I was leaving she said, "I never want to see you again." I turned to my father. "How do you feel?" "You heard what your mother said."

From The David Kopay Story

✳

# INTO THE SUNSHINE

Kopay's co-author elected to make the public disclosure of his own homosexuality by way of an open letter to his mother in the March 1975 issue of *Ms*. These are the letter's closing paragraphs:

"And so, Mother, I hope you understand why I found it necessary not just to say all this, but to say it publicly. I have tried to overcome the years of blaming myself, blaming you and the environment I was born in, and tried to live happily with myself. Now I know that my 'problems' are hardly unique, that many heterosexual men and women suffer just as much trying to live honestly with themselves. But looking back now, I don't think there was any route to who I am other than the one I had to take. And I rather like myself now.

"You came out of a backwoods Baptist culture. Your father taught himself to read and write, then became a narrow fundamentalist preacher. My own father never read an entire book. But you instilled in me a real and lasting yearning for a finer life that included music and literature, good friends, new places, people, experiences.

"You know something, Mother? Recently, I actually fulfilled your dream of following springtime around the world. I'm writing now to say thanks, Mother, thanks for whatever influence you exerted in getting me here, in making me different from all those others who never even wanted to go anywhere.

"Your loving son, Perry Deane."

The writer's mother, he says, answered with warmth and understanding. "Come out of the shadows of shame and guilt," she wrote her son. "Live your life in the sunshine. Love, Mother."

※

# VICE VERSA

The emphasis in this chapter has been on responses of mothers to homosexuality in general and in particular as it involved their children. The reverse situation also exists—the responses of a son or daughter to the homosexuality of mother.

One of the most fascinating examples of this in recent years was *Portrait of a Marriage*, the 1973 memoir by Nigel Nicolson about his parents, Harold Nicolson and Victoria (Vita) Sackville-West. Though both parents had homoerotic relationships outside their marriage, Nicolson's book concentrates its greatest attention on the attachments of his mother.

Vita Sackville-West's son had been sketchily aware of his mother's romance with a friend, Violet Trefusis, but he did not learn the full passionate extent of it until after her death in 1962 when he found a locked Gladstone bag in her sitting room in the family home at Sissinghurst. Slitting open the bag, Nicolson discovered the pages of an intimate autobiographical confession of the decade-long relationship. As Nicolson read the manuscript through, he found himself so stirred by its candid simplicity and implicit plea for forgiveness and compassion that he recognized it immediately as "a document unique in the vast literature of love." Far from "tarnishing the memory" of his mother, "it burnished it."

After both his father and his mother's female lover died, Nicolson decided to publish the memoir, believing that "an experience of this kind need no longer be regarded as shameful or unmentionable." In his completed book, he tells not only of his mother's involvement with Violet Trefusis (this came to a climax when he himself was only three years old) but of her later gentle brief love affair with fellow novelist Virginia Woolf. The real heart of the book, however, is the love which his basically homosexual parents had for one another and how it "made out of a non-marriage, a marriage that succeeded beyond their dreams."

# Mothers and Guilt

Step on a crack break your mother's back.

Children's walking rhyme

This chapter doesn't really need an introduction. Everybody knows that mothers are the classic guilt-creators. Children also function in reverse, causing mothers to feel guilty. (See the Louise Nevelson and Liv Ullmann stories in "Work, Work, Work!")

The following section contains two of the finest contemporary satires on mothers and guilt ever created—the Nichols and May dialogue of the space scientist son on the phone to his mother, and Paula Scher's brilliantly thought out "Mother Mafia" article. Guilt over mother has also overtaken Neil Simon in almost every one of his plays as well as Dan Greenburg in his books. Few children escape.

Those of us who have enjoyed the benefits of psychoanalytic therapy are partially "on" to ourselves as to *why* mother can make us feel so guilty, or why we feel so guilty in any case. I don't know that the guilt over and from mother ever completely goes away. We simply learn to deal with it.

I can still feel my insides squinch up and my heart go into pang just recalling an incident of my early life. My older brother, thirteen, came to me with his entire Christmas allowance when I was about eight, asking me to give up half my gift money to go in with him and buy a bottle of perfume for Mother. This "expensive" trip to the corner drug store would have taken half our allowances, leaving only half for everyone else we needed to remember. I selfishly refused and James then spent his entire sum on the perfume alone. As I gave Mother some dinky little item costing one tenth of my carefully parceled-out Christmas money, I was totally rebuked by James's big blue bottle of Evening in Paris nestled under the tree. This "gift of the magi" had left him with nothing for anyone else, but his gesture to Mother had been magnificent and enhanced his already paragonlike status in my eyes to the point of unbearability.

So I felt terribly guilty about James and guilty about my selfishness and guilty about not loving Mother enough to make a sacrifice. I felt especially guilty after I tried to explain to her why I had not gone along with James in his insane generosity and she hugged and kissed me, saying, "Darling, it doesn't matter—it's the thought that counts." I knew she didn't mean that and had come to love James best.

My brother and I still speak in spite of this guilt trip laid on by his selfless action (now long forgotten by him) but I have never gotten over the incident. And, of course, IT WAS ALL MOTHER'S FAULT—for being so sweet, so understanding, and simply for existing and being Mother.

*

## THESE ARE THE GUILT JOKES

A mother is cleaning her apartment, alone, humming to herself. The phone rings.

MAN'S VOICE: "Hi, Ma, I'm at the station. I'm coming right over."
MOTHER: "That's wonderful!"
MAN: "Do you still live on Seventy-second Street?"
MOTHER: "No, I'm on Ninety-first."
MAN: "Listen, is this Mrs. Seltzer?"
MOTHER: "No, it's Mrs. Green."
MAN: "Oh, I'm sorry—I've got the wrong number."
MOTHER: "Well, wait a minute. Does this mean that you're not coming over?"

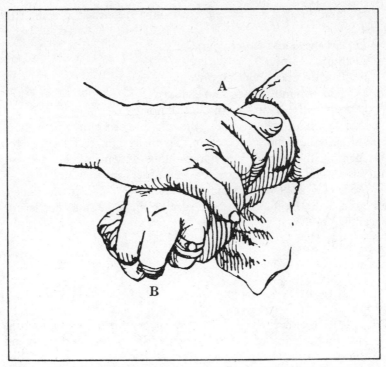

FIG. I: PROPER POSITION OF HANDS DURING EXECUTION OF DAILY SIGH.

Note: **(A)** Cross-Over Grip of Right Hand on Left Wrist, **(B)** Edge of Plain Linen Handkerchief tucked around Index Finger to facilitate tear-dabbing.

From *How to be a Jewish Mother* by Dan Greenburg

# YOU'LL BE SORRY WHEN I'M DEAD*

Dan Greenburg's fine work on "The Technique of Basic Suffering" must *not* be restricted in use to only Jewish mothers. He has suggested the Basic Facial Expression to be practiced before the mirror and if anyone catches the mother at it, she is to say:

"I'm fine, it's nothing at all, it will go away."

* It is assumed that Dan felt this was too obviously well known as a mother reflex to even mention it.

He also suggests studying with tape recorder certain key phrases:

1. "Go ahead and enjoy yourself."
2. "But be careful."
3. "Don't worry about me."
4. "I don't mind staying home alone."
5. "I'm glad it happened to me and not you."

Dan cautions: "Remember, the child is an unformed, emotionally unstable, ignorant creature. To make him feel secure, you must continually remind him of the things which you are denying yourself on his account, especially when others are present."

He also says: "Don't let him know you fainted twice in the supermarket from fatigue. But make sure he knows you're not letting him know."

*

## BUT YOU *WILL* BE SORRY

Writer Patti Goldstein says, "I hated to get up on winter mornings so I would lie in bed and reach out with my foot and open and slam drawers to make my mother think I was up and dressing. She would come to my room finally and stand there in the cold in a thin little nightgown, shivering.

" 'I'm so cold,' she'd say, 'Please get up.'

" 'Put on a bathrobe!' I'd say impatiently.

" 'How can you be so cruel?' she'd ask me, shivering. Then she'd always say, 'You'll be sorry one day because you are going to have twins just like you.' "

*

## GUILTY LAUGHTER

The so-called "silent generation" of the 1950s wasn't completely quiet. Two young undergraduates from the University of Chicago named Mike Nichols and Elaine May spoke out in a series of improvisations which sparked hysterical waves of "recognition" laughter in everyone who heard them. The dialogue following dating from the post-Sputnik period when America's brightest young space engineers were applying their expertise to John F. Kennedy's dream of putting a man on the moon, has become a classic in the literature of mother's guilt-provoking. Onstage and on records, Nichols and May provided us with the single most frequently mentioned and recalled "guilt" laugh of our time in their "Mother and Son" dialogue:

HE: Hello.

SHE: Hello, Arthur. This is your mother. Do you remember me?

HE: Mom, hi, I . . . I was just gonna call you. Is that a funny thing? You know that I had my hand on the phone to call . . .

SHE: Arthur, you were supposed to call me last Friday.

HE: Mother, darling, I just didn't have a second, and I could have cut my throat. I was *so* busy . . .

SHE: Arthur, I sat by the phone all day Friday . . .

HE: I know, I know. It was just work work work. But, darling . . .

SHE: And all day Friday night . . .

HE: I kept thinking, I gotta call Mom.

SHE: All day Saturday, all day Sunday.

HE: Mom, believe me, I felt . . .

SHE: Your father said to me, "Phyllis, eat something, you'll faint." I said, "No, Harry, No. I don't want my mouth to be full when my son calls."

HE: Mother! I was sending up Vanguard! I didn't have a second.

SHE: Well, it's always something, isn't it?

HE: Okay, honey, look . . .

SHE: You know, Arthur, I'm sure that all the other scientists there have mothers, you know? And I'm sure that they all find time, after their breakfasts or before their count-off . . .

HE: Down.

SHE: To pick up a phone and call their mothers.

HE: Honey, listen, now you have me on the phone . . . Mom . . .

SHE: You know I worry.

HE: Well, I do. That's the point.

SHE: I keep reading in the paper how you keep losing them.

HE: Mother! *I* don't lose them!

SHE: I nearly went out of my mind.

HE: Okay, honey, now . . .

SHE: I thought: what if they're taking it out of his pay!

HE: Okay, but Mother, look, darling, please. Just tell me how you are. Tell me how you are. How are ya?

SHE: I'm sick.

HE: I'm sorry to hear it. I really am. What's wrong?

SHE: Nothing. You know what it is, honey. The same thing it's always been.

HE: Yeah, sure.

SHE: It's my nerves.

HE: Yeah, yeah, yeah.

SHE: And I went to the doctor, and he told me right out, "Listen, Mrs. White." And he said, "Who are you fooling?"

HE: Yeah, yeah, yeah.

SHE: "You're a very nervous woman. A very highstrung woman."

HE: Well, God knows, that's true.

SHE: "You cannot stand the slightest aggravation."

HE: Yeah, sure, yeah.

SHE: I said, "Doctor, I know that. But you see, Doctor, I have this son. It's the truth. The boy is not lying. He's very busy. You see, Doctor, he's too busy to pick up the phone and call his mother."

HE: Honey, listen, Mom. Mom!

SHE: And when I said that to him, that man turned pale. He said, "Mrs. White, I have been a doctor thirty-five years and I have never heard of a son too busy to call his mother." That's what he said to me, Arthur. (*Pause*) And that man is a doctor!

HE: Mom. Mother. Please, dear. Will you just tell me. What did the doctor say they're going to do with you?

SHE: I may be in the hospital for a while.

HE: The hospital? Well, what are they going to do?

SHE: Well, they'll X-ray my nerves . . .

HE: Mother, why didn't you let me know? All you had to do was drop me a line . . .

SHE: I didn't want to aggravate you.

HE: Mother! How could I not aggravate myself?

SHE: Forget it. How's your hangnail?

HE: Mother, please. Just don't worry.

SHE: Arthur, what does that mean? Honey, what does that mean, "Don't worry"?

HE: Nothing, actually. I don't know. I just said the first thing that came into my head. It was a mistake.

SHE: Arthur, listen to me. I'm a mother.

HE: Yeah, well, that's the thing. You know, I should have realized . . . but I didn't. It was a mistake. I'm sorry, now.

SHE: You're very young. Some day. Some day, Arthur, you'll get married . . .

HE: Mom . . .

SHE: And you'll have children of your own.

HE: Mom . . .

SHE: And, honey, when you do, I only pray that they make you suffer the way you're making me. That's all I pray, Arthur. That's a mother's prayer.

HE: Okay, Mom. Thanks for calling.

SHE: You're very sarcastic.

HE: Mother, I'm doing my best. Now you called me on the telephone. I tried to explain how busy . . .

SHE: I'm sorry. I'm sorry that I bothered you. And look, I hope I didn't make you feel bad.

HE: Are you kidding? I feel awful!

SHE: Oh, honey. If I could believe that I'd be the happiest mother in the world!

HE: Oh, Mother, it's true. What do you think? I feel crummy.

SHE: Arthur, honey, why don't you call me, sweetheart? Look, Arthur, I know that I nag you. Look, I'm a nagging mother. What are you gonna do? No. I'm kidding. Honey, you know, you're my baby. And Arthur, you're the only baby I've got. And, honey, no matter how old you get, when you get to be eighty years old, you're going to be my baby. You know? And when you don't call me, sweetheart, I can't help it. I worry. So is it so hard to pick up a phone and call your mommy? Please, baby, please!

HE: (*baby talk*) Well, I will, I pwomise.

SHE: Do you really promise?

HE: (*baby talk*) I weally will I pwomise.

SHE: It would make your mummy so happy!

HE: (*baby talk*) If mommy's happy then he's happy. Okay, Mommy.

SHE: And Mommy wants to wish you lots of luck with your rocket.

HE: Thank you, Mommy.

SHE: And remember that I love you?

HE: I love you too, Mommy. 'Bye, Mommy. Nonny nooney. Nonny nooney. . . .

271

# GWEN'S LAW

Do not join Encounter groups.
If you enjoy being made to feel inadequate
call your Mother.

—Gwen Davis

\*

# EARL'S PEARL

It was columnist Earl Wilson who reported the case of a well-fixed Broadwayite whose mother called him one day long-distance to say she wanted to visit a sister in another city. The fare was $105. "Fine, Mother," the son told her. "I'll send you a check for $100." Replied Mother: "Thanks, and don't you worry, son, I'll get the $5 from somebody else."

\*

# SIMON SAYS

In Neil Simon's comedy *Come Blow Your Horn*, the protagonist, Buddy, has a mother who is described as "a woman who has managed to find a little misery in the best of things. Sorrow and trouble are the only things that can make her happy. She was born in this country, dresses in fine fashion and in general her speech and appearance are definitely American. But she thinks Old World, Superstitions, beliefs, customs still cling to her. Or rather she clings to them . . ."

Buddy is about to have his first experience with a girl at the opening of Act Two, but his mother picks this moment to drop in on him. Their dialogue becomes a litany of emotions, discussions of food, and guilt. Snatches of it follow:

BUDDY: Do you feel any better?
MOTHER: When did I ever feel better?
BUDDY: Mom, I hope you understand, but I've got this appointment tonight.
MOTHER: Did you have dinner yet?
BUDDY: What? Dinner? Yes. Yes, I had a sandwich.

MOTHER: A sandwich? For supper? That's how you start the minute you're away?

(*Buddy protests that a girl he knew in school is coming by and they are writing a story together.*)

MOTHER: What's the matter? She's more important than me?

BUDDY: Mom, no one's more important than you.

MOTHER: How can you say that when you worry me like this? I know you. You won't eat unless the food's in front of you.

BUDDY: *No one* eats unless the food's in front of them. Mom, I haven't got time . . .

MOTHER: (*Hurt*) You want me to go, I'll go.

(*Buddy and his mother have a tormented discussion about his father while he encourages her to leave.*)

MOTHER: Maybe I am too easygoing. Maybe if I were like some mothers who forbid their children to do everything, I'd be better off today.

BUDDY: No, Mom. You're the best mother I ever had . . . Do you feel any better?

MOTHER: How do I know? I feel too sick to tell.

(*Buddy gets his mother on her feet going toward the door, promising to come to dinner the next night, whereupon a litany about what to fix ensues.*)

MOTHER: What'll I make?

BUDDY: What?

MOTHER: For dinner? What do you want to eat?

BUDDY: Anything. *I* don't care. Good night, Mom.

MOTHER: I want to make something you like now that you're not home.

BUDDY: I like everything. Roast beef, okay?

MOTHER: All right good. (*She starts, then stops*) You had roast beef tonight.

BUDDY: I can eat it again.

MOTHER: I could get a turkey. A big turkey.

BUDDY: Okay! Turkey! Wonderful!

MOTHER: It doesn't really pay for one night.

BUDDY: (*He can't take it anymore. He practically screams*) Mom, for Pete's sakes, it doesn't matter.

MOTHER: (*Near tears*) What are you yelling? I'm only trying to make you happy. Who do I cook for, myself? I haven't eaten anything besides coffee for ten years.

# FANTASY LIFE

DR. WAYNE W. DYER:

Merely reaching adulthood does not put an end to parental manipulation by guilt. I have a friend who is fifty-two years old. He is a pediatrician of Jewish extraction married to a non-Jewish woman. He keeps his marriage a secret from his mother, because he is afraid it might "kill her" or more aptly, he might kill her. He maintains a separate apartment with all of the household trimmings for the sole purpose of meeting with his eighty-five-year-old mother every Sunday. She does not know that he is married and owns his own home where he lives six days a week. He plays this little game out of fear and guilt about being married to "Shiksa." Although he is a fully grown man who is highly successful in his own professional world, he is still controlled by his mother. Each day he talks to her from his office and lives out his bachelor fantasy.

*Your Erroneous Zones*

\*

The previous story reminds me of another true one told by an analyst of a patient whose mother wanted him to be a doctor. He became a lawyer instead, and today, in his successful busy law offices, keeps a special telephone which his secretary answers in this manner: "Dr. So-and-So's office." The number is the one the adult lawyer has given to his mother!

\*

# DEAR ABBY

My mother has been in heaven for four years. I was eight years old when the Lord took her away, but I can never forget a certain happening.

She once asked my sister or me to do a small chore for her, like carrying out the trash. We argued so much about whose turn it was to do it that Mama sent us both outside and she did it herself.

Please put this in your column for girls who are lucky enough to have their mothers. Love

MISSING MAMA
From the column of
Abigail Van Buren

✳

My mother got up every morning at 5 A.M. no matter what time it was.

—Sam Levenson

✳

# TAKING IT HARD

The experience of child-rearing can produce guilt feelings in the hearts of even the saintliest of mothers. Witness Mother Elizabeth Seton, proclaimed by Pope Paul in 1975 as the first American-born saint.

Born in New York City in 1774 and raised an Episcopalian, she didn't take her vows in the Catholic Church until after she had already been married and widowed, with five children. As the founder of the first American community of the Catholic Sisters of Charity, she was recognized in her lifetime for her spirituality and special grace, but despite her spreading reputation for holiness, she brooded about her inadequacies as a mother.

She blamed herself, among other things, for her grown son William's terrible handwriting, pointing out in a letter to a friend that permitting him to suck his fingers in infancy had made them weak.

Mother Seton died at the age of forty-three well on her way to becoming a *saint*. So much for being a failed *mother* in her own eyes.

✳

# BATTERED CHILD SYNDROME

Though the mothers of what have come to be called "battered children" do not *always* suffer guilt pangs over the physical abuses they inflict, a large number of them do. Now that the subject of child abuse is at last beginning to receive wide study, the discovery has been made that many mothers who abuse their children physically suffered similar experiences in their own childhood. That this truly vicious circle can be broken has been proved by the success of group therapy sessions sponsored by a national organization called Parents Anonymous consisting of both mothers and fathers who habitually beat their children. Founded in 1969, the organization now has six hundred chapters in the United States alone. It maintains a twenty-four-hour-a-day toll-free hotline for information and emergency guidance. The number is 800-421-0353.

✳

# THE MOTHER MAFIA

## by Paula Scher

The power of mothers to control and manipulate their offspring is age-old and widely known. Therefore the Mother Mafia has existed since man began, but the classic organization, as we know it today, began in Italy, France, England, and the United States in the 1890s.

The Victorian era was the most repressive period that women had known. The role society gave them made manipulation difficult because they continually had to control their aggressions.

Emma Rice Thompson, born in Manchester, England, in 1857, was a key founder of the British Mother Mafia. She was married to a London stockbroker, and after the birth of her third son found that family control was slipping away from her. An avid reader, Emma Rice Thompson greatly admired *Oedipus Rex* and *Hamlet*, and it is believed that these two classic pieces of literature inspired an entire movement.

Mrs. Thompson set up regular Thursday Tea Meetings with the wives of prominent lawyers, doctors, lords and of course stockbrokers. At these teas, she and the other women, most notably Lady Olivia Prickett, mapped out a strategy for increased control and manipulation of families and ultimately the world.

THE INFAMOUS
EMMA RICE THOMPSON

## 10 POINT CREDO
## FOR CONTROL AND MANIPULATION

1. It is our assumption that the process of birth entitles all mothers to total loyalty, obedience, and homage from their offspring. It is essential that mothers continually remind their children of their great debt.

2. All children are inferior beings intellectually, socially, and culturally, and will never, during an entire lifetime, assume the knowledge and position of their mothers.

3. All female children who become parents are still technically children themselves. They cannot assume the full title of "Mother." However, it is assumed that throughout their lives they will receive the education to assume this role when their mother dies.

4. The only important commandment "Honor thy mother and father" means "Honor Thy Mother."

5. All mothers are natural martyrs by pain of birth and lifelong sacrifice. To betray your mother is to betray Christ.

6. An offspring can produce no success that is great enough to please his mother or ease his debt.

7. Successful offspring must provide for their mothers to the greatest extent they can. Monetary success is of the utmost importance second only to the acquisition of power.

8. Children who fail are never to be forgiven. If the children are failures their mothers will be dropped immediately from this organization. Mothers who condone or make excuses for failure in their children are to be blacklisted.

9. Mothers are all sisters moving toward a common goal—money, power, and very good jewelry. Status in our organization corresponds directly to wealth and power.

10. Mothers may express pride to one another in the success of the offspring, but never to the offspring directly. Pride may be expressed only when it has been acknowledged that the offspring is basically ignorant and inferior.

## THE MOMIA

Emma Rice Thompson's famous credo was published in 1892 and distributed throughout the world. In the summer of 1894 Mrs. Thompson and Lady Prickett made a lecture tour visiting New York, Philadelphia, Boston, Minneapolis, and San Francisco. American women joined the organization in droves. The New York coordinator of the Mother Mafia was Frances McKinley Powers, a childhood friend of Sara Delano Roosevelt. Powers and Roosevelt felt that the organization's credo, while strong in substance, was weak in technique. Powers proposed courses for mothers in guilt manipulation. However, Emma Rice Thompson felt that debt was a much stronger tool for manipulation and the guilt theory lacked finesse. The two women feuded over theory and ultimately the American organization broke away from its English counterpart with Frances McKinley Powers as its new leader. The organization was christened "THE MOMIA" or Mothers for Overbearing Manipulation of Infants and Adolescents. Powers and Roosevelt co-authored the Movement's universally acclaimed thesis, "Theories and Practices of Guilt Manipulation." The following are excerpts.

*On health:*
"Health is the key to guilt manipulation. All children are sensitive to the fact that their births may have in some way physically impaired their mothers. It is often helpful to create an age-old ailment that exists since the birth of each child such as a bad back, recurring headaches, tendency to faint, weak stomach, etc. Make the child know that he is responsible for these ailments. Manage to have attacks when the child is about to make a decision that does not concur with your beliefs or does something which is distasteful to you."

*On Marriage:*
"Marital arguments can be a helpful instrument in maintaining total guilt manipulation of your offspring. Make the child aware of the fact that he is responsible for all your marital difficulties and the cause of your unhappy life. It is often helpful to portray your husband as a brute and yourself as a helpless partner who can only succeed in protecting the child from the father's atrocities. It is also to your advantage to have your offspring assume that you live with your husband only because you want your child to have a normal home."

*On Martyrdom:*
"Martyrdom is the most essential of all the tools of guilt manipulation. True guilt can not be established without it. When serving meat, always take the burnt piece and let your child *know* that you took it. Make sure your child is aware of your life's sacrifices for his well-being. Constantly remind him of the times you missed fashionable balls or vacations because he was ill with a cold. If these cir-

cumstances never occur, invent them."

"Theories and Practices of Guilt Manipulation" was published in 1904 and quickly became an international best seller. It brought many converts, mainly immigrant women, who had recently arrived in the United States and wanted to improve their lot in life. The most successful converts (and most famous) were Jewish mothers who quickly mastered the craft and shortly gained total control of the A.M.A., the American Bar Association and L'Eggs Pantyhose. They still maintain control of these powerful organizations and probably have amassed the largest fortune in rhinestones and furs of any single ethnic branch of the MOMIA. But they were greatly outmatched by the Irish Branch of MOMIA which ignored the showy trappings of material wealth and moved instead to consolidate political power of all major cities in the United States, and most notably in Boston, Philadelphia, and New York. The Irish MOMIA controlled Tammany Hall for over fifty years and at the same time purchased most of Brooklyn and Eastern Long Island.

The MOMIA's control of Boston was even stronger and more powerful. Led by Rose Fitzgerald (later Kennedy), the Irish MOMIA has been able to dominate every aspect of life in Massachusetts. The Irish MOMIA controls all seaports in Massachusetts, and personally owns the largest fleet of commercial ships in the United States. Their interests in steel, coal, iron, and oil are as astounding as their ability to export and import those vital resources. By carefully placing their sons in strategic political positions they have influenced legislation to the extent that their transportation monopoly is the largest legal monopoly in the world.

Sara Delano Roosevelt, the co-founder of the United States MOMIA, was also the leader of the WASP chapter of the MOMIA; by far and away the richest chapter. WASP mothers manipulated themselves into control of the entire business and financial structure of the United States. They currently maintain total control of the entire American Automotive Industry, AT&T, and Coca-Cola; plus the entire agricultural market in the United States. The success of the WASP chapter has been attributed to the fact that they were able to project the mother as a symbol of what is wholesome and good in America. The connection of Mother to patriotism was a stroke of genius. To go against Mother is to go against America. In consolidating their economic empire they found it necessary to look for international markets for their products, which ultimately brought the United States out of isolationism.

Mom, apple pie, and the American flag became causes for young men to die for.

The MOMIA which controls the Pentagon, the CIA, the FBI, and the entire intelligence community has come under scrutiny since the Vietnam War. MOMIA interference has been shown in part to be responsible for United States intervention in Vietnam and Cambodia. To counter present criticism the MOMIA has launched a media assault, blaming the faults of the nation on the break-up of the old family structure. By convincing Americans of their need for good wholesome moral values, as exemplified by the ideals of motherhood, the MOMIA hopes to maintain its control and manipulation of the human race for at least another century.

## THE FUTURE

The MOMIA is currently looking for new and greater markets throughout the world to export its products. They are concentrating mainly on the Third World nations. Florida Washington and Daisy Johnson have been secretly working on the "Black MOMIA" which would be a sister organization to the WASP, Irish and Jewish MOMIA. The code name for the Black MOMIA is Giwanga Mofooka which means "Big Mother" in Ugandanese. Washington and Johnson have found it necessary to operate under a code name because women in the Third World have been ideologically repelled by major capitalist organizations which they feel are basically manipulative of their new and growing nations.

Women of the Third World tend to be anti-feminists because they are dependent on their men for social and monetary position in their new societies. Washington and Johnson have expanded and adapted the practices of guilt manipulation to suit the special needs of Third World Mothers.

The philosophy of Giwanga Mofooka guilt manipulation:

1. All men and children have been oppressed in the past because they never grasped the western world concept of "mother worship."

2. No established nation will respect a growing young nation unless the mothers of the nation appear to be well-dressed and have a reasonably good collection of jewelry and generally keep themselves nice.

3. Behind every successful free young nation there has been a suffering, staunch, aggressive mother. Therefore, Third World Mothers are owed a share of the new national wealth.

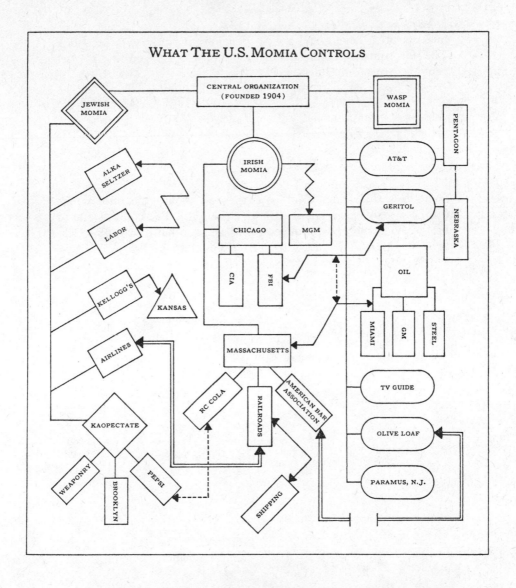

WHAT THE U.S. MOMIA CONTROLS

The success of Giwanga Mofooka is yet to be seen but the organization is strong and growing in numbers.

Other future projects of the MOMIA center around energy resource development, the search for extraterrestrial life and a continuing study in oceanography.

The Irish MOMIA is currently cultivating Antarctica where

their scientists have found a way of communicating with penguins. The scientists have confirmed the widely held suspicion that mother penguins are natural rulers.

*Push Pin Graphic*

❋

# THE REVERSE

Sometimes the saddest Mother stories of all are the ones where Mother has to accept rather than give the guilt. The child of one of Hollywood's most beautiful actresses leaped to her death off a California building. Tied neatly to her wrist was a tag reading, "Happy Mother's Day."

# Mothers and Death

Half an orphan is the fatherless child; whole orphan, the motherless.

Finnish proverb

The final severing of the child's most important early link in life—separation by death from the mother—is not the only trauma of life nor even the worst, but surely it is one of the great tragedies. It doesn't seem to matter whether the child is young, the parent young; the child middle-aged, the parent old, or what the age ratio. Hardly anyone can be indifferent to the loss of this parent and only a sadist would want to be the messenger of tidings of a mother's death.

On the other hand, I recall the untimely death at a young age of my friend Tammis Keefe. Her aging mother, alone at the funeral, broke my heart when she said, "The very worst thing that can happen is for a mother to outlive her child." Later, I was to find this is a commonly expressed sentiment. Aloise Steiner Buckley, matriarch of the famous Connecticut and New York family, has said: "I lost two daughters. That's the saddest thing that ever happened to me, even more than the death of my husband and I adored him. Never outlive your children. It's something you never get over." I am sure we have all felt the empathetic truth of this. Consider the five famous Sullivans who went down on the same ship in World War II. (After that, the Navy outlawed all siblings in one danger spot and the other armed forces followed suit.) And there are many sad examples, such as that of Rose Kennedy, who lost three sons and one daughter violently. It should be noted that there are words signifying bereaved conditions—widow, widower, orphan. But there is no word for a mother whose child has died.

My father's death, at age seventy-four, created an enormous sense of loss for me and shattered any illusions of youth and immortality. My mother's death—should I outlive her—will be even harder to bear. A friend of mine put it very well in telling of certain discussions with her analyst about her neurotic attachment and overconcern for her mother. The analyst said: "I hope you get this worked out better in the event that your mother should die before you."

There is no real way to soften up this chapter, but let's not get too morbid. I am reminded of the old joke about men at war on a great navy vessel. The first mate was a hard old salt, tough and calloused. One day a message came over the wireless that Ensign Parker's mother had died. The mate stepped to the ship's speaker, flipped the switch and yelled: "Now hear this! Now hear this! Ensign Parker's mother just died. That is all!"

The captain was aghast. He called the mate on the carpet and told him a message of a mother's death was not something to be given out lightly and that in the future he expected things to be handled with more tact.

The mate was abashed. As they steamed on, soon another message arrived. Seaman Baker's mother had passed away. The first mate flipped on the loudspeaker and barked: "Now hear this! Now hear this! All hands assemble on B deck at 1300 hours. That is all!"

At 1300 hours, the ship's crew stood in dress whites along the deck. The first mate stepped out before them and yelled: "Now hear this! Now hear this! All men whose mothers are living, take two paces forward. —NOT YOU, BAKER!!!!"

Like most mother's children, I dread the day, should it come, when *I* might be poor Seaman Baker.

※

# LAST WORDS

On the night of March 25, 1667, Samuel Pepys was, he recorded in his famous diary, "much troubled in my sleep of my being crying by my mother's bedside, laying my head over hers and crying, she almost dead and dying, and so waked." Two days later he received word that this was the day on which his mother had, indeed, died. Her last words: "God bless my poor Sam!"

❋

Last words of former Harvard president Charles W. Eliot before he died at the age of ninety-two:

"I see Mother."

❋

In 1973, under the auspices of the American Society of Psychical Research, Drs. Karlis Osis and Erendur Heraldsson began an extensive study in the United States and India of deathbed visions. Among their preliminary findings: In the United States, 61 per cent of the dying persons who experienced visions of human figures saw women—and in most of these instances, the woman was a mother. The apparition in almost all the cases seemed to be serving as a welcoming guide to the hereafter and the people who saw them appeared to die happily.

In India, only 23 per cent of the persons reporting deathbed visions saw mother-figures, but their responses were similar to the Americans. Says Dr. Osis: "All who saw apparitions of mother were in a positive mood."

❋

# IN PASSING

Here lies the body of Joan Carthew
Born at St. Columb, died at St. Cue;

Children she had five,
Three are dead, and two alive;
Those that are dead choosing rather
To die with their mother than live with their
    father.

Epitaph for St. Agnes,
Cornwall

285

# GRAY'S EPITAPH

Among the headstones in the seven-hundred-year-old cemetery at Stoke Poges which served as the inspiration for Thomas Gray's *Elegy in a Country Churchyard* there is a monument honoring the poet's mother. Gray himself wrote this inscription for it:

SHE HAD MANY CHILDREN OF WHOM ONLY ONE
HAD THE MISFORTUNE TO SURVIVE HER.

*

My mother was dead for five years before I knew that I had loved her very much.

Lillian Hellman in
*An Unfinished Woman*

*

# FIRST LADY LOSSES

First Lady Jane Appleton Pierce lost all of her three sons before she ever reached the White House. Her first boy died in infancy; the second was taken in a typhoid epidemic when he was four; the third, the family's beloved twelve-year-old Benny, was horribly mangled and killed in full view of his parents in a train wreck. Mrs. Pierce was inconsolable in her grief and, after her husband Franklin's inauguration as President, in 1853, secluded herself in the Executive Mansion almost completely. Much of her time was spent composing what Pierce's biographer, Roy Franklin Nichols, describes as "little pitiful pencil notes to her lost boy, reproaching herself for not having tried harder to express to him her great love." According to Nichols, she managed to convince her husband that Benny's death was the price God put on Pierce's winning the presidency.

First Lady Grace Goodhue Coolidge, on a July night just a little over five years after the death of her sixteen-year-old son Calvin, Jr., rose from her White House bed and set down the words to a poem which, she said later, "wrote itself." Published originally in *Good Housekeeping* in 1929, it has been reprinted many times:

## THE OPEN DOOR

You, my son,
Have shown me God.
Your kiss upon my cheek
Has made me feel the gentle touch
Of Him who leads us on.
The memory of your smile, when young,
Reveals His face,
As mellowing years come on apace.
And when you went before,
You left the Gates of Heaven ajar
That I might glimpse,
Approaching from afar,
The glories of His Grace.
Hold, Son, my hand,
Guide me along the path,
That, coming,
I may stumble not,
Nor roam,
Nor fail to show the way
Which leads us—Home.

＊

After the death of his mother in 1888, Woodrow Wilson expressed in a letter the almost universal reaction of the adult losing a parent:

"My mother was a mother to me in the fullest, sweetest sense of the word, and her loss has left me with a sad, oppressive sense of having somehow suddenly *lost my youth*. I feel old and responsibility-ridden."

# ZULU MOURNING

Before they ever collided with the white man, the Zulus were a nation. Their founding father was the ruthless chieftain Shaka, who combined an icy disposition with a brilliant military mind. In the late eighteenth century Shaka gained control of a small clan, conquered his neighbors and welded them all into a Zulu empire. He was a ferocious disciplinarian, who punished even minor disobedience with death, toughened his warriors by marching them barefoot over coals, and mourned his mother's death by making the Zulus give up sex and planting crops for a year.

> Russell Watson with Peter Younghusband
> in *Newsweek*, Sept. 6, 1976

\*

Margaret Sanger recalls the death of her five-year-old daughter from pneumonia:

Peggy died the morning of November 6, 1915.

The joy in the fullness of life went out of it then and has never quite returned. Deep in the hidden realm of my consciousness my little girl has continued to live, and in that strange, mysterious place where reality and imagination meet, she has grown up to womanhood. There she leads an ideal existence untouched by harsh actuality and disillusion.

Men and women from all classes, from nearly every city in America, poured upon me their sympathy. . . . Women wrote of children dead a quarter of a century for whom they were still secretly mourning, and sent me pictures and locks of hair of their own dead babies. I had never fully realized until then that the loss of a child remains unforgotten to every mother during her lifetime.

\*

# OH, MOTHER!

Former Secretary of Defense James V. Forrestal, hospitalized in the spring of 1949 for what Navy doctors called "excessive occupational fatigue," copied out a fragment of Sophocles from a book of

poetry beside his bed and then jumped thirteen stories to his death.
These were the final lines he copied:

> Woe to the mother, in her close of day,
> Woe to her desolate heart, and temples gray,
>     When she shall hear
> Her loved one's story whispered in her ear:
> "Woe, woe!" Will be the cry,—
> No quiet murmur like the tremulous wail . . .

✳

## MATRICIDE FIRST

Lizzie Borden took an axe
And gave her mother forty whacks
Then when she saw what she had done
She gave her father forty-one.*

✳

## PATRICIDE FIRST

While killing of the father is a common theme in the literature of
most of the world's peoples, killing of the mother is rare. Though
many psychoanalysts report that matricide turns up fairly regularly
in dreams, it is seldom acted out in person. In the statistics of
murders among family members, mother-murder is the lowest on
the list.

✳

Her death was the greatest disaster that could happen.

—Virginia Woolf
on her mother

* Although the Fall River, Massachusetts, spinster was actually acquitted of
the 1892 murder of her father and stepmother, this irreverent rhyme about the
case is still recited all over the nation.

# JOHN BROWN AND HIS MOTHER

Two years before the raid on Harpers Ferry which led to his hanging, anti-slavery crusader John Brown wrote a short history of his boyhood for a young admirer. Included in it was this third-person description of the devastating effect on him of his mother's death:

"At Eight years old John was left a Motherless boy which loss was complete and permanent, for notwithstanding his Father again married to a sensible, inteligent (sic), & on many accounts a very estimable woman: *yet he never adopted* (sic) *her in feeling:* but continued to pine after his own Mother for years. This opperated (sic) very unfavourably uppon (sic) him; as he was both naturally fond of females; & withall extremely diffident; & deprived him of a suitable connecting link between the different sexes. . . ."

＊

# GHOSTS

The only ghosts, I believe, who creep into this world, are dead young mothers, returned to see how their children fare. There is no other inducement great enough to bring the departed back.

—Sir James Barrie
in *The Little White Bird*

＊

Barrie may have written truer than he knew. Dr. Ian Stevenson of the Department of Psychiatry of the University of Virginia has traveled all over the world interviewing individuals who believe they have been reincarnated and claim to remember details of past lives. After tabulating hundreds of these (as he calls them) "cases of the reincarnation type," Stevenson has discovered a significant pattern in the circumstances of the death of the previous personalities. A high proportion were individuals who had, at the time of their deaths, certain "unfinished business." Many were young mothers. "Concern about infants and young children 'left behind,'" he says, "figures prominently in the memories and behavior of the subjects remembering the lives of such persons."

# AN ICONOCLAST MOURNS

H. L. Mencken found much to criticize about the American landscape in general, but he was exquisitely content with the particular portion of it that included his mother's house on Hollins Avenue in Baltimore. Asked, in mid-career, why he had never married, he replied quite frankly that the home she made for him was "more comfortable than any I could ever set up for myself." After her death, when Mencken was forty-five, he received a note of condolence from Theodore Dreiser. This was part of his reply: "I begin to realize how inextricably my life was interwoven with my mother's. A hundred times a day I find myself planning to tell her something, or ask her for this or that. It is a curious thing: the human incapacity to imagine finality. The house seems strange, as if the people in it were deaf and dumb."

✳

# POOR LITTLE RICH GIRL

Edna Woolworth Hutton, one of three daughters of the founder of the great five-and-ten-cent-store chain, Frank W. Woolworth, died when her daughter Barbara was only four years old. Years later, the woman famous the world over as "the Dime Store Heiress" wistfully summed up her reaction. "I hardly remember her," said Barbara Hutton about her dead mother, "but I have missed her all my life."

✳

# MEMORIES

Columnist Jim Bacon, in his book, *Made in Hollywood*, tells of visiting the Movieland Wax Museum in Buena Park. Included in the museum displays is a remarkable likeness of the late Gary Cooper in his costume for *High Noon*. Bacon writes: "Sitting in front of the wax figure was a woman in her nineties. An employee of the museum told me she came over there once or twice a month and sat for hours in front of the Cooper wax figure.

"The little old lady was Gary's mother."

# PUTTING OUT MOTHER'S LIGHT

On June 30, 1954, the deaf and almost blind mother of Noel Coward died at the height of an eclipse of the sun. Noel had a premonition that this might happen and his biographer Cole Lesley says, "it seemed to him fitting that that redoubtable lady's light should be extinguished at the same time as the sun's."

Coward had rushed to his mother's bedside. "She recognized me for a fleeting moment and said, 'Dear old darling.' Then she went into a coma . . . I sat by the bed and held her hand until she gave a pathetic little final gasp and died. I have no complaints and no regrets. It was as I always hoped it would be. I was with her close close close until her last breath . . . Fifty-four years of love and tenderness and crossness and devotion and unswerving loyalty. Without her I could only have achieved a quarter of what I have achieved, not only in terms of success and career, but in terms of personal happiness. We have quarrelled, often violently, over the years, but she has never stood between me and my life, never tried to hold me too tightly, always let me go free. For a woman of her strength of character this was truly remarkable. She was gay, even to the last I believe, gallant certainly. There was no fear in her except for me. She was a great woman to whom I owe the whole of my life. I shall never be without her in my deep mind but I shall never see her again. Good-bye my darling."

&#42;

Dick Cavett remembers his mother's dying in his book *Cavett*:

I don't think I have ever recovered completely from my mother's death. She died of cancer when I was ten, and I still can't talk about it easily. I was in fifth grade at the time, and having a dying mother was, aside from the sadness, an acute embarrassment to me. It sounds strange to say that, I know, but any kid who has been through it at such an age would know what I mean. Or would he? Some kids might enjoy the added attention, I suppose, but it killed me. I had the bad luck to be the only kid in my class, or that I had ever heard of, it seemed, who had such a thing happen to him, and it was excruciating. I already felt conspicuous because of my voice and shortness and the loathsome fact that I was considered a "brain," and this added burden of sympathy was just too much.

For me it was doubly hard because, unlike most kids, I couldn't get through the dying part without everybody in school knowing about it. Because the teachers knew my parents, solicitous inquiries were everywhere and everybody knew. My mother had been a very popular teacher in junior high school, and I remember asking my father what I could possibly say when the junior high kids I met walking home from school asked how she was. The true answer was "She's dying," but this was out of the question. My father suggested "About the same." It usually got the reply "That's good."

Maudlin sympathy angered and somehow shamed me, and whenever I overheard phrases like "poor little tyke" from supposedly well-meaning grownups I wished them incinerated on the spot. Then there were the well-meaning morons who would say, "Don't worry, it'll probably turn out to be just a problem coming from a bad wisdom tooth or an allergy of some sort," and I would conjure up a particularly hot corner of hell for them to roast in. . . .

I'm sure all of this affected me in a profound way, and I'd love to be able to get a look inside my psyche and see just how much damage was done. I think it accounts for my unconquerable streak of pessimism, odd in one who otherwise generally enjoys life . . . I suppose it's an obvious defense mechanism against my again being caught by surprise, as I was so totally and vulnerably at the age of ten.

*

My dead mother gets between me and life.

Observation made by artist
Romaine Brooks at age eighty-five

*

# A REBELLIOUS ACTOR

The late movie actor James Dean, the screen's quintessential rebel, lost his mother to cancer when he was still very young. His later comment about this:

"My mother died on me when I was nine years old. What does she expect me to do? Do it all alone?"

# HARD PRESSED TO R.I.P.

Shortly before the ceasefire in Vietnam in 1973, a New York *Times* story quoted from the diary of Charles Stockbauer, a young seminarian from St. Joseph, Missouri, who, although he was opposed to war, became a medic with the 101st Airborne. He lost his life trying to help a wounded soldier in a rice paddy. The diary entry, written on June 28, 1970, a few months before his death, was as follows: "*Narcissus and Goldmund* by Herman Hesse ends beautifully: But how will you die when your time comes, Narcissus, since you have no mother? Without a mother one cannot love. Without a mother, one cannot die."

\*

# JOHN UPDIKE WRITES

"But the *view* is so lovely," my mother said to me. We were standing on the family burial plot, in Pennsylvania. Around us, and sloping down the hill, were the red sandstone markers of planted farmers, named and dated in the innocent rectangular lettering that used to be on patent-medicine labels. My grandfather's stone, rough-hewn granite with the family name carved in the form of bent branches, did not seem very much like him. My grandmother's Christian name, cut below his, was longer and, characteristically, dominated while taking the subservient position. Elsewhere on the plot were his parents, and great-aunts and uncles I had met only at spicy-smelling funerals in my remotest childhood. My mother paced off two yards, saying, "Here's Daddy and me. See how much room is left?"

"But she"—I didn't have to name my wife—"has never *lived* here." I was again a child at one of those dread family gatherings on dark holiday afternoons—awkward and stuffed and suffocating under the constant need for tact. Only in Pennsylvania, among my kin, am I pressured into such difficult dance-steps of evasion and placation. Every buried coffin was a potential hurt feeling. I tried a perky sideways jig, hopefully humorous, and added, "And the children would feel crowded and keep everybody awake."

She turned her face and gazed downward at the view—a lush

valley, a whitewashed farmhouse, a straggling orchard, and curved sections of the highway leading to the city whose glistening tip, a television relay, could just be glimpsed five ridges in the distance. She had expected my evasion—she could hardly have expected me to pace off my six feet greedily and plant stakes—but had needed to bring me to it, to breast my refusal and the consequence that, upon receiving her and my father, the plot would be closed, would cease to be a working piece of land. Why is it that nothing that happens to me is as real as these dramas that my mother arranges around herself, like Titania calling Peaseblossom and Mustardseed from the air? Why is it that everyone else lacks the sanguine, corporeal, anguished reality of these farmers, these people of red sandstone? When was Pennsylvania an ocean, to lay down all this gritty rock, that stains your palms pink when you lift it?

Placatory, I agreed, "The view *is* lovely."

"Think of poor Daddy," she said, turning away, Mustardseed dismissed. "He has no sense of landscape. He says he wants to be buried under a sidewalk."

*Picked Up Pieces*

＊

# CLASSIC SORROW

—Frailty, thy name is woman!—
A little month, or ere those shoes were old
With which she follow'd my poor father's body,
Like Niobe, all tears:—why she, even she . . .
          married with my uncle. . . .

*Hamlet*, Act I, Scene ii

The mother from the Greek classics whom Shakespeare chose as the epitome of grief made visible was Niobe, wife of the King of Thebes and the mother of his fourteen children. According to Homer, this imperious lady was so inordinately proud of having given birth to seven sons and seven daughters that she offended the gods and was cruelly punished for it. Strolling one day with her splendid entourage, Queen Niobe caught a whiff of incense and, on investigating, discovered a group of her countrywomen making a sacrifice to Leto, mother of the gods Artemis and Apollo. She immediately broke in on the ceremony, furious that a begetter of only two babies should be honored in preference to her. Even if disaster came to two or three of her children, she described, wouldn't she still be the more blessed?

When Leto heard this remark, she sought immediate revenge. Apollo, armed with bow and arrow, hunted down each of Niobe's sons one after another and shot them dead; Artemis, with her own quiver of arrows, did the same with the daughters. The bereft mother, humbled at last, bewailed her dead children for nine days and nine nights and, legend has it, still weeps for them today. As the Greek myth tells it, Niobe was transformed into a statue on Mount Sipylus in Asia Minor and there is, indeed, a crag there in roughly human form. In summer, when the rays of the sun strike its winter covering of snow, it does seem to weep inconsolably and reminds observers that Niobe is the personification of maternal sorrow.

✳

## A WIFE WRITES A HUSBAND

Never does one feel oneself so utterly helpless as in trying to speak comfort for great bereavement. Time is the only comforter for the loss of a mother.

> Jane Welsh Carlyle, in a letter to
> her husband Thomas on the death of
> his mother, in 1853

✳

## TO END ON A CHEERFUL NOTE

Asked by store president Geraldine Stutz to come up with fresh fortune-cookie sayings for the Henri Bendel Christmas catalogue, playwright Arthur Laurents created this one:

"One good urn preserves a mother"

# "Sing Out, Louise!"

In God's great vaudeville, Mother is the headliner.

Elbert Hubbard

Every theater buff will recognize the origin of the title of this chapter. These are the first words spoken by that titanic character Rose in the Arthur Laurents-Steve Sondheim-Jule Styne musical *Gypsy*. As her young daughters, Louise and Baby, strive in an audition, Rose enters the scene, striding down the aisle, startling the audience, calling out from the back of the theater, urging her darlings on to a success for which she herself hungers. (In real life, these tormented stage children grew up to be the actresses Gypsy Rose Lee and June Havoc.)

The role of Rose was first played by Ethel Merman in the crowning triumph of a long career. The musical became a Broadway classic, the part now having been successfully revived by Angela Lansbury who played it in New York and London. It was brought to the screen by Rosalind Russell and became a staple of summer stock. Rose, the stage mother nonpareil, is a tour de force role for any mature actress-singer.

*Gypsy* has everything. It has the child whose talents are worshiped by the mother as the one who breaks and runs away from Rose's domination. And it has the child who feels herself worthless in Rose's eyes, going on to become a success as the classiest stripper the world has ever known. Everything in *Gypsy* happens because of Mother—Mother's ambition, Mother's frustration, Mother's drive, Mother's nerve, Mother's domination, Mother's energy.

297

The musical hurtles along through episodes of Rose's stage-mother zeal and overkill. She is a woman who can't "be content playing bingo and paying rent" as she sings in "Some People." But in the satirical "If Mama Was Married," the children express yearnings to be normal, to live in a house, to have a father, animals, privacy, and be out of show business ("We aren't the Lunts; I'm not Fanny Brice!"). Most of all they want to be allowed to act their age —"I'd get all these hair ribbons out of my hair and once and for all I'd get Mama out too!"

Ethel Merman, captured here in a Hirschfeld cartoon, plays the most vivid stage mother of all in *Gypsy*. Sandra Church is the youthful Gypsy Rose Lee.

Rose is the epitome of stage mothers, but there have been many others who have displayed varying degrees of loyalty, grit, and omnipresence behind the scenes. To say there have been as many stage mothers as actors wouldn't be true, of course, for many performers are their own ambitious goads, or made it in spite of Mother's objections and even indifference to their efforts. But, there have been more stage mothers than we can adequately deal with here. This chapter tries to note some of the "star" stage mothers, or those who were highly remarkable and/or visible, although you'll also find a few who might more accurately be categorized under the heading "Mothers as Fans."

※

# RATS!

Writing fact rather than fiction has its perils. As a newspaper columnist I've found that the one way to lose a really great story is to check it out. You get a terrific rumor. It has everything and fits together like a jigsaw puzzle. You can project the headline in your mind's eye. Then a sense of responsibility starts you checking up and the story usually evaporates. The characters shrink; the dialogue turns tepid; she didn't hit him with a whiskey bottle as rumored but merely brushed against him on her way to get an ice cream soda. You end up storyless.

This happened in writing of stage mothers. My favorite stage mother story disappeared and it was one I had nurtured for years. Let me tell it anyway, because it is a hoary treasure of many theater people who still believe it to be gospel and repeat it as such.

Dolores Gray's mother was, during the years of her daughter's ascendancy on the musical stage, a character and a fixture on the scene. (This much is true.) As a result of Mrs. Gray's somewhat fearsome reputation as a protector and gadfly in behalf of her blond daughter, for years Hermione Gingold was said to have a special clause written into all her theater contracts. Although Miss Gingold had never appeared in any show with Dolores Gray, apocrypha had it that she insisted on a clause stating that during the run of any show in which she appeared "at no time may Dolores Gray's mother come backstage."

Upon checking, Hermione, the doyenne of *Gigi*, *A Little Night Music*, and many other shows, said no such thing had ever happened and she had no idea how such a story got started. I was crushed.

I have added the story here as a sort of fictional tribute to stage mothers, those dramatic, larger-than-life creatures of hyperbole, hype, and sometimes hysteria. It shows how legends can spring up. And then there *is* a true story of Dolores Gray's mother in this chapter in any case.

So here's to all those mothers who react like Dalmatians to a firebell when they smell grease paint.

*

# A GYPSY BIRTH

The writer-director Arthur Laurents tells me how he was influenced to write the musical *Gypsy*. Arthur had read Gypsy Rose Lee's autobiography and seen nothing in it for the stage. Then a theatrical agent, the late Selma Lynch, casually mentioned to Arthur that she had known Gypsy's mother. Selma told him a few true tales about the ultimate S.M. and a fascinated Arthur began to visualize his musical Medea. When Arthur eventually tried to tell one of his leading lady stars, Angela Lansbury, some actual stories about the real-life Rose, she stopped him. The actress who was so critically acclaimed playing this monster onstage said, "Don't tell me anything about that terrible woman!"

*

# A PHENOMENON EXAMINED

## *by Richard Griffith*

When stage mothers first appeared is mercifully unknown, but the species is probably as least as old as the Theater of Dionysus. Doubtless they constitute a cadet branch of that long line of meddling mamas who from time immemorial have put their daughters on the auction block, as the old melodramas used to say, for sale into marriage or into some less reputable profession. Traditionally, the stage mothers motives have not been entirely mercenary; ego as well as greed has played a major part in her calculations, ego and the obvious need to fulfill through her daughter dreams frustrated in her own life. However that may be, stage mothers have to be conspicuously mentioned among important sources of grist for the mills of the gods, and a fruitful one. The road to stardom is long and tough. Somebody has to provide the energy and determination to follow it to its golden end. Surprisingly often it has been Mama, for reasons of her own.

The motives of the first *screen* mothers were considerably more prosaic. When I asked Lillian Gish why her gently bred mother sought acting jobs for herself and her two fragile little girls at the turn of the century, she answered, "Necessity!" The Gishes were one of those theatrical families so curiously common around the turn of the century who were in the theater not through family tradition, as with the Barrymores and the Drews, but because they had lost their breadwinner through death or abandonment. The mothers of these families, mostly untrained and often uneducated, took to acting because it was the only reasonably respectable profession in which they and their offspring could make a living. If the mother could act at all, or was passably good to look at, she and her brood were welcome in the touring troupes and big-city stock companies because the plays of those days, being family entertainment, had many more parts for children than is now the case.

The Smith family of Toronto, consisting of the widowed Mrs. Charlotte Smith and her children Gladys, Lottie, and Jack, became professionals by accident through a sudden need for a little girl actress to appear in a Toronto production of *The Silver King*. Gladys Smith, who got this part, soon was metamorphosed into Mary Pickford, and her mother, as Mrs. Charlotte Pickford, became the screen mother par excellence. Mighty studio moguls blanched when she approached their offices. She had only one object: to see to it that her daughter's salary increased by geometrical rather than arithmetical progression. Mrs. Pickford's financial manipulations became an industry legend. But the most interesting of these early queen mothers, and the most likeable, was Peg Talmadge.* After her hus-

---

* In her witty picture and memory book *Cast of Thousands*, writer Anita Loos says Peg Talmadge "manipulated her two beauties (Norma and Constance) to the top ranks of both films and finance. Norma wed Joe Schenck, George Jessel and other rich men. Irving Thalberg, Irving Berlin and Dick Barthelmess were suicidal over Constance. Third daughter, Natalie, wed Buster Keaton."

Ms. Loos notes that mother Peg's smile was forced at the latter wedding. "She considered Natalie's marriage as a mere substitute for movie stardom."

band deserted her, she led a hard life trying to raise her three daughters, Norma, Constance, and Natalie, and it was she who not only pushed them into pictures but kept them there. The girls thought it was lots of fun at first to be in the movies, but once the novelty wore off, they were perfectly willing to find their fun elsewhere. The movies were, after all, work, and to a Talmadge it made no sense to work if you didn't have to. Mrs. Talmadge perfectly agreed with this worldly, inartistic view of movie stardom, but until her financial goals, in the form of a series of trust funds, were realized, she insisted that the lazy Norma and the excitement-loving Constance continue to "work." The Talmadge sisters are the only stars on record who had to be bullied into continuing their stardom after the first blush of success. At the time of Mama's death, mourned by the entire movie industry, they decided that they were rich enough to satisfy even her, and retired without ceremony and without regrets.

Formidable though they were, the Mesdames Pickford and Talmadge in their single-minded concentration on family security seem rather innocent compared to the tall and somewhat sinister tales of later moms and their manipulation of talented offspring. Actresses who never quite made it themselves seem particularly determined to enjoy fame and adoration through their children. Witness the burlesque queen Belle Paget, mother of Debra Paget (who also never quite made it, at least to the top stardom), and leading woman Sara Warmbrodt, who pushed first her son (who finally eluded her) and then her very young daughter, the eminent Elizabeth Taylor, into the studio hurley-burley at an age when most mothers would have been worrying whether their teeth would come in straight. Miss Taylor's subsequent illnesses, physical as well as emotional, have been authoritatively diagnosed as stemming from the strain of having to live an emotional life for two, herself and her mother, and some of Judy Garland's problems could have derived from a similar source. Lillian Roth has publicly attributed her alcoholism to her mother's constant pressure. . . .

All this adds up to a sob story of a kind which has always delighted fans, who are not entirely displeased to learn that life is not all beer and skittles for the lovely and fortunate creatures of the screen.

*The Movie Stars*

# MOTHER CRABTREE

Stage mothers, of course, are no new development on the American theatrical scene. One of the most picturesque of the pioneer models was Mrs. Mary Ann Crabtree, who pushed her daughter Lotta into child stardom on mining town stages all over the post-Gold Rush West. Homesick for families left back East, the grizzled gold-seekers rewarded Lotta's lisping rendition of such sentimental favorites as "Little Nell" by showering her with nuggets and silver dollars; Mother Crabtree gathered them up into a leather grip which she lugged with her wherever the pair traveled. Whenever the bag grew too burdensome to carry, Mother C. traded the contents for the real estate and municipal bonds which formed the base of what became, in time, a vast Crabtree fortune. Mary Ann Crabtree trouped with her daughter for twenty-seven years, seldom allowing the star in the family as much as a dollar in spending money at a crack, but, unlike many other offspring of stage mothers, Lotta Crabtree showed no visible resentment toward her guard-dog mom. "What I am . . . and what I was," she declared after Mary Ann's death, "I owe entirely to her . . . My mother was the most wonderful woman that ever lived—and I want the world to know it."

✳

My mother was the stage mother of all time. She really was a witch. If I had a stomach ache and didn't want to go on, she'd say "Get out on that stage or I'll wrap you around a bedpost."

—Judy Garland, in an interview
with Barbara Walters

✳

# TIME WOUNDS

When Elaine Stritch was to star in Noel Coward's *Sail Away*, she introduced him to her parents, Mildred and George Stritch of Birmingham, Michigan. The Master was delighted with the ebullient, well-to-do, and swingy Stritch family. He bent over backward to amuse and please them and, the following year, sent the attractive Mildred Stritch one of his famous Christmas cards.

Time passed. Noel Coward grew busy directing Jose Ferrer

and Florence Henderson in a musical version of *The Prince and the Showgirl* on Broadway. Another Christmas came and went with no word in Birmingham from the Master. Whereupon Mrs. Stritch sent a telegram to New York. It read: "Dear Noel, I guess you have to be Florence Henderson's mother to get a card this year."

※

# SHARPER THAN A SERPENT'S TOOTH

Playwright-director Edward Chodorov is the source for this back-stage-mother saga which Chodorov calls "the best theatrical mother's story I know."

The heroine of it is the mother of Lady Hardwicke, originally an American girl who, in her premarital acting days, was known as Mary Scott. A number of Broadway seasons back, in George Bernard Shaw's *Caesar and Cleopatra*, she understudied Lilli Palmer as Cleopatra to Sir Cedric Hardwicke's Caesar.

Here's Chodorov:

"Unbelievable luck! On the very day that Mary's mother arrived from the west to visit her Mary was notified that Miss Palmer was indisposed and could not perform.

"Mary was understandably breathless. 'Mother!' she said. 'You won't believe this but *I'm going to play Cleopatra today!*'

" 'Oh dear,' said Mother. 'Do you mean that I'm not going to see Lilli Palmer?' "

※

# A CLASSIC

Sandra Berle was the classic "stage mother," over all the years, from the time Milton was a teen-ager in vaudeville until her death. In his autobiography, Berle tells this story about her:

"First, I have to tell you that I spoke with my mother every day of her life. Either I saw her or I'd telephone her, no matter where I was . . . Ripley once ran an item: 'Believe it or Not, Milton Berle has called his mother every day for the last twenty years.'*

"So one day I called her at the Essex House, and Miss Finnigan, the operator, said that Mama had left word that she was on her way down to the lobby if I called. Miss Finnigan said to hold on while she paged Mama. I don't know what it's like now, but at the time of this story, the house phones at the Essex House were in open booths right out in the middle of the lobby. After maybe a minute's wait, I heard the lobby phone pick up. Mama said, 'Hello?'

"I said hello back, and I heard Mama say in a loud voice so that the whole lobby could hear, 'Is this my son, Milton Berle?' "

✳

# REVELATIONS

Oscar-winner Joel Grey made his performing debut at age ten in the Cleveland Playhouse and, after he became a show-stopping Broadway success in such productions as *Cabaret* and *George M!*, found himself often questioned by interviewers about his days as a child actor. "For twenty years," he told me, "I assured reporters, 'No, I never was pressured by either my mother or my father. I loved what I was doing.' For *twenty years*, I said that over and over in interviews: 'No, I never was pressured.' Then, recently, my mother went on a radio talk show and the host asked *her* about how I got started. I was listening at home and was astounded to hear her say, 'Joel didn't particularly want to go into show business. I pushed him. He probably would never have done it if I hadn't pushed him so much.' Obviously," concluded Joel, "I'd blocked all that out. My mother really *was* a stage mother and I only found it out twenty-five years later!"

---

* The idea of the sentimental hardboiled comic who talks every day on the phone to Mama reoccurs. Georgie Jessel developed this real life habit into a "Hello Momma" performing telephone routine that became a classic. But attention must be paid to Mama in all cultural mediums, witness Mrs. Fanny Mailer telling viewers of *The David Susskind Show* in 1976 that her writer son Norman calls *her* every day also. On the same program, the mother of opera star Beverly Sills reported that her daughter calls *her* every day too, whereas actor Walter Matthau once told me that he calls *his* mother every *other* day. Comedian George Burns, on stage at least, went one step further. "I used to sing a song that went, 'If you can't see Mama every night, you can't see Mama at all'—a good song," says George.

# MA MINNIE

The show business career of the Marx Brothers was set into motion by their mother, Minnie, sister of Al Shean of the famous vaudeville duo of Gallagher and Shean. "Where else," theorized Minnie, "can people who don't know anything make such a good living?"

In *Son of Groucho*, Arthur Marx explains that "what the boys lacked in recognizable talent, the indomitable Minnie made up for with plenty of chutzpah when it came to button-holing theater managers and booking agents, and talking them into giving her boys a chance." (When her story was transformed into the Broadway musical, *Minnie's Boys*, in 1970, she was portrayed by the indomitable Shelley Winters.)

Later, of course, Minnie Marx's faith in her four sons was vindicated and she was an enthusiastic audience member in all the Marx Brothers' early Broadway successes, including the 1924 hit *I'll Say She Is*. Writes Arthur Marx: "Only one thing marred Minnie's complete enjoyment. . . . On opening night, Minnie was getting dressed to go to the theater. While reaching for her hat, she fell off a stool and broke her leg.

"But Minnie didn't let little things like a cast on her leg or the fact that she was in great pain keep her away from the Casino Theater that May night so long ago.

"She insisted on being driven to the theater in an ambulance. There she was carried down the aisle and to her front-row seat by two white-coated attendants—just as the curtain was going up. And she remained in her seat, with her cast-encased leg propped up on the brass rail of the orchestra pit, *kvelling* triumphantly every time one of her boys socked over a joke, until the final cheer-laden curtain call."

✳

# BLACK AND WHITE

Some stage mothers have merely been present, not pushy.

Before her death in her mid-nineties, Fred Astaire's mother lived for many years with her famous son in a separate wing of his Hollywood mansion. Mrs. Astaire had only a black and white TV set and so when her son was settling down to watch the filmed version of his appearance on *The Dick Cavett Show*, he invited his mother down to the main part of the house to see the event on his big color set. Mrs. Astaire watched for a while and then got up and smoothed her dress. "Where are you going?" asked Astaire.

"I'm going back to my own room, Fred," said Mrs. Astaire. "I really want to see how this looks in black and white."

❋

## TIMING IS EVERYTHING

One of the side effects of the new liberality in sexual explicitness on the screen is the emergence of a new breed of stage mom—what might be called "the X-rated mother." In late 1975, *The Village Voice* recorded the experience of producer Bob Roberts when he set out to film a porno version of the Patty Hearst saga. In casting about for a group of young ladies who wouldn't mind doing it in front of the camera, *The Voice* reported, "he was approached by the mothers of girls in their teens who pushed them to bare their breasts and flash the cheesecake for a chance to make it in the big time. 'The stage mother has become more modern,' decided Roberts."

❋

Out-of-work dancers who have had bad mothers get fat.

> Truism offered by
> Michael Bennett of his hit
> musical *A Chorus Line*

❋

## LIZ'S MOM

Columnist Jim Bacon tells of bumping into Elizabeth Taylor's mother, Sara, in the Polo Lounge of the Beverly Hills Hotel. She told Jim she'd just received an urgent cable from Elizabeth to hurry down to Puerto Vallarta. Jim asked what that meant. Maybe marriage? (At this time Elizabeth was waiting for her divorce from Eddie Fisher, hoping to marry Richard Burton.)

"Could be," said Mrs. Taylor. "I've been to all of Elizabeth's weddings."

❋

## GINGER'S LEE-LEE

No chapter on the Stage Mother could be complete without a mention of the late Lela "Lee-Lee" Rogers, the look-alike parent of

Ginger. In George Eells's wonderful Hollywood book, *Ginger, Loretta and Irene Who?*, the Ginger chapter is as much about Mother Rogers as the star. Says Eells: "Ginger had three great advantages over other actresses. She had herself, her mother and God in her corner." Mrs. Rogers, a devout Christian Scientist, "saw to it that even as a little girl Ginger equated what was good for her with what God wanted for her." Although Lela never quite fit the classic stage mother stereotype, together she and Ginger rushed in where Ginger alone might have feared to tread. The result has been a half century of entertainment triumphs.

Lela was one of the five pert Owens sisters of Kansas City, Missouri, and her marriage to Ginger's father, Eddins McMath, failed early on. The highly motivated Lela then progressed from stenographer to newspaper reporter to screenwriter to a stint in the Marine Corps as one of the first "Marinettes." But during her days working in Marine publicity, Lela received such a barrage of mail from little Ginger that her fellow marines nicknamed her "Mother."

After marrying one John Rogers, who adopted Ginger, Lela went back to work as a reporter in Fort Worth where she was too absorbed in her own career and "too genteel" to push Ginger toward the stage. But she was not one to stand in her child's way. "Ginger," she remembers, "wanted to go into the theater. I couldn't have prevented it." Having accepted that, Lela did everything possible to help her daughter. She wrote songs, made clothes, and invented Ginger's famous baby-talk monologue. Says Lela: "I was a regular Madame Rose. Exactly—*except* that I did it by cooperating with the circuit, cooperating with the managers, making them see that what's good for Ginger is good for them."

With Lela behind her a thousand per cent, Ginger went to Hollywood and worked like a dog. Even after her supersuccessful teaming with Fred Astaire, Ginger still called on her mother when she was in trouble. And Lela invariably rushed to her side, suggested compromises, or told Ginger when to make a stand and "tell them to get a new girl."

In Eells's view: "The multifaceted relationship between Ginger and Lela transcended that of mother and daughter. They were, according to Ginger, very good friends. Yet there is no question that Lela was the dominant force. By inclination a friendly, uncomplicated, high-spirited young woman, Ginger would on cue from her mother suddenly begin to speak, as Lela did, of the necessity of cultivating universal love of humanity to develop the magnetism an actress needed to draw audiences to her. At her mother's urging, she increased her vocabulary until her sentences were no longer means of communication but obstacle courses. Left to her natural impulses, she could be impish and amusing, but counseled by Lee-Lee that stars were a thing apart, Ginger gradually became aloof and detached."

Ginger and Lela always lived together whenever the actress was not married. Their togetherness was so complete that when either spoke, it was almost invariably "us" or "we," seldom "I." Their differences usually arose only over Ginger's men, as for instance when Lela determined to break up Ginger's romance with the married director George Stevens. At the time Mrs. Rogers behaved as if her mature daughter were a ravished virgin.

Ethel Barron once wrote that if ever an Oscar were given for the Mother Who Knows Best Award, Lela Rogers would win hands down. Lela herself agrees. "Yes," she says, "I was always there. One book said I was like a mother hippopotamus protecting her young—and that's not true . . . I was stern, I knew what I wanted. I knew Ginger would thrive by developing all sides . . . She never took a rest. We worked and developed. That's why she survived."

Lela Rogers is immortalized on celluloid as the screen mother of Ginger in *The Major and the Minor,* a comedy in which the star pretends to be a little girl. The complexities of the plot allowed Ginger, at one point, to pretend to be her own mother so that Lela gets to pretend to be Ginger's grandmother. (You have to see the movie; watch for it on television.)

As Ginger's movie career went into fade, she and her Lela remained close. In a night-club tour not long before her mother's death, Ginger made a speech to Waldorf customers on opening night, telling them, "You are beautiful people, I love you, I'd like to *can* you and send you to my mother."

George Eells closes his chapter on Ginger and Lela with this delightful anecdote:

"Through it all, fans remain faithful to this survivor. At one Eastern engagement of *Forty Carats* in 1975 an especially devoted pair—brother and sister—bought seats and two copies of Arlene Croce's *The Fred Astaire and Ginger Rogers Book* well in advance. They enjoyed the performance enormously and presented themselves at the stage door, where a doorman took the books to Ginger's dressing room for autographs. He returned to say he was sorry, but the star would not sign the books because they were unauthorized biographies. Determined to have a memento, the brother shoved their programs into the doorman's hand and implored him to have them signed. Shortly thereafter a commotion out front made it apparent that Ginger was leaving by another exit. Desperate now, the young man raced to the street and seemed about to fling himself in front of the limousine into which Ginger was scrambling. Suddenly from the depths of the interior, a voice commanded, 'Be polite. Sign! Be thankful they still remember you!'"

Lela? Natch.

※

# A MOTHER'S-EYE VIEW

The director George Cukor and I were once talking chitchat on the set of *The Bluebird* in Russia. I mentioned this book, and Cukor said one of the great "mothers" he had ever known was the woman who produced David O. Selznick. "Mrs. Selznick thought her David was the greatest man in the twentieth century and she thought so even before he produced *Gone With the Wind*. In the early days, David and I resembled one another and people constantly remarked on it. One day we were together and this happened. Mrs. Selznick indignantly objected.

"I finally said to her—'I know, Mrs. Selznick, I know—*my* mother feels the same way!'"

※

# LENA HORNE TALKS OF THE WOMAN WHO SHAPED HER LIFE

"My mother wanted me to be a star and I worked hard for her goal, though I hated it so much that when later I achieved what she wanted for me I could really not enjoy it, and neither could she, so deep was our alienation.

"But my mother was now in the grip of a dream which was that I would succeed in show business where she had failed.* I had not realized how desperately she had wanted to make it until she turned her full attention to me. She turned into the typical stage mother of lore and legend—my dreamy, impractical, rather defeated mother."

* This was when Lena was making twenty-five dollars a week in the Cotton Club in Harlem.

# TAKE THAT, III

"No promises were ever made to give him anything."

Mrs. Lillian R. Coogan's
deposition regarding the estimated $4 million
earned by her son Jackie during his reign
as a child star in the 1920s of such
films as *The Kid* and *Peck's Bad Boy*

When, in a celebrated court case of 1938, Coogan sued his mother
and stepfather for depriving him of his childhood earnings, it was
revealed that the youngster who, in 1923, "received the largest salary check ever written at that time by the film industry" ($500,000
from Joseph Schenck as advance on a million-dollar contract), was
given only $6.50 a week spending money throughout his minority.

*

# MOTHER AS A GOAD

Director Robert Parrish has written a delightful memoir titled
*Growing Up in Hollywood* in which he tells what it was like to
have a stage mother who was ambitious for all her children.

"'If Central Casting asks you *anything*, say yes,' the golden
rule from my mother to her four children: Gordon, Robert,
Beverly, and Helen. 'Can you sing?' 'Can you dance?' 'Are you
tall?' 'Are you short?' 'Do you have a blue suit' 'Red?' 'Green?'
'Cerise?' The answer was always an emphatic, unhesitating YES! If
we didn't have what was called for, my mother would make it that
night. If we couldn't sing, dance, ride bareback, swim under water,
walk a tightrope, speak Polish, or whatever, we said yes and reported for work, hoping we wouldn't actually be called upon to do
what we had lied about. Or, if we were, that we could perform well
enough to get by. The worst that could happen was that we would
be sent home with a quarter-day's pay and a threat that we would
never work again for that company . . . until they needed us.

"I worked as an actor and as an apprentice film editor on *The
Informer* for John Ford at RKO in 1935. I had first worked for him
as an extra several years earlier in *Mother Machree, Four Sons,
Riley the Cop, Judge Priest, Steamboat Round the Bend,* and other
pictures. Whenever he needed kids, he called the Watson family

(seven children of assorted sexes, sizes, and ages), the Johnson family (six), or the Parrish family (four). This way he could fill a schoolroom scene and still only have to contend with three 'movie mothers.' In fact, with these three families, the kids became so film-wise that we were not always accompanied by a parent. One of the older kids in any one or all of the families could get the required number to the studio on the bus and see that they were costumed, fed, paid, etc. Or sometimes one of the six parents would come along by mutual agreement to keep an eye on all the kids. Our three families became more or less Ford's kid stock company. He depended on us to give him no trouble, and we depended on him for work during the hard times of the Depression."

At eighty-eight the mother of the Parrish children was still working in Hollywood as an extra. "She won't take a taxi, too expensive, and we took her car away from her a few years ago," said Parrish. "So my brother, who is a senior vice-president for Coca-Cola, will be in conference and the phone will ring. 'Gordon, will you drive me over to Universal?' And he drops everything and does it."

You see, it's never easy to say no to a genuine stage mother.

✳

# A REVERSAL

As said before, not all "stage mothers" are pushy and self-confident. When the ten-year-old Noel Coward began agitating to be allowed to audition for a Christmas Pantomime, his mother agreed only with reluctance. When she took him to the theater, Noel performed and the stage manager said, "Well, Mrs. Coward, shall we say two pounds ten a week?" The neophyte performer's mother turned pale and stammered her reply: "I'm sorry but we couldn't possibly afford to pay that much."

✳

Coward went on to learn a great deal about real stage mothers, the result being a song containing these couplets:

> On my knees, Mrs. Worthington,
> Please, Mrs. Worthington,
> Don't put your daughter on the stage!
> and
> No more "buts," Mrs. Worthington,

Nuts, Mrs. Worthington,
Don't put your daughter on the stage!

Throughout most of his adult career, "Don't Put Your Daughter on the Stage, Mrs. Worthington" was one of the most-requested numbers in the Coward repertoire.

Despite "Mrs. Worthington's" enormous popularity, its effectiveness as propaganda, Coward once observed, was "negligible." In the notes accompanying the composition in the 1953 *Noel Coward Songbook*, he asserts that he hoped, by writing it, to "discourage misguided maternal ambition" and "deter those dreadful eager mothers from making beasts of themselves." Instead, a large percentage of the stage mothers who wrote to him made reference to the song with "roguish indulgence, obviously secure in the conviction that it could not in any circumstances apply to them." This, concluded the Master, "is saddening, of course, but realizing that the road of the social reformer is paved with disillusion I have determined to rise above it."

※

# MAMA'S BOY

Picture Clifton Webb
Minus mother Mabelle . . .

> Line from the Cole
> Porter song
> "Just a Picture of
> Me Without You"

The idea of the effete mama's boy whose mama was also a stage mother epitomizes itself in the actor Clifton Webb who first won cinema renown as the elegant but jealous and deranged radio commentator in the film *Laura* and later in *Sitting Pretty* and other movies as the biting, waspish baby-sitter, Mr. Belvedere, a man who was the film incarnation of himself.

The most influential and pervasive person in the actor's life was his mother, Mabelle. So much so, that once when a group of friends was playing a game in which names of plays were suggested to typify each contestant, there was a unanimous vote that the only title for Clifton had to be *Up in Mabel's Room*.

At age six, Clifton had made his stage debut in *The Brownies* under the watchful eye of his frustrated actress mother, Mabelle

Hollenbeck. She became completely responsible for her son's career as he journeyed upward from dance teacher to Broadway plays and musicals. For years, Clifton was a bright fixture of the New York stage, a man with polished diction, a worldly air, impeccable tailoring, and a host of fashionable friends. Mabelle "counted the house" at each of her son's performances, haggled over every clause in his contracts, and never failed to make her presence felt. There is a story that the producers of *Three's a Crowd* arranged for Mabelle to go to Bermuda during rehearsals, but she was stubbornly present at the dress rehearsal of the show. Finally, she was told she could sit in the back if she would be quiet. Mabelle was silent for the first four numbers—numbers in which Clifton did not appear. But finally, feeling his absence was too much, she began to shout, "We want Webb!"

Clifton's father had dropped out of sight. When asked what happened to her husband, Mabelle would say, "We never speak of him. He didn't care for the theater."

Clifton and Mabelle lived together at an estate in Greenwich, Connecticut, and in New York's Park Lane Hotel. When Webb's movie career boomed, they moved to Hollywood where their entertaining feats on North Rexford Drive became legend. In her nineties, Mabelle was still an exhibitionist, given to performing her version of the can-can. She was included in all of Clifton's social activities and though he was said to sometimes betray a momentary annoyance with his mother, he was so devoted that if she became even slightly ill he became "almost demented."

But Mabelle had her detractors. Noel Coward's secretary Cole Lesley indicates that she was "dreaded by all Hollywood." And there were traitors on North Rexford Drive. For years Clifton had employed a black maid named Theresa whose own flamboyance got on Mabelle's nerves. Theresa, totally bald, sometimes changed from a pageboy to an upswept wig between dinner courses and Mabelle would frequently chew her out. Shortly after Mabelle's death in 1960, a friend remarked to Theresa, "Well, I guess Mrs. Webb is hearing heavenly music now." To this Theresa answered: "No waaaay! Where she went, the music's hot!"

When Mabelle Webb died, Clifton began the mourning that lasted until his own death in 1966. Noel Coward noted in a letter how his old friend was handling matters: "Poor Clifton . . . is still, after two months, wailing and sobbing over Mabelle's death. As she was well over ninety, gaga, and had driven him mad for years, this seems excessive and over indulgent. He arrives here on Monday and

I'm dreaming of a wet Christmas. I am of course deeply sorry for him but he must snap out of it."

At this time, when Noel spoke to Clifton on the phone, the latter wept so uninterruptedly that Noel finally lost his temper and said sharply, "Unless you stop crying I shall reverse the charges." It was said that this had an "immediate effect." The most famous remark to go the rounds of Clifton Webb's friends was Noel Coward's final, acerbic one to him: "It must be tough to be orphaned at seventy-one!"

Clifton Webb never did snap out of mourning for Mabelle. No wonder. Her deathbed words had been:

"How is Clifton? Has he had his luncheon?"

\*

# BACKSTAGE FOR SISTER

Though her daughter was in a slightly different brand of "show business," the female begetter of evangelist Aimee Semple McPherson was as bona fide a stage mother as ever hovered in the wings. As a young Salvation Army lassie shaking her tambourine on Ontario street corners, Minnie Kennedy prayed for a woman preacher in the family. Minnie's daughter climbed the golden ladder up, up, up from the makeshift pulpit of a tent tabernacle revival meeting to the magnificent altar of her own Four Square Gospel Temple in Los Angeles, preaching to the largest congregation in the world.

Following the pattern of many another stage mom, Minnie took over the chore of handling the greenbacks which flooded in at temple collections in response to the exhortations of the lady preacher known as "the Star Salesman of God." Only after Sister Aimee was involved in a 1926 kidnaping hoax that tarnished her reputation did the mother and daughter partnership come asunder. Newspapers headlined the story when Mother Kennedy checked in at a hospital with a battered nose, charging that Sister Aimee had not only hit her but threatened to have her killed. Aimee's version was that a mild mother-daughter tiff had sparked such a wild temper tantrum on her mother's part that the older woman had flung herself on the floor and caused her own injuries.

As Sister Aimee's evangelical career continued its downward path, both mother and daughter gradually faded from public view, surfacing only with their respective death notices. Aimee died of an accidental overdose of sleeping tablets in 1944; her mother outlived her by four years.

# Oedipus and His Brothers or The Mother Lovers

GRAFFITI:
Oedipus, come home. All is forgiven.

Mother

Oh my, *my goodness*—as Edward Everett Horton used to say in all those Ginger Rogers-Fred Astaire movies. This is certainly the most "dangerous" chapter in the book—the big no-no. And you can just imagine how much worse it would be if, instead of The Mother Lovers, I had gone to press using the working title under which the material was collected for months on end. That *other* expression (dealt with in The Language of Mothers chapter), while profanely funny, was neither exactly 100 per cent accurate nor very nice.

One doesn't care to belabor the theme of mother-son incest except to say that it is possibly the ultimate sexual taboo. When Mrs. Patrick Campbell uttered that old chestnut about not caring what people did so long as they didn't do it in the streets and scare the horses, even she might have made an exception of incest, which societies from the beginning of time have considered unspeakable.

Yet history, myth, literature, psychology, and even the occasional current event prove that mother-son incest does occur in life and in nature, though unlike sibling or father-daughter incest, it is relatively rare. In *The Savage Is Loose,* a daring but failed 1975 film with George C. Scott and his real-life wife Trish Van DeVere, their movie son lusts for his young mother as he attains manhood. The three have been shipwrecked on a desert island since the boy was an infant and he has grown up with only a Bible for education. At last the boy tries to kill his father and take his mother and at one point, cries out to her the pathetic question, "Who was Cain's wife?"

For those who interpret the Old Testament literally, it does seem that after Cain slew Abel there were only three people alive on an earth waiting to be populated from the loins of Adam and Eve. Or Eve and Cain; Eve being the only woman (well, draw your own conclusions). So if you believe in this seeming sequence of events, mother-son incest begins almost at the beginning of time, being possibly the third-oldest story ever told—after the Creation and Fall. But it wasn't until 1900 in Vienna that mankind got a suitable name for this transgression.

No psychoanalytic theory has gained wider currency than the "Oedipus Complex," the term used by Freud to describe a boy's incestuous desires for his mother and feelings of rivalry with his father. By way of a quick refresher course, here is the ancient Greek legend that gave Freud the name:

Briefly, Laius, the King of Thebes, is told by an oracle that he will be killed by his son. When the child, Oedipus, is born, Laius gives him to a shepherd with instructions to abandon the infant on a mountain to die. But in keeping with the fatefulness of great myths, the compassionate shepherd gives Oedipus to someone else to raise. At puberty, journeying to Thebes, the boy kills his father in a quarrel on the road, not knowing who he has slain. He then solves the riddle presented by the Sphinx and as reward is given Jocasta, the widowed queen, as his wife. When Jocasta realizes she has wed her own son, she hangs herself. Oedipus puts out his own eyes and wanders about with his daughter, Antigone, until he is destroyed by avenging deities.

The Oedipus story has always infuriated me. Will someone please explain the poetic justice in this particular horror tale? Poor Oedipus didn't willingly lust after his mother, nor vice versa, and he didn't know he had killed dear old Dad. However, dear old Dad *did* start it all by willfully intending to kill his own son. That's what

Laius got for being superstitious and believing in oracles. He should have believed in them more fully and not bothered to try to kill Oedipus since one cannot escape "fate." Oh well, I suppose it all falls under John F. Kennedy's observation that "Life is unfair," but I do think the avenging deities should have thought twice and let Oedipus and Jocasta off with a warning.

Freud borrowed the hidden implications of this myth as his name for the "family romance" which he claimed arises in the phallic period of psychosexual development, gathering force between ages three and seven. The Oedipal situation is repressed from ages six to eleven, revived at puberty, and resolved in later life. Freud maintained the Oedipal relationship of mother and son is gradually given up because of the son's fear of retaliation from the competing father.

Freud thought this was all a universal phenomenon; he held it to be so strong that it accounts for the historical incest taboo found in most cultures. Anthropologists disagree, because there are many cultures in which no incest taboo appears. A number of psychiatric theorists have also disagreed with Freud, but whether he was right or wrong, there is now no excising the expression "Oedipus Complex" from the language and it surely belongs in the complicated language of mothers, as well as in consideration of their complicated relationship with their sons.

✻

Gaea, honored as the great earth mother of ancient Greek mythology, enjoyed a continuing amorous relationship with her son Uranus, the sky god. Among the offspring which resulted from this mother-son union were the Titans and Titanesses, the one-eyed giants known as the Cyclopes (sic) and the hundred-handed monsters called the Hecatoncheires.

✻

# BACKGROUND

. . . the nakedness of thy mother, shalt thou not uncover: she is thy mother; thou shalt not uncover her nakedness.

Leviticus XVIII: 7

"If the young wild beast were left to itself, and if the untutored mind of the child in the cradle were combined with the violence of passion of a man of thirty, then he would break his father's neck and ravish his mother."

(According to Dr. Herbert Maisch in *Incest*, this was the phrase of the French poet and philosopher Diderot, in his satire, *Le Neveu de Rameau*, that was used by Freud over a hundred years later in his *Interpretation of Dreams* as the basis of the Oedipus theory.)

*

The warmest bed of all is Mother's.

Yiddish proverb

*

# NERO AT MOTHER'S KNEE

The passion (Nero) felt for his mother, Agrippina,* was notorious; but her enemies would not let him consummate it, fearing that, if he did, she would become even more powerful and ruthless than hitherto. So he found a new mistress who was said to be her spit and image; some say that he did, in fact, commit incest with Agrippina every time they rode in the same litter—the state of his clothes when he emerged proved it.

From *The Twelve Caesars*,
by Gaius Suetonius Tranquillus,
translated by Robert Graves.

*

PSYCHOANALYST ERNEST JONES ON HAMLET:

". . . the main theme of this story is a highly elaborated and disguised account of a boy's love for his mother and consequent jealousy of and hatred towards his father . . ."

From *Hamlet and Oedipus*

---

* For more on this subject, in the honorable tradition of the linking of love and hate, see pages 67–69.

# HISTORICALLY SPEAKING

Julius Caesar's 49 B.C. crossing of the Rubicon, the narrow stream separating ancient Italy from Gaul, had an effect on our language as well as the history of Rome. The expression "to cross the Rubicon" signifies taking a step from which there is no turning back. And it all happened because of what Sigmund Freud would surely have filed as a "classic Oedipal dream." According to Plutarch (and other historians), the night before Caesar made his fateful decision to lead his troops across the Rubicon, he had a dream in which he made passionate love to his mother. Innocent of Freud's views on such matters, Caesar interpreted the dream as an augury of victory and conquest. He therefore took the step which was tantamount to a declaration of war and which did, indeed, lead to his conquest of Rome.

\*

# STENDHAL'S PASSION

The French novelist Stendhal, in the words of his biographer F. C. Green, "loved his mother with an intensity of passion remarkable even for a Frenchman." Here's how Stendhal described it himself in his autobiographical novel, *La Vie de Henri Brulard:*

> My mother, Mme. Henriette Gagnon, was a charming woman and I was in love with my mother . . . I wanted to cover my mother with kisses, and without any clothes on. She loved me passionately and often kissed me; I returned her kisses with such fervour that she was often forced to go away. I abhorred my father when he came to interrupt our kisses. I always wanted to kiss her bosom. Please be kind enough to remember that I lost her in childbed when I was barely seven . . . She died in the flower of her youth and beauty in 1790; she must have been twenty-eight or thirty. That was when the life of my mind began.

> According to another of Stendhal's biographers, Matthew Josephson, this passage "astonished Freud himself when it was brought to his attention seventy-five years after it was written."

# INCEST BRIEFS

George Burchett, the London tattooist mentioned in Mothers and Sons, remarked on the number of young men who wanted "Mother" etched onto their bodies. "Maybe a psychiatrist would say that the impulse was some kind of Oedipus Complex. But I very much doubt it."

Among the Kalangs in Java, mother-son marriages are looked upon as bringing special good fortune in the way of fertility and riches.

✳

You think Oedipus had a problem? Adam was Eve's mother.

Graffiti at Philadelphia<br>construction site

According to an old Philippine legend, the only survivor of the Flood was a pregnant woman. She gave birth to a son and when he grew to manhood they made love with the noble aim of preventing the extinction of mankind.

The following is an old incest joke, or what the mother of stage manager Murray Gitlan refers to as "an incense joke":

"Brother, you are really good in bed."

"Yes, sister, that's what Mother says."

✳

STORY CURRENT IN THE MIDDLE AGES ABOUT JUDAS:

Before he was born his mother Cyborea had a dream that he was destined to murder his father, commit incest with his mother, and sell his God. The attempts made by her and her husband to avert this curse simply led to its accomplishment. At his birth Judas was enclosed in a chest and flung into the sea; picked up on a foreign shore, he was educated at the court until a murder committed in a moment of passion compelled his flight. Coming to Judea, he entered the service of Pontius Pilate as page, and during this period committed the first two of the crimes which had been expressly foretold. Learning the secret of his birth, he, full of remorse, sought the prophet who, he had heard, had power on earth to forgive sins. He was accepted as a disciple and promoted to a position of trust, where avarice, the only vice in which he had hitherto been unpracticed, gradually took possession of his soul, and led to the complete fulfilment of his evil destiny. This Judas legend as given by Jacobus de Voragine, obtained no small popularity; and it is to be found in various shapes in every important literature of Europe.

Rev. George Milligan, D.D.
in the 1911 Encyclopaedia
Britannica (sometimes called
"The Scholars' Edition")

✳

# A MOTHER'S BOUDOIR

Love without grace is like a hook without bait.
—Anne de Lenclos .

-The Paris boudoir of Anne de Lenclos—known more familiarly as Ninon—was, for what one Victorian historian called "a preposterous length of time," a magnet for distinguished courtiers from Normandy to Provence through much of the seventeenth century. So many highborn gentlemen came to worship at her altar of love that, years later, Britain's Horace Walpole saluted her as "a veritable *Notre Dame des Amours*." Ninon maintained her position as the coquette of coquettes in the French capital until she was well into her fifties and then, unwilling to let so much exquisite experience go to waste, established a School for Gallantry designed to teach young aristocrats the art of courting and seduction. It was in her capacity of headmistress to this institution that, according to legend, she had her only real brush with tragedy.

Among the young blades who enrolled in her school in the 1670s was the Chevalier de Villiers, her own son by a Parisian gentleman who had raised the boy in ignorance of his mother's identity. Ninon recognized her new pupil immediately, but, in deference to a promise made to the father, felt she could not reveal herself to him.

So the inevitable happened. Like his father before him, the eager chevalier fell desperately in love with the worldly charmer and, mistaking maternal solicitude for passion, demanded that the affair be consummated. Ninon, grasping for an explanation for her seeming rejection, finally sought permission to tell her lovelorn son who she really was. But this, alas, only made things worse. Completely shattered by the revelation, the chevalier rushed into the garden of Ninon's establishment, drew his sword, gave an anguished cry of "Mother!" and thrust the blade into his heart.

Since Ninon, as one of her biographers puts it, "has collected apocrypha like barnacles," this tragic saga of mother passion may not be true. But Voltaire, who met Ninon when he himself was a young man, accepted it without question. "Ninon's son," he remarked, "was not as philosophical as his mother."

\*

# DANIEL AND HIS
# MOTHER?

Was the relationship between Daniel Ellsberg and his mother a key factor in the downfall of the Nixon administration in 1974? Could be. After Ellsberg's celebrated leaking of the top-secret Pentagon Papers to the New York *Times* in 1971, the White House ordered the CIA to prepare a psychiatric profile on him. Finding the resulting report too inconclusive to discredit the anti-Vietnam activist, White House plumbers G. Gordon Liddy and E. Howard Hunt burgled the office of Dr. Lewis Fielding, his Los Angeles psychiatrist. When this illegal act, with its implication of "misuse of power," was uncovered, it became an important link in the chain reaction which led to the motion for Richard Nixon's impeachment.

The original CIA study interpreted Ellsberg's entire career in Oedipal terms. When Ellsberg was fifteen, his family was in an automobile accident in which both his mother and sister were killed. Since his father was at the wheel, the CIA psychiatrist suggested that young Dan, resenting his father for "killing" his mother and later marrying another woman, turned his hostility to all those in authority over him. It was this unconscious desire to "revenge" his mother's death, the profile suggested, that led Ellsberg to his purloining of the Pentagon Papers. The CIA report declared that when Dan Ellsberg warned against the dangerous power of the Executive, it was actually his father he unconsciously longed to destroy.

✳

## SALVADOR DALI EXPLAINS WHY VANDALS ATTACK THE MONA LISA:

Knowing all Freud thought about Leonardo da Vinci, all that the latter's art kept hidden in his subconscious, it is easy to deduce that he was in love with his mother when he painted the "Gioconda." Without realizing it, he painted someone who has all the sublimated maternal attributes. She has big breasts, and she looks upon those who contemplate her in a wholly maternal way. At the same time, she smiles in an equivocal manner. Everybody has seen, and can still see today, that there was a very determinant element of eroticism in that equivocal smile. So, what happens to the poor wretch who is possessed by an Oedipus complex, that is, the complex of being in love with his mother? He goes into a museum. A museum is a public house. In his subconscious it is a brothel. And in this brothel he sees the representation of the prototype of the image of every mother. The agonizing presence of his mother gives him a tender look and an equivocal smile and drives him to a criminal act. He commits matricide by picking up the first thing that comes to hand, a stone, and destroying the painting. . . .

From Diary of a Genius

✳

# INCEST JOKE, TOAST, AND DOUBLE DACTYL

Karen, all upset, dialed her mother on the phone. Steve, her intended, had begun visiting an analyst.

325

"So what's so terrible about that?" asked Karen's mother.

"I'm worried about our marriage, Ma," cried Karen. "The doctor says Steve has a terrible Oedipus complex."

"Don't listen to that fancy talk," soothed the voice on the other end of the line. "I've watched Steve and I tell you he's a fine boy. Look how he loves his mother."

And at the San Francisco tattoo studio of Lyle Tuttle, one of the most popular "Mother" designs consists of a wreath of flowers enclosing this variation:

> The sweetest girl I ever
> kissed was another
> man's wife
> My Mother.

> Here's to the happiest hours of my life,
> Spent in the arms of another man's wife—my mother.
>
> Popular Toast

> Higgledy Piggledy
> Oedipus Tyrannos
> Murdered his father, used
> Mama for sex.
>
> This mad debauch, not
> Incomprehensibly,
> Left poor Jocasta and
> Oedipus Wrecks.
>
> Double Dactyl composed by
> Joan Munkacsi for one of
> Mary Ann Madden's *New York*
> *Magazine* competitions

*

# OH, SHAW!

George Bernard Shaw once told the actress Lilli Palmer, "I've never liked Sophocles. Has no sense of humor. Give me Euripides any

time. As a matter of fact, I always wanted to rewrite the *Oedipus*."
Lilli says Shaw paused and looked at her shyly: "Now then, tell me,
why should that fellow Oedipus get into such a state when he finds
out that he's married to his mother? It should have added to his
affection!"

✻

# CRUEL AND WICKED

The prosecutors at the Paris trial, in 1793, which dispatched Marie
Antoinette to the guillotine did not limit their accusations against
the Queen to "crimes against France" of a political nature. The at-
tackers of the noblewoman known as "the widow Capet" climaxed
their case with a denunciation emblazoned with such shocking details that many of Marie's biographers delicately gloss it over and
others ignore it entirely. The accusation was, as one prosecutor
summed it up, that "forgetting she was a mother and disregarding
the limitations set by the laws of nature, she had not been afraid to
practice with Louis Capet, her son, indecencies whose very idea and
whose mere name arouse a shudder."

The evidence presented to the jury consisted of a deposition
stating that the eleven-year-old Dauphin, imprisoned apart from his
mother, had been discovered by his jailers "several times in his bed
. . . committing indecent defilements, harmful to his health." Under
stern questioning, the deposition continued, the lad confessed that
he had initiated this practice at the urging of his mother and aunt
and "that these two women often made him lie down between
them; that there then took place acts of the most uncontrolled de-
bauchery; that there was no doubt from what Capet's son said, that
here had been an act of incest between the mother and son.

"There is reason to believe," the document continued, "that
this criminal intercourse was not dictated by pleasure but by the
calculated hope of enervating the child, whom they still liked to
think of as destined to occupy a throne and whom they wished to
be sure of dominating morally as a result of this scheme."

As things turned out, this envenomed prosecutorial overkill
misfired. When a juror asked the white-faced Marie Antoinette to
comment on these charges, her response touched even the most
bloodthirsty observers. "If I did not reply," the Queen told the
jury, with great dignity, "it was because nature recoils from such an
accusation brought against a mother." Then, turning to the crowd,

she cried: "I appeal to all you mothers here!"

"At this sublime cry," wrote two eyewitnesses, "an electric shock ran through everyone present. The *Tricoteuses** were moved in spite of themselfes and they very nearly applauded."

Despite the momentary wave of sympathy, the Queen was doomed, found guilty of other, political, charges. She was carried off to her beheading on October 16, 1793, six days before her son's twelfth birthday.

As for the incest charge, biographers who deal with the subject believe it was pure calumny. Evidence indicates that a combination of brandy, brainwashing, and beatings led Marie's son to sign his name to the affidavit accusing his beloved mother of corrupting him.

✷

# FRENCH WITHOUT TEARS

One of the classic movies about incest is Frenchman Louis Malle's understanding and tender *Murmur of the Heart*, which he both wrote and directed. In it the sensitive fifteen-year-old youngest son in a French household with two older brothers is doted on by his warm, young, and sexy Italian mother, who is more like a sister to her sons. Mother and youngest go away together for the boy to recover from a heart murmur and in the resort hotel must share a suite. On Bastille Day the mother becomes intoxicated and her eager and precocious son, tormented by puberty and virginity, goes to bed with her. In a moving aftermath, the mother tells the boy that they will reserve the experience as a tender memory but never speak of it again. The boy moves from his mother's arms with a new vigor and rather than being crippled by the happening, he immediately transfers his feelings to an adolescent girl. The ending, unthinkable in Puritan America, is a happy one.

✷

## Afterword
One of my own most interesting enlightenments regarding the

---

* The women always hideously at hand with their knitting as the heads fell from the guillotine.

Oedipus legend came when writer Elaine Dundy was quizzing me for a magazine profile. Elaine is famous for her off-beat questions and she suddenly asked, "What popular songs do you find yourself singing and why?"

After admitting that I frequently sing "Sand in My Shoes," "I Left My Hat in Haiti," and Cole Porter's "Ours" as rendered by Mabel Mercer, and used to sing "I Love You, Porgy" because it was the only song to which my cat Jasmine would come running, I realized that the number I'm most apt to do for my amusement is "That's Entertainment!" written by Howard Dietz and Arthur Schwartz for the movie *The Bandwagon.*

And, as if turns out, my favorite lyric in this catchy number?

> The plot can be hot simply teeming with sex
> A gay divorcee who is after her "ex"
> It could be Oedipus Rex
> Where a chap kills his father
> And causes a lot of bother . . .

The Oedipus myth has been written about by experts, but never more charmingly and delicately than by H.D. And why is this verse my favorite? I think simply because it's so tricky to learn and satisfying to render. And, it's taboo.

# Mother's Day

Mother's Day has long been in the top ten, third from the top, as the year's Sunday services go.

Minister's wife

I was raised a Southern Baptist Sunday School and "stay for church" goer. So Mother's Day was of some minor moment in our house, for it broke the monotony of five Sundays a year with a little tremolo of "specialness" always so welcome to children. There was invariably a sermon on the subject of mother.

Elizabeth, the mother of John the Baptist, was a big favorite, as was Sarah, who had conceived at age ninety. Generally, Mary, the mother of Jesus, was handled gingerly by the fundamentalists who considered her mostly a preserve of the Catholics and thereby dangerous. A really perceptive preacher might slip in some healthy parent-child separation psychology by telling us again the important story of Jesus disappearing into the temple at age twelve to talk to the elders and how he scolded his mother when she found him, by saying: "Know ye not, I must be about my Father's business?"

The sermon was the least of it. We were usually preoccupied with pinning on and wearing our red carnations to symbolize devotion to a mother who was still alive, noting with a thrill of fear the people who wore white flowers because their mothers were dead. My brothers and I secretly wondered and whispered about how it would feel—sometime . . . some horrible day, to be pinning on the white carnation? And there was always someone in our family pew wearing a white flower, for our grandparents had no living parents that we could remember.

The ritual of the flowers was a small thing; it only served to give continuity to our lives and to remind us for one day to be nicer, sweeter, more thoughtful of mother who could always shame us to tears anytime we slipped and "acted ugly."

Mother's Day has turned into something of a joke for the sophisticated. It is a day that brings out gritty editorials and comments on "commercialism." Even the traditionalists don't want to make too much of giving Mother her "day" when the times have changed so much that it seems like merely a sop and everybody knows Mother is either due 365 days as a fully recognized person, or let's just forget the whole thing, due to overemphasis.

But like millions of others, I still remark Mother's Day. I do send the "cute" cards and sometimes a plant or box of candy or a special note. I suppose it is all in the spirit with which one celebrates any occasion; like Christmas, either a glory or a horror. I must admit the material in this chapter is surprising. My researcher and I approached Mother's Day as a subject rather as if we were about to bridle a nasty horse, sidling up to it reluctantly. But it turned out to be fascinating and—nothing we expected.

Mother's Day is not for total ignoring, yet. The writer Martha Weinman Lear and I once worked together as production assistants for NBC. We were "immortalized," I as "The Brain" and Martha as "The Body," in a novel by Stanley Flink called *Will They Get It in Des Moines?* As years went by, Martha proved that she was not only "The Body," but "The Brain" as well.

On Mother's Day, 1975, she wrote an article for the New York *Times Magazine*. Response to her meditations about her ambivalent relationship with her mother elicited more mail than anything else she ever wrote. Martha received letters for months and is still introduced as "the one who wrote that Mother's Day piece."

Later Martha noted that the letters people sent for publication tended to be negative, even enraged, suggesting that no normal person would ever have such feelings about their mother. Yet the private response seemed to be saying, "I'm so relieved that I'm normal." Martha concluded: "I believe the intensity of both the rage and the relief come from the same source. You're not supposed to acknowledge the ambivalence you may feel for a parent or a child. The people who were enraged have feelings they don't dare face in themselves. These are feelings that people are terribly guilty about or terribly frightened about."

I am unable to reprint Martha's controversial article, but this is its telling opening sentence:

"Mother's Day, bittersweet."

✻

# A POEM FOR MY MOMMA

Dear Momma, it's Mother's Day, and I'm first in line,
To tell the world "The Greatest" is grateful you're mine!
For raising and teaching, the world's prettiest son,
Between you and me, you're Number One!

> Mother's Day poem written by
> Muhammad Ali for the *Ladies' Home
> Journal*, 1977

✻

# THE BITTER AUTHOR
# OF MOTHER'S DAY
### *by Oscar Schisgall*

One day in 1925 a tall, energetic, determined-looking woman walked into a Philadelphia hotel and marched up to a group of War Mothers, who were holding a convention. In loud tones she harangued the group, denouncing them for selling Mother's Day white carnations at a profit. Several people tried to calm her, but she was too angry to be stopped. Finally, a policeman was called, and the irate woman was arrested for disturbing the peace. Thus ended one more incident in the stormy career of Miss Anna Jarvis, who was the prime mover in establishing Mother's Day.

When Miss Jarvis was released by an embarrassed magistrate, a reporter went to see her at her home on North Twelfth Street in Philadelphia. Miss Jarvis, a handsome gray-haired woman of sixty, sat in a straight-backed chair, facing a portrait of her mother.

333

"Miss Jarvis," he asked, "why can't you stop fighting the world? You ought to be proud that you're the founder of Mother's Day."

"They're commercializing it," she answered. "Did you read what I wrote President Coolidge?"

He nodded. The letter had been in the newspapers. She had said, "I'm trying in every way possible to prevent Mother's Day from being desecrated by the greed of individuals and organizations who see in it only a way to make money."

"But, Miss Jarvis," the reporter argued, "nobody is profiting from Mother's Day in any unethical way. After all, it was you who spent years urging that the white carnation be made the emblem of Mother's Day. It was you who *urged* people to send messages of love by card or telegram to their mothers."

"In other words," Miss Jarvis said, "you're telling me that my success is also my defeat. Well, you're right, young man. That happens to be the paradox of my life."

It was not the only paradox in Anna Jarvis's life. Though she was an extremely attractive woman, she never married. In Grafton, West Virginia, where she was born in 1864, she had grown into a tall, red-haired beauty. Why did such a girl remain single?

"She had a disastrous love affair when she was young," a friend of the family said. "It left her shocked and disillusioned, and thereafter she turned her back on all men."

When she left Mary Baldwin College in 1883 she threw herself into teaching school in Grafton. Not that she needed the salary. Her widowed mother was well-to-do. A few years later Anna, her mother, and Anna's blind younger sister, Elsinore, moved to Philadelphia. Anna took a job as assistant in the advertising department of an insurance company. Through her twenties and thirties, that was her life. Then, in 1905, her mother died. It was a blow, of course, but it marked the beginning of a vital new era for Anna Jarvis.

She was forty-one, mistress of a fine home, guardian of her blind sister and chief beneficiary of her mother's estate. During the period of mourning, she conceived her vision: the establishment of a Mother's Day for everybody.

She suggested her idea to Mayor Reyburn of Philadelphia. That was the beginning of Anna Jarvis's crusade in which she insisted that deference be paid to living mothers, as well as to those who had died. From her home she conducted one of the strangest and most effective letter-writing campaigns in history. She wrote to governors, congressmen, clergymen, industrialists, women's clubs —to anybody who could wield influence. The mail that came in answer to these letters was so overwhelming—and demanded so much additional correspondence—that Anna gave up her job to devote herself wholly to her campaign.

When she found that her house was too small to serve as an office, she bought the house next door. Soon she was invited to visit other cities to speak before various organizations. She wrote and printed booklets about her plan, distributing them free. All these activities ate deeply into her inheritance, but Anna never allowed this to bother her.

These were the days when other militant women were fighting for suffrage. Anna Jarvis's aims were more sentimental, less controversial. How could a legislator fight anything as sweet and pure and idealistic as a Mother's Day? West Virginia was the first state officially to adopt the holiday; then Pennsylvania and others joined the march.

Anna Jarvis, inspired by these first triumphs, continued to write, travel, and speak. In 1914 her eloquence persuaded Representative J. Thomas Heflin of Alabama and Senator Morris Sheppard of Texas to present a joint resolution for the nationwide observance of Mother's Day. The resolution was passed by both houses of Congress.

Anna's real hour of glory came when President Woodrow Wilson signed the proclamation which urged that the second Sunday in May (the anniversary of her mother's death) be observed as Mother's Day. For Anna this triumph was not enough. There was still the rest of the world to conquer. So the writing, the speechmaking, the exhorting booklets continued, on an international scale. She was remarkably successful. In the course of her life forty-three other countries adopted Mother's Day.

Unfortunately, the triumph was mixed with frustration. "They're commercializing my Mother's Day," she was presently writing in despair to hundreds of newspapers. "This is not what I intended. I wanted it to be a day of sentiment, not of profit."

For some reason she regarded florists as her principal "enemies." Not that she didn't despise manufacturers of greeting cards and candy, and everybody else who made money of her Day. But the florists represented something special; they were profiting from her mother's favorite flower, the white carnation.

Officials of the florists' organization came to her. "*We* didn't start this, Miss Jarvis," they explained. "But now we can't stop it, and we can't help profiting by it. People *demand* flowers."

By now the money Anna had inherited was gone. Suddenly, she locked herself up in the North Twelfth Street house, alone with her sister, and refused to receive anybody. For years she kept the world out of her life. She died in 1948 in the Marshall Square Sanitarium in West Chester, Pennsylvania.

One Mother's Day before she died a reporter, pretending he was delivering a package, managed to see her. "She told me, with terrible bitterness, that she was sorry she had started Mother's Day."

—from *Reader's Digest*

❋

# ONE WAY TO GO

Jean Bokassa, president of the Central African Republic, is another one of those daring and innovative Third World leaders. To honor Mother's Day this year, Bokassa ordered all the rapists, child molesters, and mother killers taken out of the country's jails, brought to the C.A.R. capital of Bangul, and beaten to death in the market square. And we'll bet you just sent flowers.

—*Oui*, 1974

❋

# CARNAL KNOWLEDGE

Orgiastic excesses characterized what might be considered "the original Mother's Day," a Roman holiday known as the Hilaria and celebrated for three days after the Ides of March. Inaugurated in Rome in the third century B.C., the Hilaria was dedicated to a pagan goddess named Cybele, sometimes called "The Great Mother of the Gods," sometimes as "the all-Begetter, the all-Nourisher" and sometimes merely as "Mother of Nature." This revel bore little resemblance to our own gentle annual salute to Mom. Cybele was associated with drums, cymbals, flutes, and horns; thus her holidays were first and foremost *loud*. And since she was also thought to symbolize the powers of reproduction and fruitfulness in man, plants, and animals, the Roman's Hilaria was typified more by carnality than carnations.

Closer to our sort of Mother's Day was the English tradition known as "Mothering Sunday," observed on the fourth Sunday of Lent in the seventeenth century. Sons and daughters who had apprenticed themselves or taken jobs as servants made a point of returning home on this day, bringing with them small gifts or a "mothering cake" for Mum. The pastry, also called *simnel cake*, was a rich fruit cake, remembered by Robert Herrick in the lines:

> I'll to thee a Simnell bring,
> 'Gainst thou go'st a-mothering,
> So that when she blesseth thee,
> Half that blessing thou'lt give me.

Nowadays, of course, Mother's Day is big, big business—a time of rejoicing for greeting card manufacturers, florists, candy makers, Ma Bell, and Western Union, not to mention stores and restaurants featuring Mother's Day specials.

According to the Hallmark Card people, Mother's Day ranks fourth as a card-sending occasion—behind Christmas, Valentine's Day, and Easter, but ahead of Father's Day and Halloween. On an average first week in May, postmen slip more than 105 million cards into the mailboxes of American moms. The messages, says Hallmark editor Alan Doan, are often much longer than those of other card-types. "While most cards today have short sentiments, longer traditional verse is popular on Mother's Day—sometimes as long as two dozen lines." Concludes Doan: "People seem to want to send Mom as much love as possible."

＊

# "MOTHER CHURCH"

The little Andrews Methodist Church in Grafton, West Virginia, because of its early adoption of Anna Jarvis's concept, is now the recognized "Mother Church" of Mother's Day. On sale at this official Mother's Day Shrine, Inc.,* are brass plaques which can be engraved with a mother's name and birth and death dates and will be permanently displayed on a bronze tablet in the church. Prices range from fifty dollars to one thousand dollars.

* Its official name.

# AN ABBY WARNING

Mother's Day is a day of gladness to most mothers. But not for all. I should know. For weeks following Mother's Day, my desk is covered with the tear-stained letters of mothers who have been snubbed, slighted or forgotten.

Abigail Van Buren in her
"Dear Abby" column

\*

# VARIED OPINIONS

Aldous Huxley defined the Mother's Day card as "Greetings with poems printed in imitation handwriting, so that if Mom were in her second childhood she might be duped into believing that the sentiment was not a reach-me-down, but custom-made, a lyrical outpouring from the sender's overflowing heart."

\*

No man would dare say a bad word against Mother's Day in public, or a good word for it in private.

—Alistair Cooke

\*

Americans devote one day of the year to mothers, and an entire week to pickles.

Anonymous

Andy Hardy (Mickey Rooney) and "Mom" (Fay Holden) in one of the *Andy Hardy* movies. Mother Hardy was long-suffering through a series of silly son sequels. The tycoon Louis B. Mayer kept his sentimental Jewish eye on their middle-American WASP nest.

Vivien Leigh as Scarlett O'Hara and Hattie McDaniel as Mammy in *Gone With the Wind* (1939). Both these dazzling actresses won Oscars for their depiction of one of the old South's most basic black and white relationships.

Mrs. Jumbo comforts her son Dumbo (1941). Walt Disney could wring our hearts with his irresistible animal mothers. And how about Bambi's mother?

## MY YOUNG MOTHER.

Author's mother, Elizabeth.
In Mississippi gym costume,
age sixteen.

College uniform—1911.

The bride—1914.

Elizabeth and Sloan, their wedding day—1914. The best man, the bride (note bird on hat), the groom (in profile), the bridesmaids.

Young parents (Mother and Daddy) with brother James, who always appears to be smelling something terrible. Lubbock, Texas, BL (Before Liz)

Beautifully black. Dott Burns and brother Bobby.

Countess Shumofsky and some of her children—Saint Clair, Ellen McCarter, William Kent, Lloyd Lee, Gloria Donna, and Daisy. (You can read about this optimistic Rose in the opening pages.)

Big Mama Smith with James and great-
grandchild Rebecca. Gonzales, Texas

Grandma McCall with James McCall Smith and Mary Elizabeth,
later Liz. Fort Worth, Texas

## A MOTHER'S WISHES.

The Mother as Child (Liz wanted this on the jacket).

The Mother-Child stand-off (We compromised.)

The Mother dignified (Mother wanted this on the jacket).

# "Mom" and Hollywood

We never make sport of religion, politics, race or mothers. A mother never gets hit with a custard pie. Mothers-in-law—yes. But mothers—never.

Mack Sennett

I spent my formative years observing "moms," as Hollywood saw them, in the finishing school of the Tivoli Theater of Fort Worth, Texas. It cost a dime every Saturday, for going to the movies any other time was unthinkable. This study was never interrupted, censored, nor interfered with by my real mother, who was no "mom." She was *Mother*. But she was too distracted by pressing realities to try to preselect her children's movie fare. She needn't have worried. The Hays office had done most of the worrying for her.

Hollywood has used miles of film on motherhood—going all the way from sacrificing mothers like Stella Dallas (impossible!) to heroic mothers (*Mrs. Miniver*) to goody-two-shoes mothers like Andy Hardy's (not so impossible—she reminded me a little of my own) to the mother-as-a-monster (countless examples), and on and on.

This chapter deals chiefly with Mother as she has so often been seen in the movies historically and sociologically. But it also includes a few anecdotes of "real" (as opposed to screen) Hollywood moms—or mothers of persons associated with the cinema industry. These real-life, non-fiction mothers appear in this section because they don't quite fit in with the behind-the-scenes mother so often described as a "stage mother" or "a screen mother."

One of the greatest perpetuators of the mother-as-mythic-perfection was the late tycoon Louis B. Mayer, who made motion pictures entirely within the "divine" dictates of his own, in-real-life, sacrificing, unquestioned Jewish mother, combined with his socially upward yearnings for the imagined WASP puritan-ethic mother so often exalted in MGM movies. A typical Mayer dictate was the one concerning how Andy Hardy (Mickey Rooney) treated his mother, the judge's wife (Fay Holden). In this money-making series, Mayer was implacable in the rigidity of right and wrong concerning morals and mother.

In an early Hardy picture, Andy, rebuffed by his sweetheart, Polly Benedict, came to the dinner table depressed, silent, toying with his food. "You're not eating, Andy," his mother noticed. "I'm not hungry, Mom," said Andy. Mrs. Hardy then mused, "I think it's his liver." The judge responded, "If what's ailing Andrew is his liver, a lot of boys are suffering liver trouble."

Bosley Crowther reports in his biography *Hollywood Rajah* that no one laughed during the preview of this scene and Mayer became almost violent. He took the screenwriter aside and said, "Don't you know a boy of sixteen is hungry *all* the time? You tell me you were brought up in a good American home—in the kitchen! You lied to me! You've let Andy insult his mother! No boy would tell his mother he wasn't hungry! Change that line!"

The writer made the suggested revision and the scene was reshot with Andy saying, "Thanks, Mom, your cooking is fine, but I don't feel like eating." Then Mrs. Hardy comments, "I think it's his liver" and the judge says his remark. The change got a good laugh at the next preview.

In another movie in the series, *Judge Hardy and Son*, Mayer was sarcastic about a prayer where Andy offered a lengthy speech over his mother who was ill. Mayer waxed profane: "Who the hell wrote *that* prayer?" Then he dictated to the writers: "You see, you're now a Hollywood character. You've forgotten your simple, honest boyhood. You don't remember how a real boy would pray. This is how a boy would do it . . ." With that, Mayer fell to his knees and indulged in one of the dramatic impersonations that made him a legend, and possibly made MGM great. He clasped his hands, raising his eyes to heaven: "Dear God, please don't let my mom die, because she's the best mom in the world. Thank you, God."

This prayer became a stock prayer for occasions in many MGM films. Out of Louis B. Mayer's profanity, it became the prototype of the sacred in Hollywood movies of the period, evoking both the Deity and "Mom" in short, pithy, informal ways that had universal appeal. Now the whole idea is a bit embarrassing—possibly because even the most antisentimental of us can *still* see the silly, simple beauty of it.

❋

# A FAULTY MOTHER MEMORY

Faye Bainter,* Andy Hardy's mother, screwed up every mother in the world. She really did, man. Dig, who can be like Faye Bainter, man? Faye Bainter was always in the kitchen sweeping with an apron. And Anglo-Saxon—and my mother was sweating and Jewish and hollering, man. Why couldn't she be like Faye Bainter? And that's what everyone wants their mother to be. And she was a virgin. Yeah, she never balled anyone because old Lewis Stone would say, "Andrew," and that was all, man. Unless there was some kind of pollination that way—through dates, or some esoteric, mystical thing, yeah. So that's some heavy propaganda, man.

—Lenny Bruce, quoted in
*It's Only a Movie*

❋

# A NEW DAY FOR MOTHER ON THE SILVER SCREEN
### by *James Robert Parish*†

Tracing the evolution of screen mothers is a short cut to charting the changes in maternal roles in the twentieth century.

* Bruce was confused. He meant Fay Holden, who played Mickey Rooney's mother in fourteen of the Andy Hardy films. You can identify her in the photo section of this book. Fay Bainter was William Holden's mother in the film version of Thornton Wilder's *Our Town*.

† Not to be confused with Robert Parrish, author of *Growing up in Hollywood*, whose work may be found in the chapter on stage mothers titled, "*Sing Out, Louise!*"

In the early era of the flickers, two stereotypes were accepted as true by the public and film makers. The first was inspired by Will Carleton's lachrymose poem, *Over the Hill to the Poorhouse*, detailing the plight of the sweet, hard-working woman whose only waking thoughts are of her children. Then in her old age when she most needs their comfort and support, they are nowhere to be found. At least four versions (1908, 1917, 1920 and 1931) of *Over the Hill* were filmed, the most famous the 1920 rendition starring Mary Carr.

The other stereotype was the decorous young miss, idealistic to a fault, who even after wedding and giving birth to children, remains innocent. D. W. Griffith pushed this concept to the limit in his fourteen-reel epic *Intolerance* (1916), in which a demure Lillian Gish played the ethereal mother of civilization, a young woman wistfully seeking heavenly guidance while firmly swaying the new generation. World War I hastened the change of the image. Women began performing men's chores in the factories and soon (1920) would have the constitutional right to vote. On screen, the great tragedienne Nazimova appeared in *War Brides* (1916), a vivid antiwar film that had much to say about women's new rights and obligations. In a mythical kingdom, where men about to go to war are urged to marry so there will be new babies for future wars, Nazimova is a war widow who would rather kill herself than give birth to another infant for cannon fodder. For many moviegoers, this heroine's philosophy was revolutionary.

Samuel Goldwyn's *Stella Dallas* (1925) set back the cause of mother's liberation several light years. Belle Bennett portrayed the uncultured miss from the wrong side of the tracks who marries society, gives birth to a daughter and later divorces her unhappy husband so he can wed a woman of his own class. The teary finale (also the highlight of Goldwyn's 1937 remake, starring Barbara Stanwyck) finds the lovelorn mother standing outside in the cold while within the cozy mansion her grown-up daughter is marrying a blueblood.

At least her child has a future; that is enough for her, as it was for Eugenie Besserer in the part-talking *The Jazz Singer* (1927). In one of moviedom's most memorable moments, spunky Al Jolson, playing her entertainer son, comes out to perform on stage, falls to his knees and belts out "Mammy" to his beaming, proud mama sitting in the front row.* She has everything in life she wants: the

* See also pages 145–46 for more about "Mammy."

hope that her son and the father (Warner Oland) will reconcile, and a belief that her child will be happy in his life's work. She needs nothing else for herself.

But the Roaring Twenties also turned out to be a period of change for the movie mom. Exotic Gloria Swanson in *The Impossible Mrs. Bellew* (1922) portrayed a self-sacrificing wife who consents to an unfavorable divorce so her son will never know his dad is an alcoholic. The sophisticated script permitted her thereafter to begin life nearly anew with a novelist, played by Conrad Nagel.

This emancipated concept was further developed in *Dancing Mothers* (1926), in which Alice Joyce outflappers the flapper to retaliate against her husband's affair. Not only is she enticing enough to attract the suitor of her daughter (Clara Bow), but in the finale she embarks for Paris, insistent that she has the right to her own life.

The stock market crash of October 26, 1929, which ushered in the Depression, created another push for women's liberation in real life and on film. With many men out of work, it became the women's chore to keep the family together, to find some way to meet the household budget.

Sometimes the way was practical but immoral, especially if Mama was young and unmarried. In *Common Clay* (1930), blond Constance Bennett set the pattern, playing the maid seduced by the scion of the house and abandoned by him. She and her child must fend for themselves, at least until the happy fadeout. Bennett repeated this basic formula in *Born to Love* (1931) and *Rockabye* (1932).

Sometimes the unwed mother trod the streets to support her youngster. Such was the case of Marlene Dietrich in *Blond Venus* (1932) and "It" girl Clara Bow in *Call Her Savage* (1932). Swank Kay Francis had to pay a supreme penalty in two such cinema studies. In *Mary Stevens, M.D.* (1932) her illegitimate child dies during an epidemic, while in *Give Me Your Heart* (1936) she relinquishes her infant to her titled lover (Ian Hunter) and his infirm wife (Frieda Inescort).

By the mid-1930s, America was getting back on its financial feet. Mothers were again mothers, tried-and-true, and none so typical as Fay Holden who, from *You're Only Young Once* (1938) to *Andy Hardy Comes Home* (1958), portrayed the understanding, apple-pie mom of Andy Hardy (Mickey Rooney). Another late 1930s homemaker was Penny Singleton of the *Blondie* series based on the Chic Young comic. Whether being the helpmeet to her addled spouse Dagwood (Arthur Lake), looking after the family dog, Daisy, or rearing her children, Baby Dumpling and Cookie, Blondie was a contemporary, if daffy, woman who had independent thoughts. So did Myrna Loy hold her own on the *Thin Man* team, matching martinis and wits with her detective husband, William Powell.

World War II did a great deal to push females into a more favorable status. Of course, there were the traditional screen mothers who remained the courageous fortresses at home, whether it be glamorous Greer Garson in *Mrs. Miniver* (1942) or the unadorned Selena Royle in *The Sullivans* (1944). But some supported their families and helped their country at defense factories while their husbands were in military service, like Claudette Colbert in *Since You Went Away* (1944). Mary Servoss in *So Proudly We Hail* (1943) volunteered for combat nursing duty and saw her son (Dick Hogan) killed in action.

By peacetime, 1945, Joan Crawford, in her Oscar-winning role in *Mildred Pierce* was discovering that a too-protective mother can wind up with a predatory tigress for a daughter (Ann Blyth). Farm wife Marjorie Main, wed to sleepy-eyed Percy Kilbride in the *Ma and Pa Kettle* series, demonstrated that a firm hand, a loud voice, and an arched eyebrow were sufficient to keep a brood of growing kids behaving properly. In *Imitation of Life* (1959), a lush remake of a 1934 Claudette Colbert weeper, Lana Turner portrayed an energetic mama who embarked on a theatrical career to provide for her child (Sandra Dee), forgetting her daughter's emotional needs in the meanwhile. Both competed for the affections of John Gavin.

British-born Angela Lansbury, meanwhile, was revealing another side of motherhood. In *The Reluctant Debutante* (1958), *Blue Hawaii* (1961) and *The World of Henry Orient* (1964), she portrayed a well-to-do matron whose offspring are bothersome to her freewheeling existence. In *Harlow* (1966) she outdid Rosalind Russell of *Gypsy* (1962) in typifying the all-demanding stage mother. In *All Fall Down* (1961) Angela pushed momism to villainous extremes, as she suffocated the independence of her children (Warren Beatty and Brandon de Wilde). She was even more frightening in *The Manchurian Candidate* (1962) as an Iron Curtain agent who manipulated her hypnotized son (Laurence Harvey) in an effort to assassinate the President.

Despite all that, Hollywood has clung to a fond image of Mom.

There was congenial Joan Bennett in *Father of the Bride* (1950) and *Father's Little Dividend* (1951), with flibberty-gibbet Billie Burke in both; and the wholesome, well-adjusted, matronly Maureen O'Sullivan who learns she's pregnant in *Never Too Late* (1965). There was also the widow with a brood who weds a widower with his own flock, as in Lucille Ball's *Yours, Mine and Ours* (1968) and Doris Day's *With Six You Get Eggroll* (1968). Eileen Heckart earned an Academy Award in *Butterflies Are Free* (1972), showing in a comedic way that Mama can admit mistakes in rearing her child and go on to new, constructive attitudes.

How has Women's Lib affected mothers on the screen? In *Prudence and the Pill* (1968), Deborah Kerr decides that if daughter Judy Geeson can use the pill for the dating game, so can she. In *Black Girl* (1973), Claudia McNeil, who made the point in *A Raisin in the Sun* (1961), demonstrated again that Mom has always been the financial and emotional mainstay of her family. In *Summer Wishes, Winter Dreams* (1973), Joanne Woodward, having just lost her mother (Sylvia Sidney), suddenly comprehends her own life's trap and, instead of accepting her fate, contemplates alternatives as wife, mother and, most of all, woman.

From the beginning, Hollywood has stuck to the premise that, if a woman permits romance, career or ideology to overshadow her responsibilities of motherhood, she must suffer for it. Recently, though, films have tended to resolve such conflicts by leaving mother with psychological pain rather than tragedy. It's likely that future screen moms will de-emphasize the demands of their children and stress their own needs. If the trend continues, Mom may become a movie swinger.

❋

# HOLLYWOOD DREAMS

Robert Parish offered us a big "if" in saying Hollywood's mom *may* become a movie swinger. So far, she really hasn't. Even Natalie Wood, a young miniskirted mother in the swinging sixties comedy about wife-swapping, *Bob and Carol and Ted and Alice*, couldn't really get into swinging by the movie's end despite all the liberated talk and trying.

In a blistering article called "Moms, Mommies and the American Dream," Marjorie Rosen noted that the movie mom has simply not kept up with reality. The author of the book *Popcorn Venus*, writes:

"Motherhood, like apple pie, is part and parcel of the American Dream, and movies have implemented our romance with it as the ultimate feminine contribution. Through the years Hollywood has sanctified motherhood as only that industry can; with romantic crescendos on the sound track (and *not* infants crying); with soft-focused portraits of madonnas (and *not* women swollen in discomfort, overcome by morning sickness, or exhausted from diaper cleanup); and with rosy family camaraderie, even if the family is the size of a baseball team. In fact, the quality of family life on screen has often been in direct proportion to the number of kids in the home. 'Ha-ha,' throws out Clifton Webb in *Cheaper by the Dozen* (1950) when a passerby asks how he feeds all those little mouths, 'They come cheaper by the dozen!' As any welfare mother knows, that's just hogwash.

"In Hollywood, she who reproduces has been, if not divine, then at least whole or complete. Whereas, the woman who chooses career over family has always been an evil sort, and the Woman Alone, neurotic. Right from the beginning, the movies propagandized for maternalism either head-on or subtly and marginally."

Movies have almost always been anti-abortion and the writer notes that contrary to James Robert Parish, Mom's new day on the silver screen hasn't happened yet. Rosen claims that "in truth, movies haven't progressed much beyond simplistic moralizing which insisted that women's place was in the nursery and kitchen." Then there was the era of child worship which she describes as "handmaiden to the glories of motherhood." There were films like Dorothy Maguire's *Claudia* which "envisioned motherhood as a rite of passage from puberty to maturity." The forties had romantic family movies like *Meet Me in St. Louis* and there were a few movies probing "the outer limits of smother-love" (*Stella Dallas* and *Mildred Pierce*). Rosen calls *The Miracle of Morgan's Creek* and *The Pumpkin Eater* exceptions. The first "parodies our maternalistic madness" by excusing an unwed girl who bears sextuplets and the second is "a thoughtful and perceptive film about a woman (Anne Bancroft) obsessed with childbearing, empty without a full womb."

Rosen continues: "Ah, you must be saying, *since the Pill and the erstwhile Sexual Revolution, movies are naturally more sophisticated about motherhood.* More cavalier, perhaps, but films have reflected cultural changes during the last decade with the kind of reactionary simplicity they are unfortunately so expert at achieving. Disregarding a perfectly dreadful 1966 release, *Prudence and the Pill*, I can only think of one screen heroine of the early sixties— Joan Hackett in Mary McCarthy's *The Group*—who even knew that birth control existed. For the most part, those women engaging in screen sex never heard about contraception, and they *all* conceived the first time out: Carol Lynley in *Blue Denim* (on stage she had an abortion; on film she had the baby); Natalie Wood in *Love with the Proper Stranger;* Connie Stevens in *Parrish;* Sandra Dee in *A Summer Place;* and Rita Tushingham in *A Taste of Honey* are a few examples. And all these girls kept their babies. Never was there a thought about the demands of motherhood, the restrictions and burdens.

"Interesting, too, how the sexually promiscuous heroine of the mid-sixties youth-culture flicks was also an emotional vacuum for whom motherhood provided emotional roots and instant identity. Lynn Redgrave in *Georgy Girl* (1966) drives away lover Alan Bates while doting on roommate Charlotte Rampling's abandoned daughter. Finally, Georgy, that big, homely girl with an instinct to 'save the world,' marries a wealthy old man to assure retaining custody of the child. For her (substitute) motherhood is a weapon to avoid dealing with that world and with men in particular.

"*Joanna*, a 1968 British import starring Genevieve Waite as an androgynous and rootless nymphet, is perhaps the quintessential reflection of the teeny-bopper life style, so it's particularly important that motherhood is a central theme. Here three young women voice promaternalistic sentiments: One has an abortion and regrets it; another laments never having had a child by a lover who has just died; the third, Joanna, becomes pregnant by a man who'll be in jail for ten years on a manslaughter charge. Though she can scarcely care for herself, at the movie's end she returns home to await her baby, a flowered shawl around her face, an exuberant pop madonna seemingly transfixed at fadeout. . . ."

". . . Paul Mazursky's 1973 *Blume in Love* detailed how that irrepressible combination, rape and pregnancy, emerge as a reconciliatory force between estranged husband and wife, George Segal and Susan Anspach. And Barbra Streisand's 1972 vehicle, *Up the Sandbox*, stacks up smartly among the most powerful promaternalistic statements to have come out of Hollywood, then or now.

"In *Sandbox*, the industry's sole 'bankable' woman at the boxoffice plays a housewife, exasperated with the drudgery of her existence, who finds she's pregnant and suddenly discovers her basic breeding instinct. There's a lengthy final fantasy sequence in which Streisand articulates a desire for 'maybe twenty-one' children; envisions her husband violently refusing her by spouting ecological necessities like a madman; entertains an endless nightmare about abortion, which is relieved only when she floats through the operating room into a playground inhabited by happy little tots. This final image from *Sandbox* eerily calls up those last scenes from Lois Weber's *Where Are My Children?* (1916) where the babes crawl all over her childless couple as punishment for the wife's indiscretion; indeed, the two films are separated only by fifty-eight years and vast technical improvements. Spiritually, they are one."

I am inclined to think writer Rosen is right—a 1977 release, *Outrageous*, is about a drag queen and a schizophrenic girl who feels she can only prove she's "alive" by being pregnant and who lapses into catatonia when she loses her baby. The drag queen encourages her pro-maternal instincts and urges her to carry on.

Rosen closes her piece asking: "So what's wrong with glorifying motherhood in movies? Presuming that film has even the tiniest impact, the answer is quite simple. Ecologically, it's unconscionable —our planet simply can't support that much more life. And economically it enforces the status quo with traditional role expectations . . . If we hold any hope at all for true equality between the sexes, it will occur when women can choose non-motherhood happily and without stigma. Motherhood should be a *cautious* choice, not an inevitability. 'Custom,' Margaret Sanger once wrote, 'controls the sexual impulse as it controls no other.' It also controls the Hollywood impulse and prescribes the American Dream. Should you notice a woman up there on that screen in the near future, think about all this . . . and you'll see what I mean."

*

Before the establishment of the first uniform Motion Picture Production Code in 1930, it was held immoral in at least one state "for a young wife to indicate, even by knitting booties, that she was expecting a baby," according to *The Memoirs of Will H. Hays.*

# SILVER THREADS AMONG THE DARK

In her book *Broadway & Hollywood: Costumes Designed by Irene Sharaff*, the brilliant designer noted how stars put a great value on youth, sometimes exaggerating it ridiculously. "At one time," she writes, "children of stars were not mentioned or allowed to appear with their star parents in person or in photographs. Until Dietrich broke the taboo, no star would admit to being a grandparent. Motherhood, to say nothing of grandmotherhood, was associated with gray hair. In one of the first movies I watched being filmed, the star was dismayed over having an eight-year-old son in the picture. The hairdresser, leaving her face untouched by the years, sprayed her hair a silver gray so the audience would accept her as a mother."

*

# HEDDA'S MOTHER

George Eells, in his book *Hedda and Louella*, recalls the introduction of Hedda Hopper's eighty-three-year-old mother, Mrs. Margaret Furry, to her daughter's tinsel-and-glitter world:

"Assuming that her mother would enjoy meeting the current ranking film beauties, Hedda invited them to a tea in Margaret Furry's honor. Mrs. Furry, who was deaf, sat entranced and after the tea was over said, 'It was lovely, Elda.* They all had such lovely sweet faces.' 'Oh, Mother, what a pity you couldn't hear them!' Hedda said.

"When Mrs. Furry again visited Hollywood in 1941, Hedda saw to it that she had a hearing aid. Once more, Hedda gave a tea with most of the same beauties in attendance. After the festivities, Hedda asked, 'Wasn't it wonderful, Mother! Didn't you enjoy it much more now that you could hear everything?'

"Mrs. Furry responded by reaching up and gently removing the hearing aid, which she placed in its box and handed to Hedda. 'Dear,' she said, 'I want you to take this back. They had such sweet, smiling faces at the first party, but this time I could hear all the ugly things they said about other people . . .'"

* Hedda Hopper's real name.

# MORE ON MAMMY

Beautiful black mothers have been treated elsewhere, but no analysis of screen mothers can dispense with consideration of the mammy in U.S. cinema.

Donald Bogle did a colorful presentation of the black and/or tan Hollywood "Mom" in his valuable book, *Toms, Coons, Mulattoes, Mammies, and Bucks: An Interpretive History of Blacks in American Films.*

Mr. Bogle's finest analysis is of the Hattie McDaniel character in *Gone With the Wind.* He notes of this film that despite its romantic unreality, its "black-white relationships were probably closer to the real ones of ante-bellum America than any ever before presented in the movies . . . But the really beautiful aspect of this film was not what was omitted but what was ultimately accomplished by the black actors who transformed their slaves into complex human beings.

"Hattie McDaniel portrayed the O'Hara family's faithful Mammy. Boasting that she diapered three generations of O'Hara women, Mammy is proud of the mutual affection between master and servant. During the war years it is she who keeps Tara, the family plantation, going. Like earlier film slaves, Hattie McDaniel's character is motivated almost solely out of concern for the master family, but her Mammy also feels confident enough to express anger toward her masters. She berates and hounds anyone who goes against *her* conception of right and wrong, whether it be Mrs. O'Hara or Scarlett and Rhett. Not once does she bite her tongue.

"But most significantly, Scarlett and Mammy maintain a complex mother-daughter relationship, much like those which actually existed in the old South, the kind of relationship that was either glossed over or treated condescendingly in other films. In *Gone With the Wind,* McDaniel's Mammy becomes an all-seeing, all-hearing, all-knowing commentator and observer. She remarks. She annotates. She makes asides. She always opinionizes. . . .

"It is Mammy who knows—and keeps secret—Scarlett's every plot. It is she who criticizes or advises, counsels or warns, protects or defends, but always understands. When Scarlett, just widowed, privately models a flashy new hat, it is Mammy who spies the action and promptly reprimands her. When Scarlett decides to return to Atlanta to request a loan from Rhett Butler, Mammy insists upon accompanying her. 'No proper young lady is going there alone!' she snaps. She even makes a dress for Scarlett from the green drapes

that once adorned Tara. As Scarlett walks the streets of Recon-
struction Atlanta, Mammy literally clears the way, pushing aside the
renegade blacks who line the sidewalks. Later, when Butler comes
to pay a call after Scarlett is widowed a second time, Mammy,
aware that Scarlett is not grieving at all (instead she's been hitting
the bottle), informs Scarlett in the haughtiest manner, 'I done tol'
him you was prostrate with grief!' Delivered by McDaniel, it was
the most perfectly timed, the funniest, indeed the most satiric line in
the film.

"Certainly *Gone With the Wind*'s script had much to do with
presenting such an inspired Mammy. It has always been said that
once Selznick had tested McDaniel for the role, he decided that
only she could play Mammy and made script changes to meet with
the special brand of McDaniel humor. Yet through the force of her
own personality, McDaniel's character became free of the greatest
burden that slavery—on screen and off—inflicted on blacks: a sense
of innate inferiority. Her Mammy has a self-righteous grandeur that
glows. Even audiences unaware of what a fine performer McDaniel
was sensed by her mammoth presence and her strong, hearty voice
that here was an actress larger than her lines, bigger than her role.
'Best of all,' wrote the New York *Times*, 'perhaps next to Miss
Leigh, is Hattie McDaniel's Mammy.' For her performance, Hattie
McDaniel became the first Negro to win an Academy Award as
Best Supporting Actress."*

※

# MAMMY NO. TWO

No black actress ever topped Hattie McDaniel in *GWTW*. But a
close runner-up for a memorable Hollywood mammy is Louise
Beavers in the 1940 film *Imitation of Life*. A fine, amply girthed
black woman, Louise plays Delilah, the mush-mouthed servant of
a Depression-ridden Claudette Colbert in the story based on Fannie
Hurst's 1933 novel.

Louise is as sweet as molasses and hands Claudette her secret
recipe for pancake mix which eventually earns them both a fortune.
Even after she is rich, Louise calls Claudette "Miss B," massages her

* McDaniel as Mammy can be seen in the photo section.

feet at night, runs the house, and remains a servant. In the movie Louise has a big problem—she has a little girl named Peola, who grows up with Claudette's own daughter and is taken for white.

The theme of a black person passing as white was audacious for the times and although today it seems ludicrous, *Imitation of Life* can still make you cry. In the movie, Peola rejects her dear mammy who comes to the white school to bring "ma baby" her galoshes. Teacher and class are shocked when they discover Louise is Peola's mammy and not just Miss B's servant. When Peola grows up, she turns on her mother in a finishing school accent, declaring herself white, white, white.

Louise whimpers: "Peola, doan call me mother. I'se yo' mammy. Ah ain't no white mother. I'se yo' mammy." After Peola runs away, Louise dies of a broken heart. The film ends in a blast of pathos—one of the most magnificent funerals ever staged, held in Harlem, with all white horses and a hearse, lodges in uniform and marching bands playing "Flee as a Bird to the Mountain." But it is Fredi Washington as Peola, who adds the final touch, rushing out of the crowd, throwing herself, grief-stricken, on the casket of the mammy she has rejected and killed.

In his autobiography *Black and White Baby*, the singer Bobby Short says the name Peola passed into Negro slang as an expression for a very light-skinned black. He writes that his people considered *Imitation of Life* ludicrous even in a pre-civil rights 1940. To them it was a silly vision of how whites saw blacks. However, it pointed up the hideous unfairness and advantage white people had over blacks and nobody who saw it could forget the injustice. Nor can they forget Peola throwing herself on mammy Louise Beaver's coffin either.

*

# MOTHER GOSHDARN

Typical of Hollywood's protective attitude toward even the raunchiest of mothers was the switch in names for the brothel-keeping bawd in *The Shanghai Gesture*. On Broadway in 1926, the character's name was "Mother Goddam." In the Joseph von Sternberg screen version in 1941, she was introduced as "Mother Gin Sling."

Incidental information: Though this part was *not* played by Bette Davis (actress Ona Munson did it in the movies after Florence

Reed created the role on stage), *Mother Goddam* served as the title for a book written about Davis and annotated by the star herself, who approved the title.

❋

# NORA SAYRE ON HOLLYWOOD'S SPORTS CLICHÉS

". . . mothers are far more central to sports movies than wives or girl friends, and good sons make a ceremony of giving them money. Even though mothers disapprove of pool rooms or the time wasted in batting practice, the relationship with the sporting sons is playful. Paul Newman as Rocky Graziano keeps chucking his (Eileen Heckart) under the chin, James Stewart as Monty Stratton repeatedly asks Agnes Moorehead, 'How's my girl?', Gary Cooper as Lou Gehrig says again and again that his mother is his 'best girl,' and encourages her to sit on his lap. But it's clear that mothers aren't easily amused, and a fur coat rarely buys off their mistrust of the arena."

*—The Village Voice*

❋

# MAKING IT UP TO MOTHER

Many of the films of François Truffaut have a strong autobiographical vein and this was especially true of his first production, *The 400 Blows*, for which he won the best-director award at the 1959 Cannes festival. "I only understand why I made some films years after they're finished," the film-maker told *Newsweek*'s Seth S. Goldschlager. "Ten years after I made *Jules and Jim* I realized it was my way of healing the wounds inflicted on my mother by *The 400 Blows*. I had to make that first film because it was the story of my childhood. But it was a murderous film for my mother. It was only very slowly that I understood she was a woman so filled with love for her husband that she could not afford any for her children."

# MARTY, MIND YOUR MOTHER

People in show business often put their mothers into their work just as I have put my mother into this book. The lure is irresistible and besides, who else will let you use them for free?

Lily Tomlin employed her mother Lily Mae in a science fiction story written by Jane Wagner for public television. John Cassavetes used both his mother and his wife's mother in several of his cinéma vérité movies though neither was a professional actress. He liked the improvisational real quality he got from them.

Director Martin Scorsese has put his mother into several pictures. When clips were shown of Mrs. Scorsese unsuccesfully catching her umbrella in the door of Robert De Niro's cab in *Taxi Driver*, the commentator remarked that the scene never appeared in the finished movie. She quipped that it took a lot of courage to hire your mother and even more to fire her.

Scorsese tells this story: "I used my mother first in *Mean Streets* and I was having some trouble with a close-up. 'Listen,' she said to me, 'the cameraman is tired. Do you really need this close-up? I know you. You probably won't even use it.' By that point, I was rather upset, so I told her to stand in the corner and be quiet until I was ready to use her.

"I'll never forget when she said to me, 'Don't you talk to your mother that way in front of strangers!'"

# "Tarnished Cradles"

I longed to shout the whole truth to the world, that my baby was Warren Harding's baby, that we were not married in the eyes of the world, but truly married in the sight of God, and that I was proud, proud, proud to be a mother.

Nan Britton in *The President's Daughter*

Back in the U.S. "dark ages" when the combustion engine was still rather young, even a thirty-mile trip by car could involve several flat tires, a spouting radiator, and—if the car was old enough—perhaps even a chance to crank to start, thereby courting a broken arm. I especially recall the trip from Fort Worth to Dallas as high adventure back in the days before supercars and highways came to link those cities into what is now almost a unity. The best part of the old days—aside from occasionally seeing a really unfortunate car with no spare tire "riding on the rim" and making sparks on the highway—were the whispered conversations of adults.

I had lots of gossipy aunts and cousins who had plenty to say that we children weren't supposed to overhear. Somehow the confinement in a car always brought out their best gossip and their juiciest need to whisper. They were as bad as the people in *The Scarlet Letter*. And the cream of these lifted eyebrow conversations were the ones about girls "in the family way" with no husbands.

This invariably happened as we passed a certain orphanage near Dallas. The children of this orphanage had all been born to unwed mothers. Tch, tch—went the whispers. Some of my relatives seemed to feel this was truly a blot on the otherwise perfect Texas escutcheon.

In 1941 MGM braved public opinion to make a film called *Blossoms in the Dust* in which the flawless Greer Garson played Mrs. S. Gladney, the founder of this same Texas orphanage. Mrs. Gladney was a woman who lost her own child and then took up the cause of the bar sinister. I was thrilled when I went to the movie to hear Greer repudiating old fogeyism (and many of my relatives) by saying: "There *are* no illegitimate children, only illegitimate parents!" It was the best thing I'd heard since discovering how Hester Prynne won her "A."

Though the film was a real tearjerker, it was a healthy signpost of sanity on the tormented puritan road that has finally led us to the day where the mother and the child are coming to mean more than the manners, the mores and the marriage license.

I say this while noting that the unwed mother, no longer made unequivocally miserable by society, is still an unending subject of fascination. As a gossip column item, she still rates high on the "they say" scale.

*

## NOT SO COMIC

356

The "new morality" in evidence in most of the media since the 1960s was late in showing itself in the world of the comic strip. It wasn't until September of 1976 that a high school girl in *Mary Worth* admitted, as the New York *Post* reported, "to the first illegitimate pregnancy in newspaper comic strip history." Writer Allen Saunders and artist Fred Ernst, who have worked on *Mary* since 1939, "kicked the idea around" for ten years before they felt the time was ripe to introduce the subject.

*

## BAR SINISTER STATISTICS

Washington, D.C. in 1975 became the first major American city in which more babies were born to unmarried mothers than to those who were married. According to the city's Human Resources Department, 4,988 children were born to unwed moms in the District of Columbia in 1975, compared with 4,758 born to married women. Nationally, about thirteen per cent of all children born in 1975 were born to out-of-wedlock mothers.

*

## ONLY YESTERDAY

Ingrid Bergman shattered her wholesome screen "St. Ingrid" image in 1949 when she left her husband and daughter in California to fly off to Italy and mother an out-of-wedlock child by Italian director Roberto Rossellini. Such was the climate of the times that when *Stromboli*, the first film she made with Rossellini, opened in the U.S. in 1950, it precipitated protests not only from pulpits but the floor of the U. S. Senate. In railing out against Bergman, Senator Edwin C. Johnson, Democrat of Colorado, called her "one of the most powerful women on this earth today—I regret to say a powerful influence for evil." This raging emotional scandal now seems like a tempest in a teapot but it kept Miss Bergman in exile from Hollywood for exactly twenty years. Ridiculous!

# Twenty Mothers Whose Out-of-Wedlock Babies Grew Up to Amount to Something

MOTHER: Servilia
DATE: circa 85 B.C.
BABY GREW UP TO BE: Brutus
CIRCUMSTANCES OF HER UNDOING: Official Roman records tell it differently but it was common gossip around the Forum that Brutus was the product of a youthful romantic liaison between the beautiful and wellborn Servilia and Julius Caesar himself. According to that old tattletale Plutarch, Caesar, in his youth, had "been very intimate with Servilia and she passionately in love with him, and considering that Brutus was born at about that time in which their loves were at the highest, Caesar had a belief that Brutus was his own child." Some historians say that, after the fatal attack against Caesar on the Ides of March, his death-cry was not, "*Et tu, Brute*," as Shakespeare put it, but actually, "*Et tu, mi fili, Brute!*"—"and you, my son, Brutus!"

MOTHER: Bertha (or Bertrada)
DATE: circa A.D. 742
BABY GREW UP TO BE: Charlemagne
CIRCUMSTANCES OF HER UNDOING: She was a count's daughter who became the favorite mistress of Pippin the Short (do you love it?), king of the Franks, and the lady he eventually singled out to marry. Court wags made considerable jest over the fact that the couple's young son was one of the most visible guests at the wedding. (Yes, this is the same Pippin celebrated in the Broadway musical.)

MOTHER: Herleve Fulbert
DATE: 1028 or 1029
BABY GREW UP TO BE: William the Conqueror
CIRCUMSTANCES OF HER UNDOING: The most romantic version of the story goes that the seventeen-year-old Herleve, a young woman of humble origins, was scrubbing her clothes in a brook when she was spotted by dashing young Duke Robert of Normandy. He whisked her off to his castle forthwith and William was conceived that very night. Sometime before morning, says this early legend, Herleve had a prophetic dream about the conqueror-to-be. In this

dream, a giant tree grew out of her body whose branches cast their shadow not only over all of Normandy but England as well. All that was missing was the date: 1066.

MOTHER: "A lady of good family of the city of Paris"
DATE: 1313
BABY GREW UP TO BE: Giovanni Boccaccio
CIRCUMSTANCES OF HER UNDOING: The father of the creator of *The Decameron* was a fourteenth-century Florentine version of a traveling salesman. His mother, according to one story, was a king's daughter; according to another, "a widow in her lonely bed." In any case, she was loved and left, and the great storyteller Boccaccio was documented at birth as illegitimate.

MOTHER: Caterina
DATE: 1452
BABY GREW UP TO BE: Leonardo da Vinci
CIRCUMSTANCES OF HER UNDOING: All that is known is that the relationship between Catarina and a Florentine lawyer came to an end shortly after the birth of Italy's great painter, sculptor, architect, musician, and engineer. She went off and married someone else and Leonardo was raised mostly by a stepmother. Sigmund Freud, in a much-cited monograph about Leonardo, theorized that the tantalizing smile on the painter's *Mona Lisa* was inspired by a romanticized memory of his lost mother. (For another Freudian view of the *Mona Lisa*, see Salvador Dali's theory, page 399.)

MOTHER: Francesca Gonzalez
DATE: 1471 or 1475
BABY GREW UP TO BE: Francisco Pizarro
CIRCUMSTANCES OF HER UNDOING: Gonzalo Pizarro, a soldier gifted in the art of seduction, was already a married man when he began to dally with the woman who eventually became the mother of the future conqueror of Peru. She bore a total of four illegitimate sons. One of them, Hernando Pizarro, helped his brother in the brutal New World conquest that helped wipe out the exquisite Inca empire.

MOTHER: Vannozza dei Catanei
DATE: April 18, 1480
BABY GREW UP TO BE: Lucrezia Borgia
CIRCUMSTANCES OF HER UNDOING: Vannozza's paramour was the

prominent Roman Catholic churchman Rodrigo Borgia. Sitting in St. Peter's basilica on an August day in 1492 Vannozza became one of the few mothers in history to watch the father of her children become Pope. (He occupied the Vatican for eleven years as Alexander VI and openly acknowledged the paternity of both Lucrezia and her nefarious brother, Cesare. Modern scholars do not give much credence to the contemporary scandalmongers who spread the story that Pope Alexander was as passionately involved with his daughter Lucrezia as he had been with her mother.)

MOTHER:   Rachael (*sic*) Fawcett
DATE:   1755
BABY GREW UP TO BE:   Alexander Hamilton
CIRCUMSTANCES OF HER UNDOING:   While Hamilton was serving in Washington's cabinet, an opposition newspaper snidely described him as "the son of a camp girl," but the description was a bit strong. Hamilton's mother, Rachael, was actually a high-spirited beauty who rebelled against her loveless marriage to a West Indian merchant by taking a lover or two. After the husband had her arrested on charges of adultery, Rachael took up residence with a Scottish ne'er-do-well named James Hamilton who may or may not have been the father of one of America's Founding Fathers. When the scapegrace Scotsman left her, Rachael opened up a small grocery store and it was here, at the age of nine or ten, that the future Secretary of the Treasury received his first experience in fiscal management by helping to keep the books. Orphaned at twelve, he later rarely discussed his mother in public but within the family circle "recollected her with unexpressible fondness." Because it was discovered that young George Washington had paid a visit to the West Indies around the time Hamilton was conceived, it has been bruited about that *he* was the boy's real father, but most historians think this extremely unlikely.

MOTHER:   Harriet Bailey
DATE:   1817?
BABY GREW UP TO BE:   Frederick Douglass
CIRCUMSTANCES OF HER UNDOING:   A classic story of the unreconstructed South. She was a slave on a Maryland plantation; her impregnator was a white man, identity never revealed. Separated from her child a few months after his birth and sent back to work in the fields, Harriet saw young Frederick only on night-time visits,

traveling twelve miles on foot both ways to reach him. Because a whipping was the penalty for not being on the job by sunrise, the famed abolitionist editor wrote later, "I do not recollect of ever seeing my mother by the light of day . . . She would lie down with me and get me to sleep, but long before I waked she was gone." She died when he was seven.

MOTHER: Marie Labay
DATE: July 27, 1824
BABY GREW UP TO BE: Alexander Dumas *fils*
CIRCUMSTANCES OF HER UNDOING: You can hardly tell the bastards here without a program! The father of Dumas *père* was also an out-of-wedlock child. His liaison with a West Indian black lady named Marie Cassette Dumas provided the heritage that places both Alexander Dumas the elder and the younger on all those lists of prominent Europeans with Negro blood. *Fils* was the result of a youthful affair between Dumas the elder—then an humble clerk—and a Parisian seamstress. When Dumas *père* made a success of such romances as *The Three Musketeers* and *The Count of Monte Cristo*, he recognized his son officially, but the lad still suffered the cruel taunts of his schoolmates over his illegitimacy. There were compensations. "Happily," Dumas *fils* later wrote, "my mother was a good woman and worked hard to bring me up."

MOTHER: Judith Van Hard
DATE: October 23, 1844
BABY GREW UP TO BE: Sarah Bernhardt
CIRCUMSTANCES OF HER UNDOING: Judith Van Hard was pregnant when she arrived in Paris from Berlin to take up the career, as Cornelia Otis Skinner put it, "which the French glorify by the dashing name of *galanterie*." The lover responsible in this instance was probably a law student named Eduard Bernard, but later paramours were of a more distinguished ilk, including some of the most aristocratic names in Louis Napoleon's France. The courtesan's life left Judith little time for her first-born daughter but did provide the contacts and wherewithal for young Sarah to receive the early dramatic training which led to her long and flamboyant stage career. Ironically, when the twenty-year-old actress followed her mother's example by having an out-of-wedlock child of her own, both Sarah and her baby son were banished from her disapproving mother's flat. There's no lady like a reformed harlot.

MOTHER: Ulrica Eleanora Strindberg
DATE: 1849
BABY GREW UP TO BE: August Strindberg
CIRCUMSTANCES OF HER UNDOING: The mother of Sweden's greatest poet wasn't actually unwed when he was born, but it was close. A former servant, she bore three illegitimate children of the aristocratic Carl Oscar Strindberg before he decided to make things legal, just prior to the writer's birth. Strindberg wrote copiously on the subject of motherhood and at least one biographer calls him a "young Oedipus." Writing about his first wife, a maternal type, Strindberg queried, long years before Freud, "Are my feelings perverted because I want to possess my mother? Is that an unconscious incest of the heart?" Perhaps Strindberg belongs in our Mother Lovers chapter, but no, let's leave him here.

MOTHER: Flora Wellman
DATE: 1876
BABY GREW UP TO BE: Jack London
CIRCUMSTANCES OF HER UNDOING: The mother of the author of *The Call of the Wild* harkened to her own passionate cries in the company of an itinerant San Francisco astrologer who refused to marry her. She made all the papers by shooting herself in the head because, she told reporters, her lover had wanted her to have an abortion. Young Jack had a happy relationship with his mom until a day when he was about three years old and brought her a flower picked from the yard. "I was brushed aside," he recalled, "and kicked over, by a rebellious woman, striding her egomaniacal way." Up to that moment, London said, he had believed his mother to be "the most wonderful woman in the world because she said so herself."

MOTHER: Suzanne Valadon
DATE: 1883
BABY GREW UP TO BE: Maurice Utrillo
CIRCUMSTANCES OF HER UNDOING: This vivacious and voluptuous habitué of Montmartre was herself the offspring of an unwed mother. As a model for Renoir, Toulouse-Lautrec, Degas, and others, she was famous for her multiple love affairs and her artist son may or may not have been the child of the Catalan engineering student Miguel Utrillo, who acknowledged paternity. Suzanne neglected young Maurice terribly in the conventional aspects of moth-

erhood, but was thoughtful in others. Believing he should widen his sexual experience, she prodded him as a lad to go to prostitutes and actually gave him the money for it. He adored her.

MOTHER: Sarah Janner
DATE: 1888
BABY GREW UP TO BE: T. E. Lawrence
CIRCUMSTANCES OF HER UNDOING: The governess in the family of an Irish landowner, she eloped with her employer to England and lived with him there under the name of Lawrence. Their son's ambition was fueled by his puritanical mother's determination that his achievement in the world should justify her sinful life. She also was responsible, in his view, for his remaining a bachelor. "Knowledge of her," once wrote the famed Lawrence of Arabia, "will prevent my ever making any woman a mother, and the cause of children."

MOTHER: Rebecca West
DATE: August 4, 1914
BABY GREW UP TO BE: Anthony West
CIRCUMSTANCES OF HER UNDOING: She was a literary comer of twenty when she began what she called her "great adventure" with the forty-six-year-old H. G. Wells, already at the peak of his success. Wells loved her "clear open hard-hitting generous mind" but had no intention of leaving his wife. Rebecca found H.G. "everything in the way of genius and fun" and put up with the double-life arrangement for ten colorful years despite social ostracism and even some threats of blackmail. Their son Anthony grew up to be a novelist, biographer and *New Yorker* staff member.

MOTHER: Anita Maillard
DATE: December 19, 1915
BABY GREW UP TO BE: Edith Piaf
CIRCUMSTANCES OF HER UNDOING: "Three o'clock on a December morning's no time to pop out of your mother's belly to see if it's better outside than in." So said the singer Frenchmen called "The Sparrow" about her out-of-wedlock birth under a lamppost on the Rue de Belleville in wartime Paris. Her mother was a part-time *chanteuse;* her father, a freelance sidewalk acrobat. About the only thing Anita Maillard ever gave her war baby besides her life was the name Edith—for Nurse Edith Cavell, the English spy who had been shot by the Germans a few days before the little girl's birth.

Shipped off, first, to be raised by her mother's mother, the child was later given a home by a cousin of her father—in a brothel. "My mother's been dead a long time as far as I'm concerned," said Piaf when Anita died in the gutter—literally—in 1943. "Ever since she abandoned me, a month after I was born. She was never anything but the mother on my birth certificate."

MOTHER: Clarice Woolever
DATE: April 29, 1933
BABY GREW UP TO BE: Rod McKuen
CIRCUMSTANCES OF HER UNDOING:

> When I'd ask questions,
> let's not talk about it now—
> that's what Mama would say,
> your Daddy was a long, long time ago
> so I'd buy her presents
> every Father's Day.

These lines from a McKuen composition called "Love Child" say it all. He doesn't remember when or what his mother first told him about his absent father; whether he had just gone away, divorced her, or died. All he learned from her, before her death in 1972, was his father's name, and he wasn't even sure of the spelling. In *Finding My Father*, a book recounting his search for his missing dad, McKuen tells of coming to terms with his illegitimacy. "I was born a bastard," he says. "Some people spend their entire lives becoming one."

MOTHER: Romilda Villani
DATE: September 20, 1934
BABY GREW UP TO BE: Sophia Loren
CIRCUMSTANCES OF HER UNDOING: Romilda is still bitter that the smooth-talking young Roman who picked her up near the Trevi Fountain refused to marry her, even after the birth of *two* of his daughters. (Sophia's younger sister, Maria, is also a beauty.) Her prolonged struggle to raise the girls in the ruins of postwar Italy failed to destroy her Garbo-like good looks but left scars of another sort. "Everytime I think of the past," says Mama, "I am destroyed—the memories are all ugly." Ah, Mama mia, but the results were so magnificent.

MOTHER: Helen Burns
DATE: October 8, 1941
BABY GREW UP TO BE: Jesse Jackson
CIRCUMSTANCES OF HER UNDOING: She was a Greenville, North Carolina, high school girl; he was an older married neighbor. The Chicago civil rights activist has never kept his illegitimacy a secret and has even discussed it on his Saturday morning broadcasts. "Although my father's wife had three children by her previous marriage," Jackson says, "he wanted a manchild of his own. His wife would not give him any children. So he went next door." Two years later, Jesse's mother married Charles Henry Jackson and gave her boy a stepfather.

❋

# Three Unwed Mothers Who
# Precipitated Political Scandals

## SALLY HEMINGS

She was a slave on the Monticello estate of Thomas Jefferson. In 1787, when the widowed Jefferson was serving as U.S. minister to France, Sally accompanied his younger daughter to Paris for a two-year visit. During this period, it was later reported, fourteen-year-old Sally became Jefferson's "concubine" and was pregnant with her first child when they returned to Virginia. She subsequently bore a total of five children, all of whom, according to local gossip, bore a "striking resemblance" to the man who would become the third President of the United States. One of her sons, Madison Hemings, actually wrote that Jefferson was his father.

Sally and her brood became famous throughout the young American nation during Jefferson's presidency when the opposition Federalist press uncovered the story and perpetuated it through a vicious series of scurrilous poems and songs. This one, to the tune of "Yankee Doodle," and libelously attributed to "The Sage of Monticello" himself, is one of the milder examples:

Of all the damsels on the green,
　　On mountain, or in valley,
A lass so lúscious n'er was seen
　　As Monticellean Sally.
Yankee Doodle, who's the noodle?
What wife were half so handy?
To breed a flock, of slaves for stock,
　　A blackamoor's the dandy.

Despite her notoriety, Sally Hemings continued on as Jefferson's slave until after his death in 1826; she was finally given her freedom two years later by the ex-President's daughter. Sally's children had been given *their* freedom when they reached the age of twenty-one—by Thomas Jefferson himself.

## MARIA HALPIN

Ma, Ma, where's my pa?
Gone to the White House, ha, ha, ha!

Maria Halpin was the female figure in this campaign ditty cackled rapturously by Republicans in opposition to Democratic candidate Grover Cleveland prior to the presidential election of 1884.

Fanning out from a report in a Buffalo newspaper headlined, "A Terrible Tale," the saga of her relationship with the portly politician spread to pulpits all over the land and, had it been revealed a few weeks earlier, at the time of the Democratic convention, could have cost Cleveland the nomination.

The facts show there was more smoke than fire. Maria was a pretty widow in her thirties toiling behind the counter of a fashionable Buffalo department store. She "accepted the attentions" of several local men-about-town and in 1874, when a son was born to her, she named him Oscar Folsom Cleveland, charging the city's then-mayor with paternity. Though Cleveland had reservations about his responsibility in the matter, he agreed to provide for the child because he was a bachelor and the other men involved were all respectably married. Ten years after the fact, when he made a manly public acknowledgment of his brief relationship with the widow Halpin, he received the support of such nationally prominent clergymen as Henry Ward Beecher and went on to win the election. The supposed son of Grover Cleveland was later adopted into a prominent western New York family and grew up to become a distinguished professional man; Maria Halpin, after her brief, blazing hour as a campaign issue in 1884, disappeared from view.

## NAN BRITTON

As a fourteen-year-old schoolgirl in Marion, Ohio, she decorated her bedroom with photographs of Warren Gamaliel Harding, the dapper, married editor of her home-town newspaper. Later, when Harding moved to Washington as a U.S. senator, the schoolgirl crush incandesced into a full, flaming passion, and in 1919, on a couch in his Senate office, a child was conceived. Nan Britton bore Harding's baby in the same summer he was summoned into the historic smoke-filled room in Chicago and made the compromise Republican candidate for President. The illicit relationship continued on through most of the affable Ohioan's presidency, remaining a secret even in the glare of publicity brought about by the Administration's involvement in the famous "Teapot Dome" oil-lands scandal. Only after the scandal-scarred Chief Executive's death in 1923 was the nation informed that he had been unfaithful to his marital vows as well as to his presidential oath of office. Nan sought money from the Harding family for child support and when she was refused, wrote a book called *The President's Daughter* which became an immediate *succès de scandale*. Although, in the words of critic Samuel Hopkins Adams, it "titillated the prurient with the frankness of its carnal detail," it also contained some moving observations on the cause of unwed motherhood. In the book's dedication to "all unwed mothers, and to their innocent children whose fathers are generally not known to the world," the writer and mother of *The President's Daughter* included this heartfelt message:

"It is to be remembered that . . . Jesus of Nazareth did *not* say, 'Suffer little children born in wedlock to come unto me for of such is the kingdom of heaven.' Jesus loved and honored all little children and didn't bother at all about who their parents were or about the manner of their birth. He himself was born in a manger which was most unconventional."

❊

# MY DAUGHTER, THE PIRATE

Among the most colorful freebooters to sail the Spanish Main during its pirate heyday were two young women named Anne Bonney and Mary Read. Born to unwed mothers in England in the early part of the eighteenth century, both were raised and dressed as boys, passed themselves off as men to join the merchant navy, and eventually, like many of their shipmates, turned to buccaneering in the Caribbean. Captured with their ship, taken in chains, and sentenced to hang in Jamaica, they found for the first time in their lives that being female could be a plus, not a minus. Dorothy M. Johnson and R. T. Turner tell why in their *Bedside Book of Bastards:* "Both were pregnant, and in those days a pregnant woman condemned to death could at least delay the fatal day by a legal gimmick known as *pleading her belly.* Anne and Mary told the judge, 'Your Lordship, we plead our bellies,' and were reprieved."

※

# CHANGING

America's altering standards relative to the social status of unwed motherhood are clearly evidenced in the change between the first edition of *Emily Post's Etiquette*, published in 1922, and *The New Emily Post's Etiquette*, issued in 1975. Half a century ago, the nation's prime arbiter of manners failed even to mention the possibility of a wedding in which the bride was pregnant or, more unthinkable, already a mother. The current edition, put together by the original Mrs. Post's niece Elizabeth, devotes considerable space to these two alternative bridal types. Some of the *new* Emily Post's helpful tips:

—A white dress is permissible for either a pregnant bride or an unwed mother *if* the bride "does not feel that what she has done is a mistake or wrong in any way" and is " 'pure' in heart." (A very visibly pregnant bride, however, should not wear a wedding gown because it "would look utterly incongruous.")

—A veil is definitely taboo, because "the veil is the accepted and traditional symbol of virginity."

—The date on the wedding announcements should never be falsified, even when the arrival of a baby is imminent.

"Above all," says the new Ms. Post, "it should be remembered that this is a *happy* occasion, and one to be celebrated. The fatherless child is getting a father, and the mother will have his support and help in bringing up her baby. Whatever her problems and mistakes have been, they are on the way to being over. So, the wedding should be dignified, beautiful, and in quiet good taste, and the reception should match it—with gaiety and an air of celebration added."

# *Work Work Work!*

But when dread Sloth, The Mother of Doom,
    steals in,
And reigns where Labour's glory was to serve,
Then is the day of crumbling not far off.

> Sir William Watson,
> *The Mother of Doom*

In 1976, for the first time in U.S. history, statistics showed that nearly half of all school-age children (21 million) had mothers who worked outside the home. Growing up in Texas in the Depression thirties, I can recall only one mother of a friend who worked outside the home. She served, when it suited her convenience, behind the counter in a small family-owned neighborhood grocery store. But she was definitely an exception. The mothers of my small friends were simply not "career-oriented." By their own definition, they were "housewives and mothers" and that was career enough for most of them.

We did see women who worked in careers. There were our teachers, librarians, nurses, secretaries, waitresses, and telephone operators. Women worked outside the home usually only if they were young and unmarried or had fallen into serious financial straits. One of the scandals of my childhood was a woman who often came to collect garbage for her farm pigs. We hung on the back fence watching her wrestle huge cans into her Model T truck. In her greasy cap and overalls, she filled us with a thrill of horror because we had heard so much from our female relatives about how disgusting it was that this woman had chosen to "do a man's work." (Today I think of this woman as a pioneer who obviously was only doing what she liked or felt she had to do. I hope she was indifferent to public opinion and wish I had taken the trouble to try to get to know her.)

"Working mother" is a misnomer in any case. It implies that any mother without a definite career is indolently not working, lolling around eating bon-bons, reading novels, and watching soap opera. But the word "mother" is already a synonym for some of the hardest, most demanding work ever shouldered by any human. There is the transition of the pregnant woman to instant nurse, wet nurse, babysitter, cook, bottle-and-diaper washer, psychologist, historian, teacher, and guardian from the moment her child is delivered.

Unless the mother abandons her baby or turns it over to others to raise, she embarks at its birth on a career that may well last her lifetime. It is one she cannot easily give up for several decades. It can be slavery, joy in work, a magnificent career. It can be failure or triumph, but it can never be insignificant or unimportant since it is one "job" effecting the outcome of another's life.

It is astounding how many women *have* and *do* combine this hard job with other work. Working women and women seeking extramaternal careers have been the exception rather than the rule, but now they are the norm. The career mother always existed—both in the recent and distant past. One of the most entertaining parts of preparing this book was the chance to describe noteworthy "working mothers" of our grandmothers' times and before. The names of these women will be familiar to you, but you know them chiefly for their worldly accomplishments. I don't believe they have ever before been presented in the context of both their outside-the-home accomplishments *and* their motherhood.

✳

# HAS "BABY" COME A LONG WAY?

"All that is distinctly human is man; the field, the ship, the mine, the work-shop; all that is truly woman is merely reproductive—the nursery, the schoolroom. There are women to be sure who inherit much of male faculty; and some of these prefer to follow male vocations; but in so doing they for the most part unsex themselves; they fail to perform satisfactorily their maternal duties."

—Grant Allen, a well-known scientific
popularizer of the Victorian era,
in *The Forum,* 1889

\*

I'm a housewife, and a working mother, and I take Geritol.

—Opening line of 1977 TV commercial

\*

## MAMA MARY

Since invading the ranks of professional jockeydom in the early 1970s, five-foot-four-inch Mary Bacon has broken her back twice, competed with a fractured collarbone taped but protruding from her chest, been on the critical list three times, and given birth to a daughter soon after riding her third horse of the day. "Most people think I'm nuts," she declared, after being honored by a Sports Writers Association as Most Courageous Athlete of the Year. "But I'm just another working mother."

(I think she's nuts.)

\*

## MAMA MARGARET

As a young married woman, anthropologist Margaret Mead was told by doctors that it would be extremely hazardous for her ever to attempt to bear a child. She reconciled herself to this medical judgment by setting off on the field expedition to the south seas which resulted in the book *Coming of Age in Samoa* and earned her an international reputation. Then, in her thirties, Mead participated in another expedition to the South Pacific which changed her thinking profoundly. Living among a fierce group of New Guinea cannibals called the Mundugumor, she was repelled by the way they repudiated children. As she describes it in her book, *Blackberry Winter:* "Women wanted only sons and men wanted only daughters and babies of the wrong sex were tossed into the river, still alive, wrapped in a bark sheath." Witnessing this, Ms. Mead says, "I reacted so strongly against the set of the culture that it was here that I decided that I would have a child no matter how many miscarriages it meant."

The result was a daughter, Catherine, born in 1939, when the social scientist was two years shy of her fortieth birthday.

*

# REMEMBERING PHOEBE

There have been many husband-and-wife writing teams in the history of show business—Garson Kanin and Ruth Gordon come to mind, as well as Sam and Bella Spewak. One of the best Broadway-Hollywood collaborations was the one between Phoebe and Henry Ephron. The Ephrons wrote screenplays and worked in the glamorous days of Fred Astaire, Kate Hepburn, Spencer Tracy, Marilyn Monroe, James Cagney, Cary Grant, Judy Garland, etc. Just a few of their screen hits include *Carousel, The Jackpot, There's No Business Like Show Business, Daddy Long Legs.*

Phoebe Ephron was a kind of Katharine Hepburn character in real life; in fact, she reminded her very-much-in-love husband of the great Kate. And she was a wit, always a dangerous talent in a woman. It may be one reason why her now famous daughter Nora Ephron has referred to her as "the unusual and complicated woman who was my mother." There is little doubt that Phoebe's proudest efforts in tandem were the ones with Henry that produced Nora, Delia, Hattie, and Amy. Here is a portion of the tribute paid by Nora at her mother's funeral in 1971:

> I remember her teaching me to read when I was three or four, and the almost giddy pleasure that I felt that she had passed this secret art on to me before anyone else in my class knew about it. I remember how she would come home, fresh from a trip to a second hand bookstore where she had managed to scrounge a copy of a book she had read as a child. Every book she found was wonderful. They were always wonderful. She would bring us books the way other mothers brought their children toys or clothes or food. And it was as if she were giving us a part of herself . . .

She wrote the most fantastic letters. "What kind of letters were they?" my sister Amy asked me recently, "were they personal letters?" No, I guess they really weren't. They were just funny—about how the Red Sea was being divided outside her office at Paramount, and it was really made of blue Jell-O, and how so-and-so was finally getting a divorce from such-and-such and marrying the mother of his illegitimate child. My friends—first at camp, then at college—would laugh and listen, utterly rapt at the sophistication of it all.

The best way to learn to write, she often told me, is to write a letter to your mother and tear off the salutation. I don't think she made that maxim up herself. But I do know that I wrote her faithfully, because you didn't get a letter back from her if you didn't write one yourself. And I know that in writing my mother, with whom I felt completely confident, I began to become a writer.

She gave me another writing maxim which I have never forgotten. "Everything is copy," she said. Sometimes she would say it after I had had a truly thrilling experience, perhaps one I had even written about. But more often she would say it after I had made a mistake—gone to Europe when I shouldn't have, taken an assignment I shouldn't have, gone with a boy I shouldn't have—and I always realized when she said that, that someday I would be able to look back on it and—maybe not write about it, but maybe work it into a nice little anecdote.

*Everything is copy.* In the hospital, a few months ago, I went to see her one day. She knew, I think, that she was dying, and she turned to me. "You're a reporter, Nora," she said. "Take notes." That makes her sound tougher than she really was. She *was* tough—and that was good—but she was also soft, somewhat mystical, and intensely proud.

What I think she gave us, most of all, was the sense that we could do anything, anything at all, that anything was possible. Being women had nothing to do with it, just as it had had nothing to do with it for her. That is a remarkable thing to pass on to daughters. She was not doctrinaire or dogmatic about it; although she named me after the heroine of *A Doll's House*, she could not bear being called a feminist. She merely *was*, and simply by her example, we all grew up with blind faith in our own abilities and destinies.

✳

# MY MOTHER THE DENTIST

Columnist Nicholas von Hoffman, who grew up as an only child in a single-parent household, says it wasn't until he was in high school that it struck him that there was anything unusual about his mother's being a dentist. "I was always vaguely surprised to hear my friends say they went to men dentists, and to this day I get a little uncomfortable when a male D.D.S. puts his big hairy fingers in my mouth."

Looking back as an adult on his mother's decision to be a career woman, Nicholas has this to say about Anna L. Bruenn, D.D.S.:

". . . what really made her such a good parent was the serenity that came from her self-realization as a woman. Certainly there were times when Mother was angry and tired, and when her back was killing her from standing too long at the dentist's chair. But through all of that daily friction, she knew who she was, she was satisfied with the person she'd made herself into, and therefore she was absolutely unintimidated by how anybody else thought she should live.

"That was an enormous help to me. It meant she was strong enough to allow me freedom."

*

# Twelve Extraordinary Working Mothers of the Past

NAME:  Joan Angelicus
CHILDREN:  One son
OCCUPATION:  Church executive
CLAIM TO FAME:  Disguising herself as a man, she entered the Roman Catholic priesthood and, while still in her twenties, was assigned to the post of notary to the Vatican Curia. She rose rapidly in the hierarchy and, according to many church historians of the Middle Ages, was in the year A.D. 853 declared Pope, succeeding Leo IV. All went well until, in the second year of her reign, Joan became enamored of her private chamberlain, began an affair with him, and became pregnant. Her condition was kept secret until one day, riding her horse in a ceremonial procession, she suffered the pangs of premature childbirth and fell to the street. There, in full view of the crowd, a son was born. When the spectators realized that this was the result, not of a miracle but a deception, they tied

the female pontiff to the tail of her horse, dragged her around St. Peter's Square, and finally stoned her to death. The baby, somewhat miraculously, survived and grew up to be a bishop. The Catholic Church officially denies the existence of Pope Joan, but from the thirteenth to seventeenth centuries, over 150 church historians noted her two-and-a-half-year reign. Liv Ullmann's 1972 movie on the subject was "excommunicated" at the box office.

NAME: Marie Sklodowska Curie
CHILDREN: Two daughters
OCCUPATION: Physical chemist
CLAIM TO FAME: Shared Nobel Prize in 1903 with her husband, Pierre, for the discovery of radium. Awarded Nobel Prize individually in 1911 for her work on radium and its compounds. She is also the first and only mother to have her name given to a crater on the far side of the moon. Her daughter Irène shared with her own husband, Frédéric Joliot-Curie, the 1935 Nobel Prize for chemistry for the synthesis of new radioactive elements.

NAME: Miriam Wallace ("Ma") Ferguson
CHILDREN: One daughter
OCCUPATION: Governor
CLAIM TO FAME: "Me for Ma!" proclaimed the bumper stickers when she threw her sunbonnet into the ring and ran for the governorship of Texas in 1924. Undismayed by the fact that, under state law, her husband was legally entitled to all her salary, "Ma" shook so many hands campaigning that her right arm swelled to twice its size; she won by almost 98,000 votes, becoming the first American woman to be elected governor for a full term. (Mrs. Nellie Tayloe Ross of Wyoming, a mother of four, beat her by two weeks as "first governor," but Mrs. Ross was filling out the unexpired term of her late husband.) Guided closely by her politician husband, "Farmer Jim" Ferguson, himself a former governor, "Ma" Ferguson was famous for her leniency to bootleggers. During her two Prohibition years in office, she issued more than two thousand pardons, including 105 on Thanksgiving Day in 1925. She also was famous for her suspicion of things foreign. "No more of those sinful languages in the public schools," she once declared. "Stop learning our kids dirty rotten French and Spanish. If the English language was good enough for Jesus Christ, it's good enough for Texans."

Defeated for re-election in 1926, "Ma" (who secretly detested this nickname) lived up to the family motto of "Never say 'die'— say 'damn'" by running again in 1932 and serving a second two-year term.

NAME:  Henriett Howland Robinson ("Hetty") Green
CHILDREN:  One son, one daughter
OCCUPATION:  Financial speculator
CLAIM TO FAME:  She earned the nickname of "the Witch of Wall Street" when, in fifty years of wizardly wheeling and dealing, she nurtured an inheritance of six million dollars into a megafortune that made her "the richest woman in the world." She was also one of the stingiest, forcing her son and daughter to live with her for years in cramped, cold-water flats, where they cooked on a single gas plate and shared bathing facilities with a whole floor full of neighbors. Her parsimony cost her young son Edward a leg from the delay caused by her insistence that he seek treatment for an injury in a free clinic rather than consult a regular physician. (She had the severed leg buried in the family plot in Bellows Falls, Vermont, and it was reunited with Edward forty-seven years later, after his death.) At Hetty Green's own death in 1916, her entire fortune of an estimated hundred million dollars was left to Edward and his sister, with not a penny going to charity.

NAME:  Sarah Josepha Buell Hale
CHILDREN:  Five
OCCUPATION:  Magazine editor
CLAIM TO FAME:  "The most important vocation on earth," she wrote, "is that of the Christian mother in her nursery." Still, when necessity commanded, she traded her rocker for an editor's chair and earned a living for herself and her family from the age of forty until shortly before her death at ninety-one.

Sarah Hale was thrust into the labor market in 1822 when her husband's sudden death from pneumonia left her penniless with five youngsters to support—the eldest nine; the youngest born two weeks after his father was stricken. After a brief, financially unrewarding attempt to keep a millinery shop, she became editor of the magazine which eventually grew into the style-setting *Godey's Lady's Book*, one of the most influential publications of its time. In her nearly half a century as editor, she was the first American to speak out against child labor, campaigned for years against the confiscation of the earnings of working women by their husbands, and further encouraged the cause of the working mother by employing 150 women to hand-color her magazine's fashion plates in their homes. She also helped open up the field of department store clerking to women. Many clergymen of the period predicted that female salespeople would transform stores into brothels until she persuaded merchant A. T. Stewart to hire women clerks, and prove it wasn't so. Because of her efforts to persuade President Lincoln to declare it a national holiday, she is remembered further as "the Mother of Thanksgiving."

NAME: Anna Trow Lohman ("Madame Restell")
CHILDREN: One daughter
OCCUPATION: Pregnancy consultant
CLAIM TO FAME: Ensconced in a splendid brownstone at the super-social New York intersection of Fifth Avenue and Fifty-second Street, she amassed a considerable fortune vending "infallible remedies" warranted to end unwanted pregnancies, and providing refuge and/or relief to unmarried daughters of the wealthy who found themselves in the family way. She served one year behind bars on an abortion charge in 1846, but prospered at her trade for some thirty years after that, mostly, it was said, by dint of the blackmail potential of her "dread secrets" involving citizens in high places. When, thanks to evidence procured by vice fighter Anthony Comstock, she was again arrested in 1878, she saved herself from another prison stay by cutting her throat. The bulk of her wealth went to her favorite grandchild.

NAME: Margaretha (Zelle) MacLeod
CHILDREN: One son, one daughter
OCCUPATION: Dancer and espionage agent
CLAIM TO FAME: After her infant son was poisoned by a servant in Java in 1899, she separated from her husband and began a career in Paris as an entertainer known as Mata Hari. Her "Dance of the Seven Veils," performed nude, caused a sensation and brought her many influential lovers, not to mention an asking price in a French house of assignation of a thousand gold francs for *un moment* of her time. Accused of using her charms to gather military intelligence for the Germans during World War I, she was found guilty and shot by a French firing squad at dawn on October 15, 1917. She left three sealed letters: one to her twenty-year-old daughter and

two to lovers. "Don't mix up the addresses," she pleaded, at the end. "That would be fatal."

NAME:   Anna Mary Robertson ("Grandma") Moses
CHILDREN:  Ten
OCCUPATION:  Artist
CLAIM TO FAME:   At the age of seventy-seven, considering herself too old for farm work but too young to retire, this upstate New York dairy farmer's wife took up painting as a hobby. Filling her canvases with scenes recollected from her country childhood, she touched a nostalgic chord in American art buyers and was hailed as "an authentic American primitive" by critics all over the world. Her hard working schedule of five or six hours a day produced, in time, more than fifteen hundred pictures and inspired such subsidiary products as china, tiles, fabrics, and Christmas cards by the million. Undismayed by the few snobbish detractors who refused to be charmed by her spritely pictorial remembrances of things past, she kept on painting until she was past the century mark. Her credo: "I like pretty things the best. What's the use of painting a picture if it's not nice."

NAME:   Lydia Estes Pinkham
CHILDREN:  Three sons; one daughter
OCCUPATION:  Medicine-maker
CLAIM TO FAME:   Two simultaneous crises—her husband's bankruptcy and the national financial panic of 1873—impelled this Lynn, Massachusetts, homemaker to concoct and put on sale an ancient "squaw remedy" which, when marketed as "Lydia Pinkham's Vegetable Compound," made her name a household word all across America. Billed as "a Positive Cure for all those Painful Complaints and Weaknesses so common to our Best Female Population," its combination of medicinal roots and herbs was laced with a generous 18 per cent alcohol ("used solely as a solvent and preservative") and was enthusiastically endorsed by, among others, the WCTU. A large part of the success of Mrs. Pinkham's product was due to the decision of her salesman son Dan to use his mother's photograph in the company ads—a significant "first" in advertising history. In her neat black dress and white lace fichu pinned with a cameo brooch, she seemed to epitomize everybody's dream grandmother, and the profusion of the ads made her handsome elderly features more familiar in her time than any other woman except Victoria. Though Lydia Pinkham died in 1883, the celebrated "savior of her sex" is

still remembered in a bawdy song which is a hardy perennial on college campuses. This is its refrain:

> Oh-h-h-h sing of Lydia Pinkham,
> And her love for the Human Race
> How she sells her Vegetable Compound
> And the papers, the papers, they publish,
>     they publish her FACE!*

## Women's Liberation Note:

Mrs. Pinkham has long been viewed by many as a picturesque joke figure on the American cultural scene, but contemporary feminists are beginning to give her credit for at least one significant contribution to the cause. In the advertisements which she wrote herself, the lady from Lynn conducted an unending crusade against the Victorian concept that female suffering was a "natural consequence" of the human condition and must therefore simply be endured. This was a typical ad message: "Tradition says, 'Women must suffer,' and young girls are taught so . . . The mother suffered and she thinks her daughter must suffer also. It is true only to a limited extent. No excessive pain is healthy. If a young woman suffers severely she needs treatment, and her mother should see that she gets it. . . . Many a dutiful daughter pays in pain for mother's ignorance." Penetrating as it did into numberless households where "feminism" was a verboten word, the effect of this nineteenth-century consciousness-raising cannot be overestimated.

NAME: Sacagawea or Sacajawea
CHILDREN: One son, one daughter
OCCUPATION: Guide
CLAIM TO FAME: At the age of eighteen, with her two-month-old infant son strapped to her back, she set out as guide to the Lewis and Clark expedition of 1805 in its exploration of the American Northwest. Without the aid she obtained from her fellow Shoshone Indian tribesmen, it is unlikely that the explorers could ever have concluded their journey successfully. No other American mother has been honored with so many memorials. In addition to countless statues, monuments and plaques, her name is borne by a ten-thousand-foot peak in Oregon, a mountain pass and a river.

* It's even in this book's picture section.

NAME: Belle Starr
CHILDREN: One daughter; one son
OCCUPATION: Horse and cattle thief
CLAIM TO FAME: Following her five-year stint as the head of a band of horse and cattle rustlers preying on ranches along the Oklahoma Strip, dime-novel writers glamorized her as "the Bandit Queen" of the American West. She died in the arms of her daughter, Pearl, after being shot by an unknown assailant near Briartown, Oklahoma, in 1889. Later, Pearl erected an elegant monument for her mother's grave bearing this inscription:

> Shed not for her the bitter tear,
> Nor give the heart in vain regret,
> 'Tis but the casket that lives here,
> The gem that fills it sparkles yet.

NAME: Marie Gresholtz Tussaud
CHILDREN: Two sons
OCCUPATION: Museum owner
CLAIM TO FAME: The founder of the world's most famous waxworks arrived at working-mother status by way of a grisly assignment during the French Terror. The posthumous daughter of a German soldier killed in the Seven Years' War, she was raised in the home of a Swiss uncle who taught her the then-fashionable art of modeling in wax. Taken to Paris in pre-revolutionary days, she helped her uncle create the figures for a wax museum that soon became a popular Palais Royal rendezvous. After the storming of the Bastille, Marie found herself drafted for the gruesome modeling of lifeless heads from many prominent guillotine victims. When her marriage to the son of a well-to-do wine grower failed, Marie moved with her two young sons to London and, in 1802, opened up a waxworks exhibition of her own. The modeling secrets which she passed on to her boys, François and Joseph, were in turn transmitted to their sons and grandsons, keeping the celebrated "Madame Tussaud's" a favorite of London tourists long after her death in 1850 at age ninety.

NAME: Sarah Breedlove ("Madame C.J.") Walker
CHILDREN: One daughter
OCCUPATION: Cosmetics manufacturer
CLAIM TO FAME: Born into a family of black Louisiana sharecroppers, she was married at fourteen and a widow at twenty;

started her working-mother career as a St. Louis washerwoman. Her fortunes changed dramatically when, wincing at the sight of her black friends awkwardly trying to straighten their curly hair by pressing it with a hot iron, she set out to find an easier system. The hair conditioning method she ultimately devised and marketed door-to-door grew in a few years into a diversified cosmetics empire which made her the first American black woman to become a selfmade millionaire. Daughter A'Lelia Walker Robinson assisted Madame Walker with both her business and later her humanitarian activities and helped her to live in a style befitting her status in a sprawling mansion called Villa Lewaro in exclusive Irvington-on-Hudson, New York. Caught in the Depression crush, A'Lelia was forced to auction off the estate and its contents after her mother's death, but it still stands (now a home for the aged) as a symbol of one enterprising black working mother's conquest of the American dream.

✳

# THE PRICE

"You're either for or against working mothers in much the same way you're either for or against the use of nuclear energy," writes Jean Curtis in her book *Working Mothers*. "And which ever side a woman is on, pro or con, she will often find herself on the defensive, if not overtly—that is, when called upon to explain herself—then implicitly, as she feels the pressure of public skepticism.

"Only in certain situations," says Curtis, "has a mother in this society been able to work without censure. If a family is poor or the mother is the only supporter—okay. And society takes more kindly, on the whole, to mothers in the high status professions (medicine, academia), particularly if they subordinate ambition to family responsibilities. But if a woman asserts, simply, that she has the same professional ambitions as her husband, that she shares his lack of interest in committing long hours to the management of the home or the care of the children, but would like, instead, to *share* those responsibilities (not duck them) she will swiftly learn the price of her adventurousness."

# CASES OF THE GUILTS

The American sculptor Louise Nevelson is looked upon by many young feminists in the arts as the epitome of the "free spirit." But it was not always thus. Nevelson, now a great-grandmother, still remembers with pain the pulls she suffered between her career and motherhood. "I think," she says now, "people should think a million times before they give birth. The guilts of motherhood were the worst guilts in the world for me. They were really insurmountable. You see, you are depriving another human being of so many things, and the other party also knows it. That struggle blinds you. That's the price, the great price."

❈

All my life I have read that a mother should and must be home with her child.

My guilt is deep-seated. Bad conscience is part of my everyday life. I am afraid that I am doing Linn* an injustice.

But at the same time I think that she gets more from me precisely because of my happiness in a profession I love . . .

Actress Liv Ullmann in
*Changing*

❈

# TEA AND SYMPATHY

The English journalist Lynda Lee Potter sometimes gives advice in her sprightly column. Here she offers comfort to women who want careers and motherhood:

"My eldest daughter came home from school last week and said: 'I am glad you have a job. We've all been talking about it at school, and all the ones whose mothers don't go out to work wish they would, because, they say, it's a responsibility having stay-at-

* Her daughter by Ingmar Bergman.

384

home mothers, who keep getting depressed and saying their nerves are bad.' "

※

## SENATOR "MOTHER"

Declaring herself "the happiest woman in the U.S.," Mrs. Rebecca Latimer Felton made political history back on November 21, 1922, by becoming the first mother (first woman, in fact) to be sworn in as a United States senator. Truth to tell, this eighty-seven-year-old "working mother" did not manage to get *any* work done during her short-lived service on the Hill. When Senator Thomas Watson of Georgia died during an extended autumn Senate recess, "Mother" Felton was appointed to fill out his term by Governor Thomas Hardwick. (The Peach State's governor had voted against the Nineteenth Amendment giving women the vote and wanted to make a few points with his female constituents.) By the time the Senate convened again, a special election had been held and another male Georgian elected to succeed Watson. As a gesture of "gallantry," the new senator delayed presenting his credentials for twenty-four hours to give Mrs. Felton the honor of being the "first woman senator," but in her brief time in office she did not get on record with a single "aye" or "nay."

Happy to report, "Mother" Felton did, however, manage to sound forth one heartfelt, albeit unofficial, "Yea" *before* she was sworn in. Reporters asked her to comment on a speech made in London by the American Ambassador George Harvey on the topic "Do Women Have Souls?" The octogenarian "Mother" allowed as how she thought they did.

※

## QUICK COMEBACK

Representative Patricia Schroeder, the first woman Colorado ever sent to Congress, arrived in Washington as a freshman member of the House in 1973. Her initial day on the job (reported Judy

Flanders of the Washington *Star*), one of the old-timers greeted her with the question, "How can you be the mother of two small children and a member of Congress at the same time?"

Replied Representative Schroeder: "Because I have a brain and a uterus—and I use both."

＊

## MOM'S OWN YELLOW PAGES

Mother B Answering Service—Chicago
Mother's Attic (antiques)—Madison, Wisconsin
Mother's Bar—Las Vegas
Mother's Best Soul Kitchen—Chicago
Mother's Car Wash—Minneapolis
Mother's Grand Kosher Delicatessen—The Bronx
Mother's Gumbo & Bar-B-Cue House—Chicago
Mother's Nite-Club—Milwaukee
Mother's Pride Root Beer—Los Angeles
Mother's Small Loan Company—Atlanta
Mama's Trailer Ranch—Opelika, Alabama
Mother Truckers Corp.—New York City
Teen, Tot and Mom Shop—Natchez, Mississippi

# "To Grandma's"

A grandam's name is little less in love
Than is the doting title of a mother.

William Shakespeare,
*Richard III*

One unfortunate aspect of modern life has been the dividing of people up into age groups so that hundreds of older ones live isolated in retirement homes or communities while young nuclear families exist by the dictates of psychiatrist David Cooper's *Death of the Family*—as if they were walled cities afraid of some infection from experience with the old. This failure of interaction between varieties of human beings; this keeping children from their natural heritage of association with their parents' parents seems terribly barren and wasteful to me.

When families had to stay together for survival, with several generations in one house or neighborhood and when the only baby-sitter anyone had ever heard of was a grandparent, childhood experience was indescribably rich. The situation of live-in grandparents had and has its drawbacks, to be sure, but I believe it was better than the current trend toward isolation, despair, loneliness, and abandonment of the aged and the cutting off of children from their rightful relationship with a removed generation that has so much to teach.

387

I was one of the lucky ones. I knew both my grandmothers well—in fact, at various times, each of them lived in our home over long periods. This sometimes drove my father crazy; it sometimes drove my mother crazy, but I am happy for the experiences I had with these two women who were so different that they might as well have come from separate planets. All that Sallie Jemima Ball McCall and Martha Tipton Smith had in common was the marriage of their daughter and son and their grandchildren from that union. Oh, yes, they *were* both Southern Baptists, but one of them viewed her Christianity like St. Francis of Assisi and the other came on like Savonarola.

So here I was with the Alpha and Omega of grandmothers. Grandma McCall was a fragile-looking, soothing, sweet-talking, loving, generous, birdlike, cultured, well-educated, greeting card grandmother. In fact, she even looked like Grandma Moses. When we had nightmares she used to take us into her bed and tell us stories about little birds and flowers and clouds and raindrops until we went back to sleep, sure all was right with the world. (Doing this book, I learned that the expression "to see one's grandmother" means "to have a nightmare" but in my case, it was just the opposite.)

Grandma McCall had been a schoolteacher, already considered a spinster at thirty when she married an older circuit-riding country doctor in Mississippi and gave him four daughters. My mother often regretted aloud what she called "the lack of romance in Mama's life," for when Sallie Ball married Dr. Robert McCall he already had adult sons older than his bride.

However, Grandma never complained. Widowed at forty, she had moved on to Texas and was involved in life at hand, determined to pass on everything of value to the next generation. She was never idle; she tatted, crocheted, and knitted. On my sofa is an afghan she made, and on my bed, a valuable quilt with squares so tiny and stitches so small one can't imagine the patience it required. She always studied our lessons several steps ahead of us, then tutored us, so we did well in school without half trying. She entered every word contest and was so good at "twenty-five words or less" that she often won. Her room was usually stacked with boxes of cigars, crates of oranges, and other loot. She constantly read aloud to us and though she was refined and somewhat Victorian, when she performed Pearl Buck's *The Good Earth,* as we lay on the rug at her feet, she didn't leave out the sex or the childbirth or the gruesome parts. We idolized her.

No one was ever bored or unhappy long with Grandma around. She would think up a game, describe a trip, tell us a story or dig out the cracked brown daguerreotype of her father and describe how he had gone off to war against the North and died in camp of measles. "They sent home only his picture and his watch; I was just four but I remember it," she would say. She also remembered when the Yankees came to northern Mississippi and how the family had buried the silver and valuables before the troops arrived. Then she and her mother and sister hid in wagons of cotton and watched while the soldiers carried off all their chickens and hogs.

This storybook, picture-book woman, who traced her Ball ancestors back to George Washington's mother and said that she was "mostly Scotch, Irish, English," was actually an adventurer, big on progress and the future. She would save her pennies to go up in open cockpits of small planes. It was a big Sunday thrill then to take a plane ride, but the money for such frivolity was hard to come by. Grandma went as often as she could. As she put on the goggles and helmet over her knot of silver hair and lifted her long silk dress to climb up on the steps, she would say to my mother, "Don't be upset at me, baby. I know it's a selfish thing to spend money on, but I just have to do it." And we would wait on the ground looking up as the plane looped and rolled, just as thrilled as if we were up there with her.

We often competed to make Grandma say we were her favorites over our cousins, or over one another. But she was wise to us. "I have no favorites; you are all my favorites and I love you equally." This woman died at eighty-one having been bedridden for some years with a broken hip. I don't recall that her long confinement was any burden to anyone, since she continued to be her sunny, interesting, and entertaining self. Her bedroom was the focal point of life in our house and to the end, she held court there with her contest prizes stacked around her, her books in heaps, her "work" spread about and her mind clicking along a mile a minute.

So that was my perfect Grandma McCall.

My other grandmother was a real character; she was my imperfect Big Mama. (That's what everyone called her; Tennessee Williams had nothing on us!) This decidedly Irish woman was big, sturdy and solid, what one would call a *baleboosteh* in Yiddish (a bossy woman). However, like many fat people, she wasn't particularly jolly, though she had a sardonic sense of humor. Life hadn't been entirely kind to Martha Tipton, who had married a tall, thin, gangly plains boy named Jerome Bonaparte Smith when she was only sixteen. Her sweet ineffectual dreamer husband never quite lived up to the grandeur of the name bestowed by his French Louisiana mother and so getting along in the sere desert of Putnam County, West Texas, was difficult. Martha's girlhood ended abruptly in a welter of dirty diapers, eight children, cookpots, wash pots, outdoor privies, and the subsistence income "Boney" earned in various odd jobs. By the time he was better off, working as a metalsmith, and life had grown a bit easier, it was too late for Big Mama to forgive Granddaddy Smith for the enslavement he represented to her.

With a mighty fist that could slap sparks out of the offender and a tongue like a rattlesnake, Big Mama was the prototypical hen-pecking, browbeating, dissatisfied, hard-to-get-along-with Maggie to her husband's Jiggs. Her fiery temper had been inherited by some of her four boys and three girls and the result was that every family reunion or get-together disintegrated into knockdowns and dragouts. Portions of the Smiths, directed, produced and choreographed by Big Mama, were always not speaking and even when she died, there was still an assortment of brothers, sisters, sons, daughters, and cousins, on the outs.

I don't write this critically. These are the facts, for Martha Tipton Smith was a formidable example of individuality and guts. She was a child of the frontier prairie, a veteran survivor. She said what she thought and lived by her convictions. She was, in some ways, liberated before her time, for she was a cynic, a woman disillusioned with husbands, housewifery, and children. She saw the whole process as a snare and a delusion, but having made her bed, she then turned to fundamentalist religion for comfort. She believed drinking, gambling, and fornication were mortal sins; but she disapproved almost equally of card-playing, dancing, swearing, and the sexes going in swimming together. One of her more daring revolts against convention was her story of how, in the early twenties, she had made a *sleeveless* dress for a young actress who was boarding in her house. No one in Fort Worth had ever seen a woman in a sleeveless dress before but the young beauty talked her into creating it, put it on, changed her name to Adrienne Ames, and took off for Hollywood. Martha Tipton tucked the two dollars from her ill-gotten sewing caper away and wondered ever after how much she had personally contributed to the downfall of the film star. (Naturally, Big Mama considered Adrienne Ames to be a sinner; after all, she was living in *Hollywood!*)

Big Mama moved fast, struck hard, and talked later. There was always a certain amount of flying crockery in her kitchen, flopping carcasses, slashed vegetables, spattered hot grease, dripping pans under the icebox. And everything she did was larger than life— when she cut a biscuit, she didn't bother with some itsy teensy biscuit cutter, but snatched up a teacup and ground out enormous gobbets of dough. More than once I saw her throw the green and white speckled enamel dipper that still hung by the sink (as a gesture to the countrified past) at my grandfather's head. "Boney," who was loved by his children and grandchildren, admired by everyone in the neighborhood, and who amused his cronies at work, did *not* amuse her.

She had her weaknesses—one or two of her grandchildren were special to her. Her shameless favorites were my cousin Sloan and my brother James. They could do no wrong. She would let James lick his finger and stick it in the sugar bowl, or she would cut him the end piece of cake with all the icing and dare us to object. (We didn't.)

Big Mama could not get along with her daughters so she usually lived with us or with another of her sons. She got along very well with her daughters-in-law, doubtless a polished piece of pragmatism on her part. Nearly a hundred when she died, she remained cantankerous almost to the end; after she was eighty-five, she would not allow anyone to cut her toenails but my father, and if he was out of town, she would wait for him to return.

As she was half blind and increasingly dependent in her last years, the plates finally stopped flying. But Big Mama still intimidated people, and one story about her is classic. My parents came to visit me in New York and I put them up in a friend's apartment. My father wrote a letter home: "Mama, we are staying in a place that is out of this world. It has everything you want including skyscrapers out the window. We have a refrigerator full and maid service. This apartment even has a bar. It has every kind of whiskey you could imagine, why you could have any kind of drink you might want, etc." My mother read the letter and remonstrated, "Darling, you can't send this letter to Big Mama. It will worry her to death." My father exploded, "What is this? Here I am over seventy years old and I can't even write my own mother that I'm staying in an apartment where there is liquor—that's just ridiculous!"

But he didn't send the letter.

Big Mama kept up her struggle to live until the end, kicking and raging against the dying of the light. She was a tremendous fighter and I have often thought that the big scar on her leg, where a bulldog bit her as a child, might have emblematically given her the impetus to live as something of a bulldog herself. I was frightened of her. I was cautious around her. But I admired her will to survive, her honesty, her outspokenness.

Knowing these two grandmothers proved to me early in life that categorizing and stereotyping are dangerous. Grandmothers, like mothers, run the gamut. The Chinese have a negative benison that goes, "May you live in interesting times." I understand that. With my grandmothers in the houses where I grew up, I lived in interesting times. I'm glad for it.

Cross-stitch sampler kit offered in a mail-order ad in *Family Circle*

※

# MATTHEW'S GRANNY

One of the continuing delights of Mary Martin's life is that wherever she goes, she meets people who remember seeing her onstage as Peter Pan. Frequently, they ask her to "crow" for them as Peter did. One day, she heard a knock on her bedroom door at six in the morning; it was her grandson Matthew. "May I bring some friends to meet you?" he asked.

Determined to be a wonderful grandmother, Miss Martin inquired cheerily, "When, darling?"

"Now," said Matthew. "They're here."

A bunch of little boys then marched into the bedroom. Miss Martin sat up straight and tried to smile while Matthew extended one arm in her direction and made *the* introduction:

"Meet my grandmother, Peter Pan."

✽

# HAD IT!

The prolific writer Irene Kampen describes her grandmother's life with her Grandpa Trepel, a man with such a monumental temper that he once threw half a roast chicken down the toilet in a rage.

"Grandma Trepel put up with Grandpa for 77 years. She had been married to him at 14, sight unseen, the marriage having been arranged by both sets of parents when the children were born, which was the custom in the old country.

"Grandma eventually appeared on our doorstep one day and said to Mother, 'I'm through. I've left him. Let him cook his own chickens from now on. I'm never going back to him again—never!'

" 'But, Mama,' my mother said to her, 'you've been married for such a long time—77 years. You are 91 years old, Mama. Papa is 92 years old. Why have you decided to leave him now?'

" 'Because,' Grandma Trepel announced firmly, 'enough is enough.' "

✽

# VANITY, ALL IS VANITY

Gloria Safier, the New York agent, had a grandmother named Celia Selznick who lived well into her nineties. Even in her last days she was extremely vain and would fret about her appearance before making an entrance into a room. Until she died she kept the golden hair that had made her such a beauty as a young girl. So when Gloria asked her to pose one day for the sculptor Fiore de Henriquez, Celia demurred. Gloria showed Celia her own bust done by de Henriquez. Grandma studied it. "No, Dolly," she said finally. "I like you better in a picture." Gloria kept insisting her grandmother should sit for a piece of sculpture. Finally, Celia said, "Well, all right, but will my hair come out this color?"

*

## COLSON'S FAMOUS ONE

One of the most graphic evocations of the Nixon years is provided by ex-White House aide Charles Colson's much-quoted assertion (which he denies ever making) that he would walk over his grandmother if necessary to ensure Richard Nixon's re-election. Though both of Colson's grandmothers were, in fact, dead at the time, the statement nevertheless caused his mother to wince a bit. "Grandma Colson wouldn't appreciate that kind of publicity," she scolded her son. According to Madeleine Edmonson and Alden Duer Cohen in *Watergate Women*, Colson claims he refrained from twitting his mom with this rejoinder: "How do you know it wasn't *your* mother I meant?"

*

## IMPERTINENCE

The nineteenth-century clergyman and diarist Augustus Hare reminisces in one journal entry about the engagement of one of his more colorful female contemporaries, Lady Langford, who was the original of Lady Kew in Thackeray's *The Newcomes*. "Lady Langford had been very beautiful, clever and had had *une vie très orageuse*. She had much excuse, however. She had only once seen her cousin, Lord Langford, when he came to visit her grandmother, and the next day the old lady told her she was to marry him. 'Very well, Grandmamma, but when?'—'I never in my life heard such an impertinent question,' said the grandmother, 'what business is it of yours *when* you are to marry him? You will marry him when I tell you. However, whenever you hear me order six horses to the carriage, you may know that you are going to be married.' And so it was."

# WIN A BET ON THIS

Over the river and through the wood,
To grandmother's house we go;
   The horse knows the way
   To carry the sleigh
Through the white and drifted snow.

*Thanksgiving Day*
by Lydia Maria Child (1802–80)

Do you remember this famous poem, sometimes set to music as a song? Well, would it shock you as much as it did Liz Pierce and me to discover that the lyric *actually* reads:

"To grand*father's* house we go"?

Grandmother has such a strong hold on the imagination that nearly everybody we casually queried thought *she* was the protagonist of this much-quoted verse. But there it is, "grandfather," plain as pumpkins, in all the anthologies.

✳

The grandmother's correction makes no impression.

English proverb

✳

# MARY'S GRANDMA

The novelist and critic Mary McCarthy lost both her mother and father in the influenza epidemic of 1918 and was raised in part by her maternal grandmother. In *Memories of a Catholic Girlhood*, she describes how, after much nagging, her grandmother finally answered the question, "Why did you pick Grandpa?" The answer was: because she thought he would be good to her.

Mary McCarthy continues: "This archaic view of the function of a husband astonished me. But to her, as I soon learned, it was the prime, the only, consideration. 'Is he good to you?' she asked me, another night, on that same visit, speaking of my new husband. I had to stop and think, because marriage had never presented itself to me in that light. 'Why, yes, I suppose so,' I said slowly. 'Yes, of course he is.' My grandmother nodded and reopened her evening newspaper. 'That's all right, then.' The subject was closed. 'Grandpa was always good to me,' she resumed tranquilly, turning to the racing column and beginning to mark her selections for the next day's parimutuel."

✳

# GENERATIONS

At an age when many women are great-grandmothers, the anthropologist Margaret Mead became a grandmother for the first time when her daughter, Catherine, gave birth to a baby girl. Though she had spent a great portion of her life studying motherhood in primitive cultures, one aspect of her own experience came as a complete surprise. "I suddenly realized," she writes in the autobiographical *Blackberry Winter*, "that through no act of my own I had become biologically related to a new human being."

From the time of her childhood, she says, she had been able to conceive of her relationship with all of her forebears. "But the idea that as a grandparent one was dealing with action at a distance— that somewhere, miles away, a series of events occurred that changed one's own status forever—I had not thought of that and I found it very odd. . . .

"Scientists and philosophers have speculated at length about the sources of man's belief that he is a creature with a future life . . . Speculation may be the only kind of answer that is possible, but I would now add to the speculations that are more familiar another of my own: the extraordinary sense of having been transformed not by any act of one's own but by the act of one's child."

✳

# PATSY MAKES A POINT

A grandmother doesn't have to do anything except be there . . . Everybody should try to have one, especially if you don't have television, because grandmas are the only grown-ups who have got time.

From the essay, "What a Grandmother
Is" by Patsy Gray, aged nine,
quoted in *A Book for Grandmothers*
by Ruth Goode

❊

# HAUTE GRANDMA

It is the theory of social chronicler Cleveland Amory that Newport, Rhode Island's era of authentic elegance came to an end in 1952 with the death, at the age of ninety-eight, of the last of the resort's *grande dames*, Mrs. Hamilton McKown Twombly. The last surviving grandchild of Commodore Cornelius Vanderbilt, Mrs. Twombly's lifestyle can best be summarized by reporting that she paid her famous French chef a salary of twenty-five thousand dollars a year and, in her last years, owned fifteen automobiles, ten American, three English and two French, all painted in her own special shade of maroon. (Her chauffeurs, footmen and maids wore livery of a matching hue.) In *The Last Resorts*, Amory demonstrates that Mrs. Twombly shone, however, as a grandmother as well as a *grande dame*. An instance when the two identities overlapped was in 1935 when a beloved grandson invited Mrs. Twombly to his wedding in California. Amory's account of it:

"Mrs. Twombly was, even in those days, already in her eighties and a plane trip was out of the question. Nor, since the passing of her private railroad car, would she consider a public train. Driving, too, presented a problem. There was always the chance, during those dark days, of being recognized in the back seat of her Rolls Royce and meeting up . . . with foul play. But go West the Newport *grande dame* would, and she finally decided on the perfect solution. For six thousand miles, going and coming, Mrs. Twombly's maid, dressed as Mrs. Twombly, rode in the back seat of the Rolls, and for six thousand miles, going and coming, Mrs. Twombly, dressed as Mrs. Twombly's maid, rode in the front seat."

# NABOKOV'S

Vladimir Nabokov wrote about his aristocratic Russian grandmother in the years before the Revolution:

In a flowing silk gown and net mitts, a period piece rather than a live person, she spent most of her life on a couch, fanning herself with an ivory fan. A box of *boules de gomme*, or a glass of almond milk, were always within her reach, as well as a hand mirror, for she used to repowder her face, with a large pink puff, every hour or so, the little mole on her cheekbone showing through all that flour, like a currant. Notwithstanding the languid aspects of her usual day, she remained an extraordinary hardy woman and made a point of sleeping near a wide-open window all year round. One morning, after a nightlong blizzard, her maid found her lying under a layer of sparkling snow which had swept over her bed and her, without infringing upon the healthy glow of her sleep.

From *Speak, Memory,*
*An Autobiography Revisited*

❋

# ED'S ADVICE

"My recommendation to any kid planning to have a nice permissive childhood is to have loving parents who come to see him often treat him with generosity and affection, and leave him in the care of an infatuated grandmother."　　　—Ed McMahon

❋

# JUST FOR THE RECORD

"Little Red Ridinghood sat down by the side of the bed.

"I have brought you some eggs and a jar of honey and some butter," she said, as she bent over the bed. "But what great big ears you have, Grandmother."

"The better to hear you with, my child!" said the wolf.

"What great big eyes you have, Grandmother!"

"The better to see you with, my child!"

"And oh, what great big teeth you have, Grandmother!

"The better to eat you with, my dear!"

So saying, the wicked wolf sprang on Little Red Ridinghood and ate her up.

From *The Fairy Tales of
Charles Perrault*

✻

# *Granny Jokes*

On a bright May morning, Mrs. Flynn, her smile as radiant as the day, set forth on an outing with her first grandchild. Before the carriage had proceeded two blocks, she was delighted to run into a neighbor.

"What a beautiful baby!" gushed the friend.

"You think this is beautiful?" clucked the grandma. "You ought to see her pictures!"

Given charge of little Murray and Melvin for the afternoon, Grandma Goldstein decided to give them the treat of a soda. Just as they reached the corner drug store, a friend approached. "*Ay*, what nice, handsome boys," she rhapsodized. "Tell me, how old are they?"

"The doctor is four," explained Grandma, "and the lawyer is six."

✻

# *Four Fabulous Grandmothers*

## ST. ANNE*

The canonical books of the New Testament contain nary a mention of her, but St. Anne, venerated as the grandmother of Jesus, is nevertheless one of the most beloved saints in Christendom. She is patron saint of Brittany and of Quebec's Ste. Anne de Beaupré, the

---

* In 1955, novelist Frances Parkinson Keyes wrote an affectionate portrait of *St. Anne, Grandmother of Our Saviour* that became immensely popular. Mrs. Keyes was inspired to write her book, she told readers, after she heard of the difficulty of a friend's granddaughter in accepting the story of the Nativity. "I don't understand why Mary and Joseph had to go to a stable," the little girl complained. "Why didn't they just go to Grandma's?"

second most famous healing shrine in the world. There are close to four hundred Roman Catholic churches dedicated to her in the United States alone.

The story of Anne's conception of Mary, found in the apocryphal Book of James, has its own touch of the miraculous. Mourning her long childlessness after many years of marriage to a prosperous Jerusalem resident named Joachim, Anne wanders into her garden one day and is made even sadder by the sight of a nest of baby sparrows. Suddenly, as she weeps, an angel appears and promises her a child. At the same moment, an angel comes also to Joachim with the same message. The two rush joyfully into each other's arms at the gate of the city and, as prophesied, they become the parents of the woman called "the mother of Our Lord."

During the Renaissance, St. Anne became a popular cult figure in Europe and the many artists of the period who painted her include such giants as Giotto and Leonardo. The Council of Trent in the sixteenth century banned further depiction of such apocryphal figures, and Luther and other Reformation leaders acrimoniously derided her. But the affection of Catholics for Jesus's grandmother was too deeply ingrained in tradition to vanish from memory. As a result, many churches still exhibit relics of the mother of Mary and visitors today who attend mass in the church of St. Anne in Jerusalem are told by their guidebooks that this is "the birthplace of the Blessed Virgin."

## ELIZABETH FOSTER GOOSE

Many American scholars are of the opinion that this grandmother from colonial Boston was *the* "Mother Goose" of nursery rhyme fame.* When, in 1692, at the age of twenty-seven, she became the bride of a widower named Isaac Goose, she became the stepmother of his ten children and thereafter gave birth to six babies of her own. As these little ones gradually grew to adulthood, Mrs. Goose made the transition to grandmother and, like countless other grannies before and since, enjoyed amusing the new generation with rhymes recalled from her own younger days. One of her sons-in-law, a Boston printer named Thomas Fleet, decided to publish these remembered ditties in pamphlet form and thus came into being, in 1719, *Songs for the Nursery, or Mother Goose's Melodies*, and the

* For some alternative theories, see page 438.

400

subsequent literary immortality of the Fleet children's grandmom. Mother Goose, meanwhile, went on reciting her rhymes in the flesh to still another generation of youngsters. In 1757, when she died, she was in her ninety-third year.

Bibliographic alert: Despite the exhaustive scouring of New England libraries and attics, no copy of Thomas Fleet's original American *Mother Goose* collection is now known to exist. If one ever turns up, it will be worth a fortune.

## ELIZABETH TAYLOR

Actress Elizabeth Taylor became a grandmother for the first time in 1971, the same year she celebrated her fortieth birthday. The child, christened Leyla, is the daughter of Miss Taylor's older son, Michael Wilding, Jr., and the former Beth Clutter of Portland, Oregon. In the beginning, Elizabeth was a demonstrative and doting grandma, showering little Leyla with Christian Dior clothes and burning up the long-distance wires for news of her. After daughter-in-law Beth left Michael's hippie commune in western Wales, returned to the United States, and divorced Michael, contact between grandmother and grandchild diminished. But even though Beth's new husband has legally adopted Leyla, Elizabeth still keeps and displays pictures of Leyla to anyone willing to look.

Michael presented Elizabeth with a second granddaughter, Naomi, in 1975, the offspring of an informal liaison with an English girl named Johanna Lykke-Dahn. When I interviewed the violet-eyed Elizabeth in London that year, she had just returned from picnicking with her children and the new baby in the fields where she had spent her own English childhood. Miss Taylor, who has now definitely supplanted Marlene Dietrich as *the* "Glamorous Grandmother" of the decade, beamed and said, "The baby is wonderful. She spit up all over me!"

## QUEEN VICTORIA

Kaiser Wilhelm II of Germany called her "the most unparalleled Grandmama that ever existed" and most of his multitude of cousins (including Czarina Alexandra of Russia and Queen Marie of Romania) doubtlessly felt the same way about the Queen Empress who ruled the greatest Empire the world has ever known. Though

Victoria was not always happy with her role as mother,* she was an adoring "Gangan" to the offspring of her own nine children and insisted on being at hand for the birth of each grandchild, sitting patiently for uncounted bedside hours with the various mothers-to-be. Christening and birthday presents flowed out from Windsor in a stream as steady as the Thames and included everything from bassinets to hand-knitted quilts to (as a birthday gift for the grandson who grew up to be Kaiser) a royal deed to Africa's Mount Kilimanjaro. In her lonely old age, when all of her own progeny had left home, Victoria enjoyed having one or another of the grandchildren around as company for, she wrote, "to have no children in the house is most dreary." But, after a crowded castle Christmas, she echoed the sentiments of many another grandma with her observation that, "It is always sad when a large family party disperses, but on the other hand, I need a little quiet." As for her effect on her grandchildren's behavior, she had a universal grandma's complaint. "I feel very deeply that my opinion and my advice are never listened to," she wrote her favorite granddaughter, Princess Victoria of Hesse. "It is almost useless to give any."

A *great*-grandmother many times over at the time of her death in 1901, Victoria breathed her last in the arms of grandson Wilhelm and it was he who actually measured her for her coffin.

*

# GRANNY GROWS YOUNGER

. . . just as childhood emerged in the fifteenth century, adolescence at the beginning of the twentieth, and youth at midcentury, so, too, has a new generation of women—products of medical technology—appeared on the scene today. These women do not fit any of the old stereotypes. They announce, with as much surprise and incredulity as they expect to find in their listeners, that they are *grand*mothers! And in the near future they will be *great*-grandmothers, for the four-generation family is almost inevitable.

Traditionally the image of the grandmother has been one of a benign little old lady delightedly serving roast turkey and pumpkin pie to a large family. It has now become common to speak of glam-

---

* For more about Victoria as a mother, see page 119.

orous grandmothers. As, indeed, many of them, still only in their late forties or fifties, are.

Jessie Bernard in
*The Future of Motherhood*

# Other Mothers

"Oh, Auntie Em, there's no place like home."

Dorothy, returning to Kansas,
at the end of *The Wizard of Oz*

Everyone who has ever loved or cared for a child, even momentarily, has been an Other Mother.

The screenwriter Joel Schumacher is an Other Mother of two black youngsters in the Save the Children Program. The actress Betty Beaird is the Other Mother of two Vietnamese orphans. Countless friends have told me their stepmother stories—pro and con. For myself, I have had my nieces and nephews Bryson, Malissa, Karen, Roxanna, Sloan, and Rebecca—courtesy of my brothers—as well as my true godchild, Sidney Simms.

I had the privilege of Other Mothering little Miss Sidney from the time she was born until she was almost two. That made her mine forever, and now that she is a grown-up, beautiful, blond TV producer in Dallas, it makes no difference to me. She is still the little girl who used to always say she wanted a "blue" ice cream cone for some imaginative reason known only to her.

My personally most important Other Mother from the past has been covered in the Beautiful Black Mothers intro, but I've had other Other Mothers also . . . the rare, birdlike Helen McCall Cheslyn, who is known to me as Auntie . . . the three fun-loving,

405

energetic women who were my father's sisters—Mary Eula (she gave me a part of her name), Iris, and Hassie. (Mrs. John Pate, Mrs. Ed Scott, Mrs. Bryson Sherrill, Sr. of Fort Worth.) Two of my most beautiful Other Mothers were my older cousins, Mary Emma Whaley (Mrs. Anthony Raye of Houston) and Mardell Scott (Mrs. Ivan Hollingsworth of Fort Worth.)

Today my most important Other Mother is my therapist, Mildred Newman. Her "other mothering" enabled me to make more sense of all aspects of this book and of my relationship with that mother supreme, my own.

Some of the Other Mothers to follow are really surprising. I hope you will be as beguiled by Lana and The Computer as I am.

✲

# THE KING AND MOTHER SMITH

England's George III, best remembered as "the king who lost America," was born prematurely. He was a fragile infant and, because of his unexpected arrival, there wasn't time to round up some wellborn lady of the court to serve as a wet nurse for him—the usual custom with heirs to the throne. Instead, he was placed on the breast of "the fine, healthy fresh-coloured wife of a gardener," a Mrs. Mary Smith. This worthy lady was as robust of spirit as she was of form. According to Alan Lloyd, the king's biographer, when she was told the royal baby could not possibly sleep with her, she responded proudly: "Then you may nurse the boy yourselves." In the end, she had her way. Years later, George gave Mrs. Smith full credit for his survival. "To her great attention," he stated, "my having been reared is owing."

✲

# HULL HOUSE

The world-famous settlement house founded in Chicago by Jane Addams, provided a home for countless children without mothers. Discussing this with the writer Adela Rogers St. Johns, the spinster social worker said: "They all became mine."

# WINNIE'S OTHER MUMMY

Winston Churchill's mother, Jenny, was so caught up in the fashionable English social whirl that, as a child, he scarcely saw her for weeks at a time. During these crucial years, he was looked after by his beloved Nanny Everest who, according to his son Randolph, was "the principal confidante of his joys, his troubles, and his hopes." In *Savrola*, the single novel Churchill wrote as an adult, he described a similar Nanny who nursed his hero from birth "with a devotion and care which knew no break." The book's leading character makes this observation about her:

> It is a strange thing, the love of these women. Perhaps it is the only disinterested affection in the world. The mother loves her child; that is maternal nature. The youth loves his sweetheart; that too may be explained. The dog loves his master; he feeds him; a man loves his friend; he has stood by him perhaps at doubtful moments. In all there are reasons; but the love of a foster-mother for her charge appears absolutely irrational. It is one of the few proofs, not to be explained even by the association of ideas, that the nature of mankind is superior to mere utilitarianism and that his destinies are high.

❊

# AN EXPLANATION

Kaye Ballard, in her night-club act, expounds her theory on why all mothers have the same stock answers to their children's questions. "They all go to a school for mothers, and have to take a final. All those who fail become aunts."

❊

# GRAVESTONE

The Stepchild[ren] of the deceased
remembering with gratitude
her kindness to them, in their
tender years, place this stone.
Ye Step-mothers!
Follow her example & ye
shall not lose your reward.

Memorial to Mrs. Elizabeth Strong,
died 1775, aged fifty-five, in Old Burying
Ground, New Marlborough, Mass.

# MISUNDERSTOOD

Few characters in history or fiction have received shorter shrift
than the stepmother. In the fairy tales she is invariably wicked.
Now a group called "The Step Family Foundation, Inc. is trying to
clear up some of the misunderstanding and prejudice which its
founder, Jeannette Lofas, says is virtually inescapable in most
steprelations—particularly for stepmothers.

"Rejection and fear is a natural thing . . . the stepfamily might
be considered analogous, psychologically to what happens physically in organ transplants," says Jeannette.

Stein & Day published a marvelous book titled *Living in Step*
after Jeannette and Ruth Roosevelt discovered that even the National Institute of Mental Health had nothing on steprelations. Then
Jeannette formed her foundation at 333 West End Avenue, NYC
10023.

There are an estimated 50 million people in America involved
in steprelationships so there must be a lot of stepmothers. It is interesting that a study made in 1976 showed that stepchildren today
are apparently as contented and happy as children living with both
their natural parents. Stepchildren do work that is just as successful in school as other children. Dr. Paul J. Bohannan, an anthropologist at the University of California in Santa Barbara conducted
the three-year research for the Western Behavorial Sciences Institute.

So maybe if Cinderella and Snow White were living with us
today we wouldn't have the strong motive for their successful and
somewhat frightening fairy tales.

\*

# USEFUL

"A good stepmother is as rare as a white raven," goes an old German proverb. Now we know this is no longer true. But the wicked
stepmother of the fairy tales serves a purpose as Bruno Bettelheim
tells us in his wonderful book *The Uses of Enchantment—The
Meaning and Importance of Fairy Tales*. (I would recommend this
book to every mother and other mother!)

". . . the typical fairy-tale splitting of the mother into a good (usually dead) mother and an evil stepmother serves the child well. It is not only a means of preserving an internal all-good mother when the real mother is not all-good, but it also permits anger at this bad 'stepmother' without endangering the goodwill of the true mother, who is viewed as a different person. Thus, the fairy tale suggests how the child may manage the contradictory feelings which would otherwise overwhelm him at this stage of his barely beginning ability to integrate contradictory emotions. The fantasy of the wicked stepmother not only preserves the good mother intact, it also prevents having to feel guilty about one's angry thoughts and wishes about her—a guilt which would seriously interfere with the good relation to Mother.

"While the fantasy of the evil stepmother thus preserves the image of the good mother, the fairy tale also helps the child not to be devastated by experiencing his mother as evil—a benevolent spirit can counteract in a moment all the bad doings of the evil one. In the fairy-tale rescuer, the good qualities of Mother are as exaggerated as the bad ones were in the witch. But this is how the young child experiences the world: either as entirely blissful or as an unmitigated hell. . . ."

*

# ALL HERS

It's a safe guess that one of the most beloved Other Mothers in twentieth-century literature is Alice, the no-nonsense nanny who, in A. A. Milne's children's classic, *When We Were Very Young*, takes Christopher Robin to see the changing of the guard at Buckingham Palace. Was Alice a real person? Emphatically yes, according to the author's son. As a grown-up, Christopher Milne has excised the "Robin" from his name but not his fond memories of the woman who bossed his nursery back in the 1920s. *The Enchanted Places*, his memoir of the childhood years, is dedicated to:

> Olive Brockwell
> "Alice" to others
> But "Nou" to me.
> To remind you of those enchanted places
> Where the past will always be present.

Later in the book, the erstwhile companion of Winnie-the-Pooh writes: "I was all hers and remained hers until the age of nine. Other people hovered around the edges, but they meant little. My total loyalty was to her. . . . Was she a brilliant teacher? Not specially. She was just a very good and very loving person; and when that has been said, no more need be added."

✳

## CARE TO LEAVE A MESSAGE?

Telephone answering services seem to be especially fertile grounds for the nurturing of surrogate mothers. The actress Barbara Harris had to fire her service when the operators became too maternal. "They started taking over my life," she complained, "like little mother hens."

Almost apropos of this, but not quite, was the message received by Elaine May on *her* answering service after a call from her female parent:

"Mrs. Mother called."

✳

## A MONSTER'S OTHER MUMS

The late, great Hollywood horror-film heavy, Boris Karloff, grew up as just plain Willie Pratt in what he called "the serene London suburb of Enfield." The youngest of his mother's nine children, the actor-to-be was reared after her death mostly by an amiable older stepsister. Two other mother surrogates of slightly lesser significance were the housemistresses of his alma mater, Uppingham, one of Britain's finest public schools. More than fifty years after leaving Uppingham, the man who frightened millions of moviegoers out of their seats as Frankenstein's monster, still lovingly remembered these two latter ladies by their pet nicknames, "Big Bum Ada" and "Pee Drawers Elsie."

# JOHN'S MIMI

Beatle John Lennon was raised by his Aunt Mimi, his mother's sister. In the 1960s, at the height of Beatlemania, he persuaded her to leave her home in Liverpool and move into a luxury bungalow he bought for her in the seaside resort of Bournemouth. He also presented her with the M.B.E. medal awarded to him by Queen Elizabeth* and a large, engraved-to-order plaque. On the plaque is the phrase Aunt Mimi addressed to John almost every day of his adolescent life: "The guitar's all right, but you'll never earn your living with it."

※

# Five Extraordinary Surrogate Mothers

## JOSEPHINE BAKER

This Cotton Club alumna, daughter of a black St. Louis washerwoman, was awarded France's Legion of Honor for her innovations as a jazz interpreter at the Folies-Bergère; won the Croix de Guerre for her heroism in the French resistance during World War II. After the war, she added surrogate motherhood to her talents by establishing an interracial orphanage outside Paris. There, youngsters of varying ethnic backgrounds and nationalities knew her not as one of Europe's most exotic superstars but as the no-nonsense substitute "Maman" who, in giving of herelf, gave them a new lease on life.

## ROSINA LHEVINNE

This Moscow-born piano virtuoso spent the better part of her ninety-six years sharing her arcane knowledge of the keyboard with a long list of star pupils including such recent concert greats as Van Cliburn, John Browning and Misha Dichter. More than merely a brilliant teacher, she melded "the autocracy of Catherine the Great and the informality of a taxi-driver" to guide her students in everything from table manners to costume to the complexities of male-female relations. Rosina became, said one adoring protégé, "at one with what you are doing."

* Later John took his medal back to return to the government as a political protest, even though at the time of the investiture, Paul McCartney had described the Queen as being "just like a mum."

## ANNIE SULLIVAN MACY

"The Miracle Worker" who taught the deaf and sightless young Helen Keller to speak dedicated a lifetime to helping her charge break free from the dark, silent prison in which she found herself after a childhood illness. Partially blind herself, Helen Keller's adored "Teacher" even sat beside her in classes at Radcliffe transmitting the lecturers' words in finger-language to her eager pupil. In time, the name of Annie Sullivan Macy became almost as famous as that of her protégée—a symbol of stubborn, dedicated surrogate motherhood at its most inspiring. Some advice of "Teacher's" which Helen Keller passed on to others: "No matter what happens, keep on beginning."

## NANA

Surely the most famous animal mother surrogate in the history of the theater. She is the Newfoundland dog who, thanks to the whimsical fancy of J. M. Barrie, serves as a nursemaid for Wendy Darling and her brothers in *Peter Pan*. Grumpy Father Darling's banishing of Nana to the doghouse precipitates all the dramatic action of the children's adventures in Never-Never-Land.

## TIM AND THE COMPUTER

This extraordinary surrogate mother combine has made a notable contribution to the history of research into chimpanzee speech. In the Robert M. Yerkes Primate Research Center at Atlanta, graduate student Timothy Gill has been raising a chimp named Lana who lives in a Plexiglas room with a computer console. Lana pushes coded buttons to say, "Please, Tim, move into room" or "Please, Tim, groom Lana," or whatever else she wants to express. Lana also makes signs in a rigorous syntax dubbed Yerkish grammar. Tim and the computer are the only "mothers" Lana has ever known, so much so that at night when Tim goes home, Lana has been known to punch out "Please, Machine, move into room" and "Please, Machine, tickle Lana."

# *Animal Queendom*

What tigress is there that does not purr over her young ones, and fawn upon them in tenderness.

St. Augustine

I hardly know what to say about the concept of animal mothers as a subject, except that like everybody else, I am a sucker for the heroism and ardor and sacrifice that seem built into most of nature. (There are exceptions, as you'll see.) There was always a lot of discussion in my home about "the soul" and whether it went to heaven or hell when you died. And how you had to be sure it didn't go to the wrong place. I can still recall my mother's patient descriptions to us, repeated ad infinitum (because we were stubborn little kids) that the chief difference between human beings and animals was that the latter had no souls.

Therefore, as she told us, their indiscriminate open sex behavior was not immoral since they did not know "right from wrong" and as they could go neither to heaven nor hell, it didn't matter much what animals did, so long as they didn't do it in your house or where you could be offended by it. Privately, we rejected this thesis, anthropomorphizing our animal friends like mad, dressing our cats in doll's clothes, assuring ourselves they could read and write and speak if only we were patient enough, giving them human character traits they probably wouldn't have wanted to possess. (In this, we were aided by the movie cartoons of the day which invested animals with all the worst traits of people.)

413

Mother had to do her "animals have no souls" lecture every time we required the assuaging of our grief—as my grandmother, Big Mama, wrung the neck of a chicken to fry and we watched its flopping death throes, horrified, or when a dog, cat, goldfish, rabbit, armadillo, or other pet died, or when we wept at some poor creature squashed flat on the Texas highway.

My mother thought it would make us feel better to know animals had no souls and thus their deaths were not to be taken so seriously. But it didn't help and when I think of some of the animals I have known, I wonder. The only really "soulful" eyes in the world belong to the dog or cat who sits on your lap or at your feet commiserating when you cry. (No animal of mine has ever ignored my grief, but plenty of humans have turned a deaf ear.) Oh well, my point is only that, in considering animal mothers, one is supposed to believe they only operate out of an evolutionary instinct for survival of the species. But it seems to me theirs is mostly a love unsullied by the neurosis of higher animals.

Simplistic? I hope so.

I simply adore the animal mothers of this chapter—the odd and the predictable and the two who have made me cry the most in movies, those devoted creations of Walt Disney—the mothers of Dumbo and Bambi.

In fact, I noted watching NBC-TV's *Saturday Night Live* how they super slogans under the shots of innocents in the studio audience, holding these onlookers up to ridicule with phrases like WEARING RUBBER UNDERWEAR, or, HIS UNDERARM DEODORANT JUST FAILED. The worst insult the show's writers ever hung on an unsuspecting guest, however, was the following: LAUGHED WHEN BAMBI'S MOTHER DIED.

Animal mothers may not have "souls" but they are surely the mothers with "soul."

※

# Some Record-setting Mothers Among Animal Queens

*Mother with the largest and heaviest baby:* The blue whale or Sibbald's rorqual. Her young may be twenty-five feet long at birth and weigh up to 7.99 tons. The blue whale calf's growth from a barely

414

visible ovum weighing a fraction of a milligram to a weight of thirteen to seventeen tons in twelve months is the most rapid growth in either the animal or plant kingdom.

*Most prolific mother:* The largest litter on record is thirty-six, held by the tenrec, an insect-eating mammal from Madagascar.

*Oldest cat mother:* Although most cats do not live beyond twenty-one years, there is a well-authenticated case of a female tabby owned by Mrs. Alice Moore of Drewsteignton, Devon, England, who was put to sleep on November 5, 1957 in her thirty-fifth year. Her name was "Ma."

*Bird mother who lays the largest egg:* The ostrich. Her eggs are six to seven inches in length and four to six inches in diameter. They require about forty minutes for boiling.

*Bird mother who lays the smallest egg:* The green and grayish white Vervain hummingbird of Jamaica, known as the "Little Doctor Bird." Her eggs look like large pearls with an over-all length of only half an inch.

Statistics from
*Guinness Book of World Records*

❋

# SWINGING MOM

"No human mother could have shown more unselfish and sacrificing devotion than did this poor, wild brute for the little orphaned waif whom fate had thrown into her keeping."

One of the most famous animal mothers in literature is Kala, the African ape who nurtured the lad who becomes the immortal Edgar Rice Burroughs hero, Tarzan of the Apes. The son of an English lord and his delicate wife, the future jungle monarch is orphaned at the age of one when his mother dies and his father is killed by rampaging apes. Little Lord Greystoke might have been slain too, had it not been for Kala, who is mourning the loss of a baby of her own. Here's how Burroughs describes the adoption:

"When the king ape released the limp form which had been John Clayton, Lord Greystoke, he turned his attention toward the little cradle; but Kala was there before him, and when he would have grasped the child she snatched it herself, and before he could intercept she had bolted through the door and taken refuge in a high tree.

"As she took up the live baby of Alice Clayton she dropped the dead body of her own into the empty cradle, for the wail of the living had answered the call of universal motherhood within her wild breast which the dead could not still.

"High up among the branches of the mighty tree she hugged the shrieking infant to her bosom, and soon the instinct that was dominant in this fierce female as it had been in the breast of his tender and beautiful mother—the instinct of mother love—reached out to the tiny man-child's half-formed understanding, and he became quiet.

"Then hunger closed the gap between them, and the son of an English lord and an English lady nursed at the breast of Kala, the great ape."

Tarzan and Kala maintain a warm mother-son relationship until the ape is killed by a cannibal with a poisoned arrow. At this tragic turn of events, writes Burroughs, "Tarzan's grief and anger were unbounded. He roared out his hideous challenge time and again. He beat upon her great chest with his clenched fist, and then he fell upon the body of Kala and sobbed out the pitiful sorrowing of his lonely heart.

"To lose the only creature in all his world who ever had manifested love and affection for him was the greatest tragedy he had ever known.

"What though Kala was a fierce and hideous ape! To Tarzan she had been kind, she had been beautiful.

"Upon her he had lavished, unknown to himself, all the reverence and respect and love that a normal English boy feels for his own mother."

❋

# THE CASUAL CUCKOO

And being fed by us you used us so
As that ungentle gull, the cuckoo's bird,
Useth the sparrow.

*Henry IV*

The most written-about bird in English literature is not the robin, not the nightingale, not even the lark, but the cuckoo. Sometimes (as by the poet Edmund Spenser) the cuckoo is assigned the role of "messenger of spring." More often (as in the Shakespearean quotation above) it is used as a symbol for the shirking of maternal responsibility. The English hen cuckoo *never* builds a nest for her young. (Her American cousins don't share her lazy habits.) The cuckoo surreptitiously deposits her eggs in the nests of other bird-mothers, often cavalierly tossing out eggs already there to make room for her own. The cuckoo eggs are then hatched by the duped nestbuilder while the cuckoo mother flies off with nary a backward glance. Though there are several other bird-mothers which emulate the cuckoo in foisting off their offspring for others to nurture, the cuckoo, for some reason, is the one most often chosen by the poets in their search for metaphors of Mom at her least lovable.

# AN ORPHAN

Much of pertinence to the human condition is observed by Charles Schulz in his *Peanuts* cartoon strip. However, the characters therein, none of them adults, do not deal much with the vagaries of motherhood. An exception was the moment when Snoopy set off to find his animal mother about whom little was known. When he thought he had found her and rushed across a field toward a barnyard shouting "Mom! Mom! Mom!" he had to admit it was a case of mistaken identity and that to him all beagles look alike.

※

In the eyes of its mother every beetle is a gazelle.

Moroccan proverb

※

# THE DEVOTED BIRD

Storks are proverbially devoted to their young. When a thatched roof caught fire in Denmark a few years ago, the mother bird stuck to her nest, covering her young and, as the flames rolled nearer, beating her wings violently to keep the youngsters from suffocating in the smoke. When the fire was extinguished, she was black with soot, but her babies were saved.

Small wonder that the baby-bringing legend attached itself to this tender fowl. And that belief is not so silly as it sounds. For the original thought was that the stork who came to preside on the family roof embodied the soul of some ancestor and took the liveliest interest in each anticipated descendant. So he it was, people came to think, who fetched, from that well or spring the village called "the children's fountain," not the expected baby's body but its little soul.

Donald Culross Peattie
in *Reader's Digest*

\*

## *Leo Fable*

There was great commotion among all the beasts, as to which boasted the largest family. They came to the Lioness, asking "How many do you have at birth?" "Just one," she replied, "but that one is a Lion."

\*

## MATERNAL GENES

Mary Welsh Hemingway, writer Ernest's widow, tells in her memoir, *How It Was*, of a visit the couple made in 1954 to Spain where they met Luis Miguel Dominguin, then the country's supreme matador. At a *tiesta*, a testing of bull calves, Luis Miguel explained the ingredients that create the best animals for the bull ring. The genes of the stud bull, he said, determine the young calf's bone and muscle structure. But, he told Mrs. Hemingway, the animal's courage and combative instinct—*that* he inherits from his mother.

418

# LIKE MOTHER LIKE BABY

The gestation period of a mother rhinoceros is eighteen months, longer than any other animal except the elephant. Rhino babies, which weigh about seventy pounds at birth, may not rank high on the cuddlesome scale but they demonstrate one extraordinary and unique trait. According to animal writer Jean-Pierre Hallet, they are "the only young animals in Africa who will fight courageously, and fight to the death if they have to, in defense of their mothers." Even a three-foot-high rhino, says Hallet, will charge again and again at a gang of native poachers to protect the arrow-studded body of his dead mother. The baby must be killed or captured before the poachers can touch the mother.

*

# THE MOTHERLY ELEPHANT

There was once a kindly she-elephant who accidentally stood upon a hen. She was much distressed, especially when she looked down and saw all the little chickens running about, cheeping.

"Poor little motherless creatures!" she exclaimed. "I will be a mother to them!"

And gathering the chickens tenderly underneath her, she sat down upon them.

From *A Dictionary of British Folk Tales*

*

# SACRIFICE

Snake mothers, for the most part, seem indifferent to their offspring. The ones who lay eggs usually slither off afterward with nary a backward glance; those who give birth to their young live lose interest the minute the little ones emerge and wriggle away. An exception is the giant python of the tropics. Though this monstrous mother may grow to thirty feet in length and is powerful enough to

419

crush the life out of an ox, she is both tender and self-sacrificing when it comes to looking after her young. After she lays her eggs—often as many as a hundred—she gathers them into a heap around which she coils herself, covering them so that her head rests in the center on the top. She continues on in this role of living incubator, completely without nourishment for herself, for the two months it takes for the eggs to hatch.

*

Ladybug, ladybug, fly away home,
Your house is on fire, and your children will burn.

Nursery rhyme

*

## BUT THIS IS RIDICULOUS

Mink mothers have been known to allow their youngsters to eat them alive when their milk ran short in the suckling stage.

*

## BE FRUITFUL AND MULTIPLY

Baby cockroaches grow up in a month and a female can begin a family twenty-four hours after reaching adulthood. One mother can produce as many as 180 offspring in 303 days. As insect mothers go, the cockroach is generally considered to be a good one.

*

## *Eight Irresistible Animal Mothers*

### BAMBI'S MOTHER

Walt Disney was performing at his peak when he took *Bambi*, the novel of Felix Salten, and adapted it into a cartoon film in 1942. The doe who is the mother of the adorable fawn Bambi represents the ultimate in sacrifice, and oceans of tears have been shed by hard-bitten sophisticates almost from the moment the grazing Bambi and his mother hear the hunter's first shot. Bambi's mother says, "Man is in the forest!" Naturally, she is killed making sure her baby is safe, and though Bambi's father appears soon after to take heroically over, we are never compensated for the loss of Bambi's mother. I cannot resist adding here, incidentally, that one of the most acute and entertaining things I have ever seen is Burt Reynolds' impersonation of Bambi's father. I hope sometime you will get to see him do it on the Johnny Carson show and I only mention it because I doubt there'll ever be a Father Book.

## ELSA

After being raised as an intimate in the family of a Kenya game warden, this tawny African lioness readapted herself successfully to life in the wild, mated and became the mother of three rollicking cubs. The account by her former mistress, Joy Adamson, of Elsa's experience, entitled *Born Free*, became both a best-selling book and a movie box-office biggie and song.

## ELSIE

The cow the Borden people affectionately refer to as "America's greatest lactress" came into being back in 1936 as a bovine cartoon character designed to plug the company's evaporated milk in medical journal ads. Reader response was so enthusiastic, the petal-wreathed Elsie soon was swishing her tail in major newspapers and magazines all across the land and was, as one marketing magazine put it, "the prime moo-ver" of Borden dairy products. At a live dairy exhibit at the 1939 New York World's Fair, so many people asked Borden cowtenders "Which one is Elsie?" that the company picked a cuddlesome Jersey to serve as its four-legged good-will ambassador on a full-time basis. In the years since, this real-life Elsie and her ten or so successors have made thousands of in-cow appearances and received the keys to over two hundred cities. Elsie's consort Elmer is now almost as famous as she is and their offspring Beulah, Beauregard, and the twins Larabee and Lobelia, all occasionally get into the marketing act.

## MRS. JUMBO

I'll bet you forgot her name! Well, she is the circus mother of the appealing Dumbo and the prototype of the defending mother. After the stork pays Mrs. Jumbo a visit and her baby is born, the other elephants gather to admire the arrival. But the baby suddenly sneezes and his huge ears fly out and flop to the ground. The catty female elephants are flabbergasted and sarcastically name him Dumbo instead of Jumbo. Many large crystal Walt Disney tears fall from the eyelashed eyes of Dumbo and Mrs. Jumbo as she cuddles him protectively in her trunk. After other circus people mistreat her baby, the mother causes such a commotion that she is chained up as a mad rogue. Dumbo, of course, eventually saves her by becoming a star— the first flying elephant. They wind up in a streamlined circus car. Anyone who has ever seen *Dumbo* surely remembers Mrs. Jumbo and her little pink doily nightcap as well as her singing the song *Baby of Mine*.* Sob, gulp, sigh!

## KANGA

She was the motherly marsupial resident of the Enchanted Forest conjured up by author A. A. Milne as a backdrop for his stories of Winnie-the-Pooh, Piglet, Eeyore, et al. A firm believer in Extract of Malt as a Strengthening Medicine, she spoons it out generously to her child Roo and anybody else who comes to call.

## LASSIE

When the film *Lassie Come Home* first opened at Radio City Music Hall in 1943, New York *Times* critic Bosley Crowther proclaimed that only "the hardest heart can fail to be moved" by this wrenching saga of a boy and his dog. Sure enough, the loyalty, perseverence, and finely tuned homing instinct of the brown and white collie heroine earned her such a following that she went on to a long series of successful motion pictures and also branched out into radio and TV. Though the character "Lassie," inspired originally by English novelist Eric Knight, was a female who mothers pups and "mothers" other animals and humans in distress, "she" was portrayed in both films and TV by a series of males. It is one of Hollywood's rare instances of transsexual casting.

* Verna Felton was the voice. The nightcap is in the photo section.

## MEHITABEL

She was the free-spirited feline created by New York *Sun* columnist Don Marquis as a pal for archy the literary cockroach. Here, in
archy's lower-case *vers libre* style, are some of Mehitabel's observations on motherhood:

> i look back on my life
> and it seems to me to be
> just one damned kitten
> after another . . .
> it is not archy
> that i am shy on mother love
> god knows i care for
> the sweet little things
> curse them
> but am i never to be allowed
> to live my own life . . .
> i hope none of them
> gets run over by
> an automobile
> my heart would bleed
> if anything happened
> to them and i found it out
> but it isn t fair archy
> it isn t fair
> these damned tom cats have all
> the fun and freedom . . .*

## STRYELKA

This Soviet-born dog of indeterminate breed made frontpage headlines all over the world in August 1960, when she and a canine companion became the first living things to make a successful earth
landing after orbiting in space. That Stryelka's seventeen airborne
circuits of the globe had no adverse effects on her maternal potential was proved early in 1961 when she gave birth to a family of
healthy puppies. (Conceived on the ground; the father was *not* her
space-rocket-mate.) In June, the fluffiest of the brood, Pushinka

---

* Mehitabel's lament reminds me of a charming story told by the poet Helen
Bevington in her book *When Found Make a Verse Of*. A black kitten,
certified as male, grew up to demonstrate herself a female by giving birth to a
litter of five kittens. Whereupon Mrs. Bevington's son promptly named the cat
mother "Madame Ovary."

(the name means "fluffy" in Russian), was presented by Soviet chief Nikita Khrushchev to President John Kennedy's young daughter Caroline as a gift. Pushinka also ultimately became a much-publicized mother, after mating with the Kennedy's Welsh terrier Charlie (a distant relation, of Asta, of *Thin Man* movie fame). One of her pups went to the family of then-married Peter and Pat Lawford. The other two went to the winners of an essay-writing contest for schoolchildren. One of the most imaginative entries failed to win one of Stryelka's grandpups because the writer omitted a return address. It read: "I will raise the dog to be a Democrat and bite all Republicans."

✳

# AND ONE LAST "ANIMAL MOTHER"

Mrs. Mary Toft of the market town of Godalming in Surrey became a nine-days-wonder in eighteenth-century England when she let it be known that she had given birth to a rabbit. Actually, a full litter of rabbits, fifteen in number.

Mrs. Toft's story was that, shortly after becoming pregnant in the spring of 1726, while working in a field, she had been startled by the sudden appearance of a hare. This fright, she told the world, had reacted on her reproductive system, and the result, in November, was what pamphlets published all over England were soon calling "this Extraordinary Delivery."

The wife of a journeyman clothier and the mother already of three normal children, Mrs. Toft was widely believed. The local apothecary who served as midwife testified to having felt the rabbits leaping in the mother's womb. Many in Godalming had actually seen the rabbits. Nathaniel St. Andres, "Surgeon and Anatomist to his Majesty," came to scoff, but changed his mind when he himself helped Mrs. Toft deliver two more rabbits. His published account of the matter, padded with confusing medical jargon, added more fuel to the fire until, as Alexander Pope put it in a letter to a friend, "all London is divided into factions about it."

It took a special investigation· ordered by King George I to wind the wonder down. He dispatched Sir Richard Manningham, one of the chief physician-accoucheurs of the day, to report on the case. Manningham quickly offered his opinion that Mrs. Toft was a hoaxter with an artful talent for concealing baby rabbits about her person. On December 3, when the lady was caught in the act of surreptitiously trying to *purchase* a rabbit, his suspicions were confirmed. Four days later, she made a full confession.

"The Rabbit Woman of Godalming" lived out the rest of her life in comparative obscurity, but her niche in history seems secure. Voltaire discussed her at length in a book; Hogarth used her to illustrate an engraving entitled, *Credulity, Superstition and Fanaticism*. And, tucked in cosily amid its roster of distinguished generals, authors, scientists, statesmen and divines, Britain's scholarly, sober-sided Dictionary of National Biography devotes a full two and a half columns to her bizarre excursion into counterfeit motherhood.

# Liberated Mothers

No woman can call herself free until she can choose consciously whether she will or will not be a mother.

Margaret Sanger

For mothers, the idea of being liberated is an incredible one. For thousands of years it was an impossible one. Almost any pregnancy brought to term still almost automatically bends the mother to at least fifteen years of some kind of responsibility, servitude, and, at the least, emotional dependency. Having money and servants or having no sense of duty and responsibility never quite work, either, to completely free the mother from the bond forged between herself and her child. But there have always been liberated mothers and now there are many more of them and tomorrow there will be so many more that hopefully a day will come when we will wonder what the quaint term "liberated mothers" was all about.

This chapter on some famous liberated mothers is another of the self-creating phenomenon of this book. It generated itself, for I never sat down and said "we'll have a chapter on liberated mothers." But as the research grew, so did the questions. What is one to do with a mother like Nell Gwynn? She was an "unwed mother," yes—but she was also something far beyond that. And where does one file a mother who earned the nickname of "Labor's Joan of Arc"? She was a "working mother," of course, but a good deal more.

So, in a way, this is a chapter of mothers who were "more than." Most of them are from the past but all of them seem to represent, for one reason or another, the aspirations and goals of what has come to be one of the greatest social movements of our time—the recognition of women as equal human beings.

❋

## LADY G.

The period of the early Middle Ages is not exactly famous for its liberated mothers, but one who certainly deserves that appellation is the beautiful wife of Leofric, Earl of Mercia, a few years prior to the Norman Conquest. Local chroniclers called her Godgifu, but we know her as Lady Godiva. According to the well-known legend, the people of her district were suffering so grievously under Leofric's oppressive taxes that she begged her husband to ease their burden. He agreed, on the unlikely condition that she would ride naked through the Coventry market, shielded only by her long tresses. Her fulfillment of these immodest terms made her immortal.

Historians (and artists) still disagree on the manner in which Godiva rode her horse through Coventry—astride or side-saddle—but there's firm documentation as to her motherhood. Her son Aelfric, later renowned as a soldier, succeeded his father as Earl of Mercia and gave Godiva several grandchildren. If his mum's canter in the buff left any deep psychological scars, records don't show it.

❋

## THE KING'S WHORE

Elen Gwynne commonly called Old Madam Gwynne,
being drunk with brandy, fell in a ditch neare
the neat houses London and was stifled.

Thus, in July of 1679, did a London newspaper report the demise of the mother of actress Nell Gwynn, paramour to King Charles II of England. The brandy-gulping Madam Gwynn was, as Victorian biographers liked to put it, "a lady of easy virtue" and didn't give little Nell much of a childhood after her birth in the Coal Yard Alley of Drury Lane. But the spirited onetime orange-seller was a loyal and affectionate daughter to the end. Her mother lived with her for many years and when the old woman died, the

428

"magnificent obsequies" Nell provided were the talk of London. A local wag described the funeral this way:

> No cost, no velvet did the daughter spare;
> Fine gilded 'scutcheons did this hearse enrich
> To celebrate this martyr of the ditch;
> Burnt brandy did in flamming brimmers glow,
> Drunk at her funeral, while her well-pleased shade
> Rejoiced, even in the sober Fields below,
> At all the drunkenness her death had made.

As a mother herself, the actress whom Samuel Pepys called "pretty, witty Nell" was fiercely protective and, despite her shaky social status, made sure that King Charles did right by the two sons she bore him. It was the King's nature to take his love affairs casually and he avoided commitments whenever possible. Nelly's techniques for getting what she wanted were characteristically forthright. One oft-repeated story of her attempts to get a title for her firstborn son involved her standing with the baby on the balcony of a house Charles built for her. As the King approached on horseback, she shouted down to him, "If you don't give the boy a proper title this instant, I shall drop him to his death."

And Charles II (so the story goes) cried back: "Madam, don't drop the Duke of ——!"— and that's how he got his title.*

In another story, Nell, when entertaining the King, called one of the youngsters to her, saying, "Come hither, you little bastard, and speak to your father." When Charles chided her, "Nay, Nelly. Do not give the child such a name," she replied, "Your Majesty, what else can I call him?"

In any event, Mother Nell got her wish. The paternity of both the boys was eventually acknowledged by the King and both were given the titles she wished for. Charles also did right by their mother. His deathbed request to his brother James II, "Let not poor Nelly starve," was faithfully carried out.

❊

# THE GRANNY OF FRANKENSTEIN

"Childbirth," observed thirty-five-year-old Mary Wollstonecraft in

---

* Charles Chaplin, in his autobiography, states that one of his most vivid childhood memories was of his own actress mother entertaining him by dramatically acting out this Nell Gwynn balcony scene.

the spring of 1794, "is not smooth work." Still, the unmarried author of the feminist classic *A Vindication of the Rights of Women* was up and about only a day after the birth of her "vigorous" baby daughter Fanny and soon after, the happy new mother was proudly telling friends: "My little girl begins to suck so MANFULLY that her father reckons saucily on her writing the second part [of the book]."

When American ex-soldier Gilbert Imlay, the father of the child, deserted Mary, the author who had cried out in print against the prevailing female dependence on men, proved her mettle by getting a job to support her one-parent family. At the same time, she embarked on a regimen of child rearing that was much in advance of eighteenth-century tradition. "I must suppose," she once wrote, "while a third part of the human species . . . die during their infancy, just at the threshold of life, that there is some error in the modes adapted by mothers and nurses."

Mary's own methods centered around the theme of "simplicity" and she planned to write a book expanding her ideas but never managed to complete it. Six months after her 1797 marriage to the political philosopher William Godwin, Mary became a mother for the second time and did not survive the experience. (So crude were the methods of treatment during the ordeal that at one point she had to endure having her surplus milk extracted by suckling puppies placed on her breast.)

Daughter Fanny, cut off from her mother's enlightened child-rearing methods, did not go on to "write the second part" of Mary's trail-blazing book. She committed suicide as a young woman. Daughter Mary, whose birth caused her mother's death, grew up to write another classic, *Frankenstein*.

✻

# HER EPITAPH

There is a word sweeter than Mother, Home, or Heaven—that word is Liberty.

> Statement included in an 1873 woman's suffrage speech by Matilda Joslyn Gage and written out by her ever afterward in the autograph books of her followers. It is now chiseled on the stone marking her grave in Fayetteville, New York.

# FREE LOVE CANDIDATE

The first mother to proclaim herself a candidate for the office of president of the United States was Victoria Claflin Woodhull, famous for her outspoken views on free love. The mother of a son and daughter, she was nominated at a convention of the National Equal Rights Party on May 10, 1872, sharing the ticket with the Negro leader and former slave, Frederick Douglass. Undeterred by defeat, she gave the White House a second try twenty years later, this time with another woman as vice-presidential candidate. On Election Day 1892, not one vote was cast for her.

\*

A mother is not a person to lean on, but a person to make leaning unnecessary.

—Dorothy Canfield Fisher in
*Her Son's Wife*

\*

# SUSY B.

Spinster Susan B. Anthony, the great nineteenth-century suffragette, had no children of her own. Gertrude Stein and Virgil Thompson commemorated her in an opera as *The Mother of Us All*.

\*

# "MOTHER" JONES

Before the yellow fever epidemic in Memphis in the summer of 1867, Irish-born Mary Harris Jones was a happily married mother of two sons and two daughters. After the pestilence had passed, she was a childless widow with, as she put it later, "no tears left." Almost overnight, the contented homebody was transformed into the woman who would be famous as "labor's Joan of Arc," one of the most militant trade-union organizers in the American labor movement.

The American illustrator Rose O'Neill, "Mother of the Kewpies," did her bit for liberated mothers via this 1915 suffrage propaganda postcard.

The social consciousness of Mary Jones derived first from her late husband, an iron worker who was an ardent trade unionist. Secondly, it came from her experiences as a widowed seamstress in Chicago. The dramatic difference between the homes of the wealthy industrialists in which she did her stitching and the living quarters of the poor laboring people among whom she lived, drew her into hoping she might diminish that difference. For the next fifty years Mary Jones traversed America, preaching her one-word gospel: "Organize!"

No one now remembers when she first was given the affectionate nickname of "Mother" but that is what she eventually became to coal miners in West Virginia, Pennsylvania, and Colorado; to cotton-mill workers in both North and South, and garment workers in New York City. Her "motherliness" manifested itself in particular when, as a longtime paid organizer for the United Mine Workers, she fired off her biggest verbal guns at the horrors of child labor, both in and out of the mining camps.

She also, on occasion, used the institution of motherhood as a weapon in her struggle against labor injustices. During one Pennsylvania miners' strike, she organized a battalion of young miners' wives to stand guard at the mine entrances. Mother Jones's mothers, each with a baby cradled on one arm and a broom or mop in the other, successfully managed to keep out the scabs until the strike was over.

Before her death in 1930 at the age of one hundred, Mother Jones saw many of her dreams come to fruition: better child labor laws; bigger union representation in the mines and mills—and votes for women. Today she is immortalized also as the title of a popular West Coast magazine. But for her first ninety years, Mother Jones proved over and over that even without the privilege of suffrage she could make her presence felt. It was just as she had once told a convention of suffragettes: "You don't need a vote to raise hell!"

*

## "MOTHER BLOOR"

When Mrs. Ella Reeve Ware Cohen Omholt died in 1951, at the age of eighty-eight, the headline on her New York *Times* obituary identified her as the "matron saint" of the American Communist Party. For more than fifty years, in hobo jungles and union halls, on picket lines and protest marches, and as often as not in jail, she was hailed or vilified as "the mother of the revolution to come."

Born in 1862, the daughter of a "rich Republican" on Staten Island, Ella Reeve first broke away from the conservative family mold when, as a young mother of two, she was attracted to the cause of women's suffrage. By the time all of her six children were born (two died in infancy), she was a full-fledged radical, applying her fiery tongue and indomitable energy to lost causes from Boston to Burbank. In Chicago in 1906 to investigate the meat-packing industry, Ella decided she needed a male escort to accompany her into the stockyard saloons where she hoped to pick up information. She persuaded a young Welsh compatriot named Richard Bloor to guide her on her rounds and henceforth was famous all along the radical grapevine as "Mother Bloor." (Novelist Upton Sinclair used many of her findings in his muckraking stockyards exposé, *The Jungle.*)

433

The three-times-married "Mother Bloor" joined the Communist Party in 1919, served on its national committee until she was in her eighties, wrote countless articles for *The Daily Worker* and was held in such high left-wing esteem that, for years, her birthday was an annual excuse for Communist picnics. But as much as she longed for the revolution to come, "Mother Bloor" adored the country she fought so hard to change. Incapacitated in her last months by a stroke, she failed to recognize many of the visitors who came to pay her homage. She *did* remember the words to all four verses of "The Star-Spangled Banner" and sang them daily.

❋

### MOTHERS!

Can you afford to have a large family?
Do you want any more children?
If not, why do you have them?
DO NOT KILL, DO NOT TAKE LIFE, BUT PREVENT
Safe, Harmless Information can be obtained of trained Nurses at
46 Amboy Street
NEAR PITKIN AVENUE, BROOKLYN
Tell Your Friends and Neighbors.    All Mothers Welcome.
A registration fee of 10 cents entitles any mother
to this information.

—Flyer for the first birth-control
clinic in America opened
October 16, 1916, in the
Brownsville section of Brooklyn
by Margaret Sanger

❋

## ROSA'S TURN

Mrs. Rosa Parks, a Montgomery, Alabama, seamstress, has been called "the mother of the civil-rights movement" because in 1955 she refused to give her seat on a bus to a white man and was arrested. The ensuing black boycott of Montgomery buses lasted more than a year, until the U. S. Supreme Court declared that the Alabama laws permitting racial segregation in public transportation were unconstitutional.

※

# ETERNAL PROBLEM

The earliest known reference to birth-control techniques appears in an Egyptian papyrus dating back to 1850 B.C. Women desiring to avoid pregnancy were advised to use a contraceptive concoction, the key ingredients of which were honey, soda, and crocodile excrement.

※

# THE FORMIDABLE MRS. P.

In 1963, Mrs. Malcolm Peabody, the mother of the then-governor of Massachusetts, Endicott Peabody, made national headlines when she was arrested during a civil rights demonstration in St. Augustine, Florida. Traveling with a group of Episcopal bishops' wives, the seventy-three-year-old matriarch undertook the journey with the full understanding that she might be arrested and explained this in advance to her daughter Marietta Tree, then on the U.S. staff of the United Nations.

Felicia Warburg Roosevelt, in her book *Doers and Dowagers*, reports that, at the time of Mother Peabody's Florida trip, Marietta and her husband Ronald Tree were entertaining Britain's Queen Mother in Barbados. Marietta spent a good deal of time during the visit listening to the radio for news from St. Augustine, so much time that Mr. Tree felt it necessary to apologize to the Queen Mother for his wife's absence. "You must forgive Marietta," he told her. "Her mother is taking part in a demonstration and I think Marietta would like to see her arrested, since it would prove an important point."

When it came time for the Queen Mother to leave, she said good night to Marietta and added, "Mrs. Tree, it's been a delightful evening and I do hope your mother gets arrested soon."

# A FREE LADYBIRD

Many people assume, says Lynda Johnson Robb, that her mother, Lady Bird, the wife of LBJ, the thirty-sixth President, "lived in his shadow, to do his bidding." "Definitely not so," asserts Lady Bird's daughter. Amazed to hear that Lynda and her husband had a joint checking account, the independent Lady Bird told her daughter, "I wouldn't have a joint checking account with the angel Gabriel!"

*

I've become a mother. That's why women grow up and men don't.

—Kathleen (Mrs. Eldridge) Cleaver

# Mother Mix

The mother is a matchless beast.

Spanish proverb

I owe a great debt to the Fort Worth Public Library and without the New York Public Library, there could have been no *Mother Book*. Like many other children, I grew up as a person in love with words. I became an inveterate reader and collector of things printed, even the backs of condiment bottles if there is nothing else. My life today is a welter of notebooks, scraps of paper, index cards, news clips, and ill-assorted files. And books.

It is no wonder that the commonplace book is one of my favorite art forms. When I first read Shakespeare and understood that the Elizabethans carried wax tablets at their waist in order to jot down the wisdom of creatures like Polonius, I felt an instant kinship with them. My idea of heaven has always been the collecting of odd assorted bits and the vain hope that they might be assembled into something making a cohesive whole. So I ask the reader's indulgence for my love of my own book. It has not, of course, been written, so much as assembled and organized.

As a child I wanted to read long before any aptitude was visible and used to lie looking through the books on our shelves thinking if I stared long enough, the meaning would become clear.

When I did learn to read, long before school, I became a worshiper. My mother had bought all of our books because the bindings were handsome, so I read things totally outside my ken, including

*Mechanics of the Boiler Room,* a distinguished-looking green leather volume I remember fondly even to this day. There were some German texts mixed in the books bought for "looks" and I always felt quite frustrated that they refused to yield up their secrets.

The discovery that they let you take out books for free in a place downtown called the Fort Worth Public Library was the happiest day of my young life. I fell into reading adventures like Alice down the rabbit hole. I always shuddered and passed quickly through the front doors into the familiar library smell as fast as possible because there were eerie mammoth tusks and a genuine Chinese rickshaw with a sinister mannequin between its handles at the entrance.

When I reread these pages I am delighted over and over again to find special favorites in the material. Like a kid in a candy store I am always finding my "favorite" thing which changes from reading to reading. But Mother Mix really is just about my favorite chapter. And it is what it says it is—a lot of tag ends that didn't fit specifically elsewhere but were the irresistible end.

I especially commend to you here the theory of Mother Goose and the political aspects of countries and motherhood. Every time I read these I find them "indescribably delicious," but then I am a lunatic for words, an information magpie manquée. And anyway, how can you pay any mind to a person who still fondly remembers *Mechanics of the Boiler Room?*

✳

Old Mother Goose when she wanted to wander
Would ride through the air on a very fine gander.

## MORE ON MOTHER GOOSE

While Mrs. Elizabeth Foster Goose of eighteenth-century Boston* is the odds-on favorite of Americans for the title of "the *real* Mother Goose," she had some well-documented predecessors. In 1697, twenty years before the American Mrs. Goose made her debut in print, the French fairytale collector Charles Perrault brought out a book subtitled *Contes de Ma Mère l'Oye—Tales of*

* For more about her, see page 400.

*My Mother Goose*—and it is known that in England, children were reciting the rhyme noted above even earlier.

Nursery-rhyme scholars, a persistent albeit fanciful bunch, theorize that *the* original was Queen Berthe, the wife of Pepin (or Pippin) and mother of Charlemagne.* According to Ceil and William S. Baring-Gould in *The Annotated Mother Goose*, because of the size, or perhaps the shape of her feet, Berthe was called *La Reine Pédauque (or Pédance)*, otherwise *Berthe, au grand pied,* "Queen Goosefoot," or "Goose-Footed Bertha." In legend, she is represented as "incessantly spinning, with hordes of children clustered around her."

*Another* Berthe, the wife of France's Robert the Pious, however, also had a goose connection. The Baring-Goulds say that she was "so closely related to her husband that on his marriage to her, he was excommunicated from the Catholic Church. The result of this near-incestuous union (it was whispered) was the birth of a monster—a creature with the head of a goose."

The point is, nobody knows for certain *who* "the real Mother Goose" was, any more than we know about the *real* Cinderella, Little Red Ridinghood, Jack the Giant-killer or Jack the Ripper, for that matter.

❋

# OUT OF THE MOUTHS OF TYCOONS

Greek tragedy is the sort of drama where one character says to another, "If you don't kill Mother, I will!"

—Spyros Skouras

❋

# THE WISDOM OF HARRY

The playwright Harry Kurnitz was sitting around one night kibitzing with the boys and they started telling mother stories. Said Kurnitz: "If you have had one mother, you have had them all."

* For more about *her*, see page 358.

# LOVE LETTER

*Dear mother,* he wrote with his finger on the back of an envelope, looking up, between every few invisible words, at the unnoticing woman opposite, *this is to tell you that I arrived safely and that I am drinking in the buffet with a tart. I will tell you later if she is Irish.*

—Dylan Thomas in
*Adventures in the Skin Trade*

\*

# MAMA MEDEA

What's a not-so-nice mother like Medea doing in a chapter like this? Frankly, I couldn't think where else to put her. She is a mythic mother all right, but nobody's *Arrangement in Gray and Black.* She is the classic bad mother, but where to consider her badness? Let's just mix her in as the example of mother enlarged and gone wrong.

This legendary Greek sorceress is a paradigm of the "woman scorned." After her fervid love affair with Jason the Argonaut ended and the handsome adventurer deserted her to marry someone else, Medea extracted a terrible revenge for his faithlessness. She murdered both her rival and *her own children* by Jason.

Today a mother like Medea would be a big headline in the New York *Daily News.* Her ultimate unnatural maternal act caused her to be immortalized by Euripides in a dramatic tragedy first produced in 431 B.C. It has proved an irresistible theme for playwrights, artists, and musicians ever since.

My writing colleague Diane Judge has the best Medea story I know. Once while watching a Greek production of the play brought to Broadway on tour, Diane was listening to the translation into English over a headset at the City Center. As Medea went totally berserk on stage, spouting Greek and chewing scenery, another performer spoke a line in Greek about her.

The translator then said calmly into Diane's astonished ear: "Here comes a *very* sick mother!!"

# PRETENDING

Though only mythic males are credited with having become "mothers," it has been common in many cultures for men to *act* as if they have given birth. In the custom known to folklorists as *couvade* (from the French word for "hatch"), the mother of a newborn infant gets up as soon as possible and returns to her customary routine while the father takes the baby to bed and is treated as if *he* were the one who had just delivered. Though now no longer common, this custom existed in India, Borneo, South America, and many parts of Europe. The prevailing theory is that *couvade* was partly a ritual for asserting paternity and partly for protecting the newborn against malevolent spirits. The idea was that a woman was not competent to do this herself because, according to primitive beliefs, she was "unclean" after confinement. The father therefore took her place and, protected by various charms, guarded the child and the household against the onslaughts of any demons in the neighborhood.

The most common "sympathetic" ailment suffered by husbands during their wife's pregnancy is a toothache.

*

# THE GOOD OLD BAD OLD DAYS

This is as good a spot as any to record a fact that seems to have been overlooked in most histories of television's swaddling days—America's first fully sponsored daytime TV program to go network was called *Okay, Mother*. Though I never saw this program, I have been howling at stories about it for years thanks to my researcher for this book, Liz Pierce, and our late friend Jim Elson, who both worked on the show. Little did I dream that one day Liz Pierce and I would have a chance to help immortalize *Okay, Mother* in *The Mother Book*.

The program went on the air November 1, 1948, starred Dennis James, and by 1950, was still, in the eyes of television critic John Crosby of the New York *Herald-Tribune*, "the most terrible daytime program I've yet run across." Crosby's analysis of *Okay,*

*Mother* remains one of the landmarks of the now almost lost art of TV criticism:

> Mr. James or his henchmen—who, I suspect are trolls—round up two or three hundred mothers every day. I don't know how they do this. I imagine it's something like an elephant hunt. The beaters fan out in the New Jersey veld, setting fire to the bush and shouting their weird cries, and gradually they drive the poor, hunted mothers into the kraal. Then each day the mothers are shipped to New York for exhibition.
>
> I must confess they don't seem to mind being exhibited. . . . Almost every single one tries to get her face into the camera and, by George, almost every single one succeeds. Most easily domesticated mothers I ever saw.
>
> "Who's the girl with brush and broom?" shouts Mr. James.
>
> "Mother!" cry the captives dutifully.
>
> "Who's the girl who chases gloom?" says Mr. James.
>
> "Mother!" is the riposte to this one. (No, they don't have to push any teak logs around, Junior. They just have to yell "Mother" at appropriate intervals.)
>
> . . . Mr. James—I throw this in as limply as possible—is tall, dark, husky and handsome, and I suspect he appeals not only to the girls on the set but to the ones at home. Thousands of them probably swoon over their ironing boards every day, causing—I devoutly hope—endless casualties. Mr. James may easily have set fire to more mothers than any man since Nero.
>
> There isn't much else to tell you about this program. Mr. James, from time to time, recites what he calls Mothergrams, a form of verse I shan't inflict on you. Occasionally, he vaults two or three rows of mothers to land squarely on the lap of a mother in the upper tiers, busses her roundly and vaults back—easily the most specialized form of exercise I ever saw . . . Just why he should get mixed up in this mother thing, I don't know. Maybe he needs the money. Maybe he never had a mother. Or maybe—this is my theory—the whole thing is a freak of transmission, a collision between a cumulus cloud and a low pressure area, which produces a picture that never took place at all.
>
> If that last theory is true, I apologize to Mr. James and to mothers everywhere. I now propose to adjourn to my favorite saloon where I shall sing "Mother's Day Falls Once a Year but Every Day is Mother's Day to Me" until closing time. Or until they throw me out.

It was John Crosby's conclusion that "if anything will kill motherhood in this country, this is the one that will do it," which confirms my long-held conclusion that American mothers are a hardy bunch. *Okay, Mother* continued on, often with the highest viewer rating of any daytime show, for three and a half years, and motherhood rose above it.

✳

# ECONOMY LESSON

"If 20 per cent of the estimated 27 million mothers in urban areas of developing countries do not breast-feed, the loss in breast milk is $365 million. If half of the other 80 per cent do not continue to breast-feed after the first six months, the total loss reaches $780 million. These estimates . . . clearly understate the situation; losses to developing countries more likely are in the billions."

—Alan Berg, in Population Bulletin

✳

## *Oldest*

"Medical literature contains extreme but unauthenticated cases of septuagenarian mothers such as Mrs. Ellen Ellis, aged 72, of Four Crosses, Clwyd, Wales, who allegedly produced a stillborn 13th child on May 15, 1776, in her 46th year of marriage. Many early cases were cover-ups for illegitimate grandchildren. The oldest recorded mother of whom there is certain evidence is Mrs. Ruth Alice Kistler (née Taylor), formerly Mrs. Shepard, of Portland, Oregon. She was born at Wakefield, Massachusetts, on June 11, 1899, and gave birth to a daughter, Suzan, in Glendale, California, on October 18, 1956, when her age was 57 years 129 days."

—Guinness Book of World Records

✳

## *Youngest*

The illustrious Guinness Book has no report on the world's youngest mother, probably because there is considerable medical controversy surrounding the reported statistics.* It's safe to say, however, that the most highly publicized mother of a very young age was little Lina Medina who, in 1939, delivered a baby when (according to her Peruvian Indian mother) she was still four months shy of her fifth birthday. Lina's baby, a lusty six-pound boy, was delivered by Caesarean section in a Lima maternity hospital surrounded by an audience of thirty-five astounded physicians. Observed one of them about the seventy-pound little girl who began menstruating before her first birthday: "Lina is a miniature woman."

Lina's bewildered mother had no idea who the father of her new grandchild was and Lina herself seemed not to understand what had happened. According to some reports, she was raised at first believing the infant in the family was a new baby brother, but she did eventually learn the truth. The education of both young mother and son was underwritten by Dr. Gerardo Lozado, the surgeon who had delivered the child, and Lina later went to work as a secretary in Lozado's clinic, gradually fading from public view.

When the first announcements of Lina Medina's motherhood came out of Peru in 1939, many doctors expressed doubt as to the accuracy of her stated age. Be that as it may, there have been many authenticated cases of motherhood among girls under twelve. Another Peruvian obstetrician, Dr. Rolando Colareta, has stated that he has seen four mothers under the age of eleven and in 1957, he delivered the child of a young mother named Hilda Trujillo who was four months short of being ten.

✳

A fond mother produces mischief.

Spanish proverb

✳

LIZ NOTE: This reminds me of the *New York* magazine cover of the elegant mother whose son is in a wheelchair. She says: "Of course, he can walk. Thank God, he doesn't have to!"

* Nathan Rappaport, a reader of my syndicated newspaper column, writes me that he sent a letter to the Guinness people inquiring about the record book's omission of statistics on the "Youngest Mother." The editors told Mr. Rappaport about Lina Medina, adding that the information is not included in their book "as a matter of policy, as the book is seen by very many young people and this is not the sort of thing we think should be published."

# MORE MOTHER THAN MEETS
# THE EYE

In her study, *Music for Patriots, Politicians and Presidents*, musicologist Vera Brodsky Lawrence presents a number of songs the rebellious American colonists vocalized fortissimo protesting British rule. One of them was called "The Mother Song" and it went like this:

> We have an old Mother that peevish is grown,
> She snubs us like Children that scarce walk alone:
> She forgets we're grown up and have Sense of our own;
> > Which nobody can deny, deny,
> > Which nobody can deny . . .*

By the time of the American Bicentennial, of course, all such bitterness had disappeared, as is evidenced by the July 1975 issue of *The British American Magazine*. It featured a red, white, and blue cover with this handwritten message across it: "Happy Birthday, America! Love, Mum." †

✳

# BE NICE DON'T FIGHT

An example of the overindulgent mother was the mother in the "Little Willie" verses popular in America in the early part of the

---

* Around this same period, Benjamin Franklin coined the term "Mother of Mischief" to describe the Stamp Act, recognizing that if the act passed, it would create a serious rift between the colonies and Britain.

† The Revolution actually *was* a revolt against mum in the opinion of Lloyd deMause, Director of New York's Institute for Psychohistory. In a speech to members of the American Association for the Advancement of Science in 1976, he offered the theory that children in eighteenth-century Europe grew up in cruel environments that induced them to accept punishment and avoid rebellious behavior. American children of the same period, however, had strong and loving mothers, and were later unhappy when they were denied love by their mothers or symbolic substitutes. When the symbolic Mother England withheld her love, the Americans quickly rebelled. The Revolution, said deMause, was thus a massive "regression-rebirth fantasy," which is the re-experiencing of the events of birth.

twentieth century. A Freudian would surely have some pungent observations to make about this odd verse form. The examples of it below are presented without comment:

Little Will, with father's gun,
Punctured Grandma, just for fun.
Mother frowned at the merry lad:
It was the last shell father had.

Willie, with a thirst for gore,
Nailed the baby to the door,
Mother said, with humor quaint,
"Willie, dear, don't spoil the paint."

Little Willie hung his sister;
She was dead before we missed her.
"Willie's always up to tricks.
Ain't he cute? He's only six."

Willie poisoned his father's tea;
Father died in agony.
Mother came, and looked quite vexed:
"Really, Will," she said, "What next?"

❊

# MA JAIL

In March 1977, a cross-country drifter named Daniel Duncan, falsely imprisoned for four years, was set free after proving that he was in custody in Kansas on the day of the Long Island robbery for which he had been convicted. As the handcuffs were removed, the thirty-five-year-old prisoner told reporters he felt no bitterness about his experience. "Prison," said Duncan, "is like a mother in a way."

❊

Freud is the father of psychoanalysis. It had no mother.

—Germaine Greer in
*The Female Eunuch*

# Some Mythic Males Who Gave Birth

NAME:  Adam
NATIONALITY:  Edenic
CHILD:  Eve
METHOD OF CHILDBEARING:  "And the Lord God caused a deep sleep to fall upon Adam, and he slept; and he took one of his ribs, and closed up the flesh instead thereof; And the rib, which the Lord God had taken from man, made he a woman, and brought her unto the man." Genesis 2:21–22.


NAME:  Atum
NATIONALITY:  Egyptian
CHILDREN:  Shu and Tefnut
METHOD OF CHILDBEARING:  According to one legend, he begat them by spitting; according to another, he created them by masturbating.


NAME:  Hephaestus
NATIONALITY:  Greek
CHILD:  Pandora
METHOD OF CHILDBEARING:  On orders from Zeus, he created her in his smithy.


NAME:  Zeus
NATIONALITY:  Greek
CHILD:  Athena
METHOD OF CHILDBEARING:  Walking beside a lake in Libya, he was smitten with a violent headache and roared with pain. Shortly thereafter, out of his skull jumped the goddess Athena, fully armed.


NAME:  Avalokitesvara
NATIONALITY:  Indian (Buddhist)
CHILD:  Tara
METHOD OF CHILDBEARING:  She evolved from his tears.


NAME:  Vishnu
NATIONALITY:  Indian (Hindu)
CHILD:  Lakshmi
METHOD OF CHILDBEARING:  He produced a lotus from his forehead and on the leaf was his future consort.

NAME: Ymir
NATIONALITY: Icelandic
CHILDREN: A male and female giant
METHOD OF CHILDBEARING: They emerged from his armpit.

＊

## THE DUKE LOVED IT

A rowdy exception to America's typical, sweetly sentimental "mother" songs was a 1943 hit inspired by the turbulence of the East Texas oilfields. Written by a hillbilly singer named Al Dexter (born Albert Poindexter) it became one of World War II's biggest musical blockbusters or, depending on your point of view, "a national scourge," as *Life* magazine put it. The critics notwithstanding, this was the song hummed by the Duke of Windsor during a visit to wartime Washington:

> Drinkin' beer in a cabaret
> And was I havin' fun!
> Until one night she caught me right,
> And now I'm on the run.
>
>> Lay that pistol down, Babe,
>> Lay that pistol down
>> Pistol-packin' Mama
>> Lay that pistol down.

＊

## THEATER STORY

OSWALD: Give me the sun, Mother.

Curtain line of Ibsen's *Ghosts*

There is a story ("probably apocryphal") told by W. H. Auden about the dramatic actress Minnie Maddern Fiske, who had the reputation for always demanding the last word. Playing Mrs. Alving in the above play, she was faithful to the Ibsen lines all during rehearsals, but on opening night the finale went thus:

OSWALD: Give me the sun, Mother.
MRS. ALVING: No!

Drawing by O. Soglow; © 1932, 1960 The New Yorker Magazine, Inc.